POVERTY, U. S. A.

THE HISTORICAL RECORD

ADVISORY EDITOR: David J. Rothman

Professor of History, Columbia University

THE
PRINCIPLES
OF RELIEF

EDWARD T. DEVINE

Arno Press & The New York Times
NEW YORK   1971

Reprint Edition 1971 by Arno Press Inc.

Reprinted from a copy in
The University of Illinois Library

LC# 74—137162
ISBN 0—405—03132—7

POVERTY, U.S.A.: THE HISTORICAL RECORD
ISBN for complete set: 0-405-03090-8

Manufactured in the United States of America

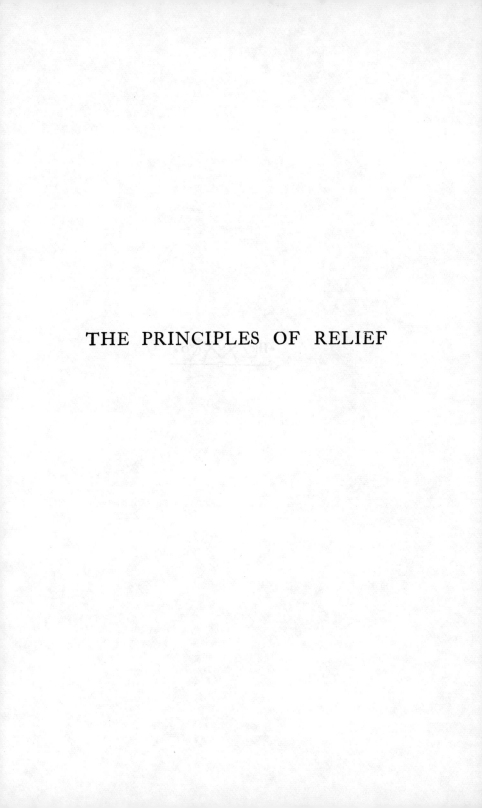

THE PRINCIPLES OF RELIEF

THE

PRINCIPLES OF RELIEF

BY

EDWARD T. DEVINE, Ph.D., LL.D.

AUTHOR OF "THE PRACTICE OF CHARITY"

GENERAL SECRETARY OF THE CHARITY ORGANIZATION
SOCIETY OF THE CITY OF NEW YORK

New York

THE MACMILLAN COMPANY

LONDON: MACMILLAN & CO., Ltd.

1904

Norwood Press
J. S. Cushing & Co. — Berwick & Smith Co.
Norwood, Mass., U.S.A.

CONTENTS

PART I

PRINCIPLES

PART II

TYPICAL RELIEF PROBLEMS

v

PART III

HISTORICAL SURVEY

PART IV

RELIEF IN DISASTERS

APPENDICES

PART I

PRINCIPLES

CHAPTER I

SOCIAL DEBTORS — THE PROBLEM

THE industrial and social progress of the nineteenth century has led to an enormous increase of wealth and to a higher average standard of both efficiency and comfort. This progress has not at all points proceeded with that equitable distribution which would accord with our sense of justice and the problem remains of dealing with such forms of social injustice and remediable hardship as have survived or have arisen as an incident to progress. The relief problem, which is to occupy our attention, is only a part — although a clearly defined and manageable part — of this undertaking. The normal family in the community is self-supporting. There are some who, because of inefficiency or misfortune, are dependent in part or in whole upon others ; or who, if not relieved by others, live at a standard below that at which their physical vitality and moral character can be maintained. It is our present task to consider comprehensively the elementary principles upon which the community should afford relief to those who are thus dependent. The entire range of public and private relief, organized and unorganized, institutional and personal, must be passed in review — leaving necessarily many by-paths unexplored, but making clear at least the nature of the general relief problem, and enabling the student, it may be, to understand the various parts of our existing relief system, and those upon whom rests the responsibility for leadership to forecast the directions in which the relief policy should be developed.

The very existence of the need for relief, as a phenomenon of general social interest, is often overlooked, and is nearly always recognized but tardily. There are, indeed, some advantages in concealing it, or at least in discharging whatever obligations it involves in as private and personal a manner as possible. So long as all the charitable relief required can be supplied by relatives, by neighbors, or by those who act from a direct sense of religious obligation or other similar personal motive, the community does not become conscious of it as a relief problem. However desirable it might be to continue these primitive conditions, they inevitably disappear with the growth of towns and cities, and even in rural communities with the widening of economic and social relations. Whenever it becomes the rule that those who ask for aid find themselves either by preference or by force of circumstances turning to strangers or to those who are not bound to them by the strongest ties of family or religious kinship, it becomes a matter of concern for the community as a whole, and not merely for the two individuals in question. When the need is not merely to relieve the hunger of an individual who is without food, but to consider whether the individual is doing what he can to earn his own food, and whether he has an opportunity to earn it, or whether the circumstances which have incapacitated him from earning it may be so modified as to save others from reaching the same state — the matter is one of social concern.

As soon as the need of preventing disease becomes paramount to the duty of nursing an individual sick person; as soon as the possibility is recognized that, by preventable sickness, by unsanitary housing, by avoidable accidents, by premature death, by industrial distress, or by any other cause, wholly or partly social in character, families may become dependent, it becomes of vital social concern to examine all such causes of dependence and to devise such systems of relief, of alleviation, and of cure as may be found practicable and desirable.

It is idle to deny that the problem of relief has thus become a vital social problem in American communities, as it has long been in older countries. This is by no means equivalent to saying that there are more dependent families, that poverty is on the increase, or that the distribution of wealth in general is less equitable than in earlier or more primitive conditions. It is rather that society has

become conscious of its responsibility for the relief of distress, and is awakening to its obligation to devise effective
and remedial systems of relief for such dependents.

The class of social debtors is not recruited from any one
occupation, or from any one economic or social group.
The learned professions, the mercantile and clerical vocations, artisans skilled and unskilled, contribute each their
fair quota of those who for a longer or shorter period are
dependent upon public or private relief. Religion, race,
nationality, and color require in the records of charitable
societies as many subdivisions as in the census. By no
means all of those who have small and irregular incomes
become dependent. Meagre or irregular income is, of
course, a usual precedent condition of dependence, but
there is an uncounted multitude whose earnings are irregular or meagre who, nevertheless, do not become social
debtors, and who maintain a standard of living which
conserves their physical vitality, and enables their children to attain a better position than that which they have
themselves occupied.

The relief problem is not directly concerned with
attempts to elevate the general standard of living, or to
influence the general distribution of wealth. It deals rather
with social accidents — with individual families, whatever
their previous station, who, through sickness, death of
breadwinner, or exceptional misfortune of some kind, lose
their position and are either temporarily or permanently
unable to regain it, or to adjust themselves to any other
position of normal self-support. The aggregate number
of those who are thus submerged in the onward movement
of commerce and industry may be great, but it affords a
relief problem only in those communities which are so far
advanced in civilization as to recognize social obligations
and in which there are at least some resources available
for relief.

Whether a particular family is dependent is to be judged
not by an absolute standard, but with reference to the prevailing conditions. Where there is general prosperity and
a considerable social surplus, it is possible to find families
temporarily dependent and fairly entitled, in the interests
of the community, to a helping hand from their fellows,

who, under harsher conditions, might instead, with the same earning capacity, be looked upon as fairly successful and as contributors to the common welfare rather than as social debtors. The helping hand to which such families are entitled under the more prosperous conditions is one that will enable them eventually to stand alone, not one that will carry them. As we shall see later this involves skill and familiarity with the principles and methods of efficient relief. Dislike of organization and a dread of extending it to the delicate and intangible task of charity, are responsible for much real hardship and neglect.

Granting that relief partakes of a social as well as of a personal character, and that it produces a definite social effect, there are some who think that that effect is pernicious, because it is in some way in conflict with the beneficent operation of the law of evolution. From an evolutionary point of view the pressure of population on the means of subsistence is supposed to prevent the survival of the unfit, and therefore to be a good thing for society. Instead of becoming dependent, those who cannot maintain themselves should, in this view, be allowed to perish. There should be no interference with the natural results of competition, and those who are submerged should not receive charity, which is but the robbery of the prosperous and successful of a portion of their subsistence. This, however, is an unwarrantable deduction from the great truths which constitute the doctrine of evolution. Charity may be of a kind that will transform the unfit into such as are fit to survive, and still more readily, charity — or, to use a more appropriate term, an enlightened relief policy — may alter the conditions which create the unfit. It is doubtful if modern charity often increases the birth-rate or diminishes the death-rate of the criminal or the pauper. What it does is to give to the children of the dependent and the anti-social classes a chance to pass from the associations and surroundings of their parents into a position of self-respect and self-support. It gives to those who are physically disabled, but otherwise valuable, members of the community, an opportunity to regain their health and strength, or, if incurable, to live with less of suffering and more of kindly care. By segregating the epileptic and the feeble-minded, and preventing them from producing off-spring, it may even hasten the elimination of the unfit — a process which by natural selection proceeds but slowly. It provides for the aged and infirm, for the insane and those who are otherwise afflicted, a more suitable main-tenance, but under conditions, with some exceptions which should be remedied, that do not impede progress.

If there is an active policy directed to that end, the pressure of population may accomplish the beneficent results which scientists have claimed for it without impos-ing extraordinary hardship upon individuals. What is demanded to insure this result is that individuals, and sometimes a considerable number of persons, shall be entirely removed from the ordinary economic and social competition and supported in one form or another from the surplus of human society. The burden in this way becomes a definite one of which the community is con-scious, and the extent of which can be clearly ascertained. It is of comparatively little importance from our present point of view whether the surplus is drawn upon by taxa-tion or through the channel of charitable donations. While it is conceivable that the burden might be so great that it would become a serious drain upon productive industry or upon normal consumption, there are no indications that this would happen at the present time in American communities.

The main purpose of the present volume is to aid the citizen who is conscious of a sense of obligation for the relief of poverty, and more especially those who look for-ward to active volunteer or professional service in any branch of social work, to recognize the character and extent of such service, to become familiar with its guiding principles, and to apply those principles to such practical tasks as they may encounter. With these objects in view, after a discussion of relief as an incident of progress and as a social policy, and a concrete description of the stand-ard of living as a basis from which to estimate what relief is required, two illustrations are presented of the modern conception of preventive and effective relief, in the elimi-nation of disease through the coöperation of the medical

profession with social workers and others, and the movement for tenement-house reform.   The relief of the poor
in their homes, the breaking up of families, and the care of
dependent children and of dependent adults outside their
own homes, lead naturally to a consideration of four of the
more important causes of need : family desertion, intemperance, industrial displacement, and immigration.   The
relief of the poor in their homes is the natural starting
point of all charitable activities, and an account of the
sources of such relief is supplemented by the consideration
in a separate chapter of the manner in which relief is
modified by the constitution of the family.   For example,
a family of orphans, or a widow with small children, presents very different problems from those of single unencumbered adults or of married couples without children.
In the chapter on the breaking-up of families certain principles are enumerated, the neglect of which is responsible
for some of the serious aspects of the problems of dependent children and dependent adults.

Supplementing the statement and application of principles in Part I, there is given in Part II a digest of seventy-
five illustrative cases.   The end in view in presenting these
summaries of actual case records is similar to that which
leads to the preparation of digests of judicial decisions for
the use of members of the bar and law students.   There
is no desire to demonstrate the success of any particular
method of treatment, or to reflect credit upon any particular charitable agency, but rather to show in the most helpful and direct way what is the real nature of the problems
with which charitable societies and citizens have to deal.
In some instances an account is given of the relief afforded
and the results which followed ; in others little more than
a statement of the situation as it was presented at the time
of application.   But these very contrasts are typical.
There are circumstances in which initial steps must be
taken on superficial indications, while in others there is
opportunity at the outset for thorough inquiry and deliberation.

The reader who examines all of these records at one
time may find them on the whole discouraging rather
than otherwise.   Selected almost at random and not

edited with a view to enlisting sympathy in behalf of the families, they will at least convince the student that for the relief of destitution something more is required than money, groceries, clothing, or fuel. It will become clear that these are not relief but only the instruments through which relief may be effected.

That there are those who are unattractive, unappreciative of kindness, and ungrateful for charity is only too apparent from the records, as it is only too obvious to any who come into first-hand contact with the poor. Yet these also may need help and in the long run may well repay effort put forth in their behalf. If, however, in the interests of accuracy and due proportion it had seemed advisable to modify the case records in any particular, I would have desired to do this only in making them bear more frequent and emphatic testimony to the good qualities of the poor, — to their fortitude, their faithfulness, to their heroism and their charity. It is because of the reality of these qualities that we are justified in maintaining a hopeful attitude towards our relief problem.

CHAPTER II

THE ESSENTIALS OF A RELIEF POLICY

It should be possible to formulate the general principles upon which charitable relief is to be given to dependent families, whether the source of such relief is the church, a relief society, the public treasury, or a private individual; whether such relief is temporary or long continued; and whatever the particular form of relief may be, *i.e.* whether money, food, fuel, clothing, tools, or some such special relief as medical treatment, legal advice, assistance in finding employment or transportation to another locality. The relief of distress is a much neglected field of research and discussion. There are innumerable leaflets and even books of respectable dimensions detailing for memorial or for practical purposes the work of particular charitable agencies and of individuals who have labored for their fellow-men. There are works of reference dealing with the administrative history of poor-relief systems, with laws of settlement, and with the financial aspects of public relief. The charity organization movement has called forth an extensive literature which treats of many aspects of the relief problem, but from a critical rather than from a constructive standpoint; and in so far as it is constructive, it deals mainly with coöperation among charitable agencies, rather than with the principles applying to the relief of individual cases of distress.

Within the past few years a noticeable change has taken place in the conferences of charities, in the discussions among social workers, in the special periodicals devoted to social problems, and in the more general daily and periodical press. A new unity has been discovered underlying various charitable activities which centre in the homes of the poor. It has become apparent that relief societies, charity organization societies, religious, educational, and social agencies, and public departments charged with the care of dependents, form practically a single group with many common interests, methods, difficulties, and dangers.   It is found that for all alike the task of creating a normal, well-balanced family life is important. All are equally interested in determining the extent to which charitable relief should be drawn upon to supplement the income already earned, or to supply the necessities of life when the income has been entirely cut off. While each smaller group will naturally have its own peculiar problems, the number of questions that are of common interest to all agencies which for any reason contribute to the care and relief of needy families and dependent persons has become sufficiently great, and their importance sufficiently clear, to justify more adequate treatment than they have yet received.

Preceding and accompanying this new recognition of the larger boundaries of social work, there may be discovered a related series of changes in the conception of charity and of social obligations.   At the same time that those who are engaged in divers branches of social effort discover the essential unity of their task, they become conscious that the task is not so simple as they supposed, and that its magnitude has not been at all appreciated.

Primitive man, in destroying the lives of those who have become dependent from sickness or old age, and in exposing superfluous infants, acts intelligibly, if not in accordance with the familiar and humane instincts of civilized man.   With the growth of sympathy and of the sense of family, community, and racial responsibility, the duty of man toward his dependent fellow-creatures is less easily defined.   A larger number of individuals are moved to acts of pity, kindness, and benevolence ; the conception of charity as a universal obligation springs up and receives a religious sanction ; the church inculcates the duty of giving ; the state assumes the burden of relief of certain kinds and degrees of distress ; voluntary associations are formed under the charitable impulse ; and individuals feel a distinct pleasure in ministering to the unfortunate.   In this middle stage of development, tradition and custom are the most important factors in determining the direction of charitable effort. The idea that personal reward, either in the present or in a future life, will follow acts of charity, is dominant. Social standing and public acclaim await those who perform conspicuous acts of benevolence. With the development of social classes based on heredity, on differences of income, and on differences of employment and vocation, there arises a class feeling which modifies the charitable instincts of each class, and prescribes the relations of a charitable character among such classes.

These may be looked upon as intermediate stages in the development of the general problem of relief, and they are naturally stages of perplexity and incomplete adjustment. The idea of charity, attractive and inspiring at one stage of social development, becomes in time obnoxious, and as a permanent element in the relation between classes, it becomes an anomaly. Religion no longer lends its sanction to all acts prompted by the charitable impulse. Larger tasks are now suggested for the state, bearing some resemblance to the modest measures for the relief of distress formerly undertaken, but differing in so many ways and resting upon such new premises, that they alienate, rather than attract, those who have been most completely identified with the traditional distribution of relief. Charitable people, as John Stuart Mill pointed out over half a century ago, "have human infirmities, and would very often be secretly not a little dissatisfied if no one needed their charity ; it is from them one oftenest hears the base doctrine, that God has decreed there shall always be poor."

The inquiry arises as to whether relief cannot take a larger and more useful place in the life of the community, whether it cannot be made the means by which society will distribute with a nearer approach to equity the burdens which fall upon individuals through social and industrial changes, from which the community as a whole derives great advantage ; whether, moreover, relief measures cannot be devised of sufficient magnitude and efficiency to enable society to eradicate completely great evils with which it has heretofore temporized ; whether particular social problems, such as those arising from immigration, congested population, war, public disaster, and even industrial displacement, cannot be dealt with comprehensively and intelligently with a view to the total elimination of the bad conditions.

Business, domestic life, religion, and education has each its recognized and definite place in the social economy. Education, for example, is recognized as the means through which society passes on from one generation to another the accumulated results of civilization; the means by which the workers of each generation are trained, at least up to the point of efficiency of their immediate ancestors, and their capacity for further progress, if possible, increased. Relief may eventually come to be recognized as equally entitled to serious consideration, and to a definite place in our permanent social arrangements.

The relief policy of the community might then be defined in terms as definite as those by which we describe the educational processes. By wisely formulated relief measures, society would transfer to the community as a whole, certain of the burdens naturally imposed upon individuals by industrial progress. The community would no longer permit its weakest members to suffer vicariously that others might gain. Industrial changes from which the community as a whole profits eventually, displace skilled labor that has been a source of adequate income to the worker and his family, but under the new conditions is so no longer. A sound relief policy would seek out from among the families that become dependent as a result of such changes those who suffer most severely, and put them as nearly as possible in a position as eligible as that from which they were displaced.

Diseases due to unsanitary conditions, or to social causes beyond the reach of the individual, will be more effectively guarded against, and when they cannot be prevented, the expense and loss of income will be borne by relief agencies, public or private ; and the aim of all such agencies will be the speedy restoration of the individual to a position of complete support. Diseases which are distinctly social in character, *i.e.* communicable, curable, and preventable, will be attacked with increased vigor and confidence.

Scientific discoveries are often, perhaps usually, essential preliminaries to the adoption of adequate relief measures. For example, the discovery of the method by which yellow fever is propagated, enabled the Military Government in Cuba, in 1901, to adopt remedial measures, as a result of which the island was freed from the scourge of yellow fever in an incredibly short time, although for two hundred years it had never been entirely absent. The development of aseptic surgery has prevented the greater part of the loss of life formerly resulting from gunshot wounds and accidents of various kinds. Increased knowledge concerning the communicability and curability of tuberculosis will similarly, assuming sensible and adequate relief policies, reduce the death-rate from this most dreaded disease.

Although scientific knowledge is a preliminary, it is not a substitute for relief. In many instances, as in the case of tuberculosis at present, there is a wide gap between the existing state of scientific knowledge and the practical results in social welfare. This gap may not infrequently be bridged by judicious relief measures, and often it is impossible to bridge it by any other means. Instead of a mere dole given by the casual stranger whose easily excitable sympathies are moved by the sight of physical suffering, and who hopes for increased public esteem and for religious reward as a result of his action, relief has become a large social policy, resting, as in the beginning, upon benevolence in its true sense, a desire for the good of others ; and upon philanthropy, a regard for fellow-man : but taking the form of genuine beneficence which is the accomplishing of good, as distinct from well-wishing ; and upon a democratic and social sentiment, which is the best of all forms of philanthropy.

In a progressive society industrial changes are likely to be made with great rapidity, and the number of persons who find themselves stranded because there is no longer a market demand for the particular skill which they possess is therefore likely to be larger than in a stable community, where changes are infrequent.[1] The

[1] Such a family was that of the Italian, Attila Rossi, described on page 218, an architectural draughtsman, who, in spite of his handicap in

mental and physical strain upon the individual members
of a complex and progressive community is also likely to
be greater than under primitive conditions.   As a consequence, health will frequently be endangered and the
physical constitution undermined.   Excessive demands
may be made upon individuals, such as could safely be
borne after a period of complete adjustment, but in the
interval much hardship may be entailed upon those whose
capacities and acquirements are least quickly modified to
meet the new conditions.   Rapid industrial and social
changes are likely to be accompanied by a shifting of
population, reducing the strength of family ties, and increasing the extent to which the individual members of a
community, when they become dependent, must rely upon
the community as a whole, rather than upon their immediate relatives, for relief.

For all these reasons and others of a similar character
that will suggest themselves, the place of relief in a progressive society is naturally a large and permanent one,
even aside from all of the causes upon which emphasis has
ordinarily been placed, such as the congestion of population in cities and the injuries to wage-earners resulting
from industrial crises.

Such recognition of the place of relief is not pessi-
mistic, as might at first sight appear.   On the contrary, it
implies a confidence in the efficacy of relief.   It implies
that the beneficiaries of such a system of relief as would
be inaugurated are constantly and ever rapidly changing ;
that there is no such thing as a permanent class of dependents, but rather a succession of individuals or groups, who
on a *laissez-faire* or a half-hearted policy would become dependents, but on a policy of *thorough* relief are caught up once
for all into a position of self-support and entire self-respect;
into a position of public usefulness and public esteem.[1]

The recognition of the need of a consistent relief policy

not speaking English, had been employed for over a year, and lost his
position only by the closing out of the architectural branch of an important building firm.

[1] For a fuller discussion of the meaning of *relief*, and of such other
terms as *prevention, reconstruction,* and *elimination,* the reader may consult the chapter entitled " Some Elementary Definitions," in the author's
" Practice of Charity," 2d edition.

and the adoption of public measures in accordance there-
with, brings the only possible reconciliation between
democracy and charity. It solves the riddle of the relation between charity and justice; it gives firm ground for
those who are unwilling to pass by human misery without
an attempt to alleviate it, and who at the same time believe
in human progress, and refuse to place themselves in an-
tagonism to the forces of civilization. As soon as relief
becomes adequate in amount from the social point of
view, the act of giving and receiving ceases to be one involving shame to either donor or beneficiary, assuming that
fraud is eliminated, and that the treatment accompanying
the relief is intelligent and sympathetic. A sound relief
policy demands, however difficult the task, a clear demar-
cation between those who are and those who are not to
receive relief. Many crude and unsuccessful attempts to
find such a line have been made. The naïve exclusion of
Italian immigrant families from the bounty of one lady
who had decided that they were " unworthy," because it
occurred to her that they were taking employment which
belonged to native American citizens, is, after all, a typical
illustration of the manner in which this line is frequently
drawn. One person of catholic views will consider only
whether there is actual present destitution; another will
add a test of residence, such as is common in poor-law
relief statutes; a third will limit his charity to " worthy "
applicants, i.e. those whose past lives meet with his
approval; and a fourth will make as a condition of assistance some promise in regard to the future. Besides
these avowed conditions, there are others less freely
admitted, and even less consciously recognized by the
benefactor. When a euchre club, a majority of whose
members happened to be Presbyterians, relinquished a plan
for devoting the surplus funds on hand at the end of a
season to a public playground in a crowded district on
learning that the playground was frequented chiefly by
Roman Catholic children, it afforded an instance of the
manner in which the instinctive consciousness of kind
sometimes operates in determining the direction of charitable gifts. Those who are especially impressed by the
far-reaching consequences of intemperance, may consider

it wrong to give to any person who uses, or has habitually indulged in, alcoholic beverages.   Another will under no circumstances aid able-bodied men, while others draw the line in such a way as to discriminate against deserted families, or old persons who are supposed to be suitable candidates for the almshouse, or chronic invalids, or those who are afflicted by contagious disease.   Sometimes the basis of discrimination appears to be nothing more than a personal prejudice, or an arbitrary and unaccountable choice of beneficiaries.   Usually, however, it is a more or less conscious recognition of a personal or group obligation toward a particular class.   To some extent such selections and exclusions neutralize or supplement each other, a particular charitable resource arising in the community for each class of dependents, and nearly every one who is in need finding himself a qualified candidate for the benefits of one or more individuals or groups.

The question arises whether from this maze of special resources for relief and cross currents of desire to aid, from the apparently hopeless tangle of real needs and of fraudulent claims on the one hand, and on the other of arbitrary whims, carelessly accepted traditions, and deliberate adoption of one or another set of tests, there can be detached any clear principle of general application.

There is no doubt that there are grave disadvantages in the existing state of confusion.   The poor who are in need of relief, or who think that they are, should not be set the problem of analyzing the psychological eccentricities of possible donors.   They should not be subjected to the hardship of finding themselves in an excluded class for reasons which have nothing to do with generally accepted standards of conduct ; and it may be almost equally dangerous for the applicant for assistance suddenly to find himself richly rewarded for the unsuspected possession of some qualification which has no importance for himself, but which, for personal reasons, commends him to the one whose aid he has sought.   If to any extent this state of affairs can be remedied, the result will be conducive to morality and a more equitable distribution of charitable gifts.   The existence in a community of a general bureau of information to direct applicants to this or that agency

c

mitigates, but does not radically cure, the evil. Such a bureau may save time to both donors and applicants, but it does not really coördinate the various parts of what should be a charitable system, or justify the actions of the well-to-do in the eyes of the unfortunate. To accomplish these desirable results, it is essential that some definite understanding should be reached; and if it is impracticable to propose one that would be entirely acceptable to all concerned, it may at least be possible to establish certain elementary principles and to eliminate some of the causes of confusion. Even if the one who is in need of assistance knows or can readily learn under what conditions it may be obtained, and if an agreement can be reached among the multitudinous agencies and the large number of individuals who respond to appeals for assistance, it may still be that many would be discontented with the result, but it would then be possible to test the results of the policies agreed upon, and applicants for relief would at least know upon what to rely.

It may be objected that this in itself is precisely the principal evil to be avoided; that relief funds are dangerous to the exact extent to which people are taught to rely upon them. This objection disappears if it is found possible to restrict relief to those who ought to rely upon it. If fraud and misrepresentation can be eliminated, it ought to be practicable to exclude those who should not receive assistance. Provision would be made for those in whose income there is necessarily a permanent deficiency, and for those who, by assistance for a limited period, can be brought from dependence to normal self-support. Inasmuch as the existence of relief funds cannot well be entirely concealed, or the existence of charitable individuals truthfully denied, there would seem to be little advantage in continuing a sense of uncertainty for the doubtful result of preventing possible dependents from taking such a course as will lead to dependence upon them. Uncertainty cultivates the speculative and gambling spirit, and nothing more surely leads to dependence than the introduction of the gambling element into the plans of one who is already near the margin of dependence. To know that, if certain reasonable conditions are complied with, relief will be provided in case some misfortune should render it necessary, may well be of incalculable assistance in exorcising this very speculative spirit. The relief policy should not be of a kind that will cause the general course of life to be shaped with reference to it; but if it is of such a kind as to cause a feeling of security that disasters of an unpreventable kind will call forth sympathy and practical assistance, a stimulus will result to rational living.

The principle for which we are seeking is to be found in the formulation and general acceptance of the idea of a normal standard of living, and the rigid adoption of either disciplinary or charitable measures, as may be found appropriate and necessary for those families and individuals whose income and expenditure do not conform to such standard. An approach to the adoption of such a principle has already been made from various directions. The general acceptance of the obligation in the last extremity to support life, to make provision for orphan children, to care for the sick and disabled, and to provide burial, is, in effect, the primitive form in which the principle of the standard of living is accepted. The sanitary code, nominally in the interest of the community, but really, if the motives supporting it are fully analyzed, quite as much from an altruistic concern for those to whom it is applied, imposes conditions much beyond this elementary requirement. In the larger cities, where the prevailing standard would otherwise be lowest, it is often in fact kept very high by positive enactment. Overcrowding in living and sleeping rooms is prevented, a normal supply of light and air is secured, suitable precautions against fire and other dangers to life and property are prescribed; a definite standard of cleanliness and decency is deliberately established; measures are taken to prevent moral contamination of those who would be most exposed to it, and who, if left to themselves, would be helpless against it. To these might be added the voluntarily accepted obligation to give a good elementary education to all children, and the policy not infrequently extended to adults through a system of night schools and popular lectures, and carried into the realm of higher education through state universities, grants to higher and technical educations from the public treasury, and in other ways.

The two instances that have been cited of the acceptance by the public of a normal standard of living happen both to imply corresponding action on the part of the state or its political subdivisions. In the first instance cited the state acts through its system of public charities; in the second, through its health board or other sanitary or police authorities.

There are other equally striking instances in which the principle is enforced through wholly voluntary agencies. The agreement common in trade unions not to work for less than a prevailing rate of wages, the agreement to purchase only in stores in which satisfactory conditions prevail, and to purchase goods made under reasonable conditions, are illustrations. In these instances the primary object is generally supposed to be merely economic gain. The concerted action is taken in part to secure an advantage over other competitors in the distribution of the total income of industry. Very soon, however, when there are strikes or industrial disputes of other forms, an appeal is made to the sentiment of the community to sustain a standard of living, and statements are made, designed to show that under the prevailing conditions the income will no longer maintain the old level. Within the labor organizations the establishment and maintenance of a reasonable standard of living acquires constantly increasing prominence and increasing vital significance. It is more clearly recognized that the standard of living is not merely a collective name for the commodities enjoyed at a given time, but that, if it is to have real meaning, the elements which enter into the standard must be of real importance to those who enjoy them, and that they must be prepared to make real sacrifices, and to struggle, if need be, for their continued enjoyment. The method of enforcing these considerations upon those who do not appreciate them may be brutal, and, on the surface, uncharitable. Scorn and abuse may be the weapons adopted rather than patient and considerate attempt to enable those who fall below the standard to attain it. Gradually, however, the milder methods of education and persuasion, and, when practicable, material assistance, may be expected to take the place of the cruder and more cruel weapons. For our present purpose, the significant fact is, that practically the entire body of organized labor recognizes the necessity of a standard of living, both in its material and in its psychological aspect, and may be counted upon to support a relief policy which rests upon the fundamental proposition that the community should not be indifferent to the distinction between those who have a normal standard and those who have not.

The first deduction from this principle to which attention may be called is that it is neither advisable nor necessary to provide relief for those whose standards are normal. To recognize a right to support as distinct from a right to be placed in a position in which self-support is possible, would be fatal to the continuance of those economic motives upon which our entire industrial system rests. Where there is in the family one or more able-bodied, adult bread-winners, so that the natural and normal income of the family is sufficient to maintain the standard of living, charitable relief should invariably be refused.[1] An elementary consideration is that no one should be given a choice between support of himself and family by his own efforts and support from unearned and charitable sources. Practically, it is true, the question never arises except with complications of attempted fraud or neglect of family or some other condition which may call for discipline, supplemented, if necessary, by the temporary, or even the permanent care of members of the family who can be protected, it may be, only by removal from the home.[2] These modifying considerations, however, should not be allowed to obscure the fundamental principle.

That there is a similarity in the effect on character between charitable gifts and that which is obtained by

[1] The relief, for example, supplied in the case of John Williams (p. 239) is seen to have been entirely unjustifiable.

[2] The decision recorded in the case of Campbell (see p. 208) should have been that the family was entitled to no relief, unless the forcible removal of the children from the influence of such parents as are described, be regarded as relief — a step which does not seem to have been considered advisable in this instance.

inheritance or in other ways independent of the individual services of the recipient, there is no denying; but the comparison will yield as much reason for accepting as for rejecting the principle recommended. One family which has furnished to the republic a remarkable number of distinguished citizens has seen in the same and immediately following generation one after another of its most promising young men utterly ruined from having received liberal sums of money by legacy or bequest. At the other end of the social scale, an instance has come to the writer's attention of a woman of middle age who had supported herself as a domestic until she received an unexpected legacy of a few hundred dollars, as the result of which she immediately became an inmate of the alcoholic ward, and on her discharge found that her capacity for self-support had vanished. No statistics of the effect of legacies on rich and poor are available, and it is doubtless true that they may be of benefit as well as of injury. In other words, those to whom is presented the choice between a life of comparative idleness and a continuance of those habits of industry which have previously been acquired, may resist the temptation to choose wrongly. Since, however, charitable resources have not been shown to be greater than are required for real needs, the community is clearly justified in refusing to present this choice, either through public or through private beneficence.

It is equally true that those who find themselves unable to maintain the standard of living which is accepted by the community as normal should have assistance, and that such assistance should always, if possible, be of a kind that will eventually remove the disability. The best occupation for a sick person, says a shrewd and sensible physician, is to get well. The best occupation for any family whose income is below the minimum which permits a normal standard of living is to raise it, and one of the wisest occupations for their neighbors, from either a selfish or an altruistic point of view, is to encourage this process.[1]

The third deduction to be made from the recognition of the standard of living is that there is such a thing as a

[1] In this connection one may profitably study the cases of Friedrich, Sheehan, Caspar, Sidney, Bowles, and many others described in Part II.

criminal failure, justifying correctional, disciplinary, and protective measures. The man who, from an appetite for strong drink or from the survival of migratory instincts, or from any other unsocial and antisocial motives and impulses, fails to provide for his own support and that of others who are naturally dependent upon him, may require segregation or punishment before relief methods are applicable. The faults of the head of a family should not become a reason for refusing relief to its other members, but his faults may require attention before relief is advisable. Such punishment or segregation may not always be practicable.   The one who is responsible for the neglect, maltreatment, or desertion of the family may have escaped beyond the jurisdiction of the state, or it may be that there is an absence of legal evidence, even when the facts are notorious.   These practical difficulties, however, point to modification in the penal code or in the practice of the courts, and in no way affect the governing principle.[1]

The fourth and final consideration to which attention may be called is the necessity for an accurate knowledge of the facts, the elimination of fraud, an investigation sufficiently thorough to leave no doubt whatever of the amount of income, of the expenditure necessary to maintain the proposed standard of living, of the personal and special resources of the family, and of all other facts essential to a sound judgment as to the extent to which charitable relief is required.   Absolute privacy in regard to one's personal and domestic affairs is inconsistent with a sound policy of relief.   Publicity, however, in regard to such affairs, such as is sometimes given by the sensational public press, or by irresponsible almoners, who undertake to collect funds, is entirely unnecessary.   The requisite knowledge of the circumstances need not be shared by many, but the few upon whom the responsibility rests should have full and reliable information.

[1] Ample demonstration of the necessity for discipline and reformation will be found in illustrative cases set forth in the present volume.   Attention may be asked especially to the cases of Dolan, p. 224, Campbell, p. 208, Bonner, p. 227, and Jones, p. 227.   In some instances recourse is necessary to the criminal law, but in others, notwithstanding grave moral shortcomings, a complete reformation and improvement have been brought about entirely by personal influence.

If these four conditions are observed: I. discrimination based upon full knowledge; II. disciplinary treatment of those who are criminally responsible for dependence; III. relief with intelligent oversight for those who cannot maintain a normal standard of living; IV. the refusal of all charitable support to those who can — there may be practically unlimited increase in the funds available for relief, without either danger of pauperization or danger of exceeding the need.

When the actual earning capacity of the family is below the point of physical or moral well-being, the deficiency may ordinarily be made up by outside aid. Whenever possible, assistance should be of such a kind as to increase the earning capacity and so make further aid unnecessary. When the deficiency is, however, inevitable and permanent, the aid must be likewise permanent. This is the fundamental and comprehensive principle of relief. It is subject to certain limitations, to which attention will be called in due time ; but the principle itself should not be lost in the consideration of exceptions and limitations. The principle that relief may properly be supplied to make good a temporary or permanent deficiency in the wage-earning capacity of the family, is not to be confused with the practice of the old English poor law in providing relief in aid of wages. We are not to supply relief in order that employers may get the benefit of underpaid labor ; we are not to encourage, directly or indirectly, the payment of wages below the normal and self-supporting standard, in the expectation that a part of the income of wage-earners will be supplied from charitable sources. Charitable relief is not an efficient lever with which to raise the standard of living among those who have normal wage-earning capacity; it is only when from some definite reason the family is below the level of normal wage-earning power, that relief is justified. Relief is not a substitute for wages in whole or in part, but is a substitute for income necessary for the supply of the necessities and the ordinary comforts of life, when such income cannot be earned.

There are two persistent delusions from which we need thoroughly to free our minds. One of these is that there

is something meritorious in the mere act of giving relief,
regardless of the need for it and regardless of the adaptability of the particular form of relief to the need. The
other is that the sole or principal danger is that the
relief extended is likely to pauperize the individual aided,
and that therefore an elaborate series of precautions must
be devised to enable relief to be given safely. We are
accustomed to think of every charitable act and of all missionary effort as beyond measure of price, as precious and
praiseworthy beyond human calculation. Entire candor,
however, and sober reflection demand a revision of these
estimates. Every charitable intent and every missionary
impulse are indeed of infinite value to those who feel such
impulse and perform such act; but, concretely, from the
standpoint of one whose needs have given rise to the
impulse and act, their value may be very slight indeed.
The interests of humanity, and especially of those who
need effective aid, are paramount, and many things done,
from good motives are injurious and not helpful. Not
all men and women are by nature, or can easily be made
to become, effective practical workers in a charity organization society, or a social settlement, or a day nursery,
or the social activities of the church. When, therefore,
a limited number, however small, find themselves by an
irresistible inner call, by a consciousness of the power to
accomplish, set apart for the reclamation of the social
debtors and the creation of social conditions which shall
lessen the number of the dependent, there is greater cause
for felicitation than if a wave of superficial interest
sweeps over the community leaving little but a vague
unrest as a sign of its passing.

The second error of which we should strive to be free
is that of fixing attention exclusively on the safeguards,
necessarily more or less artificial, with which we seek to
surround our charity in order that it may not pauperize.
Perhaps it will best aid us in reaching a right perspective
to be reminded that people become dependent in other
ways than by receiving relief. To be born and nurtured
among squalid and indecent living conditions, to have the
physical strength undermined by disease, by undernutrition and abuse, to be given a perverted education in a

school of vice, to be deprived of suitable parental care, to
be compelled to struggle hopelessly for the support of
one's family against adverse industrial and social surroundings over which the individual can exert no effective control, to become enslaved by drink or other animal appetites, are dangers as great, some of them indeed
far greater, than to be given unearned money. The
danger of being pauperized by relief is a real one, but it
should not become so exaggerated as to blind us to other
dangers, nor what is much more likely, should it lead us
to underestimate the need for relief or the beneficent
result which it may accomplish.

Modern charity, whether inspiring individual acts of
generosity or concerted movements of great social significance, differs so widely from the mediæval type that it is
difficult not to feel some sympathy for what is probably the
vain attempt to find a new name for it. This modern
charity is distinctly social, as contrasted with the indi-
vidualistic character of earlier almsgiving; it is democratic, as contrasted with the aloofness of the giver of the
doles; it is constructive, as contrasted with the disin-
tegrating and demoralizing effect of impulsive gifts.

Relief funds, under the influence of the modern spirit,
are no longer to be regarded as sums forever set apart to
be expended in meeting an annually recurring number of
cases of destitution of particular kinds, merely because
those cases fall within the stipulated categories. With
this idea in mind, great apprehension not unnaturally
arises at the creation of any large relief fund, because experience has shown that in almost any community the number of unfortunates of the class for whom it was intended
will readily arise to absorb the entire available fund. The
modern idea of relief funds is different. They are regarded
as sums of money from the expenditure of which certain definite results are to be obtained. By caring for consumptives,
for example, in a rational way, and adopting suitable sup-
plementary measures, the scourge of tuberculosis is to be
eradicated and further expenditures for the relief of consumptives thus made superfluous. By providing for crippled children in appropriate hospitals, or at least under
competent surgical advice, a large proportion are to be

cured, and hand in hand with this care is to go such educational and sanitary work as shall greatly reduce the number of preventable cases. A large expenditure, comprehensively planned and made with courage and determination, thus takes the place of a bungling and inadequate expenditure which reaches results rather than causes, and which must be continued indefinitely because the sources of distress remain untouched. The danger of a relief fund is reduced to a minimum if it may be freely used to attack the evil on all sides, and if those who manage it are inspired by at least the possibility of accomplishing definite results. It is not solely a question of the amount of the available fund. The large expenditure to which reference has been made necessarily includes a very considerable outlay for the personal oversight and intelligent direction through which alone the fund becomes in any genuine sense a relief fund. Effective control is less practicable in the case of families that are aided in their own homes than with inmates of institutions, but a certain degree of control and coöperation can always be secured if there is trained and competent service.

Modern charity has invaded the field of municipal and state administration, influencing the use of public funds — here again, however, not for palliative, but for thorough-going remedial measures. It is not that government has been asked to extend its operations into many new fields, but rather that in the tasks which have longest been recognized as appropriate public functions there shall be a new spirit and new standards of efficiency. The care of the dependent poor, the provision of parks and playgrounds, sanitary inspection of dwellings, elementary education, correctional and reformatory work, and even certain aspects of ordinary police duty, are now subjected to the searching scrutiny of practical workers in charitable societies, who insist upon some positive evidences of the modern spirit of brotherhood and humanity on the part of those who are chosen as the servants of the community.

And so modern charity is aggressive, clear-sighted, practical ; mingling with its pity for human woe a knowledge of the resources of modern science for its alleviation, and finding for all the injustice and oppression that exists some redress in law or in an enlightened public opinion. In the following chapter, the attempt will be made to set forth more concretely the conception of the standard of living to which we have given a central place in the formulation of the general theory of a relief policy.

CHAPTER III

THE STANDARD OF LIVING

IN attempting to describe in detail what is demanded by the standard of living in the larger cities of the United States, it will be better at the outset not to consider principally dependent families or those which are at the lowest round of income and expenditure. To apply the standard to the case of those who are thus situated is the principal task of the practical charity worker, but in order to ascertain what measure is to be applied, we must consider the circumstances of those who have not encountered exceptional misfortune and whose earning capacity is not abnormally deficient. We shall not, of course, discover a clearly defined class with identical incomes or with uniform expenditures. On the contrary, on account of the great diversity in the number of persons constituting the family unit, in the relative number of wage-earners, in occupations, in the percentage of time employed, in the exceptional expenses of various kinds, and in the degree of judgment exercised in the use of money, it will be found that no two families are in exactly the same position. Notwithstanding this, it is possible in general terms to describe some of the elements of usual expenditure, from which sufficiently clear calculations may be made for practical purposes when it is desired to ascertain whether a given individual or family is falling below it.

Possibly food is the most elementary necessity of life, but in the plans of a majority of the families in question it is fair to say that the problem of rent is one which receives earlier attention and causes greater anxiety; and it is possible that if the items for which provision must be made were arranged in the order of their importance to the majority of the poor in the great cities, among the unexpected features of such a table would be, that in advance of both food and shelter would appear provision for burial, so strong and universal is the desire not to be buried in a pauper grave. Some form of life insurance sufficient to meet the burial expenses of the individual insured may therefore be enumerated first, however distasteful the idea of burial insurance may be to those who are in more comfortable circumstances, and however expensive the prevalent forms of insurance may appear. The insurance may take the form of membership in a mutual benefit society of some kind, or it may be an incident to a local political organization, or to membership in a church, but in a large number of instances it will probably be in the nature of "industrial insurance," obtained by small weekly payments, the amount of the policy varying with the length of time for which payments have been made, and other conditions specified in the contract.

For shelter a family of five persons will require not less than three rooms, and even with eight or nine persons in the family, five rooms will usually in a city of tenement houses be considered reasonable provision. It is also essential that the building used for dwelling purposes shall be constructed in such a way as to give to the tenants a reasonable amount of light and air; protection from fire; lighted halls, and safeguards against any special dangers to life and limb, such as result from buildings which are structurally defective. As it is obvious that the number of rooms is not of itself a test of the adequacy of the apartment, various attempts have been made, by prescribing the number of cubic feet for each family or the number of cubic feet for each occupant of a room, to establish a satisfactory minimum. Such progress has been made in the building laws that it is perhaps sufficient to say, for the more enlightened communities, that the standard of living requires compliance with the statutes and local ordinances which have been enacted. There is no community, however progressive, in which such provisions are not frequently violated.

The ordinary diet of American working people is abundant and varied. It includes daily use of meat, vegetables, milk, fruit, and coffee or tea. The ordinary budget, therefore, from which shortcomings are to be measured, is exceptionally high, at least as far as the quantity and variety of articles of food are concerned. Possibly not so much can be said as to its preparation or as to the extent to which it is adapted to the physiological needs of the people. Reformers are therefore rightly directing their energies toward improvement in cooking, in the selection of foods, and in the forming of dietaries that are well adapted to the kind of labor to be performed. In a word, it may be laid down for our purpose that the standard of living must include enough to eat, both for adults and children, and not too small a number of different articles of food. It may be added that in a normal family life the meals are served regularly, the entire family participating in a common meal usually three times a day. Of course individual wage-earners may find themselves at a distance from home at meal time, especially at the time of the midday meal, and may therefore be obliged to eat at restaurants or from a dinner pail. The practice, however, among many of those for whom the economic struggle is most severe, of feeding at any time without regard to a formal meal, is a distinct and unfortunate departure from normal family life. Especially pernicious is the practice of giving to children a few pennies to buy cakes or other things to eat when they are hungry, instead of providing a regular meal to be eaten under the oversight of the mother, or in company with the entire family; and all such irregularities must be looked upon as a departure from a satisfactory standard.

The household furniture deemed essential in the families of restricted income in American cities, is mainly the product of the modern factory. There are fewer heirlooms and heavy pieces of substantial furniture than in the country, or in the cities of European countries. It is apt to be light, showy, and not especially durable. On the other hand it can be easily moved, it is well adapted to the special needs of modern life in cities, and can be purchased on instalment; that is, on monthly payments, the aggregate of which will, however, be beyond the cash value of the articles purchased. On the whole, being light and of materials that can be more easily cleaned, it is probably to be preferred to the more lasting and costly furniture that it has replaced. A stove, a table, several chairs, a sofa, a bureau, cooking and table utensils, carpets, rugs or oilcloth, and two or more beds, according to the size of the family, may be enumerated as the requisites, and to these will be added, almost universally, some pictures, inexpensive mirrors, a clock, and probably a few books and ornaments. The addition of a sewing-machine, which is not at all uncommon, may be regarded as a means of livelihood, or as an economy in the making of clothes and in enabling them to last a longer time, rather than as an article of furniture.

Clothing is an important item in the family budget, although the kind and quantity vary so greatly that it can be described only in the most general terms. It is sufficient to say that besides working clothes, for which discarded suits originally made for other purposes are not deemed satisfactory, there must also be available a decent suit for holidays and formal occasions, and that, especially in the northern cities, where there are great extremes of heat and cold, there must be clothing adapted to each season. For winter, underclothes as well as outer garments of sufficient warmth are essential, and in summer also, undergarments are perhaps the rule rather than the exception. Shoes and hats are, of course, to be included and a moderate allowance for collars, ribbons, and other ornamental articles of apparel.

The standard of living is rapidly tending to include, if it does not already include, ready access to running water, a separate bath-room and a separate toilet-room for each family, and many other conveniences and decencies which need not be enumerated, since they depend upon local accidental customs and conditions. A plentiful supply of pure water, clean streets and pavements, good public schools, opportunity for religious worship, freedom to congregate and hold public meetings for any lawful purposes, even-handed justice in the courts, an honest and efficient administration of the law, full participation in the selection of law-makers and other public officials, and the exercise of other political, civic, and social rights and privileges, are, equally with the features described more in detail, component parts of the standard of living. If justice in a given case should be denied, it may be quite as much the duty of a charitably disposed neighbor to aid in securing it as it is to provide food or shelter.   The refusal of the right to vote to those upon whom this right is conferred by the constitution and law, may be as much an infringement of the standard of living as the payment of inadequate wages, or the withholding of material relief.

Medical attendance, under which should be included the care of the eyes and teeth, and other needs involving the services of specialists, obstetrical services, and necessary surgical attendance, and care, if necessary, during convalescence from illness, is included in the standard of living, waiving for the present the question as to whether it should be met entirely from the ordinary income, or whether, like public education and privately supported libraries, it should come in part from public appropriations and private munificence.   Newspapers and access to public libraries are all but universal.

Finally, rational living demands not only time but opportunity for rest, recreation, and social enjoyment.   Entire freedom from ordinary labor one day in seven, freedom from the necessity of working more than ten hours in each twenty-four, and in many occupations more than eight hours in the twenty-four, are the essentials, and still further deductions are likely to be made for ordinary holidays averaging eight or ten in the year, and sometimes, especially in the summer months, for Saturday half holiday.   It is not material for our present purpose whether these deductions are at the expense of the employee or the employer. If employees are in position to obtain this free time at their own expense, and value it sufficiently to allow the deduction to be made, then the additional free time is a part of their standard of living just as are their food, their shelter, and their freedom from work on Sunday.

It is not possible to obtain a clear conception of the prevalent standard of living merely by enumerating the goods which at a given moment are in the possession of the families under consideration; it is necessary to follow

D

their fortunes through an entire generation, or, what is equivalent, to consider the position of the children, the middle aged, and those of advanced years in the household economy. We must find out what happens in sickness, in hard times, and at times when there is a distinct reversal in the family fortunes. The family is on the right side of self-support only when, one year after another, in hard times as well as in periods of prosperity, they are able to remain independent ; they must be able to provide insurance against accident and death ; they must be able to keep the children at school until they are physically and mentally ready for work; they must be able to obtain sufficient relaxation and recreation to prevent premature breakdown of the physical system. Those who do not have the expense of rearing children, and who are therefore deprived of support from their own offspring when grown to manhood, must lay aside, either in the form of insurance or in that of savings, enough to provide for their own old age.

The standard of living, whatever physical comforts it includes at a given period of life, must be understood to imply an income which will take the individual of the normal family safely through the ordinary vicissitudes of life without reliance upon charitable assistance, although not indeed necessarily without mutual interchange of many courtesies and favors from friends and neighbors. If the income is earned not by the head of the family alone, but by the wife and one or more children, it should be larger in amount, other things being considered, than if it is due entirely to the earnings of the natural breadwinner, since there should be a deduction from the earnings of the children, even if of wage-earning age, to provide for their future household expenses; and, if the earnings are in part by the wife, there should be a deduction to provide for the assistance which under such circumstances should be given to the household work.

It is a somewhat venturesome though tempting undertaking to express in terms of money income the standard of living to which the average family which remains entirely independent of charitable relief has actually attained. If it is difficult, because of the great diversities in individual families, to describe concretely the actual commodities, comforts, services, and privileges which the standard of living demands, it is equally difficult, although there is, perhaps, less actual diversity, to estimate what income is necessary to secure these particular necessities and comforts in a given city at a given time. Recognizing the tentative character of such an estimate, it may be worth while to record the opinion that in New York City, where rentals and provisions are, perhaps, more expensive than in any other large city, for an average family of five persons the minimum income on which it is practicable to remain self-supporting, and to maintain any approach to a decent standard of living, is $600 a year. Those who receive less than this sum are almost invariably dependent, in part, upon others for some of the things which have been enumerated as forming a part of the standard of living, or they are deprived of things which are essential according to the opinion of their neighbors and friends. This is not to say that an income of $600 a year is sufficient to maintain the standard of living of a skilled artisan or even of those who are engaged in many occupations which are ordinarily described as unskilled. It is rather an estimate of the absolute minimum below which earnings cannot fall without either constituting a just claim upon the consideration of the charitable, or at least arousing the apprehension of those who look forward to the effect upon the rising generation of a meagre supply of the necessities and decencies of living.

If a considerable number, constituting a natural group, are found to be in receipt of an income of less than this amount, it may be impracticable for charitable assistance to make good the deficit; and it is even true that an attempt to supplement ordinary wages by charitable relief would have the effect of continuing an inadequate scale of wages or particular occupations for which there is no longer any legitimate need. It is only when individuals or individual families, for personal or accidental or temporary reasons, fall below the standard, that charitable assistance can effectively intervene. In other words, as has been pointed out in other connections, the relief policy cannot be made to raise the general standard of living, but it should be so shaped as not to depress it. A recognition of the standard of living must enter as an element in determining what course to pursue, and especially in determining what amount of relief is required to meet individual needs. If it is true that the living conditions, for example, in New York City, require an income of $600 for a family of five persons, then, after making due allowance for whatever earnings and supplementary income are possible, the relief provided should be not less than the amount required to make up that sum. In other words, those who are aided as a part of a general and systematic scheme of relief should be aided to live at the normal standard of living, and should not be tempted or required to live below it.

It must be borne in mind that the amount suggested, $600 a year, is purely relative, and is subject to change. Between 1900 and 1904 there was a very perceptible increase in the cost of living, which is, perhaps, fairly represented by a very general increase in rentals of from fifty cents to three dollars a month in the east side tenement-houses which were subjected to inquiry upon this point. If the average increase was as much as a dollar and a half, this represents an increase in the item of rent in the smaller apartments of 20 per cent, and if our estimate of the standard of living were to be made for the end of the period named, it is possible that it should be increased from $600 to $700, since, as has been said, within the same period there was a great increase in nearly all other items of the cost of living as well as in rentals. If, however, the average conditions of the past decade be considered the amount first named is probably not too low.

The importance of the standard of living can best be appreciated when we consider not merely of what it consists at a given time, but the changes which it is undergoing. The most striking indication that there has been a continuous change for the better is revealed by a study of vital statistics. This is the diminution of the death-rate : the prolongation of human life, and especially the prolongation of the period of childhood, and the consequent better preparation for the working period of life. In the ten years between 1890 and 1900 there was, in the language of the census, " a remarkable and most satisfactory decrease in the death-rate." In what is known as the registration area,[1] presenting an aggregate population in 1900 of nearly 29,000,000, the death-rate declined from 19.6 per thousand in 1890 to 17.8 per thousand in 1900, notwithstanding the fact that there was a more complete record and therefore a more complete return of deaths for the census of 1900.

During the same period there was a decrease in the death-rate of nearly all European countries, closely approximating that given for the registration area of the United States, indicating that the improvement is not due to local or accidental causes, but to the advance of sanitary and medical science; to a general improvement of economic and social conditions or to other similar causes operating throughout the civilized world. The fall in the death-rate of what is now Manhattan Borough of New York City was from 26.7 to 21.3, or over 20 per cent. This decrease is attributed to the advance in medical and surgical knowledge, — especially in the line of preventive medicine; improved sanitary surroundings and cleaner streets; and a stricter inspection of milk and food.

In Boston the decrease was from 23.4 to 20.1, and the causes assigned were: improved water supply; improved sewerage; abolition of the old vault system, and the substitution of water-closets; additional public parks; and improved health regulations.

In Buffalo the death-rate decreased from 18.4 to 14.8, and from a very complete analysis of the death-rate during the ten years, with tables showing deaths in each year by ages and from certain causes, it appears that the greatest decrease is in the number of deaths recorded among children under five years of age, the largest percentage of decrease being among those under one year. This is attrib-

---

[1] This area in 1890 included Connecticut, Delaware, District of Columbia, Massachusetts, New Hampshire, New Jersey, New York, Rhode Island, and Vermont, with the cities therein, and 83 cities of 5000 or more population in other states. In the census of 1900, the area included the states named above, with the exception of Delaware, and with the addition of Maine and Michigan, and included 153 cities outside the states named, having a population of 8000 or more. The comparison, therefore, is not between identical areas.

uted to preventive and remedial agencies, summarized as follows : —

Control of the milk supply by licensing and supervision of milk-dealers; inspection of outside dairies supplying milk, and the exclusion of the produce of dairies in unsanitary condition; the enforcement of strict regulations requiring the immediate reporting of contagious disease (among which tuberculosis is included); inspection of infected premises, and strict quarantine during the disease, with complete disinfection after its termination; obligatory vaccination of school children, free baths, public and private, for bath and laundry purposes. Tenement-houses and lodging-houses are repeatedly inspected, and made to comply with sanitary regulations, and other municipal improvements are made of a similar character.

The most encouraging fact about this decrease in the death-rate is that it has occurred not only in the last ten years, but that, with minor fluctuations, it has continued for over half a century, and probably much longer, wherever registration statistics are available.

From the doctrine that there is in each community a definite standard of living, and that charitable relief is concerned, not with raising or lowering it, but rather with eliminating the obstacles which particular individuals and families have in realizing the standard, and in securing the withdrawal from the industrial class of those who are unfit for a place in it, there result certain conclusions which must not be overlooked. The first of these is that the community must provide sufficient hospital accommodation for the sick.

There are many kinds of diseases which can be treated effectively only in hospitals or sanatoria, for which the actual provision offered is everywhere totally inadequate. Crippled children, consumptives, and those who are afflicted by cancer, are the most conspicuous illustrations ; but it has been demonstrated that many other forms of disease, which have heretofore been neglected or treated only at home, can be treated more effectively in hospitals. In cases of confinement from childbirth, properly equipped maternity hospitals offer greater safety and more satisfactory care than is possible even in the homes of the well-to-do, and certainly greater than can be secured, as a rule, in the tenement-houses.

At the present time the hospital system in American cities appears to be in a transitional stage. There exist endowed hospitals, hospitals which are supported by annual contributions and payment of fees by patients, and those which are supported by public appropriations ; and many institutions rely, in varying degrees, upon all such sources of income. The financial problem of both public and private hospitals has become increasingly serious. In New York City alone there are twenty private hospitals, which, at the time of this writing, have an aggregate annual deficit of nearly half a million dollars, and officers and managers are anxiously scanning the future to determine whether there is any manner in which the encroachment upon endowment funds, or the increase of indebtedness, may be prevented and the hospitals enlarged to meet the ever increasing demands upon them. Frank Tucker, in an article in Charities of January 2, 1904, proposed the creation of an endowment of $10,000,000, under the control of an independent board of trustees, to meet this deficiency. This paper gave rise to an extended and spirited discussion, in the course of which Dr. F. R. Sturgis suggested that the city should cease to make any payments to private hospitals, and should expend the funds now devoted to that purpose to the maintenance and enlargement of its own institutions. Dr. Sturgis suggested that some of the existing private hospitals should be discontinued, by mutual consent ; that the remaining ones would receive only patients who are able to pay for their board ; and that indigent patients would be cared for by the city in its own hospitals. If the hospital system should indeed develop in this direction, it is probable that we would eventually have what might be called a hospital hotel or boarding-house, in which patients would pay for their boarding, while each would make his own arrangements as to medical care with a physician of his own selection, precisely as if he were living in his own home or an ordinary hotel or boarding-house. There are those who distinctly favor a differentiation, in this manner, between the professional care and the board, both of which are now provided by the hospital. The facilities of the hospital hotel, with its service of nurses and attendants, would be equally at the disposal of all physicians for patients who need to be removed from their homes, and who are in a position to pay for care in private hospitals. While so radical a departure from the existing system would seem improbable, it is quite within the possibility of the immediate future that there shall be a sharper distinction between those who are indigent and are therefore legitimate public charges, on the one hand, and who, as a result, will be cared for in public hospitals, or in private hospitals at public expense; and, on the other, those who can pay for their own treatment, or who can at least pay something for their care, the remainder being made up by income from endowment or by private donations. The recognition of this distinction, and the assumption by the city of the expense of caring for those who are unable to pay anything for their support during illness, would probably reduce the financial problem of the private hospitals to manageable proportions.

When once the community has passed through the pending revolution, and is adjusted to the conditions made necessary, on the one hand, by our congested population and the substitution of tenements, flats, and apartments for private houses; and made possible, on the other, by the advances in medical and surgical science and in nursing, it will be found that the care of the sick in hospitals is not only more efficient, but is much more economical.

At the moment, this adjustment not having taken place, there is much confusion in the hospital situation. Many patients are treated without charge who could afford to pay a proportionate cost for treatment. The income of the hospitals has come in part, as has been indicated, from private contributions, in part from paying patients, in part from public subsidies, and in part from the voluntary service of physicians and others. No clear and consistent policy has been followed by the city and state governments in the making of appropriations, and there has been great diversity among the hospitals in their requirement of pay from patients. Affiliation with medical colleges has introduced another element, since in such hospitals the supply of patients as material for instruction and practice becomes as important as any other aspect of the hospital administration.

Because of the uncertainty on the part of the charitable public as to the extent of the imposition practised by patients who are not really indigent, and the further uncertainty as to how far the hospitals are really needed for purposes of medical instruction, response has been less freely made than the case demands to the appeals for that part of the support of the hospitals which must come from them. The medical profession, aside from those who are directly interested in the hospitals, — a weighty exception, since a large and increasing number of influential physicians are connected with the hospitals in an advisory capacity, — naturally looks askance at the growth of the hospital and dispensary system, especially at the free treatment of the class that has heretofore paid for the services of a family physician. Medical associations have, therefore, insisted upon greater discrimination on the part of the free hospitals and dispensaries, and a rigid investigation of applicants, to ascertain whether they should not be excluded as able to employ a private physician. The hospital, as a strictly eleemosynary institution, would naturally accept this policy; as interested, however, in medical education, it must welcome a large number of patients, and especially those who offer an interesting and fruitful field for observation and study. The actual development of the hospital system will be influenced by all of these considerations.

Our present purpose is merely to point out that in addition to these facts, which are well known, a sound relief policy on the part of the community is in harmony with the interests of medical institutions in favoring a considerable increase in hospital facilities and a liberal support of the existing institutions; but is likewise in harmony with the demands of the medical profession that discrimination should be exercised in the selection and admission of patients, and that the increase should come, not by continuing to receive patients who are normally self-supporting, but rather by seeking out and securing necessary treatment and care for those who are now neglected or who are vainly attempting to keep their place in the industrial world, to which they might be restored after a longer or shorter period of suitable material and medical relief.

The lengthening of adult life to which attention has been called should naturally operate to lessen the need of child labor, and consequently to defer the period at which wage-earning occupations begin. This is, however, one of the phases of social progress in which there has been the greatest inequality. In many communities the industrial and social conditions have permitted a shocking sacrifice of child life, and the movement for legislation to prohibit child labor affords one of the best illustrations of the social effects which may naturally be expected to follow from the recognition of the need of a comprehensive policy. Laws prohibiting child labor in mines, factories, stores, and offices, and requiring school attendance, are essential for the physical and mental welfare of the child. The laws on this subject, in the various states, are seriously defective and curiously diverse: for example, the age below which child labor is prohibited varies from four to ten years; eleven states and territories have no restriction whatever as to age. The number of employments in which children may not work also varies greatly — from all employments during school hours in one state to mining only in another. Seven states require compulsory school attendance throughout the entire period during which employment is prohibited. In New York State, until 1903, according to the child-labor law, a child could not begin work under the age of fourteen, except during the vacation of the public schools. Under the compulsory education law, however, children between twelve and fourteen need attend school only eighty days in the year, and were thus left free to work for the remainder of the school year. The temptation for false affidavits was one to which parents yielded on a large scale.

Here, as in other instances, the matter of prime importance is to determine upon a standard [1] and then unflinchingly to apply it, by act of legislature, by charitable assistance when the law results in undue hardship, and

[1] See Florence Kelley, "An Effective Child Labor Law," Annals of the American Academy of Political and Social Science, May, 1903.

by the creation of a public sentiment which will severely condemn any deviation from it. Such a standard should prohibit the employment of children under the age of fourteen, should require attendance at school throughout the full term during which the schools are in session, to the age of fourteen, and to sixteen years if they are not at work between fourteen and sixteen, and should further require that children between the ages of fourteen and sixteen shall be able to read and write the English language before they can be legally employed.[1]

The principal argument which advocates of advanced legislation for the protection of children have been obliged to meet is that their labor is often essential to the support of a widowed mother, or of a mother who has been deserted by the natural breadwinner of the family, or of one whose husband is in prison or is incapacitated by illness from the support of his family. The most superficial consideration of this argument will show that it is one of comparatively little weight. Widows who are dependent upon the earnings of children from ten to fourteen or sixteen years of age are by no means so large an element in the population of any community as the constant reiteration of the dependent widows argument would suggest; in fact, the total number of widows in the working population is commonly overestimated. Some widows are provided for by insurance, or by the helping hand of relatives and immediate friends; others have older children, beyond the age in which legal protection is needed; others are left unencumbered by offspring, or with a family of such moderate size as can be supported by the unaided efforts of the mother. The comparatively small number who remain may, indeed, be without a sufficient income from their own wages and from other natural sources; but surely these are not so numerous, nor is the amount required to supplement their incomes so great, that it will not be cheerfully borne by their charitably disposed neighbors or by philanthropic agencies.

[1] In Massachusetts the law at present extends this requirement to the age of twenty-one, with a proviso that if they are regularly attending a night school, and over fourteen years of age, they may be employed.

Temporary charitable support, if the alternative becomes necessary, is better than premature employment. Regular pensions, given, if this be preferred, in the form of scholarships as a distinct reward for keeping children in school, are not demoralizing if wisely administered and if accompanied by uplifting personal influences. It is neither natural nor possible for a widowed mother to carry the double burden of earning an income and making a home for herself and her children ; and under a social regimen in which the male head of the family is universally the normal wage-earner, it can scarcely be pauperizing to substitute for his earnings, when he is removed by death, a regular income from some suitable charitable source. For the children to be set at heavy tasks before the mind or body is ready for them, is very likely to sow the seed of disease and physical weakness, from which dependency and eventual pauperism may result. Even the mother herself may be injured by undertaking physical burdens beyond her capacity more readily than by finding her load lightened by the kindly consideration of neighbors and friends, or even, if the former is not sufficient, by an allowance from some suitable relief fund.

The advocate of legislation for the protection of children must, therefore, be prepared to advocate for the limited number of families that are necessarily dependent upon the earnings of children a pension or scholarship system either from public or from private sources. Let the responsibility be frankly accepted, and let not the maintenance of a high standard of protection for child life be discouraged by exaggerated fears of the effect of charitable assistance as a substitute for juvenile earnings.

There are many who are in danger of falling below the standard through sickness, or lack of normal physical development, who are rescued by means of summer outings, playgrounds, and healthful recreations for which the facilities are provided as a part of the relief system of the community. By increasing the physical vigor of growing children, by providing a needed rest for tired mothers, and by securing an opportunity for convalescence, the fresh-air agencies perform a most important function in maintaining a reasonable standard.

Another conclusion which may justly be drawn from the principles that have been presented is that material relief itself may often be used in such a way as to enable the one who receives it to become independent of relief. This is most clearly brought out in the contrast between small, irregular grants, made from time to time to supply the bare necessities, when the applicant for relief has reached the point of destitution, and the loan, at one time, of a considerable sum of money, which, by enabling one to start in business or to continue in a small business already established, or to fit one's self for some new vocation, transfers the beneficiary of such loan, once for all, to the ranks of the self-supporting. Two or three important charitable agencies conduct, as a regular part of their activities, a special self-support fund, from which such advances are made, as nearly as possible, on a business basis, although, in the absence of absolute security, there is always the risk that the loan will not be repaid in whole or even, perhaps, in part. The providing of an artificial leg, of a set of mechanic's tools, of a membership card in a trade-union, of a uniform, or a waiter's suit, sometimes enables the one who obtains such assistance to secure a position which would otherwise not be open to him. To provide the fixtures and stock of goods necessary to open a modest business of some kind, may be the best and most radical form of relief.

The degree of success of this form of material aid is not to be measured entirely by the success of borrowers in returning the principal of their loans. While the maintenance intact of the original fund through the repayment of all loans would be the ideal, it may, nevertheless, be regarded as a fair measure of success if by such means families are made to become independent of continuous relief, who would otherwise be in need of it; and charitable loans should, in fact, be restricted to those for whom there is a possibility that this will be the outcome. Where there is a certainty of repayment, even if this certainty rests only upon the personal character of the borrower, loans can ordinarily be obtained on a commercial basis, and where this is possible there should be no recourse to philanthropy. Loans from a self-support fund, the principal of which is advanced from philanthropic motives, will ordinarily not bear interest, but some motive for prompt repayment is nevertheless desirable, and this may be secured either by demanding a moderate rate of interest, or by insisting upon an indorsement from some friend of the borrower, for whom it would be nearly or quite as great a hardship to pay the loan as for the borrower himself.

In all forms of relief, consideration should be given to its effect upon the standard of living of the family immediately affected. In order that relief may be educational, it must often include more than bare necessities. This is true both of care in institutions and of home relief; but there is an important distinction. Relief in an institution may be more readily adjusted so as to meet exactly the individual needs of the inmates. Relief for families in their homes must be more varied in character and in amount, taking account of the habits and customs of the social group to which the family belongs, and enabling the family to do those things that are regarded as essential to self-respect, and that will win and retain for them a fair measure of the regard of the neighborhood.

We may reserve for separate chapters two of the most striking illustrations of the modern conception of preventive and effective relief, viz., the elimination of disease through the coöperation of the medical profession with others who are in positions to contribute to that desirable end; and the movement for housing reform.

CHAPTER IV

THE ELIMINATION OF DISEASE

THE prevention of disease has been thought to be the special concern of the medical profession. This is, however, no more the case than that the improvement of housing conditions concerns only architects, or that the improvement of morals is of interest only to the clergy. There is a distinct mutuality of interest between physicians and those who labor for the improvement of social conditions. The struggle which physicians and health boards and sanitarians maintain, with greater or less success, to reduce the death-rate is, after all, only one phase of the warfare against bad social conditions. The death-rate is only a concrete sign of the existing state of the conflict with poverty, injustice, and crime : with the causes of human misery. "Social salvation," remarks C. Hanford Henderson, "must come about by changing men's ideas and bodies and homes, not separately, but contemporaneously." To lower the death-rate, involving as that does, under existing conditions, the decrease of needless suffering, the improvement of our physical bodies, and the elevation of our ideas, is, therefore, an integral part of social reform, and is an essential part of any comprehensive relief policy.

In the reduction of the death-rate the first place is given instinctively to the services of the physician and the surgeon in their treatment of individual cases, and this is as it should be. The maintenance of a high professional standard in the practice of medicine is of the utmost social importance. It is not a matter which concerns primarily the individual practitioner. For him the only thing necessary to his reputation and his pecuniary emoluments is that he shall be a little more skilful and successful than his fellow-practitioners. But for the community as a whole it is the general level of the efficiency and knowledge and skill of those who are to be intrusted with the health and lives of the people that is of concern. Medical education, therefore, and laboratory research are properly charges upon the community as a whole, and although their guidance necessarily remains in the hands of doctors of medicine, there should be quick public appreciation of every public-spirited act which makes the hospital of greater utility for purposes of instruction and the medical college of increasing breadth and efficiency.

On the other hand, physicians might take that part of the general public which has shown an interest in social welfare increasingly into their confidence, and might welcome more emphatically than heretofore the coöperation of the public press, of charitable agencies and public officials, including not only health boards, but those who from any point of view come into contact officially with the living conditions of the mass of the people. Such increased confidence and coöperation might profitably extend to clergymen, to employers of labor, to labor leaders, and to many others whom we do not think of primarily as interested in the problems of medical science, but upon whose aid the community must rely if the conclusions of investigators and those who practise medicine are to be made the basis of universal public policy.

A friend of the author once wrote in a personal letter that in his opinion physicians are, on the whole, the most bigoted body of men that he knew, with a single exception. Possibly the force of this severe and undeserved reflection will be somewhat mitigated by the explanation that he was interested in the manufacture and sale of a proprietary remedy. But whatever basis there is for the charge that some physicians continue the guild spirit in an age to which it is ill adapted should surely be removed. There are everywhere indications that the air of mystery surrounding the treatment of disease is clearing away, that the individual patient is frankly told much more than formerly of the nature of his disease, of the reason for this and that course of treatment.

There may still be justification for innocent temporary

deception and for professional reserve, but it certainly is true that the general tendency among physicians whose standing and practice are most assured is to speak frankly, to assume a modicum of common sense and general intelligence on the part of patients who show these qualities in other relations of life, and to rely for public respect upon their real skill in diagnosis, their acquired judgment as to treatment and remedies, and their familiarity with the literature and with the unrecorded professional experience which together place, of course, an impassable gulf between the competent physician and his best generally informed patient.

A similar change may be expected in the attitude of the profession toward other groups of workers whose social aims are similar to the aims of public-spirited physicians who wish to reduce the death-rate and to lessen human suffering. There are many things which might be done by others than physicians if these others could be confident that in doing them they are moving in the right direction; if physicians would offer them the necessary direction, encouragement, and support; if their personal relations with physicans were sufficiently intimate to permit the correction of errors before they had become serious and before the workers in question had done something inadvertently to invite ridicule or contempt.

The county and state medical organizations afford, in part, the machinery through which such increased coöperation might be secured. These organizations have rendered excellent service of a negative kind to the community in preventing loose and unsafe legislation, and have also participated in positive movements for social betterment. It may be that the trade-union element, the mutual benefit element, the class-interest element, or whatever that element should be called which socialists are trying to develop among workingmen, and which is so conspicuous a feature of Wall Street, has been present also in these organizations. There is no special occasion for criticism if that is the case, and yet the ideal undoubtedly calls for the organization of the professions primarily not for self-protection, but in order that through such organization more effective coöperation with the best social tendencies

E

may be possible. It is a question only of the point of view. The test of whether it is worth while to belong to an organization is not what it contributes to one's income, but the extent to which it increases one's power for useful service to mankind.

The Rockefeller Institute in New York and the Chicago Institute for the Study of Infectious Diseases are made possible by special endowment. Both of them will naturally find useful materials in the experiences of the charitable institutions, the settlements, the hospitals, and certain of the city and state departments; and will in turn contribute materials for the more fruitful prosecution of the work of these agencies. Those who favor a democratic organization of society, and who like to see workers get the maximum satisfaction from their daily work, might conceivably long for the time when special endowment or subsidies for such purpose would not be necessary; when each physician who has the capacity for research and the taste for it might afford to devote some time to it; and when such special labors as require the prolonged and continuous attention of the investigator might still in some way result from the mutual sacrifices of the medical profession itself.

Those who are engaged in the relief of distress, unless they are mere automata, are inevitably led on to the consideration of preventive measures. Among all the causes of undeserved destitution, sickness is the most conspicuous. It is certainly most unsatisfactory to be taking part in the relief of families who are in distress because of illness, and at the same time to realize that forces are at work and conditions are present which are undermining the health of others, and leading inevitably to the situation in which relief will be required. The personal indignation which is aroused by the neglect of such forces and conditions would be a valuable ally in securing the changes which physicians well know to be essential. The social force which might easily be developed among charitable visitors, professional and volunteer, among clergymen and church visitors, among trade-unionists and social reformers, can scarcely be exaggerated.

One of the diseases whose insidious and evil effects

are most frequently encountered by those who are called upon to inquire why a family cannot be self-supporting is malaria. It not only increases the hardship of wage-earners, causing irregularity of work and reducing physical energy, but it makes precisely the difference between self-support and dependence for many of those who are already near this dreaded border line. It attacks adults as well as children, and its full effects upon the economic position of the family may not be obvious until many years after the fever has been acquired. Is it not then important, if we would lessen the burden of poverty and the need for charitable relief, to do everything that science has demonstrated that it is possible to do to lessen the number of its victims? If it is true, to quote Dr. Howard's language, that perfectly satisfactory proof has been gained during the past few years that mosquitoes "are responsible for the transmission of the malarial germ from the malarial patient to healthy people,"[1] is it not incumbent upon us to utilize to the full every influence that will compel the adoption of the remedy which is thus indicated, viz., the extermination of the mosquito? Is not the time already longer than should have elapsed between the demonstration and the public policies which are its logical result? Should we not attack malaria in every community in precisely the spirit in which the military governor of Cuba acted upon the results of the experiments and demonstrations at Havana? The conquest of yellow fever as a result of demonstrations made at Columbia Barracks near Havana, in 1900–1901, that the disease is communicated through the medium of a certain species of mosquito, is one of the most brilliant achievements of medical science. The United States military government, during its brief existence in Cuba, not only freed the island of yellow fever, but also made great strides in the control of malaria and of tuberculosis. At the time of a visit by the author, in 1902, there were to be seen two interesting, tangible indications of these changes. In a corner of one of the general hospital wards there was a small enclosure the walls of which were wire screens. It was separated only

[1] " Mosquitoes : How they Live ; How they carry Disease ; How they are Classified ; How they may be Destroyed," L. O. Howard.

in this way from the remainder of the ward. In this room it was the practice to isolate any patients suspected of yellow fever. No mosquito could get into it, or if by any chance one did, it was not allowed to get out alive; and this was all the protection that was deemed necessary; whereas but a few weeks before isolation was accomplished by removal to a distant building across a ravine with many attending inconveniences and hardships. The change in the attitude toward malaria was illustrated by two large wards standing side by side, one built a year later than the other. Both were some three feet above the ground. Beneath the one built first, when malaria was supposed to arise as an exhalation from the damp ground, there was a concrete floor which cost the government $2000. The theory was that this would keep the malaria down and incidentally would permit a more complete disinfection after the flushing of the floor of the ward. Beneath the second ward there was the natural gravel which cost nothing. It is needless to say that the recoveries were as numerous in the one ward as in the other, and that cases of malaria did not develop in either.

Under a military government, action may instantly follow scientific discovery. All that is necessary is that there shall be an intelligent chief and efficient subordinates; but in a republic appropriate action on the part of health boards, state or local, and on the part of physicians themselves, is likely to be taken only when there is coöperation on the part of other leaders of public opinion. The treatment of disease, and especially sanitary measures for the prevention of disease, must be discussed elsewhere than in medical journals and at the meetings of medical societies. Physicians and investigators, as soon as the demonstration is complete, must be ready to take steps to create public opinion, and then must summon as allies in the new crusade all those who come into contact with disease, distress, and bad social conditions from other standpoints than that of the medical profession. It is generally understood that physicians must be leaders, but they cannot lead effectively unless they are in constant and intimate relations with all these other groups—relations which must be established gradually, and which should be a constant asset immediately available when new situations of this kind arise.

Defective eyesight, decayed teeth, an imperfect carriage, are, from a social point of view, not merely causes of individual suffering and occasions for the exercise of professional skill. They are also causes of poverty; causes of irregular employment ; causes of undue restriction in the field of possible industrial opportunity ; causes which may lead to physical deterioration in offspring. Such defects as these can be remedied, if the public sentiment of the community is alert to remedy them. Knowledge which individual parents may scarcely be expected to possess exists, nevertheless, in the community, and should find expression through the health board, through the school board, or through some other recognized agency. It may indeed be that the remedy would be found to lie chiefly in the education of parents and in the education of future generations; but whether thus indirectly or by more direct means, the prevention of disease, for which the combined efforts of physicians and of others are requisite, remains a fundamental and a most neglected public duty.

The most striking illustration is a movement which has but recently been inaugurated, but which is making rapid headway, and will for some time to come give the greatest scope for effective coöperation. This is the concerted movement for the prevention of tuberculosis. There has been a rapid transition in the public mind from submissive despair to eager hopefulness, from pessimism to impatient demand for fruits of the new knowledge which has been gained. There has been a slow dawning of public conviction that if, as physicians say, tuberculosis is curable, it must be cured oftener ; that if, as bacteriologists have demonstrated, it is preventable, it must be prevented ; that if it is communicable, then there is a moral responsibility to stay the infectious plague. The problem is how to utilize for the good of mankind the knowledge that we have ; how to extend that knowledge where it will have potent influence in the prevention of needless disease and death ; how to bridge over the gap between what is written in medical books and what is written in the sunken cheeks of the consumptives, of whom one may easily see a thousand or more in a single day if he will merely visit the hospitals of the city of New York, where less than one in twenty of the entire number is to be found.   Personal interest in this subject does not often need to rest upon an altruistic basis.   Nearly every family has lost a member or close friend, or looks forward with apprehension to an impending loss.   It is this catholic impartiality that makes almost inevitable a concerted movement against the disease; yet the impartiality is not complete, for consumption feeds upon overcrowding and alcoholism and undernutrition, so that again it is found that from him that hath not is taken away even that which he hath, and that the destruction of the poor is their poverty.

The lines upon which coöperation appears to be possible at the present time between the medical profession and agencies for social betterment are at least four : —

I.   The promulgation through personal interviews, through public lectures, through leaflets, through newspapers and the periodical press, through clubs and classes, through the schools and colleges, and through every other practicable channel of public education, of the idea that the consumptive must properly care for his sputum ; that tuberculosis should be recognized and treated at the earliest possible moment ; that nutritious and suitable food is essential, and that the physical presence of a consumptive who is intelligent and conscientious is not necessarily dangerous to others.

II.   The opening of numerous and not too populous houses of rest for advanced cases — where there shall be every attempt to make easier the closing hours of life, to detect and help any hopeful case, to provide for outdoor exercise and indoor recreation, to permit occasional or even frequent visits from friends under proper precautions, and in general to create those conditions of cheerfulness and physical comfort that will lead patients readily to enter and to remain whenever the conditions in the patient's home are such as do not permit him to remain there with comfort and safety.   They may properly be maintained either by local taxation or by private benevolence, and they should be numerous enough to make long journeys unnecessary and to remove all inducement to overcrowding.

These houses of rest may profitably be supplemented by endowments or by generous private gifts for individual patients to show how much can be done in even apparently hopeless cases if ideal conditions are attained. The interests of humanity and of science alike require numerous experiments even with advanced cases to see whether at least some of the more distressing features cannot be still further mitigated.

III. The erection of well-equipped sanatoria for the treatment of lung diseases, favorably situated as to climate, as to altitude, as to remoteness from congested populations, as to scenery, and in all other respects, in order that no known condition favorable to recovery shall be absent if it is feasible to secure it. In these hospitals there should be ample, even lavish, provision for the essentials of treatment. There should be no hesitation to provide everything in the way of grounds, and buildings, and maintenance ; and above all there should be no parsimony as to professional services and no lack of opportunity for laboratory research and experiment.

To the charge that this would be the creation of a favored class of public dependents, it is to be replied that these things are not done solely for the sake of the particular patients who may be cared for, but for the sake of the entire people. We are in the midst of a desperate warfare; and just as we would give every protection to a garrison that was battling for the homes and lives of all, so we would concentrate here, upon the human bodies that are struggling with the bacillus which is our common enemy, every element of strength that will enable them to resist the disease. Every patient saved, or even taught simple hygienic precautions, is multiplied into a regiment for the further conquest of new fields. If we could at one stroke cure all our consumptives, it would undoubtedly be a boon to that particular body of people ; but their gain would be insignificant indeed when compared with the great gain which would accrue to those who are now sound and well, and to generations still unborn, in the removal of the disease which we must still class as the "captain of the men of death."

Liberal appropriations, therefore, to enable us finally to

make headway against tuberculosis, are preëminently justified in the extraordinary position in which we are just
now placed.   It is no more of a scourge than formerly.   The
difference is that we know more about it; and there is
added reproach in every year in which that knowledge remains merely a means of hardship to the consumptive poor,
through increasing their difficulties in finding and keeping employment and in moving from place to place, and
does not show itself in the conquest of the plague.

Whether these more expensive and elaborate hospitals
for treatable cases should be built and conducted by the
state, or by the local municipalities or by private means,
is a question which may be decided differently in different
communities.   In New York, where the state tax at the
time of the present writing has passed the vanishing point
and become a fiction, while local taxation is a heavy burden, the policy which has been adopted of at least one
state hospital in the Adirondacks seems clearly justified,
and it is doubtful whether better results would not be obtained if the plan of county support of individual patients
were entirely abandoned.   Similar hospitals erected and
endowed by private philanthropy, making special provision for those who can afford to pay small sums for maintenance, would admirably supplement this action of the state.

IV.   Besides the educational propaganda, the houses of
rest, the hospitals for incipient cases of tuberculosis, or, as
it is better to say, for lung diseases or for diseases of the
throat and lungs, there is indicated still a fourth line of
action.   We need far more knowledge than is at present
available as to the relation between overcrowding and
tuberculosis, not only in living and sleeping rooms, but in
business offices, printing establishments, and similar places
of employment; as to the relation between occupations
and the disease; as to the extent to which the disease is
really what the Germans call it, a house disease; especially as to the infection of the cheaper tenements —
where, of course, the most advanced cases among the poor
gravitate, since with the duration of illness they naturally
move into cheaper and cheaper rooms as wages are reduced
and finally cut off entirely, and as savings are then gradually exhausted.

That there is frequently direct infection in business offices, even where salaries are high, hardly admits of question. That in the cities there are many rooms in basements, where the direct sunlight never enters, where ventilating systems, if they are provided, are apt not to be in working order, or at least not to be working, and where employees are in too close contact, is also susceptible of easy demonstration. But these things need to be made matters of record, and a basis established, first, for voluntary reform by proprietors and managers of these offices, who are often merely ignorant or thoughtless; and then, so far as the evil is not remedied voluntarily, for restrictive legislation by health boards or by local or state legislative bodies. It may be also that the erection of high office buildings will be found to have some direct bearing upon the prevalence of tuberculosis. The primary task will be an inquiry as to the number of persons whose usual supply of light and air in working hours does not reach a carefully determined minimum, and as to the existing safeguards against direct infection.

When plans were submitted in a large city recently for new public bath-houses, many were quick to express surprise that they were to be only one story in height to permit use of skylights. That the architect and the charity expert who had planned them had been determined above all to be sure that bathers should be amply supplied with air and sunlight, as well as with water, is a cause for congratulation, and that the wonder of the aldermen and others who objected to the plans is typical of uneducated public sentiment in general is equally cause for regret.

We need also far more experience and knowledge than we now have as to the wisdom of aiding individual patients to remove to a more favorable climate, and as to the means of supporting them at a distance from their homes. The ethics of aided transportation of consumptives are still rather crude and undeveloped, and the complementary ethics and public policy of restricting immigration and interstate migration of consumptives also need further elucidation. This fourth suggestion is, therefore, that there is need of investigation of certain social aspects of the disease, in which there is fully as much opportunity for coöperation between the medical profession and lay societies and individuals interested in the social welfare as in other lines that have been indicated.

In New York City, in the light of the extraordinary success of the Tenement-House Committee of the Charity Organization Society in its movement for tenement-house reform, it was in 1902 decided to inaugurate a committee on the prevention of tuberculosis in the same society in which there should be ample representation of physicians, of men of business experience, and of men and women who were identified with other movements for social reform, thus affording that combination of scientific knowledge, of medical experience, of business efficiency, and of social enthusiasm that will permit some real contribution to the application of our existing knowledge to our recognized existing evils. This committee has been energetically and successfully at work.[1] In Chicago, Boston, Washington, Buffalo, and St. Louis similar plans have been inaugurated, and other cities are taking steps to crystallize public sentiment on the subject.[2]

There is another field in which the next step in reform appears to await an impetus from outside the medical profession. The practice of midwifery is virtually without regulation, except in five or six states, chiefly for the reason that physicians are reluctant to assume any responsibility for it, and have apparently cherished the hope that it would either die out altogether from natural causes or that public sentiment would eventually call for legislative prohibition.

In a period of six years, from 1891 to 1896 inclusive, there appears to have been in New York City a slight decrease, probably about 3 per cent, in the number of cases attended by midwives. It is known, however, that many cases are not reported. It has been estimated again that

[1] The first annual report of this committee, published in 1903, is expanded into a "Handbook on the Prevention of Tuberculosis," 388 pages, with important contributions on many aspects of the subject, including a valuable statistical study, by Lilian Brandt, of such social phases of the disease as are referred to in the preceding paragraphs.

[2] There has also been organized a National Association for the Study and Prevention of Tuberculosis, with headquarters in New York City.

in 1898 midwives attended 45 per cent of the births reported; that in 1900 the percentage increased to 49, while by 1903 it fell again to 45 per cent. Whichever of the two periods may afford the more accurate indication of present tendencies, it would appear that the midwife, in New York City, at least, is being only very slowly, if at all, displaced by the physician. It is possible that the proportion of midwifery cases is merely kept up by the inflow of immigration. In confirmation of this view is the fact that a very large proportion of the cases occurring in the families known to the United Hebrew Charities are now treated by the physicians of a free lying-in hospital, whereas only seven years ago nearly all were attended by midwives.

That the midwives are in large part totally ignorant of aseptic treatment, that many cases result fatally because of their lack of knowledge and skill, and that a very much larger number of women suffer more or less permanent injury from such defects, is generally believed. Whether the remedy lies in a prohibition of midwifery; in an increase in the amount of free treatment provided by charitable institutions; in an increase in the number of women physicians; in the official regulation and licensing of mid-wifery; or in the *laissez-faire* policy of the present, is a problem in which social considerations are quite as important as those which are of direct professional importance to physicians.

Assuming that the number of deaths from puerperal fever is a trustworthy index of the comparative efficiency of physicians and midwives, the author caused an investigation to be made as to who was responsible for the treatment in each of the 46 deaths from this cause in the first three months of 1902 in Manhattan Borough, New York City. It was surprising to find that in 21 of these cases the patient was under the exclusive charge of a physician, while in 21 cases, an exactly equal number, the patient was originally attended by a midwife, although in most of the latter cases a physician was called after the fever had developed. Eighteen of these 46 patients died in hospitals, all of these having been treated outside by physicians and removed to the hospital shortly before death. In two cases it was probable that abortion had been produced by unknown persons. In four cases the physician believed that infection was due to the nurse employed by the patient, who was ignorant or did not observe instructions. In two cases physicians had reported that midwives had been employed where investigation showed the statement to have been incorrect. It is probable that the official records at the department of health do not show all deaths from puerperal fever, since the opinion has been freely expressed that there are cases in which death occurs from this cause, but is reported to have occurred from some other cause. These statistics, although the period may be too brief to justify any generalization, point toward the conclusion that infection resulting in death occurs as frequently in the practice of physicians as in that of midwives, and they point also toward the conclusion that the regulation of midwifery and the licensing of such as have shown their competence would probably lessen or eliminate the existing evils resulting from their practice. If so, the fact that the use of the midwife is a long established custom among immigrants of several nationalities, the lower expense and the widespread preference for employing the services of women in this capacity would become decisive in deciding what legislation should be enacted.[1]

Other illustrations of the advantage to society from such coöperation as has been described lie at hand if they are needed. Twice in as many years the physicians of New York joined with the reformers, the charity workers, the clergymen, the public press, and a host of good citizens to defend the charitable institutions of the state from what they believed to be vicious political attack, and the acquaintance and common experience gained in those controversies proved to be of great service in later, more agreeable tasks. Physicians in public offices, not only in health and sanitary departments, but in such allied branches of the public service as street cleaning, in administrative positions connected with charitable and correctional work, in public education and in legislative bodies, give everywhere evidence of the value of medical

[1] "Obstetrics in the Tenements," Ralph Folks, Charities, Vol. IX, p. 429.

training and experience as a preparation for such service. As leaders of public opinion, through the medical journals, through the transactions of learned societies, through public addresses, through letters to the newspapers, and especially through personal contact with men and women who have the special genius and the peculiar qualities that fit them to act as leaders, physicians count for more than at any previous epoch.

In the emphasis which has been placed upon the value of this social service and the need for increasing it, there is no disposition to underestimate the social importance of the ordinary daily routine of a physician's private practice.   Philanthropists who give universities, libraries, and hospitals, thereby do much to promote social welfare, as do other business men by introducing a higher standard into their relations with their own employees.   And yet if we had to choose between such occasional and incidental acts of altruism, and the contributions to human progress made by these same "captains of industry" in the daily conduct of their various enterprises, we would scarcely hesitate to choose the latter.   It is preëminently so of the medical profession.   The legitimate call of public duty will never make such demands upon individuals, and will never be addressed to so large a proportion of the profession as to obscure the call of the individual who, whether for pay or merely in the extremity of his need, demands attention. The plea for increased coöperation confidently assumes that there will result from it not less but greater usefulness to the individual patient.

Improved sanitation, pure air in living and sleeping rooms, simple and nutritious food, and appropriate dress, abstinence from the use of alcohol and harmful drugs, and, in the cities, multiplication of small parks and playgrounds in the crowded districts, are chief among the means for the prevention of disease; and the authoritative argument for these things must come from the physician.   In the widespread movement for housing reform, to which we shall recur in the next chapter, physicians have taken an active part.   The intimate relation between improved housing and the prevention of disease is obvious.

CHAPTER V

THE HOUSING PROBLEM

THE problem of rent takes precedence in the minds of those who live in the tenement-houses of great cities over the problems of food and clothing. It is a striking coincidence that it is also with reference to shelter that the conception of a normal standard of living has been most clearly attained. Among the three primary essentials to life, it is in the character of the dwelling to be occupied that the importance of maintaining a minimum standard has been most clearly recognized, and in fact has already become a function of government. The principle may be said to have been established that it is a duty of society to make it impossible for any of its members to live in houses below a minimum standard prescribed by law. It is not alone the vital importance of insuring normal housing conditions that has brought about this recognition, for it may be that a normal supply of normally nutritious food is equally important. The possibility of securing necessary food and clothing depends chiefly on the efforts of the individual consumer, while housing conditions are only in a very limited degree under his control. For this reason the maintenance of a standard of shelter is more readily accepted as a duty of government. Another circumstance which has favored the early establishment of this principle is that the factors which make up a normal standard for dwellings are susceptible of enumeration, of exact definition, and of quantitative measurement. In regard to food, legislation can hardly do more than protect the consumer against adulteration and fraud. It cannot prescribe the amount or the quality of the daily rations of the community. To determine a legal minimum standard of clothing would be still more difficult. Sumptuary laws have not attempted to do more than to prevent excess in the direction of individual indulgences.[1]

It is comparatively simple, on the other hand, to regulate the construction of dwellings so as to secure an irreducible minimum of light and air, a certain degree of decency in the provision for sanitary requirements, and safeguards against fire and other dangers. It is easy, also, to make laws in regard to overcrowding, although the practical problem of enforcing such laws has yet, in the main, to be solved. This idea, now so widely accepted, of maintaining a normal standard in housing conditions, has not been evolved by a process of abstract reasoning. It has been forced upon us by the intensity of the evils which result from the unchecked operation of the *laissez-faire* principle. Those evils are found in their most acute development in cities in which there is a rapidly increasing population within a naturally limited territory. The most conspicuous example is the borough of Manhattan in New York City; but similar conditions have produced similar effects in other cities, of which Edinburgh, Scotland, and San Juan, Porto Rico, may be cited as examples. Referring to the conditions in New York City, at the time of its report, the Tenement-House Commission of 1900 says: —

"The most serious evils may be grouped as follows : —

"1. Insufficiency of light and air, due to narrow courts or air-shafts, undue height, and to the occupation by this building or by adjacent buildings of too great a proportion of lot area.

"2. Danger from fire.

"3. Lack of separate water-closets and washing facilities.

"4. Overcrowding.

"5. Foul cellars and courts, and other like evils, which may be classed as bad housekeeping. . . .

"The tenement districts of New York are places in which thousands of people are living in the smallest space

---

[1] In the seventeenth century, the Massachusetts General Court forbade the use of tobacco publicly or privately before strangers, and the purchase of "any appell, either wollen, silke, or lynnen, with any lace on it, silver, golde, silke, or thread." "Economic and Social History of New England," Weeden, Vol. I, p. 226. Other colonies had similar statutes.

in which it is possible for human beings to exist—crowded together in dark, ill-ventilated rooms, in many of which the sunlight never enters, and in most of which fresh air is unknown. They are centres of disease, poverty, vice, and crime, where it is a marvel, not that some children grow up to be thieves, drunkards, and prostitutes, but that so many should ever grow up to be decent and self-respecting. All the conditions which surround childhood, youth, and womanhood in New York's crowded tenement quarters make for unrighteousness. They also make for disease. There is hardly a tenement-house in which there has not been at least one case of pulmonary tuberculosis within the last five years, and in some houses there have been as great a number as twenty-two cases of this terrible disease. From the tenements there comes a stream of sick, helpless people to our hospitals and dispensaries, few of whom are able to afford the luxury of a private physician, and some houses are in such bad sanitary condition that few people can be seriously ill in them and get well; from them also comes a host of paupers and charity seekers. The most terrible of all the features of tenement-house life in New York, however, is the indiscriminate herding of all kinds of people in close contact; the fact that, mingled with the drunken, the dissolute, the improvident, the diseased, dwell the great mass of the respectable workingmen of the city with their families."

The conditions in Buffalo present a marked contrast to those of New York City, as thus described. Quoting from the Special Report on Housing Conditions in Buffalo, prepared by two Buffalo members of the Tenement-House Commission, we learn that "the tenement-house evil in Buffalo is practically confined to two districts — the one inhabited principally by Italians, . . . the other inhabited by Poles. . . .

"It would seem," says the report, "that there is no necessity whatever of the existence of the tenement-house system. There is plenty of room for houses of moderate height, easily accessible from all parts of the city by the present means of transportation, and there is room for very much larger growth under the same conditions. It seems possible, therefore, by the enforcement of sufficiently strict regulations, to exterminate gradually the evil as it exists, and to prevent its development in the future. These are the lines upon which the enactment of law should proceed, and if the time is to come when more unfavorable housing conditions must prevail, then the evil day should be postponed as long as possible."

The law drawn by the Commission to remedy these evils was enacted by the Legislature, and there was created in the city of New York a distinct Tenement-House Department intrusted with the enforcement of its provisions. The first commissioner of this unique department was Robert W. de Forest, who had been chairman of the Commission which made the report and drafted the proposed law, and the first deputy commissioner was Lawrence Veiller, who had been secretary of the Commission, and secretary also of the Tenement-House Committee of the Charity Organization Society. It was this committee which, in December, 1898, initiated the movement which within a brief period of three years had culminated in the sweeping victory for tenement-house reform in the city where housing conditions were recognized as worse than elsewhere in the civilized world. The new law tenements afford the greatest possible contrast with those of the dumb-bell type, which were erected with great rapidity up to July 1, 1900, when the new law became operative. The foul " air-shaft " of the old law buildings immediately gave place, so far as new buildings were concerned, to a large, well-ventilated court, and no house built under the new law may contain any room that is not adequately lighted and ventilated. In the dumb-bell tenements ten rooms out of each fourteen were usually almost totally dark and without ventilation, but under the steady pressure of competition, immediately created by the new and the more desirable houses; the demands of business, resulting in the replacing of some of the worst of the old buildings by warehouses, factories, and shops; and the operation of the new law, there has already come about a great transformation in those housing conditions which have so long been the despair of all who knew them, and which are so effectively described in the report from which paragraphs have been quoted.

F

The Tenement-House Department, under the judicious and efficient administration of those who had done most to bring about the enactment of the new law, has instantly been recognized as an embodiment of the idea that the social welfare of the great body of the working people is the legitimate object of state and municipal concern. The Tenement-House Department, although a new departure in many respects, fell heir to certain duties which had previously devolved upon the other departments. So far as the interior of the houses in which the bulk of the people live is concerned, it virtually is the Health Department. Sanitary inspection, the correction of unsanitary conditions, and the vacating of buildings unsuitable for human habitation devolve upon it. It brings about the improvements in housing conditions from which result less sickness and a lower death-rate and greater decency, and a nearer approach in many ways to rational family and home life.

It was fortunate that the introduction of the new law coincided with the introduction of an efficient administration. Imperfect as the old laws had been, it was found by the investigation of 1900 that practically every new house constructed was built to a great extent in disregard of those provisions. The violation of existing tenement-house laws was one of the most flagrant abuses discovered, although even if they had been built as the law directed they would have fallen far short of a reasonable standard. It is said that every new tenement-house built under the jurisdiction of the Tenement-House Department, has been made to conform with the requirements of the law in every detail. New buildings are inspected at stated intervals, and if any important defect is found, it is immediately remedied or work on the building is stopped by the Department. The law contains a provision that no tenement-house shall be occupied for habitation until a certificate is granted by the Tenement-House Department that it has been built according to law in every respect. Aside from this inspection of new buildings the Tenement-House Department, under the new law, systematically inspects occupied tenement-houses, whether old or new, and a system has been introduced by which frequently recurring violations of law cause a house to be classed as a neglected house, resulting in a special inspection and a prosecution of the owner, or an order that the building shall be vacated until satisfactory evidence has been given that the defects which have led to the action will be remedied. By the power to vacate a tenement-house the Department has been enabled to remedy defects far more effectively than by the procedure of tearing down a house as unfit for human habitation, since the property loss involved by this process and the inherent legal difficulties are so great that for practical purposes the power might almost as well not exist. Under the special provisions of the law prostitution was successfully driven out of the tenements, the effective remedy in this instance being a provision that the house itself becomes subject to a penalty of $1000 if after receiving notice from the Tenement-House Department that prostitution is being carried on, the tenant is not ejected within a period of five days.

Although it is true that, "in America, there are few cities to-day, outside of New York, where there exists a tenement-house problem, and few where there exists even an acute housing problem," [1] it is also true that in many of the smaller cities of the country there is material for the development of serious evils.

It is significant that the thirty-seven cities in the United States with a population between 50,000 and 100,000 had, in 1900, a death-rate very little below that of the six cities of 500,000 inhabitants and over. The death-rate for consumption, the "house disease," is even closer, being 21.9 per 10,000 population, compared with 22.3 for the largest cities. Both the death-rate from consumption and the general death-rate are actually greater in these smaller cities than in the cities which have from 100,000 to 500,000 inhabitants.[2] Evidently the small city is not

---

[1] "Tenement-House Problem," Vol. I, p. 131. The New York Commission found the germs of a tenement-house problem in Boston, Pittsburg, Cincinnati, Jersey City, and Hartford, and bad housing conditions in other cities. As a result of the agitation begun in New York City in 1900, investigations have been made in many other cities, and important legislation has been enacted in several states.

[2] "Handbook on the Prevention of Tuberculosis," p. 75. Published by the Charity Organization Society, of New York City, 1903.

without its grave sanitary problems, some of which, such as drainage and water supply, are closely connected with housing, and evidence is not wanting that there exist evils similar in kind, though not in extent, to those found in Manhattan "dumb-bells" or "barracks."

Four cities of the second class in New York State are Rochester, Syracuse, Albany, and Troy, each with a population of more than 50,000.[1] In a visit made to these cities by the author in the year following the report of the Tenement-House Commission,[2] it was found that in only one of them was there any system of sanitary inspection, except the investigation of complaints voluntarily made by tenants and other citizens, although in each case the representative of the health bureau who was interviewed expressed the opinion that systematic inspection of the entire city at regular intervals would be desirable.

In these cities and in others like them throughout the country protection from infection and from unsanitary conditions which sap vitality, retard recovery from disease, and increase the liability of contagion, is the greatest unrecognized need—unrecognized, since there is no adequate recognition of the need nor adequate provision for meeting it. It is not amiss, therefore, to emphasize a demand for regular, systematic, responsible sanitary inspection by local boards of health, including not only the investigation of complaints, but the independent discovery of things to be remedied. It is absurd to leave such discovery to tenants, who may be ignorant, or to neighbors, who may be timid and indifferent. Inspection should be educational in character, including definite oral advice, and possibly even the incidental distribution of suitable leaflets.

Early restrictive legislation should be enacted to make impossible the reckless exploitation of life and physical vigor induced by the possibility of overcrowding any given acre of ground, if it happens to be favorably situated with reference to opportunities for employment.

---

[1] In 1900 Rochester had a population of 162,608 ; Syracuse, 108,374 ; Albany, 94,151 ; Troy, 60,651.

[2] The results of the observations made in this visit were embodied in a report submitted to the second New York State Conference of Charities and Correction.

The law must say definitely: so much space must be left absolutely free for the circulation of air; so much protection from fire must be given; so much of light in the public hallways; so much of decency in toilet and bath.   This is the irreducible minimum fixed by the sovereign state as a condition to which all houses that are to be used as dwellings must conform.   Such regulation is not interference with the laws of competition.   It is but fixing the plane above which legitimate competition may run its course.

There should be either a state law or local city ordinances covering the evils most likely to occur.   Such law or ordinances might, for example, definitely prescribe the height to which buildings not built with elevators may be raised; the extent to which houses must be fireproof; the amount of space upon the building lot which must be left unoccupied, and the minimum cubic contents of each room.   This list is by no means exhaustive, but it indicates the kind of subjects upon which legislation might suitably begin.

The housing problem is unique in certain respects.   It is not strictly analogous, for example, to the relief problem involved in the supply of food and other necessities to those who are of deficient wage-earning capacity. There is in each case the recognition of a normal standard, but the method of enforcing it is necessarily different. In the one case the deficiency may be made good from charitable sources; in the other, it can be made good only by seeing that the buildings are properly constructed in the first instance, or reconstructed, if they are unfit for use as they are.   Action by the state is, therefore, necessary in connection with the housing problem to supplement charitable relief, which may, indeed, be called upon when there is not income enough to pay the rental of an appropriate dwelling.   As in the case of ordinary charitable relief, and as in the case of hospitals, the controlling consideration is that a decision must be made as to what is a reasonable standard, and we must then stick to it, accepting the consequences, however burdensome.   The puerile cry that tuberculosis cannot be eradicated because it would cost a large sum of money to accomplish that result, must be calmly disregarded; that relief cannot be supplied on a comprehensive and adequate scale, because relief funds may lead to pauperization, cannot be granted; that the housing problem is beyond solution, because for the state to prescribe the conditions under which houses may be erected and occupied is an interference with the ordinary laws of trade, is an argument not worthy of serious consideration. Normal living conditions require a minimum standard of housing accommodations, a reasonable chance for recovery from sickness, and a supply of the material necessities of life — not because these are necessarily the most important things in life, but because they are an essential physical basis for rational living.

Legislation and inspection are not the whole of improved housing. It is effected also by improved transportation facilities, by certain other centrifugal tendencies in modern life, such as the distribution of power through the electric current,[1] and by the erection of model tenements, whether on a business or on a philanthropic basis. Every really model dwelling which is a profitable investment certainly raises the standard of neighboring dwellings, creating new demands on the part of tenants, and reassuring doubtful owners as to what it is commercially possible for them to do.

Every improvement in the standard of housekeeping by which foul cellars and courts are cleaned not only adds to the comfort of particular tenants directly concerned but exerts an influence in raising the standard of all competing dwellings. The training of janitors and housekeepers, voluntary association among themselves for mutual improvement, and the exaction of a higher standard of efficiency and of greater responsibility for the conditions in the houses under their care, appear to be probable developments of the near future.

Educational propaganda, official inspection, and reasonable legislative enactment to prevent the development of

---

[1] When water power or steam is used for direct power it is natural that factories and residences should be grouped in great towns and cities. The easy transmission of power in the form of electricity permits a wider distribution of mills and of homes.

bad conditions are, therefore, the threefold means of maintaining a normal standard.   So far as the responsibility for preventing the worst evils of unsanitary housing has been assumed by the government, it has been removed from the scope of ordinary relief agencies.   There remains, even in communities which have gone farthest in administrative control, a field of activity for private charity. The element of adequacy in the normal standard of shelter cannot be absolutely and uniformly secured by legislation. It has been suggested that three rooms may be assumed to be the normal minimum for a family of five.   If this be the correct standard, it is then the part of relief agencies to see to it that the families under their care are not encouraged or allowed to be overcrowded according to this standard.   The desirability of economic independence must not be so exaggerated as to obscure the importance of securing adequate shelter.   If, for example, a family of five, living in three rooms, could become self-supporting by taking in a lodger, it may well be better that the deficiency in the income should be supplied than that the lowering of the housing standard should be permitted. The question must be considered, also, when it is proposed to place with collateral relatives a child or old person whose home has been broken up.   It is important to know, before deciding on such arrangement, whether or not the addition of one member to the family will mean, for all, overcrowding, according to the accepted minimum. Another temptation to countenance in individual cases a housing standard below the normal is met by relief societies when a housekeeper is paid by free rent of basement rooms, which may be fairly good as basements go, but are nevertheless inadequately lighted, damp, and otherwise undesirable to live in.   Clearly it is essential in such a case not only to give no encouragement to the objectionable plan, but to see that the family is enabled, by whatever means may be required, to move into proper rooms, or at least to move out of the cellar.

In cities which have not yet definitely provided for a certain standard in construction, the responsibility devolving on relief agencies is even heavier.   Nothing then can be taken for granted, and it is necessary to be on the alert for evils which, in other cities, are provided against by law. It will require more ingenuity to correct the evils when they are discovered if there is no explicit statute, but, with the coöperation of local health authorities, a way can usually be found.

Among the more recent and authoritative sources of information on this subject are the comprehensive work, in two volumes, entitled "The Tenement-House Problem," edited by Robert W. de Forest and Lawrence Veiller, in which is embodied the report of the New York Tenement-House Commission of 1900; and the report, also in two volumes, of the operations, for the first eighteen months of its existence, of the Tenement-House Department, created in accordance with the recommendations of the Commission above named. With these may be studied to advantage the report of the City Homes Association of Chicago on "Tenement Conditions in Chicago for 1901," edited by Robert Hunter; the successive annual reports of the Octavia Hill Association of Philadelphia, and the report of the New Jersey Tenement-House Commission of 1904; report on "Housing Conditions in Cleveland," by the Housing Problem Committee of the Cleveland Chamber of Commerce; "Housing Conditions in Jersey City," by Mary B. Sayles, published in the Annals of the American Academy of Political and Social Science; "Housing of the Working Classes in Yonkers," Ernest Ludlow Bogart; "The Slums of Great Cities," E. R. L. Gould, Seventh Special Report of the Commissioner of Labor; "Housing of the Working People," E. R. L. Gould, Eighth Special Report of the Commissioner of Labor; "The Social Evil," Report of the Committee of Fifteen, New York; "How the Other Half Lives," by Jacob A. Riis.

CHAPTER VI

THE RELIEF OF FAMILIES AT HOME

HAVING completed our survey of those relief policies which affect more or less directly all classes of the community, we may now turn to more distinctively charitable tasks. Among these we are to distinguish on the one hand the relief of the poor in their homes, and on the other, the care of children and of dependent adults who do not remain in their homes.

Those who, not being aged or disabled by illness or by any such complete mental infirmity as would make institutional care essential, still require help at their own homes, constitute the most complex and diversified class. In statistics of public relief, they are often distinguished from almshouse inmates as being in receipt of "partial support." An inference naturally drawn from this classification of paupers as those who are receiving "full support" and those who are receiving "partial support," has been of great comfort to advocates of public outdoor relief, since nothing appears more plausible than that it is cheaper for a community to give partial than to give full support. Those who hold that relief in the homes of the poor should not be supplied from public funds, or that it should be reduced to a minimum, contend, on the other hand, that full support is the more economical, since the number of beneficiaries is universally less when only full support is offered. It is obvious that many persons would accept aid from the public treasury if allowed to remain at home, who would not wish to become inmates of a public institution, even though the amount of aid which they receive at home is less than the cost of their maintenance in the almshouse.

Almsgiving to street beggars, or to those who apply at the door, is another method — however reprehensible —

of giving aid to applicants in their homes. The homes which such mendicants may claim are, indeed, likely to be low-class boarding-houses, casual shelters, or other makeshifts as devoid as possible of all the elements of a normal home. Since, however, money is given outright, and no attempt is made to control the action of its recipients, it must be classed, like that distributed by public officials, with aid given to the poor in their homes.

Vastly more important than either of the above, whether greater or less in actual amount, is the relief distributed by clergymen, deacons, and others who represent the churches in their care of the poor; and voluntary associations, founded either for the purpose of caring generally for the poor or for the care of some particular class, such as widows with young children, or working upon a basis of nationality or a community bond, as, for example, in New York City, the St. George's Society and the New England Society, both of which, although social rather than eleemosynary, have nevertheless created relief funds for the aid, respectively, of destitute Englishmen stranded in the community, or destitute persons of New England origin.

Doubtless it would be found that the aid given by private individuals to those who appeal to them personally, if any tabulation of such aid were possible, is even greater in amount and of even greater significance in its social aspects than what is disbursed by such organized charities as have been just mentioned. When we speak of relief given to the dependent poor in their homes, it will be understood, then, that we include what is given in this way by individuals, by relief agencies, by churches, and by public officials charged with the relief of destitution.

Certain broad differences are clear between relief in the homes of the dependent and relief given in institutions, or in any other manner. The normal family, which is the unit of society, depends for the means of livelihood upon the exertions of one or more of its own members. It is self-contained — independent of outsiders. Its domestic circle is sacred. The standard of living may be high or low. The income may be liberal or the necessities of life barely supplied. Between the family which is thus self-dependent and that of the true pauper there is a most striking contrast. The pauper type, whether in receipt of beggarly alms or of generous income, is a shameless and insolvent social debtor.

The self-dependent and the pauper classes do not, however, together constitute the whole of human society. There are some whose earning capacity, when exerted to the utmost, does not suffice for the means of livelihood; there are some who are temporarily disabled and have been unable to provide in advance for such a calamity. While many of these are isolated individuals, for whom institutional care of some kind may be advisable, there are others who are grouped in families and for whom the essential elements of normal family life, aside from financial income, remain or may be supplied. It is a task of the greatest difficulty and delicacy to distinguish such cases, and a great responsibility is assumed by those who undertake to supply the relief which will enable family life to be continued, when this must be done otherwise than by the normal earnings of its members. It is true that in particular instances an equal responsibility may be involved in a refusal to supply such relief, with the consequent breaking up of the family. In other words, the responsibility of those who are in position to aid and to whom a direct appeal has been made, can be met only by reaching a sound conclusion as to whether or not the conditions are such as to call for relief at home.

It is for this reason, primarily, that official relief from the public treasury and ordinary almsgiving are unwise and harmful. The conditions under which alms are given to passers-by, and the conditions under which public relief is disbursed, are universally unfavorable to any adequate consideration, on the part of the giver, of the following questions: first, whether the home conditions are such as can safely be perpetuated through relief; second, exactly what kind and amount of relief are required; and third, whether there are natural sources, other than the one to whom the appeal has been made, from which any needed relief should be supplied. It may justly be questioned, also, whether churches are in position to give dispassionate answers to these questions, except as relating to their own members. One of the chief concerns of the church organization as such is to hold the allegiance of those already affiliated with it, and to secure the adhesion of others. It is only in rare instances that a relief system under the control of the church or auxiliary to it can be carried on with efficiency and success. There is no reason to expect that strict observance of correct principles of relief will invariably promote the religious objects recognized by the churches, or that church membership can be increased or maintained, under existing conditions of sectarian divisions, by a legitimate use of relief funds.

If, then, public relief funds, indiscriminate almsgiving, and relief by churches should eventually be discontinued, the particular task of supplying relief to dependent families in their homes will fall upon private individuals and such voluntary associations as may be formed with this end in view ; — and private charity, individual or associated, is precisely the best reliance for such relief. In so far as it is organized, it should be unsectarian ; it should not be subsidized from the public treasury, but should be spontaneous, voluntary, and of a broad, catholic spirit, even if some place is allowed for patriotic or religious motives in its form of organization.

If a society were to be organized in a community in which there is no general relief society, and it were expected that it would undertake only this particular task, it might well take some simple descriptive name such as the Society for the Relief of Distress,[1] or the Provident Relief Fund.[2] General relief has in fact been undertaken by societies which differ widely both in their names and in their methods; and if there is no society for organizing charity or for promoting social reform, it will usually be more advisable to found a society with broad scope which will undertake among other things either to supply relief as one of its corporate functions, or to obtain relief from private individuals or from miscellaneous relief sources, if it is deemed that these are sufficient for the purpose. It

[1] A society under this name, commonly known as the S. R. D., exists in London and works in coöperation with the Charity Organization Society.

[2] This is the name of a fund from which temporary relief is supplied to families found upon investigation by the Charity Organization Society of the city of New York to be in need.

is now not uncommon for the charity organization society, the associated charities, the bureau of charities, the association for improving the condition of the poor, or the provident association to undertake itself directly to give relief and also to promote coöperation among charitable agencies and individuals, and to work for such changes in the laws and in their administration as to ameliorate the condition of the poor.[1]

There is scarcely any city with a population of ten thousand in which there are not the beginnings of some society which with more or less modification of plans and methods might readily occupy this position. It is essential that each city should build upon its own historical foundation. It is also desirable that there should be such a degree of uniformity in various cities as will lead to easy communication and comparison of results. These two ends will be found not to be incompatible if they are both kept in view. The danger is that one or the other will be completely disregarded. A newcomer who happens to be familiar with the form of organization in another city will, with greater zeal than prudence, attempt to draft immediately the identical institution with which he is familiar upon the new community; and, on the other hand, those who have given no attention to the progress made in other cities will follow blindly their traditional customs, and if a new condition arises will attempt to meet it with no guidance whatever from the score of instructive attempts that may have already been made to meet the same condition elsewhere.

There is no reason why there should not be far greater uniformity than at present in nomenclature, and progress is already noticeable in the free interchange of experiences among various cities. If a broader work is to be undertaken than that which is implied by the two titles first suggested, the choice would appear to lie between the

---

[1] Cf. page 351 for a statement of the advantages of obtaining relief as it is needed, case by case, as an alternative to a relief fund. Such a society as here suggested may obtain and disburse relief on either plan. If it is deemed best to have a relief fund, it may still be possible to obtain relief, case by case, replacing in this way amounts temporarily advanced from the relief fund.

brief and expressive United Charities and the title which is perhaps more widely used than any other and may possibly be regarded as somewhat more modest than the other, Charity Organization Society. The current abbreviation, C. O. S., is familiar in national conferences, and is in not infrequent use both in England and America. The older title, Association for Improving the Condition of the Poor, is admirable as a description, but is too cumbrous for common use and is apt to degenerate, as it has in some cities, into the infelicitous "poor association." To justify the name Associated Charities or United Charities, the society should occupy a unique and commanding position in the community. It should not be one among rivals, but should really be an agency which will bring into immediate intimate association the charitable activities of the entire community. It has been suggested that the name Charity Organization Society implies some attitude of superiority on the part of those who are undertaking, as their name suggests, to organize the charity of the community. If the society goes farther and offers to provide instruction for professional and volunteer workers in the social field, this again is thought to imply an assumption of superiority of knowledge on the part of those who offer themselves as teachers. Both of these criticisms rest upon a fallacy. The giving of instruction and the organization of charitable endeavor are tasks for which some provision should be made. Those who are doing these things are by that fact debarred from undertaking other things which may be of equal or greater value. Even the college faculty does not lay claim to greater culture or wisdom than belongs to clergymen, lawyers, and artists, made up as these professions are largely of men who have earlier been students in the university. The particular individuals who constitute the college faculty may be more or less capable than those who are their contemporaries in age. They are probably only the peers of the individuals who have previously been their associates. Some individuals become teachers of the youth of future generations, others take up other tasks. Neither the hand nor the foot is justified in claiming to be the superior. And so of the task of organizing charity. To secure a division of work and joint effort, where that is advisable, is neither a higher nor a lower task than the doing of the work itself; and for a society to undertake the organization of charity is by no means to lay claim to a superior task. The name is a suitable one because it is already associated in the public mind with thoroughness of investigation, with coördination of agencies, and coöperation among them, with adequacy of relief, with volunteer personal service for the poor, the suppression of mendicancy, and the promotion of social reforms. While it must assume whatever natural repugnance may exist to the idea of "organizing" so intangible and spiritual a thing as charity, it is quite possible to make it clear from the outset that organization is not mechanicalization; that organized charity is but the union of law and love, as it was formulated by Mark Hopkins in an eloquent passage before any charity organization society had yet been established. "Law and love! these are the two mightiest forces in the universe, and thus do we marry them. . . . As in all right marriage there is both contrariety and deep harmony. Law is stern, majestic, and the fountain of all order. Love is mild, winning, the fountain of all right spontaneity — that is, of the spontaneity that follows rational choice. Love without law is capricious, weak, mischievous ; opposed to law it is wicked. Law without love is unlovely. . . . Such a union is demonstrably the only condition of perfection for the individual or for society, and when it shall be universally consummated the millennium will have come."

The charity organization society pleads for law and for love. And thus we join them — organization and charity, law and love, mind and heart, the charitable impulse and the sensible action.

CHAPTER VII

RELIEF AS MODIFIED BY CONSTITUTION OF FAMILY

ON the basis of social status it will be convenient to distinguish among families who are to be helped : —

I. Orphan or deserted children, constituting a family.
II. Unmarried man or widower without children.
III. Unmarried woman or widow without children.
IV. Married couple without children.
V. Married couple with children.
VI. Widow or deserted wife with one child.
VII. Unmarried woman with illegitimate child.
VIII. Widower or deserted husband with children.
IX. Widow or deserted wife with children.

I. It happens occasionally that a family of orphan children, or children who are worse than orphaned because of desertion or imprisonment or other misfortune which deprives them of their natural protectors, are so related to each other, and are of such ages, that it is advisable for them to remain a family group. It is no infrequent sight for an older sister or brother to be responsible for the care of younger brothers and sisters during the entire working day, because of the employment of both parents or of the only surviving parent. So numerous are these " little mothers " that a society has been formed especially to provide outings and other forms of assistance for them. Less frequently the maintenance as well as the oversight of younger brothers and sisters falls upon such children as are of working age. If before this need arises one or more have already become wage-earners or are in position to earn a fair income at once, the situation does not necessarily call for outside assistance. Natural affection and a praiseworthy ambition to take the place of the breadwinners

of the family may lead to sacrifices as great and to results
as successful as those which are seen in hard-working
parents. If it is an older sister upon whom this burden
falls, it may indeed be one of crushing weight, and may
call for endowments and physical endurance which are
rarely to be found in any class.

In such families as this there are likely to come crises
when, on account of sickness or the loss of work or experiences which bring exceptional financial obligations, a
helping hand is advisable. Such occasions should be
anticipated by those who are in such natural and intimate
relations with the family as to learn about them, without
the necessity of formal application to church, relief society,
or others. It will not weaken the character of children
so situated to have such help. It is, indeed, wise to guard
against the danger of teaching the lesson that begging
pays, but under the circumstances described this is not the
great danger. This lies rather in the possibility that such
heroic and splendid efforts as are being made toward self-
support may fail, and that the seeds of bitterness for
neglect and for lack of human sympathy may take root.
Not that there is really a lack of such sympathy, but it may
for one accidental reason or another fail to find its legitimate object, and there may exist, along with the very qualities which cause so difficult a task to be undertaken, a
sensitiveness which shrinks from wide acquaintance or
ready response to neighborly overtures. The danger, as
in so large a number of cases, is less the undermining of
character than the failure to build up character. It has
too often been assumed that the only problem for the
charitable is to refrain from destroying the character of
the independent, self-respecting normal citizen. This is
indeed essential, but very often it is a widely different
duty which confronts the community. The task is rather
to bring up to the level of normal citizenship those who, if
left to themselves, will be overwhelmed by their adverse
condition, or who, if of adult years, are lacking in the qualities which are so highly prized.

II. The problem of single men, whether unmarried or
widowers, would seem to be a comparatively simple one.
If disabled by illness or accident, the hospital presents it-

G

self as the natural refuge in case there is no accessible home with relatives or friends. If able-bodied, it must be assumed that in periods of normal industrial activity employment of some kind is to be had which will yield at least enough remuneration for their own support. And yet the problem of the care of homeless men is found in practice not to be so free from complications and difficulties. Among those who present themselves as single, homeless men asking for aid in finding work, or for relief in the form of meals and lodgings, there are in fact some who are not without family obligations, but who have deserted their families and have afterward found themselves unable to earn even their own living; or if not unable, at least ready to seek help and not above the use of misrepresentation and fraud in attempting to secure it.

Furthermore the army of professional beggars is chiefly recruited from the class of single, homeless men, and of these a large proportion are not really able-bodied, although their own account of the origin of their afflictions is of course never to be relied upon. This is not the place to discuss vagrancy, which is essentially a police, rather than a relief, problem. The pseudo-charity which creates and supports vagrancy is entitled neither to respect nor to defence. Demonstrations that not more than one in ten of those that ask for help on the street at the door is "deserving," have little weight with those who readily respond that they would rather aid nine undeserving persons, than allow one who is deserving to suffer. Those who give habitually to beggars should, however, learn that giving to the tenth, if indeed one in ten is "deserving" in the sense in which that term is thus used, is more injurious than giving to the other nine. The gift without the giver is not only bare, it is an active agent of injury. The conscience which is relieved by giving to ten beggars in the chance that one may be in need, is a naïve and unenlightened conscience. The possibility of securing the necessities of life by this means, thwarts remedial measures. To give money or its equivalent on easy terms to able-bodied, homeless men, is not a neutral act, but one by which serious, direct responsibility is incurred.

It is by no means the case, however, that there is no

field for charitable endeavor among the unattached, homeless men, and even among those who have become professional mendicants.   There are few of them to whom, at one
time or another, there does not come a desire to break
loose from his associations, from the deceit and from the
unmanly dependence, and to take an honorable place in the
industry and the social life of the community.   A helping
hand in finding employment, or it may be in supplying
tools, suitable clothing, or even transportation at the oppor-
tune moment, may be so clearly justified that its omission
would be little less than criminal.   The reality, however,
must be distinguished from an attempt at imposition.   It
is precisely in the plea for money for such purposes as this
that experienced mendicants are most successful.   It is
essential, therefore, that the donor, or some one who can
act in his stead, shall keep an eye on the beneficiary, shall
see that he goes to work and remains at work, or shall take
such other reasonable precautions as will bring the greatest
chance of success.   There is no reason for discouragement
in occasional failures, or in the fact that improvement may
be slow ; but sincerity of purpose may rightly be insisted
upon, and so far as the more intelligent and capable men
who form a considerable element in the mendicant class are
concerned, it may be anticipated that, given a start in the
right direction, they will speedily make their own way.

It is in dealing with applications from single, homeless
men, more perhaps than in any other branch of philanthropic work, that discrimination and experienced judgment
are essential.   There must be a quick and sympathetic
appreciation for the tale of a boy who is really desirous
of returning to his home after his first experience in
feeding upon the husks of the swine.   There must be a
long memory for faces and voices, and characteristic incidents or expression in the narrative of the applicant, even
when all have been more or less disguised by the mere lapse
of time, or by dissipation or other cause.   There must be
an impartial fairness in considering whether there may be
an element of justice even in a palpably absurd story, or at
least of some unexpressed need which can be met.   There
must also be firmness and courage in applying appropriate
remedies when discipline rather than relief is required,

and withal a capacity for developing ever increased sympathy, and consideration, and patience, and hope, however large the number of irreclaimable human beings one has met. For it must not be forgotten that none is irreclaimable except relatively, that until one has infinite resources at his command he is not justified in assuming that any particular individual could not have been saved by other and different means than those which had been tried in vain. It is the part of wisdom to recognize the point beyond which, with the resources at hand and with a given attitude on the part of an applicant, nothing whatever of good can be accomplished, and to leave further dealings with those who are in position to apply other remedies; but this is far from forming or expressing any final judgment upon the ultimate outcome, even in those cases.

So far as applications from homeless men are concerned, then, the task is to single out those who have family ties, and to attempt, if possible, to restore them; and to rescue from a life of unworthy dependence those who by reasonable encouragement can be fitted into their natural places as self-supporting wage-earners; to secure for such as need it hospital and custodial care, and to give direction and counsel in regard to employment to such as can become self-supporting only through this form of aid. It is true that the responsibility for finding employment rests primarily upon the individual himself, quite as much as the doing of work after being employed. In the rapid shifting of opportunities for employment, however, from one place to another, and the numerous artificial disturbances of the normal course of industry, it is not strange that many who are able to work satisfactorily are without the initiative essential to the finding of work. The free state employment bureaus, and, to a still greater extent, the development of employment exchange advertisements in the daily press, meet this need, and sometimes a simple direction to one of these sources of information is all that is requisite.

There will remain those who cannot be helped by relief or by personal counsel, and who insist upon preying on the public and living the life of professional beggars. They prefer to live without regular employment, and are both in intent and in fact offenders against the law of the land. There is no choice but to prosecute and deal with such offenders as criminals. Through the system of probation and suspended sentence, and through timely efforts at reformation at the moment of discharge from prison, something may be accomplished even with these men, and among them, as among original applicants for relief, will be found individuals who are very responsive to personal interest and encouragement.

III. A deep-rooted instinct that woman is entitled to protection prevents the throwing upon the charity of the community of any large number of girls or young women who are absolutely homeless; they are not, however, entirely unknown. Runaway girls who become stranded in a strange city; women who are at a distance from their friends, or who have but recently been discharged from a hospital; and more often women who have outlived their years of active service as domestics, and who have drifted away from those upon whom they have any special claim, are found in considerable numbers in the cities among applicants for relief. Unless enfeebled by illness or age, or placed at a disadvantage by vicious habits or offensive traits of character, there is little difficulty in finding work for such applicants when able-bodied and supplied with references as to efficiency and character. Their natural resource is the employment bureau, although careful precautions should be taken against fraudulent employment agencies which are sometimes used as a decoy for houses of prostitution.

There is a legitimate but very limited demand for temporary shelters for the few who must be cared for until employment is found, or until there can be communication with relatives or friends. There may well be, at least in the larger cities, a public lodging-house, in which under suitable restrictions shelter may be provided for those who are not properly almshouse inmates, and who can readily place themselves, if given shelter for a day or two. The women's lodging-house, if one is established, should be distinct from that conducted for homeless men, and lodgers should be given private rooms and wise matronly oversight. In smaller towns it will be feasible to care for such applicants in a suitable boarding-house

or a private family. Convalescent homes pleasantly situated, and sufficient in number or in accommodations to
enable patients to remain until they have fully recovered
health and strength, are specially needed for wage-earning
women whose resources have been exhausted by illness, or
who are not in position to be cared for by friends. For
superannuated domestics and those who are past service
on account of mental or physical infirmities, the usual resources after their own savings are exhausted, in the
absence of relatives able to support them, is the almshouse,
and, for exceptional cases, the private homes for the aged.

It is a fair question whether for these more than for any
other class there cannot be made a valid argument in
favor of state old-age pensions. The normal family
contains within itself the element of continuing self-
support. The growth of children coincides with the decay
of wage-earning capacity in the parents; and even if there
are no children, the strength of the wife may offset deficient earning capacity in the husband, or, if both fail,
there are in the two sets of relatives double chances of
natural outside aid. The unmarried man has a much
greater range of employment, and for various reasons,
some of which at least are not likely to be altered, has,
other things being equal, greater money-earning capacity.
The woman who is dependent upon her own resources,
under existing conditions, finds her living expenses greater,
rather than less, than those of the unmarried man. The
only considerable offset to the economic disadvantage at
which she is placed is the greater natural readiness of
brothers, married sisters, or more distant relatives to provide a home for her in case of need. For those of whom
we are speaking, viz., women who have spent the normal
working life in domestic service or in other employment
which prevents their taking part in a normal home life,
this resource is greatly lessened. They may well be at a
long distance from their immediate kindred, and by the
very nature of their employment are likely, to some extent, to be estranged from those upon whom they might
otherwise establish a claim.

For them, therefore, if for any, the state might wisely
make such provision as is made for soldiers and for those

who have served the community in certain branches of the
civil service. Unless and until some such provision is
made, there should be great liberality on the part of the
charitable public in meeting the needs of disabled homeless women ; but this provision should, of course, take
account of the efforts made by the applicant to provide for
her own needs. If there has been frugality and industry,
and a disposition to help others, it may be anticipated that
more agreeable forms of relief can be supplied than if
these qualities have been lacking. An impossible standard,
however, should not be set up, and the principle is that
reasonable assurance of care in case of unavoidable misfortune will operate as a motive to thrift, rather than the
contrary. It is quite possible that some of those who are
now inmates of almshouses throughout the country could
be removed and cared for with greater personal consideration without in the least undermining character or discouraging prudence and application in the younger. It is
certain that greater consideration, increased respect for
individual likes and dislikes, and in general a higher
standard of comfort in the almshouses, is compatible with
every necessary precaution against pauperizing the community. This is a danger which is to be guarded against
by discrimination in admission, by diligent inquiry for
relatives, and by individualizing those who are admitted,
rather than by withholding the comforts and decencies to
which applicants have been accustomed.

Among the unmarried women and widows who apply
for relief, there will be some who are of vicious character,
or who are so addicted to drink or other stimulants that
only reformatory discipline and perhaps medical treatment
will be of any avail. In the plea that has been made for
special consideration for the protection of homeless girls
and women, these needs must not be ignored. Sternness
and decision in applying the only remedies from which
there is any hope of success are as essential here as in
dealing with homeless men.

IV. It is astounding that among applicants for relief
there is occasionally found the case of a young native-born,
able-bodied, unencumbered married couple. The natural
inclination of one to whom such an application is made is

to deliver an incisive and stimulating lecture, and send the applicants unceremoniously about their business, and, on the whole, perhaps no more judicious treatment could be suggested. Even when there is a handicap of inefficiency, of physical incapacity, of ignorance of the language, or of lack of acquaintance in the neighborhood, a very conservative course with reference to material relief is advisable. Those who remove to a new community, especially if it is to a foreign country with strange language and customs, assume a responsibility which for the common good must largely be left upon their own shoulders. In casting aside the acquaintances, friendships, and other social ties which are so often of direct advantage in solving the problem of earning a living, a risk is necessarily assumed, and it will be mischievous to implant the idea that this risk is less than it really is.

V. Accident, illness, or some sudden shifting of industrial conditions may justify relief for a married couple, and in old age the fact that both man and wife have survived will create no presumption against assistance, if the conditions otherwise demand it. The assumption that the mere existence of children in the family gives a claim for relief which would otherwise be denied, is one to which may be traced a vast amount of harmful giving. The test is not the number of children or the presence of any other single condition in the composition of the family group ; it is rather a question as to whether the family is helpable ; whether any radical relief is possible ; whether any beneficial result can be accomplished. If the relief perpetuates unwholesome or vicious conditions, it is equally to be condemned whether applied to a childless couple or to a family with many children ; whether applied to the old or to the young ; whether given to a dispossessed widow with small children, or to a homeless man.

Opportunities for industrial training leading to self-support need not be denied to single men or women, or to married couples without children. There is no reason why the expense of such training, however, should not, if practicable, be thrown upon the beneficiaries. The problem is different from that of training children, the product of whose labor can ordinarily have but slight market value.

In institutions for children, sound educational policies are usually incompatible with attempts to make an income from the product of the industries employed in the training of the children. Adult men and women, however, may more readily be put at employment in which the deficiencies of their earlier education may be made good, habits of application and industry developed, and even some degree of skill attained; while at the same time the product of the work done may be made to meet the entire expense of such training, while affording a bare living wage to those who are trained.

For aged couples there are in some cities private homes, and there is also a tendency, which is to be encouraged, to provide accommodation for aged couples in the public almshouse. With the safeguards to which attention has been repeatedly called elsewhere, there is no need of the inhumanity of separating husband and wife when they become dependent upon the public for self-support.

VI. A widow with one child, if able to do housework, may usually be self-supporting at domestic service. If better adapted to some other form of employment, she may prefer to make some arrangement for the care of her child, either in a home of her own or at board. It is found that there are many families who will readily receive for general housework, or for some special branch of household service, a mother with a child, allowing for the board of the child on a fair basis of exchange toward the compensation of the mother, and of course allowing the mother also to give so much time as is necessary to the care of her child. In many instances this arrangement is far better both for the child and for the mother than employment which causes them to be separated during the day, even if the remuneration of such employment is enough to provide a caretaker to look after the home, and to care for the child, or to pay for board of the latter in a private family. Much depends, however, upon the circumstances of the case as to the choice among various plans. Aside from the presence of some cause of distress such as might be otherwise present, there is nothing in the social status of a widow with one child which would make dependence upon charity inevitable. With a young infant, with a child requiring

exceptional care, and especially in a period of distress or
of transition, such as might immediately follow the death
of a husband who has been the breadwinner of the family,
financial aid might be advisable, and there may always be
such changes resulting from the death of father, brothers,
or others from whom assistance has been obtained, as
will create temporary need.   Other things being equal, a
widow with an infant child has naturally greater burdens
than a childless woman, but she has also a greater motive
to application and good habits, and if qualified physically
and by experience for any one of many occupations, she
will have little occasion to ask for outside help.

VII. The considerations which lead us to prefer that a
widow or deserted wife with infant child should find such
work as will enable her to keep her offspring with her,
apply with redoubled force when the child is born out of
wedlock.   The unmarried mother who is separated from
her child is deprived of a safeguard of which she is sometimes in sore need; and separation, whether the child is
placed in an institution, or given to a foster-mother, or
abandoned completely, is likely to result in the child's
death.   The mortality in foundling asylums has always
been notoriously high ; and while the chance of the foundling for life in a good boarding home is greater, this is
only brought about by a degree of vigilance and personal
devotion that is rare.

It is recorded by those who have had long experience in
the care of dependent children, that mothers who relin-
quish their offspring at birth as a rule gradually cease to
care for them, and seldom attempt to reëstablish the natural relation.   Subsequent illegitimate births are more frequent, and this may sometimes be directly attributed, on
the testimony of the mother herself, to the fact of the separation in the first instance.   Foundling asylums and
maternity hospitals which care for mother and child for a
suitable period and subsequently place the mother with
the child at domestic service, or at other suitable employment, therefore do their simple duty toward both child
and mother.   In New York and Boston a separate agency
for the particular purpose of providing situations, mainly
in the country, for mothers and infants, has demon-

strated its great usefulness,[1] while in Philadelphia and
other cities similar work is done by the Children's Aid
Society.

It is believed that the foundling asylum to which a
new-born infant might be brought and deposited by the
mother, with no requirements that the latter should make
herself known, served as a perceptible check upon infanti-
cide, and that there was a time when this awful crime
occurred more frequently than can readily be conceived.
On the other hand it is held that the existence of such
institutions, making easy the abandonment of children,
removed a deterring check upon illegitimacy. A change
of plan, by which mothers are induced to enter the institution with the child, has been for the better, although the
subsequent separation often permitted prevents the reap-
ing of the full possible benefits of the change.

If the point at which the problem is taken up is the
care of the mother and child after birth, there is no better
solution than that of finding situations in good homes for
such as are by nature and experience suited to this kind
of employment. It is essential, however, that the character and standing of the employers be thoroughly ascertained, and it is advisable that those who have aided in
finding such employment shall keep in touch with the
mother by correspondence, or still better by personal
visits. In fact, of course, the problem does not begin at
the point which we have assumed. Guidance and counsel
before confinement, removal of any social causes which
lead to this form of dependence, and educational influences begun far back in childhood are the true beginnings,
and in the last of these attention should be directed toward
the reformation and training of the two sexes alike.

VIII. It is conceivable that a widower, upon his wife's
death, should find himself seriously embarrassed in making provision for the care of his children, even though his
income had been amply sufficient to care for the entire
family. In the normal family the contribution made by

[1] Known in Boston as the Charity for Aiding Mothers and Infants, and
in New York as the Agency for Providing Situations in the Country for
Destitute Mothers with Children — a branch of the State Charities Aid
Association.

the mother to the common welfare is fully equal to that of the father even though it is not so readily measured in dollars and cents. The loss of the mother may well be held to reduce by one-half the effective income of the family, even though she does not earn a dollar of money, and even if the father contributes his share in the training and discipline of the children and in the heavier part of the household work. It does not follow, however, that normally the loss of the wife causes the family of the wage-earner to become dependent upon outside aid. It may be expected to result in a distinct deprivation of physical comforts, besides the greater and immeasurable loss of companionship and guidance. There should, however, be a margin between the standard of living, which is to be fully realized only when both heads of the family are living and in good health, and that lower level of self-support beneath which charitable assistance becomes necessary. In many instances even the higher level may be maintained if one of the children, especially if a daughter, is old enough to take up the household cares, or if some near relative of the husband is in position to step into the vacant place.

Whenever a home can be kept in such ways for half-orphan children, there will not infrequently result rather more of parental affection and moral training and the other elements of the home that has been broken by death, than when they are cared for outside the family, whether in institutions or in foster homes. This is a point, however, upon which generalization must be made with caution. A father whose daily task gives little or no opportunity for personal contact with his child may find it a duty to intrust it to foster-parents, or may find that only by boarding it in an institution for children can he give it the education and the physical care to which it is entitled. The guiding principle is that an able-bodied man cannot consistently with self-respect accept charitable aid in the support of his children, unless under very exceptional circumstances, and then only in the expectation of cancelling whatever obligations he may have incurred.

What is true of the widower is equally true of the

husband who, through the desertion of the mother of his
children, is left doubly responsible for their care.   Fortunately such cases are rare.   The act of abandonment by
the mother, although no more reprehensible than desertion
by the father, indicates so unnatural a disposition that one
is readily reconciled to a belief that the children will fare
better in the hands of strangers.   The husband's brutal-
ity may indeed often all but justify flight from a bare instinct of self-preservation ; yet all experience shows that
even in the most extreme cases of this kind a neglected or
abused wife will escape only with her children, or after
some permanent provision for their safety and care has
been made.   Reluctance to resort either to legal remedies
or to any other outside protection is the rule, and this
attitude is repeatedly maintained in the face of the most
earnest entreaties on the part of neighbors and friends
to institute legal measures for punishment and protection.

IX. In the central place of all charitable literature
stands the widow and her fatherless children; from the
earliest times her need has been recognized to be imperative
and unique.   Others may be brought to dependence by un-
toward misfortune ; old age and infirmity have aroused a
degree of sympathy akin to that felt for helpless children ;
but for the widow, upon whom through the death of her
husband has devolved, in addition to the duties which she
was already discharging, the necessity of becoming the
family wage-earner, through the performance, it may be,
of tasks to which she is physically unfitted — a change
resulting inevitably in a lowering of standards, in the giving up of a home, in parting with valued possessions, or
in the giving up of cherished plans for her children ; for
the widow and the fatherless there has always been pity
if not charity; there has always been recognized a right
to special consideration, even if there has often been
lacking that encouragement which would have been best
for her and for her children.

After all deductions are made, it will remain true that
widows are most often legitimately entitled to relief;
and yet it may be as well to be sure that the deductions
are made.   Let it be borne in mind, first, that it is one
of the fundamental duties of the male heads of families

to make some provision for the care of the family in case of death. This can be done through life insurance, through membership in some well-managed benefit society, or through systematic savings. It can hardly be expected that the average wage-earner will lay aside a sum sufficient to provide for a long period for his family in case of his own death; but it is precisely the period of readjustment, lasting, it may be, but a few weeks or months, in which the need is greatest, and an available sum in cash, even if it be but a few hundred dollars, may easily prevent any recourse whatever to charitable aid. Again, a widow may have children old enough to contribute to the family income, or there may be near kindred whose financial aid is not to be classed with that of strangers.

There are those, again, and perhaps these are the larger number, who do find themselves able to manage without the aid of their own children or their kindred. These are the women who have been independent before marriage and find themselves in position to resume the occupations through which they have earned their living, and those who have such a degree of energy and adaptability to circumstances that they put themselves into relation with the life of the community, offering some service for which there is a demand, and obtaining sufficient remuneration to provide either at home or at board for themselves and for those who are dependent upon them.

A charitable worker in one of the large cities has expressed to the writer the belief that any able-bodied woman of average natural ability can manage to support herself and her children if there is enough insurance to provide for the necessities of the family for a few weeks, or if she is aided to tide over this period of readjustment to her new conditions. The occupations to which such women as this worker has in mind would turn are those of laundress, seamstress, office cleaner, housekeeper, and perhaps in more exceptional cases, newsdealer, saleswoman, etc. This estimate is probably too sweeping, or at least, if true that the average mother can and does accomplish the result, it cannot be denied that it is done only at the risk of her own health, and too often with real deprivation on the part of the children. It would be better for the mothers, for the children, and for society to curb, rather than to encourage, the ambition to be self-supporting when this means that the income is to be earned by the efforts of the mother of a family of small children. Occupation which separates the mother from her children for the entire working day, and for six days in the week, is certainly unsuitable. It is rare, indeed, that any plan can be devised for providing a satisfactory substitute for a mother's direct personal care and oversight.

It will not be unreasonable that some contribution toward the support of the family should be made; but in the cities where rents and the cost of provisions are necessarily high, it can be made to cover the entire income only in exceptional cases. The increase in the number of occupations open to women has enabled many to pass from the ranks of the ordinary wage-earners to the more skilled and professional vocations in which hours of duty are lower and remuneration higher. Applications for relief are rare from those who are engaged in these higher occupations, and when they do occur are usually to be attributed to illness or to some exceptional misfortune.

What has been said of the normal deficiency in income applies only to the widow with dependent children who has no profession or skilled trade, and whose husband has made no effective provision for her support. The deserted family presents problems distinct from those involved in the relief of widows, and these will be considered in another chapter. After a long separation, or one that is likely to be permanent, and after due efforts at reconciliation or prosecution, as the case may require, the deserted wife with dependent children may sometimes properly be regarded as virtually in the position of a widow with children. Relief may be as necessary, and as fully justified, in the case of a deserted family as in that of a family in which the male wage-earner is disabled by illness or removed by death. This is true, however, only on condition that the criminal deserter is dealt with as such, and it is essential that the relief supplied shall be of such a character, and given under such conditions, as shall not encourage desertion on the part of others.

Every type of family group is encountered in the examination of the records of charitable societies. The proportions, however, vary in different cities, and in the same community they vary with changes in industrial conditions. Widows, deserted families, aged persons, remain a less variable factor, especially in the older communities, and from one year to another. In the centre of migration homeless men increase in number, and in regions where there are many deaths among wage-earners in dangerous occupations the number of widows and orphans becomes abnormally large ; but representatives of all will be found wherever an application bureau is opened, or where there is reason to believe that response will be made to appeals made to individual charity. The unity and the responsibility of the family are the first consideration in deciding upon the natural source of relief in any case, and the modifying consideration is the responsibility of the neighbor, or, more broadly expressed, the responsibility of society for relieving distress in such a manner and with such safeguards as will strengthen individual character and the feeling of responsibility on the part of the individual for the welfare of those who through family or other ties have claims upon them.

CHAPTER VIII

THE BREAKING UP OF FAMILIES

THE breaking up of a family by any outside agency is justified only when it is merely the outward expression of a destruction which has already taken place. The stern scriptural injunction, " Whom God hath joined together let no man put asunder," gains increased solemnity and force when children are born of the union so that the family bond includes the relation between parent and child as well as that between man and wife. The separation of husband and wife, the removal of children, the involuntary displacement of an aged member of the family, are the more usual forms of separation which are included under the expression the breaking up of families. Any one of these may be dictated by mere caprice ; circumstances may exist under which public opinion will approve any one of them ; conditions may arise under which the strong arm of the law may give its sanction to such a course. The presumption, however, is against either compulsory or voluntary breaking up of the family except by the natural and evolutionary withdrawal of children who have attained their growth and who come to rely upon their own exertions or establish new families of their own.

The family is the ultimate unit of our social organization. Other social institutions are supplemental to it, and it is not an unfair test of their value whether they strengthen and support the family and the ends for which the family exists, or on the contrary tend to disintegrate the family and to thwart its objects. Even the church does not relieve the family of its duty as a religious institution, but only aids and supplements it. The school only takes up the work of education where the family leaves it, and

H 97

upon the latter remains a responsibility parallel with that
of the school and extending far beyond it.   Hospitals and
other agencies of medical relief are expedients for restoring as quickly as possible to their active and normal
places in the family those who are disabled from performing their part.   Homes for aged persons and for incurables are agencies for the care of that limited proportion
of the class to which their inmates belong, for whom,
because of exceptional reasons, a normal life has become
impossible.   Orphan asylums and other institutions for
children are primarily to provide shelter and training for
children who are deprived of their natural birthright in
the opportunity for a growth and development in the
family, and for the parental care which, to the child, is
the chief element in family life.   The social club, the
boarding-house, the tenement-house, the employment of
women in factories, the higher education of women, all of
these, and countless other social innovations and institutions, are judged instinctively more by their influence
upon the family than by any other single test, although
each will naturally involve other considerations of greater
or less importance.

The application of the test is not always easy.   For
example, if it be asked whether homes for aged persons
supported by charitable contributions have the effect of
removing from the family those who should be supported
by their children or other near relatives, it is necessary to
ascertain how far the inmates of such homes really have
such relatives and how far it would be possible for them to
provide a home for the aged dependents in their own
families; how far such support, if given, would deprive
young children in the same families of the opportunities
now afforded to them; and how far, if at all, there would
be a reduction of the physical comforts now secured both
by the aged persons and by families who are by the
present plan relieved of the burden of their support.   Such
facts as these lend themselves to statistical inquiry.
There are other more subtle but equally vital facts which
it will be necessary to ascertain.   What is the effect upon
young children of the example set by their parents, when
the latter too easily throw off the burden of caring for

their own aged parents or their near relatives? Is there a social disadvantage in the policy of sacrificing the most fruitful and active years in caring for those who no longer contribute to the family income and who are of no direct service? In other words, using the language of natural selection, will the community which merely from sentiment cares for its aged dependents by uneconomical methods compete successfully with the community which disregards such sentiment and places those who are past active service in institutions where they can be supported on some uniform, and therefore economical, plan? Is there a conflict between the economic and moral standards, and, if so, which should prevail? If our homes for aged men and women are found to be as humane as, and more economical than, the plan of caring for the aged members of our families at home, their numbers should doubtless be increased and multiplied. If we reach the conclusion that they should be utilized only for those who are absolutely without near relatives or friends able to care for them, it may still be necessary to increase their number merely to provide adequately for all persons who are in this unfortunate position.

There is involved also the relation which they should bear to the public almshouse. The theory of almshouse administration has been that the conditions must be made less attractive than the home which the average hardworking member of the community can provide for himself in his old age. Otherwise there will be no inducement to make such provision, and the number of those who accept the public bounty will tend constantly to increase. In an ideal administration sufficient discrimination might be introduced so that those who become public dependents solely through misfortune can be surrounded with a somewhat greater degree of comfort than is provided for the shiftless, the intemperate, and the improvident. It would then become a question whether the almshouse thus conducted might not care for all who cannot be kept at home by their own relatives, either with or without private assistance.

The actual situation in most communities of the more advanced states is that there is little, if any, formal classi-

fication in the almshouse ; although there are in the smaller
almshouses an individualizing of inmates and a natural
grouping according to personal affinities which is better
than any other classification could be, and there is also
increased diversification among institutions.

Within the past twenty-five years the standard of comfort in almshouses has steadily improved, while at the
same time there is no tendency that can be discovered to
increased abuse of the public bounty. In fact, there are
probably to-day fewer almshouse inmates who should be
cared for by their relatives than there were a quarter of a
century ago, when the discomforts and privations of the
almshouse were much greater. This fortunate result is
brought about by a more general introduction of the practice of making some investigation when application for
admission is made and the exercise of wider discrimination both in admissions and discharges. The actual
population of the almshouse has not only not kept pace
with the increased population, but has, in New York and
some of the other more populous states, actually diminished. This is, of course, due in part to the removal from
the county almshouses of children and of many special
classes of defectives, such as the insane, the epileptic, and
the feeble-minded, who are now cared for in state institutions; but even after due allowance for this has been
made, it still remains clear that the increased decency and
comfort of the almshouse have not led to increased pauperization, and that it is perfectly possible for the community to provide adequate deterrent checks against such
tendencies other than the repellent plan of making the
almshouse a place of actual physical discomfort and privation. It is probable that the prejudice against the almshouse, while it is useful in stimulating every possible
effort to avoid becoming public dependents, has the
marked disadvantage of keeping in a state of actual want
and suffering outside the almshouse some who would
be distinctly better off within it. The duty of the
charitable would seem to be to emphasize the fact that
it is no disgrace to accept public care if it is necessary ;
the disgrace, where there is any, lying only in the
course of action that leads to dependency, rather than

in the particular method by which that dependency is relieved.

There is not sufficient accommodation in the private homes for aged persons to receive all who are entitled to better care than the almshouse affords, nor is this press-ure caused by a general tendency to get rid of the care of the aged persons by shunting such responsibility to the public or to private institutions. In other words, there is still considerable margin for the wise institutional care of aged relatives before the danger point of demorali-zation is reached, and there are doubtless several thousand persons in the United States for whom admission should be secured either to a well-managed private institution or to a reformed and improved almshouse, unless, indeed, the plan of providing funds to pay the board of these persons in private families is preferred.   There is much to be said in favor of this alternative ; but the discussion is beyond the scope of the present chapter, since in either case the beneficiary would not remain a member of the family to which he naturally belongs.

A similar series of questions arises in regard to the social effects of medical institutions, but they are easily answered.   Hospitals, whether public or private, homes for convalescents, and institutions for the treatment of special kinds of diseases, such as alcoholism, insanity, and consumption, do not as a rule have a tendency to break up families prematurely or improperly.   When the patient is curable the brief stay in a hospital or other institution, by restoring health, permits a continuance of family relations. One exception may be noted in some of the state hos-pitals for the insane where there are many slightly de-mented old people who could be cared for with perfect ease at home or even in the county institutions.   The high reputation of these hospitals is responsible for the readiness of relatives to send such patients to them.

Harmless senile patients, who are incurable, may safely and with increased comfort to the patient as well as with greater economy, be boarded in carefully selected homes if they do not have relatives able to care for them.   Small psychopathic hospitals, in which acutely insane persons may be taken for brief periods of observation and treatment, often restore their patients to their families without the necessity for formal commitment to an asylum.

The essential feature of the normal family is the relation between parent and child. Questions affecting the claims of grandparents and grandchildren, and of collateral relations frequently arise, and must be considered on their merits. If through long association or special circumstances such relatives become in fact integral parts of the family, their position should be safeguarded, but a clannish superstition which demands great sacrifices, possibly at the expense of children, for the sake of relatives who are not really part of the family is of doubtful social value.

By one serious menace is the integrity of the family endangered. The removal of children for destitution, for ungovernable conduct, and for improper guardianship is a state policy which has had an extraordinary development, especially in New York and California, within the past generation. It is true that there have always been children who, because of the death of their parents, because of their destitution, or their unfitness for parental responsibilities, have required some substitute for the natural protection of their own family, and it has long been recognized that children were entitled to some protection at the hands of the state against neglect, even if from their own parents. In some American communities the state itself undertakes to provide, either in public institutions or in foster-homes selected by itself, for those who become public charges. In the city of New York such children are, for the most part, cared for in private institutions, chiefly under the control of religious bodies, but maintained under what is practically a contract with the city at public expense. In other parts of the state the same system is in force, although the county authorities also place children in many instances in foster-homes either directly or through societies which exist for that purpose.

From the maze of complications and difficulties in which the whole question as to when children should become dependent is involved, a few principles emerge : —

I. Children should remain with their parents if the latter are of good character and have sufficient income for their support. Simple and obvious as this proposition appears, it has been frequently violated in the past, and in the city of New York its violation has been so widespread and continued as to create in the minds of many residents and, in rare instances, even in the minds of future immigrants beyond the seas, the idea that, by coming here and putting themselves into relations with the proper persons, it will be possible for them to rid themselves of the expense and burden of looking after their children. The rules of the State Board of Charities, under which children are now received and retained in public institutions, and the action of the Department of Public Charities under those rules, have checked this tendency to some extent, but have by no means eradicated it.

II. Parents who are of good character, but who, without assistance, cannot earn enough to support their children at home, should, as a rule, receive such assistance, and the breaking up of the family should thus be averted. In 1898 the Charity Organization Society of the city of New York inaugurated a plan by which a representative of the society called daily at the office of the Department of Public Charities to examine the applications which had there been made for the commitment of children on the ground of destitution, and after necessary inquiries, to select those who might appropriately be aided at home, as an alternative to this separation of mother and children. The result of this experience, set forth in the succeeding annual reports of the society, demonstrates beyond possible controversy that assistance can wisely be provided from private sources for a considerable number of such families.

III. If children are removed because their parents are morally unfit guardians for them, this removal should be unconditional. There should be no hesitation in transferring the legal guardianship in such cases; there should be usually no opportunity for intercourse between parent and child, and no obstacle should be placed in the way of such disposition of the child as is best for its own welfare. Without passing at present upon the relative merits of institutional care and the system of placing out children in families, it is clear that whichever is best for the child should, in cases of improper guardianship, be adopted with the least possible delay. The care provided by the state should continue as long as the interests of the child require, and should not be influenced by the importunities of relatives. Increased precautions are doubtless necessary not to remove children upon this charge unless the facts warrant it, as the danger of injustice both to parent and child is always present; but if, after careful review of the circumstances, a court decides that the parents are unfit to care for it because of moral depravity, or that the child is living under degrading conditions, the child should be so disposed of as to prevent the effective claim to the services of the child as soon as he is old enough to have a money value to the parent who has been declared to be an unfit guardian.

IV. If children are removed because of their own incorrigible conduct, the expense of their maintenance in a disciplinary institution should be borne by their parents, and the period of their detention should be as short as is consistent with the objects in view when commitment is made. This involves the principle of an indeterminate sentence, since the temporary guardians will be the best judges as to when the conduct of the child is sufficiently improved to warrant his return to his parents. Neither incorrigible conduct nor improper guardianship, however, should be used as a mere cloak to enable parents to shift the burden of caring for their children upon the city; nor should a child committed as ungovernable be retained merely because the parents are believed to be unfit guardians. If, when the question of discharging the child arises, the unfitness of parents to care for their children is called into question, this should be definitely passed upon by a court, and if they are unfit, because of viciousness or immorality, appropriate action should be taken upon this basis.

V. Orphans, abandoned children, the whereabouts of whose parents are unknown, and others who for any exceptional reason may be treated without regard to their parents or other relatives, do not raise any question as to the breaking up of a family, and, as in the case of children whose parents are pronounced unfit guardians, they may be cared for by whatever methods are believed to be best for

themselves.   If, however, there are older children able to
make a home for their younger brothers and sisters, it
may be, and often is, expedient to keep the family together,
as in the case of parents of good character.

VI. The children of destitute parents for whom no
adequate private assistance is forthcoming, in a community which has no public outdoor relief, must necessarily be cared for either in institutions where they may
be placed by their parents, or by a system of boarding in
private families, without legal adoption or other transfer
of guardianship from the parents.   The latter have done
nothing to sacrifice their claim upon the children, and yet
the children cannot be permitted to suffer.   Theoretically
this is the class of children for whose sake chiefly the great
institutional system of New York City has grown up.   The
managers of those institutions, having in mind children of
this class, indignantly and with some justification deny that
their institutions have a tendency to break up families.
In their eyes the institution is like a hospital, in that it
provides temporary care for one who will shortly be
restored to the family, but for whom proper provision cannot at the moment be made.   As the children of the well-
to-do are sent to the boarding school, so the children of the
poor are sent to the only place where corresponding opportunities are provided by the city for the poor.

There is a definite place for the institution in the care
of some of the children of this class as well as in the care
of children who are ungovernable, and for the temporary
care of children whose parents are unfit guardians, and
who should eventually be placed in foster-homes so far as
good homes can be provided.   Private charity should reduce the number of children committed solely for destitution as far as possible, and only the remainder, who for
exceptional reasons cannot be aided at home, should become public charges.   The commitment of children for
destitution does sometimes lead to the breaking up of
the family, and it should be avoided whenever the deficiency in family income can be made good without injury
to parents or children.   There are instances in which the
temporary care of children in institutions during a period
of illness or other misfortune really has the effect in the

long run of keeping the family intact, and full recognition of this public service should be made. The danger, however, that the separation will be extended beyond the period for which it is justified, and the disadvantages of even a brief separation of children from their parents and their reception into a large institution where their individuality is lost sight of, should also be recognized. The breaking up of families by the removal of children for insufficient reasons, the accompanying loss of a sense of responsibility on the part of parents, failure on the part of parents to make even reasonable efforts to care for offspring, the desertion of families in order to secure the commitment of children, the refusal of near relatives other than parents to play their part in the carrying of burdens of this kind, and the easy-going complaisance of public officials in accepting as public charges those for whom other provisions should be made — these are serious evils, constituting a public menace, which in many communities a few courageous, high-minded, public-spirited citizens are vigorously and effectively combating.

CHAPTER IX

DEPENDENT CHILDREN

To preserve a normal family life for growing children, to keep children, even with sacrifices and even by external relief, with their own parents when they are fit guardians, and to prevent the breaking up of any family until the evidence is clear that the physical and spiritual welfare of one or more of its members make it absolutely necessary, are primary considerations of a sound relief policy. Such. efforts, however, will not always prove successful. Unfortunately there are parents who are demonstrably unfit to rear the children whom they have brought into the world; there are orphan children for whom no home offers with near relatives and for whom the parents have made no provision. There are children whose parents or natural guardians are disabled by illness, not only from earning their support, but from giving them such care as would justify material relief. There are instances in which a widow with many children may more wisely submit to the removal of one or more to enable her to care for the remainder with or without aid, although, as has been pointed out, the presumption is in favor of the family's remaining intact, if this is possible.

Death, sickness, abuse, neglect, or sheer inability may therefore, here or there, leave to the community the responsibility for the care of dependent children. In primitive communities either of two courses is likely to be followed. Exposure and hardships may lead to the death of a large proportion of such orphaned or neglected children, leaving but a remnant of exceptionally tough fibre to survive, or they may be taken in by neighbors to become virtually integral members of the family which thus formally or informally adopts them. Numerous instances

107

might readily be cited of the adoption by kind-hearted neighbors of whole families of children with or without some claim of relationship. When, for any reason, the number becomes noticeably large, the church or private individuals are likely to establish homes in which such children are gathered for education and maintenance, and finally the support of such asylums is apt to be undertaken in whole or in part by the state. Childless families desiring young children for adoption, or those who wish to secure inexpensive service, giving maintenance as compensation, repair to these asylums, and a system of indenture or placing out grows up as a means of disposing of the children who come into the asylums. In some instances the managers of the orphan asylums take the initiative, and seek homes of a suitable kind for their children at whatever age they deem suitable. Eventually there arise societies for the express purpose of placing children in foster-homes, and these societies may either maintain a small home for the temporary care of children until they are suitably placed, or, as in a few instances, they may adopt a plan of boarding their children in private families, pending a more permanent disposition.

The institutional care of children has been marked in the past by notable philanthropic endowments and large annual gifts, by religious zeal, and by remarkable personal devotion. The introduction of a system of subsidies from the public treasury, which has later in some instances been modified into what is virtually a system of contract payments by the state or one of its minor civil divisions on a per capita and per diem basis, has had the effect of lessening private contributions, and when not held rigidly in check by some plan of supervision on the part of the state, has led to an abnormal growth in the number of institutional children.

The drift toward an excessive institutional population of children is checked by three distinct influences, the absence of any one of which may be regarded as an indication of a low standard of responsibility for child life. The first of these is the appreciation of the value of the normal family life to which attention has repeatedly been called. The second is the tendency to develop alternative, and even a variety of methods, some of which will be more or less experimental in character, for helping children who are deprived of parental care.   Human nature revolts at the attempt to force a multitude of children, made dependent for a great variety of reasons, into a single channel, and to assume that a single method of dealing with them is necessarily better than others which can be devised. This feeling will show itself in the adoption of makeshifts for individual children, full of danger it may be, but giving to the exceptional child an opportunity for the natural development of his individuality.   Then clubs and other definite plans spring up, societies for educational ends, for physical recreation, for providing employment and other special purposes come into existence.   The institutions under the pressure of outside competition and under the guidance of managers of greater than average initiative and individuality, differentiate among themselves, and the word "institution" finally comes to stand for agencies which differ as greatly among themselves as from the outside agencies.

The third consideration is the desire on the part of the average citizen and taxpayer to economize in the expenditure of public funds, and to be assured of a maximum return for expenditures that are made.   It is observed that under a lax administration there is a temptation to parents to give up their children for a few years during which they are a financial burden, and on the part of collateral relatives to shift readily to the state the task which, if no provision were made or if it were strictly administered, would be undertaken by themselves.   Either institutions or placing-out agencies when paid upon a per capita basis for their services are likely to regard an increase in their numbers as neither objectionable nor alarming, contrasting the condition of those for whom they care with the more obvious instances of neglect and hardship in the period before the children reach them.   It is natural to regard easy admissions as charitable and humane. Private citizens or state officials intrusted with financial responsibility are generally the first to discover that there is another side, that a policy of indifference on the part of the state may readily result in the acceptance of many who would better be with their own parents, or for whom provision can be made by friends or relatives, or who, if admitted at all, need remain only for very brief periods.

These three considerations, therefore, — the financial, the desire to discover new, and possibly better, methods, and the natural preference for normal family life, — may be counted upon to counteract the development of great institutions. Aside from the inertia which causes a community to remain satisfied with an institutional system when it once exists, and the opportunity which arises to create a monument by endowments or other benefactions which may take the form of a building and facilities for caring for children, the most important factor in the growth of institutions has been the religious element. It is easy in the institution to organize definite religious instruction, and to make upon the minds of the children in the formative period definite religious impressions. In the absence of a state religion and of any power on the part of the state to dictate a religious profession, there has, nevertheless, been a general recognition that religious instruction cannot be ignored, and that the state is justified in going so far as to provide that an orphan child may be placed by the state in a religious institution managed by those who are of the same general faith as the child's parents. When this principle has once been recognized, it inevitably leads to a rapid development of institutions of markedly religious character, and to a demand on the part of the churches that neglected and orphaned children shall be gathered into them, partly in order that their physical welfare may be the better cared for, but chiefly that their spiritual salvation shall be as far as possible assured.

To counteract the tendency toward an increase of institutional population arising from this motive, the obvious policy on the part of those who prefer placing out in families would be to recognize the same principle in the placing out of children. If children were placed in families of their own religious faith or that of their parents, and if after being placed there were proper supervision both of secular and of religious education, the religious motive would cease to operate in favor of institutions. Placing-out agencies have been curiously reluctant to recognize this, or to place due emphasis upon it. The argument in favor of the requirement which is now frequently embodied in statute that children who are to be placed in foster-homes shall, if practicable, be placed in homes of their own religious faith or that of their parents is based, of course, not upon the interests of the churches but upon the welfare of the child. It is not that the state is powerless to choose and therefore resorts to this expedient in desperation. It is accepted for the reason that it is found in experience not advisable that a radical change should be made in the religious environment of the growing child. Children who are old enough to have received definite religious impressions, when suddenly placed under conditions in which the ideas and forms to which they have been accustomed are looked upon with indifference or with contempt, do not as a rule discard them and adopt new ones, although they would readily have adopted the latter had they known no others. They are likely on the contrary only to lose their own faint but tender impressions, and to attain no effective substitute for them. This applies less, it is true, or not at all, to very young children, but it is applicable to so large a proportion of the total number who are placed out that it may wisely be accepted as a general rule of action. Respect for parental rights may also have weight, although more emphasis has been placed upon this than it deserves. Parents have the right to bring up their own children in accordance with their own ideas, and are guaranteed freedom of worship for themselves and their children, but there is no inalienable post-mortem right to have one's religious faith perpetuated in his children at the expense of others; and in the case of neglected or orphaned children for whom responsibility must be assumed by the state, the latter must be considered free to adopt whatever policies are approved by experience.

Assuming proper inspection of admissions and discharges and vigilance in enforcing the legal, and as far as possible insisting upon the moral, obligation of parents and relatives to support their children, there may still remain in populous communities a large aggregate number of children for whom provision must be made either in institutions or in foster-homes found for them by state officials or organized agencies. Against the placing-out system has been urged the notorious laxity in selecting homes, with which some societies and institutions have frequently been charged, and the absence of efficient supervision in children who have once been placed. As a natural result it has been practicable for unscrupulous persons to obtain children for improper motives and to exact unrecompensed labor from them with impunity. It is also alleged that the system has lent itself to proselyting on a large scale, especially to the placing of neglected Catholic children from the great cities in Protestant rural homes. Both of these charges, however, relate to incidental abuses of the system rather than to essential features. As a matter of fact, under pressure from the state boards of charities and other outside sources, and by the voluntary adoption of more approved methods, agencies that have been engaged in placing children in foster-homes have freed themselves to a great extent from just criticism in these particulars.

Two objections, which go more nearly to the foundation of the placing-out system, may be urged. In effect the placing-out system is an attempt to transfer the burden of dependency from the cities to agricultural communities. Applications, it is true, are received from villages and smaller towns, but at least to some extent the placing-out system may be looked upon as a part of the movement back to the land. In so far as it is a part of this movement, it represents a transitional and a rapidly disappearing phase of national life. The burden of dependence cannot in the long run be shifted successfully in this manner from a commercial and industrial community to one that is agricultural. While many children for whom homes could be found are healthy in mind and body and are of good family stock, many others are in a degree dependent because of crime or indulgence, physical weakness, or inefficiency on the part of parents, traces of which are likely, sooner or later, to be discovered in the offspring. Some of the children have already come to be classed as incorrigible or are abnormal mentally or physically, but even those who are most attractive and desirable must pass through an unproductive period in which they are an economic burden, with comparatively little assurance that they will remain after they have turned the balance and are contributing to the family income more than their cost. It may be that children in the family ought not to be considered a burden. It may be that the compensations from the very beginning outweigh the costs, and yet in the majority of cases of adopted children it is certain that there is a financial burden, and that an appeal must be made to the charitable impulse, or to the sense of loneliness on account of the loss of an own child, or to the prospect of partial recompense by services in later years.

Several states, finding that children who have been brought from distant cities have later become public charges or inmates of reformatories, have passed laws regulating the placing-out of children by foreign societies or non-residents, in some instances requiring local incorporation or the giving of a bond to insure that a child who becomes a public charge will be received by the one who has placed it. This is but one, although the clearest, indication that methods must be devised, whether institutional or of the placing-out type, that will enable children to be cared for within the community in which they have become dependent, that the larger wealth of the cities must in some way offset directly the greater burden of dependency, that in so far as dependency in children is a result of social maladjustments and abuses, these must be corrected where they exist; and as a means to that end that their results shall be fully realized by those who reside where they occur. In the long run the community which has a higher standard of family life and a greater margin of average comfort does not render a kindness to the community in which there is a greater amount of misery and distress by removing individuals and relieving the less fortunate community from the consequences of its own shortcomings. Surplus gifts from the community which is in the happier state may indeed be used to correct the evils in neighboring, or even distant, regions, but there should be no levelling down, and no such shifting of burdens and injuries as will endanger the

I

higher standard. On the other hand placing-out agencies as they develop and extend their activities are likely to accept an increasing number of charges from country and village homes; and if dependent children, whatever their origin, are boarded at the expense of the state or of private charity there is a due equivalent for whatever economic burden is transferred.

A second objection of an even more vital character is that the attempt to find an indefinite number of private families for the children who are charges upon organized charity, or upon public relief, ignores the well-founded modern tendency toward the increased employment of professional skill. To care for dependent children is a more difficult task than to care for the normal children of an average family, difficult as this also is. Oftentimes essential qualities are lacking in the child, and it is a matter requiring extraordinary experience and skill to develop them. A trained expert is needed to detect the traces of abnormality and degeneracy. Even for the child who is entirely normal there must be found some substitute for the painstaking attention which fathers and mothers may naturally be expected to give to the development of their offspring.

The trained nurse and the trained kindergartner have assumed duties which in the ordinary family were formerly universally performed by parents. It is recognized that maternal affection is less potent than training and professional skill even in such delicate tasks as those which are now frequently transferred for a consideration to the nurse in illness and to the kindergartner in the period at the beginning of elementary instruction. There is a similar place which must be filled by some efficient representative of the community in the development and oversight and care of dependent children. The assumption that this care can best be given by childless married couples who have a great variety of reasons for desiring to adopt children, or by families in which, whatever the number of children, there is felt to be room for one or more foster-children in addition, is an assumption which requires for its successful support experience on a large scale and through an extended period. The probabilities would appear to lie in the other direction. It would seem as if in an institution where experiences can be more readily compared and deductions made from the observation of a large number of children, there could be developed that trained skill and scientific grasp of the subject that are essential. The family in which parents are rearing and caring for their own offspring is the natural social unit. The relation between foster-parent and placed-out child, when this relation is established by a third individual or a society organized for the purpose, is a less natural one, and there is little argument by analogy in its behalf based upon the normal family. The community is compelled, under modern conditions, to face, practically as if it were a new problem, the task of fitting the dependent child into his place as a self-supporting and self-respecting member of the industrial and social organization. If the institutions for the maintenance and education of children have not been of a character to perform this task with complete satisfaction in the past, it is, in view of the considerations that have last been urged, a duty to consider whether they cannot be so modified and improved as to fit them more adequately to perform it. It will simplify the problem if it be granted that what can reasonably be expected is not the production of geniuses or of exceptionally endowed individuals, save in rare instances for which no plan can be consciously devised, but rather the bringing of those who are thrown upon charity fairly into the ranks of self-supporting citizens. We may hope to bring them to a place where they are no longer social debtors, but may be content, if, by accomplishing so much as this, the actual pauperism existing in the community is so far reduced, as well as the number who are likely to become criminals, and thus a double burden upon the community measurably reduced.

In reply to this objection it may be urged that those who are engaged in placing out children, and especially such as supplement their free homes by a system of boarding homes for wayward children and for those who are later to be returned to their parents, are, equally with institutions, developing special skill and expert knowledge. While there is much truth in this it can hardly be claimed at the foster-parents, who are the ones that are most continuously in contact with the children, can be expected to devote their energies exclusively to the problems involved in the care of children, as do even the subordinate employees of institutions. The officers and agents of the placing-out society may well become experts, but after all the direct responsibility for training and caring for the children does not fall upon them.

Institutionalism has also its pronounced evils. Aside from its tendency to abnormal ·growth and the danger of resorting to it in demonstrably unsuitable cases, both of which dangers may be guarded against, there are inherent dangers in institutional life even for those who are properly accepted as charges upon the state or upon private philanthropy. Institutionalism is defined by R. R. Reeder, superintendent of the New York Orphan Asylum, as "a combination of rote, routine, and dead levelism"; as "law and coercion, without liberty or individual initiative." Mr. Reeder's ironical advice to those in charge of institutions is "to employ people who have had experience in institutionalism, for they are more certain to have studied the best methods of properly suppressing the child, so that he will give a minimum of trouble"; and to remember that "the more the child is suppressed the less dynamic he is and the less liable to break through your well-articulated and grooved system." The mere fact that this systematic suppression and reliance upon routine methods is dubbed institutionalism is an indication that institutions have a tendency to err in these directions. Indeed, it is freely charged by those who have had exceptionally good opportunities for observation, that it is almost impossible to conduct an institution of any considerable size on any other plan. The superintendent of one large institution casually remarked, in answer to a question as to what he did with boys who were about to leave the institution after an average stay of five or six years, that he then began to study their individual tastes and inclinations, that, in fact, it was "really necessary when a boy got to be fourteen or fifteen years of age that he should be individualized." This implies, of course, that the thousands of children passing through this particular institution are not individualized until this stage, unless the superintendent did himself and his institution a grave injustice; that thousands of children are treated *en masse* until the problem arises of fitting them into some position on their discharge. There is obviously a wide and deep gulf between such a system and the sense of responsibility felt by a conscientious father for the development of the personality of his sons and daughters, or the love of a mother for her individual children.

It is said that children come out of institutions almost wholly unfamiliar with the thousand proficiencies and accomplishments which the boy at home, on the street, or in an ordinary school picks up as a matter of course. The institutional child does not learn how to handle matches with safety, because the electric light or the gas is always adjusted by some employee of the institution who is assigned to this duty. He does not learn the value of money, because purchases are made by steward or superintendent, and the procedure is wholly removed from the personal knowledge of the inmates. There is no analogy between the transactions of the institution and those of the ordinary wage-earning family, and the children have no means of becoming acquainted with either. Protection from fire, from accident, and from illness are matters which concern the authorities of the institution, whereas in an ordinary family the responsibility for such things is shared to some extent by the different members of the family, and increasingly by the children as they grow older. A manager of one comparatively small institution relates that when a group of boys from the institution was skating on an ice pond, and one of them being separated from the others broke through and was in danger of drowning, his associates were helpless, being confronted by a situation which had no analogy in their previous experiences, and, incredible as it appears, turned their backs to walk toward the institution; while some boys of the neighboring village, no older than those from the institution, seeing from a distance what had happened, ran to the spot and rescued the drowning boy. A dentist who had a considerable practice in a large institution was struck by the comparative docility of those children and their ready submission to whatever pain his operations made necessary, and this he attributed to their drill in accepting quietly whatever experiences came to them and the sense of futility of resistance which had been implanted. The suppression of exceptional characteristics because of the trouble which they cause, the failure to awaken any sense of responsibility or power of exercising rational independent choice or of forming sound judgment, and the absence of opportunity to acquire those fundamental conceptions which together enable one to play his part naturally and easily in association with his fellow-men, are, then, the gravest objections which have been urged against institutions for children.

There are in several different institutions men and women seriously engaged in the attempt to demonstrate that these evils are not inherent, and that they may be conquered by the breaking up of large aggregates into small groups, formed as nearly as possible on a family basis ; by the employment of skilled teachers and matrons, and a reduction of the number of children assigned to each ; by removal from the city, where land is too valuable to permit room for out-of-door recreation, to country sites, where children may be brought into contact with woods and fields and rivers ; and by the introduction of features directly calculated to supply those experiences and opportunities which fall as a matter of course to the lot of the ordinary child. Such institutions are ridding themselves of institutionalism, of that mechanicalization which is an ever present danger. In one or two notable instances the revolt against institutionalism has gone so far as to lead to the introduction of a plan of more or less complete self-government, and all who are interested in the development of a rational system of care for children are watching with interest the results of this extreme policy. In other instances a degree of freedom has been introduced which approaches or fully equals that of the average family, although government remains entirely in the hands of the superintendent and officers. By avoiding uniformity of dress, by throwing together children of different ages, and above all by a flexible curriculum administered by instructors who are seeking constantly to adapt their teaching to the needs and capacities of individual children, progress is being made toward the development of institutions which will be free from criticism.

Contemporaneously with this improvement, however, there has been developed in a few places a high standard of placing-out work to which it is appropriate to recur after what has been said about institutions, since a large proportion of the children who are temporarily cared for in institutions are eventually placed in foster-homes. The principles upon which homes should be selected have now been carefully worked out and formulated. One of the best statements of these principles is contained in a paper presented by Homer Folks to the International Conference of Charities at Chicago in 1893, entitled " Family Life for Dependent and Wayward Children." It is first of all necessary that there shall be obtained from the applicant for the child a full statement concerning the constitution of his own family, and of employees or other persons residing in the family; concerning the occupation of the head of the family and his circumstances of life, — if a farmer, for example, whether he is owner or tenant, size of his farm, kind and amount of live stock, — if in clerical or professional life, particulars concerning summer and winter residence; number of rooms occupied by family, and intention of applicant concerning future career of the adopted child; religious affiliations; distance from nearest church; distance from school, whether public, parochial, or private; length of school year; agreement as to period during which child should be sent; whether the family has ever received children from other charitable organizations; and description of child desired. Mr. Folks adds the following searching questions : Would the child eat with the family; with whom would it sleep; would it attend social gatherings with the family, and be treated in all respects as one of their number? What is the principal motive in desiring to receive the child in the home? This statement is but the beginning of the essential inquiry concerning the applicant, although the answers to these questions, rightly interpreted, will often be sufficient to lead to the immediate rejection of the application. References will naturally be given by those who desire to adopt children, and it will do no harm to address inquiries to those who are mentioned by the applicants as in a position to give information. Independent inquiries, however, addressed to clergymen, teachers, and to neighbors who are found to be in a position to express an independent judgment, are far more valuable, and there will be no difficulty, if a little trouble is taken, to secure the names of such persons. Besides the statement from the applicant, however, and letters from those suggested by himself and from others whose names are secured independently, a personal visit to the home in which it is proposed to place the child is found in experience to be absolutely essential.

The sad tragedies resulting from the omission of these safeguards are a warning that, however troublesome and expensive such inquiries prove to be, they cannot wisely be omitted. The practice of taking a group of children into a new community, and giving them out to persons who have assembled in response to a glowing appeal, with no assurance except a perfunctory public indorsement from a local committee, is scarcely less reprehensible than the habitual daily exercise of personal discretion on the part of the superintendent or public official based solely on the appearance of the applicant, and the assumed capacity of the interviewer to judge human nature sufficiently to make an offhand decision on such meagre data. Rigid investigation of those who desire to adopt children is again, however, only the initial step in a judicious system of placing out children. Subsequent supervision based upon correspondence and frequent visits, and the exercise of trained intelligence in detecting evidences of ill treatment or maladjustment between child and home, are equally indispensable.[1] Occasionally a second or third home must be tried before a satisfactory permanent adjustment is made. Responsibility for health, education, and moral development are assumed by the individual or society that places the child in a foster-home and thus determine the environment in which he shall live. This

---

[1] Mr. Folks, from whom I have already quoted in regard to the selection of homes, says that the principal feature of subsequent supervision should be unannounced personal visits by an expert agent.

responsibility is a continuing one, and to be discharged properly it is as necessary to know the conditions after six months, a year, or five years, as at the time of placing. Until the child has grown to maturity constant supervision is required. Visits may be more or less frequent, according to circumstances, but must be of sufficient frequency to keep those who are responsible in the first instance reliably informed concerning the conditions. Even legal adoption, although it shifts responsibility to a great extent, does not completely absolve those who have originally assumed it, since in some communities the formality of adoption may not be adequately safeguarded.

The writer was once asked what it would cost to send a thousand children from the streets of New York City to free homes in the West. The inquiry was not an unnatural one, coming from a man who had amassed a great fortune, and whose own boyhood had been passed in a New England village. Having no personal knowledge either of city waifs or of organized methods of placing children, he assumed, or, perhaps it would be more accurate to say, had been informed from a certain class of books and newspaper articles which deal superficially with social problems, that there are at large an indefinite number of children who can be gathered bodily into a child-saving net, and taken hither and yon as the catcher may fancy, and that the only expense involved is the railway fare. If, in answer to the inquiry, it had been said that the thousand children could be taken West and placed out at a per capita expense of $20 or $25, this sum might no doubt have been instantly forthcoming; and if it had been attempted to carry the donor's wishes into execution, sad havoc would have resulted. A few happy chances would have resulted from the attempt, but many children would certainly have been taken who are better off at home, in spite of the fact that that home happens to be in the city; and others, who would appear at the outset to have been placed pleasantly enough, would in a very few months have run away from their new homes, perhaps on just provocation; while still others, in the course of time, would have found themselves sorely in need of protection or guidance or help which no one would stand

ready to give, since the philanthropy of the original donor
would have been exhausted by his gift, and he would have
provided no substitute to stand in his place.   One cannot
remove a thousand children from their homes, or even
from their temporary lodging-places, however unsatisfactory they may appear to an onlooker, without accepting
the responsibilities implied in the act.   In answer to the
inquiry the following letter was sent : —

   " Dear Sir : —

   " Pursuant to your request that I should send you
information as to the cost of sending 1000 boys to the
West and placing them in homes, I beg to say that I have
had made three estimates representing somewhat different
methods of placing out children, and also, I must add,
somewhat different degrees of efficiency and thoroughness.
None of these estimates, however, is as low as that which
I gave you offhand over the telephone when your inquiry
was made, as I did not make sufficient allowance for the
expense of subsequent supervision and for various incidental expenses, most of which are itemized in the
accompanying estimates.

   " Estimate A gives a total of $233,700, or approximately
$235 per capita for 1000 children.   You will notice, how-
ever, that this provides for close supervision of the children until death, adoption, or coming of age ; it provides
for a complete outfit of clothing for each child placed out,
and also a very considerable item for the board of a maximum of forty children, who, although placed in free homes
at the outset, are returned for one reason or another, and
must be boarded at least temporarily, and in some instances
for a considerable period.   Experience shows that children
who, because of personal unattractiveness, physical deformity, or some other reason, cannot be placed in free
homes, may usually receive all the advantages of a good
home if their board is paid for at some such rate as $2 per
week.   This estimate includes an adequate allowance for
the travelling expenses, not only at the outset, but also
for the occasional transfers from one home to another ;
for medical and surgical care of children who need such
treatment, and other similar items, which in the other
estimates are not allowed for, as it is there assumed that

such expenses will be met as the need arises, either by
existing charitable agencies of some kind or by the foster-
parents. In other words, the estimate of $235 includes
everything which is necessary to find a suitable home,
prepare the child for it, place him there, and insure that
he shall receive during his minority a good elementary
education, proper attention to his health, and the continued attention of a responsible agency which will at
once remove him to another place if the first proves in
any way unsuitable.

" While the total amount seems large, it is, in my judgment, conservative and not extravagant, and perhaps it
will not seem to you that $235 is more than one should
expect to expend in providing a home, an education, and
living expenses for a boy for an average period of ten
years, or a maximum period of sixteen years.

" It should also be added that of course this whole sum
would not need to be made available at the outset, as this
expenditure would extend over a total period of sixteen
years. If the entire sum were provided at the outset, a
corresponding deduction might be made for interest.

" Estimate B is made by a society which has placed out
a large number of children. I am of the opinion that the
estimate does not include sufficient provision for such
previous inspection of the homes as will insure the selection
of good homes. Such as it is, however, the estimate, as
you will see, is considerably lower than estimate A, and
amounts to $91.15 per capita.

" Estimate C is supplied by two gentlemen who have
had extensive experience in the state of Minnesota, where
the placing out of dependent children is carried on directly
by the state. Their estimate is itemized, and is $166.40
per capita.

" My own opinion is that neither estimate B nor estimate C should be accepted, for the reason that they do
not take sufficient account of the expenses of care for the
difficult cases. On the Minnesota plan, children who cannot be placed in free homes are, in fact, cared for in a
state institution. Of course, it would be entirely possible
for those who were carrying out this plan to turn over the
difficult cases (such as are boarded under estimate A) to a

charitable institution. This, however, is only to shift the burden which should be recognized as a part of the task of placing out 1000 children. It would be impossible that one should anticipate at the start all the personal idiosyncrasies, physical weaknesses, and even the moral deficiencies which would eventually be disclosed by 1000 boys.

"Coming, therefore, to a direct answer to your question, my estimate would be that to place 1000 boys in free homes, whether in New York State or in the West, would cost about $75,000 initial expense; and to give them the subsequent supervision which should be supplied to any children thus placed elsewhere than in their own homes, would bring the total expense to about $235,000.

"While there is necessarily some guesswork in the above, as, for example, in the number of children for which it would be necessary to provide board, I think that I am safe in saying that a thoroughly responsible society, which represents the very best methods of placing-out work, would assume the responsibility of carrying through the plan if the amount named in estimate A were placed at their disposal; while the other society mentioned would doubtless undertake the work on the basis of their estimate."

ESTIMATE A

I. AGENTS FOR PLACING-OUT AND SUPERVISION (including travelling expenses of agent and children) : —

10 agents for first three years at $1750	$52,500	
6 agents for second three years at $1750	31,500	
4 agents for third three years at $1750	21,000	
2 agents for final seven years at $1750	24,500	$139,500

II. CLOTHING : —

1000 outfits at $15	$15,000	
Outfits for children who are boarded out, and for those who must be placed more than once :		
First 5 years at $1000	5,000	
Second 5 years at $500 . . .	2,500	$22,500

III. ADMINISTRATIVE EXPENSES: —

Rent for 10 years at $600 . . .	$6,000	
Clerical services:		
First 10 years at $1200 (2 clerks at $600 each)	12,000	
Six years at $600 (1 clerk) . . .	3,600	
Office supplies, 16 years	1,600	$23,200

IV. PRINTING: —

First year	$500	
8 years at $200	1,600	
7 years at $100	700	$2,800

V. POSTAGE: —

3 years at $500	$1,500	
7 years at $100	700	
6 years at $50	300	$2,500

VI. BOARD: —

40 children for 5 years at $100 . .	$20,000	
20 children for 5 years at $100 . .	10,000	
10 children for 6 years at $100 . .	6,000	$36,000

VII. MISCELLANEOUS EXPENSES: —

Medical and surgical treatment, etc., especially for boarded children . .	$7,200	$7,200
		$233,700

Annual cost of placing out and keeping under continued supervision an average number of 1000 children: —

I.	10 agents at $1750	$17,500
II.	Clothing (first year)	2,300
III.	Administrative expenses . . .	2,000
IV.	Printing	200
V.	Postage	400
VI.	Board of children not in free homes . .	4,000
VII.	Miscellaneous expenses	800
	Total	$27,200

Assuming that the children are kept under supervision on an average eight years, the average cost for each child would be $217.60.

ESTIMATE B

For placing out each child (including expenses of investigation, travelling, clothing, etc.) . . .	$51.40
Supervision, at $4.40 per annum, for an average period of five years	22.00
Preliminary training at a farm-school (which is found useful both as a training and as an opportunity for observing the peculiarities of the child) . . .	17.75
	$91.15
Total cost for 1000 children at $91.15	$91,150.00

ESTIMATE C

The cost of supervising in free homes 1000 dependent children, received at the average ages and supervised until each child is 18 years of age, — estimate based on conditions existing in Minnesota, except its capacity for assimilating this number in satisfactory homes : —

	1st year	2d year	17th year
Superintendent	$1,800	$1,800	$1,800
Superintendent's travelling expenses	400	400	600
Four agents	4,800	4,800	—
Agents' travelling expenses . .	2,200	2,200	—
Stenographer and clerk . . .	500	500	500
Rent	300	300	300
Office maintenance	50	50	50
Office furniture	400	10	—
Postage, printing, and stationery .	400	400	200
Telegraph and telephone . . .	120	120	60
Annual report	150	150	150
Travelling of children in the state .	2,000	200	—
Clothing	11,000	300	40
Emergent board	400	700	250
Total	$24,520	$11,930	$3,950

First year	$24,520
Second year	11,930
Third, fourth, and fifth years	36,000
Sixth to sixteenth years, inclusive (11 years) . . .	90,000
Seventeenth year	3,950
Grand total	$166,400

CHAPTER .X

As there are children who from orphanage or other cause cannot be cared for in their own homes, so there are also adults who, through advanced age or physical incapacity arising from some other cause, cannot support themselves, and for whom there are no relatives or friends ready to offer maintenance and shelter. In the chapter on the social consequences implied in the acceptance of a normal standard of living, it was pointed out that hospitals for the sick have not yet reached their full natural development, and that we may expect that many for whom as yet no provision has been made, will be received as patients at the expense either of the taxpayer or of private philanthropy. Whichever bears the burden, it is essential that those who can pay for treatment and maintenance shall do so, either on the present ordinary plan of fees for care actually received, or by an insurance system of regular payments by the month or quarter, in return for which care is given when needed. Many of those who now become public charges could readily meet the actual expense involved if it could thus be distributed, and there are many who would prefer thus to keep free from obligations to others. This applies, however, to out-patient dispensary treatment, to secure which patients call in person at dispensaries, and to treatment given from such institutions to patients who are cared for at home.

Somewhat more completely dependent are those who become patients within the hospital, because they have not homes in which they can be properly cared for, or because from the nature of the illness hospital care is deemed advisable. For the majority of these, also, care

127

in the hospital is only a form of relief, for the family separation is but temporary and the purpose is the easiest possible restoration to ordinary home life. The incurable, or those suffering from chronic disease involving a long period of institutional care; isolated individuals, who although not seriously ill are, on account of physical incapacity, not quite able to earn their own living; and the less efficient members of classes variously afflicted, such as the blind, the crippled, and the epileptic, form a series of dependent groups for whom provision must be made. To some extent private endowments and even societies relying upon annual contributions have supplied institutions to meet these needs. There is, however, plainly apparent a tendency for private philanthropy to withdraw from this field, and to occupy itself rather with those who are more easily reclaimable, and with preventive tasks of which the aim is to lessen the number who become dependent upon others. This tendency is one which may wisely be encouraged. Institutional care for those who cannot be cured, for those who can look for release from their infirmities and afflictions only in death, is certainly a most appropriate task for the state. It is true that if the state neglects it, it will be performed in some fashion by private charity, but it is admitted that the amounts likely to be invested by private philanthropy in constructive social work and also in relief will not be sufficient to support all of those who, whether by their own fault or that of others — or without fault on the part of any — are dependent, and at the same time provide genuine relief in its more accurate sense for those who, through effective relief, may be removed from the ranks of the social debtors. A division of work is therefore essential, and if the arguments presented against public out-door relief are valid, the division lies along the line of institutional care from the public treasury, and relief at home from private sources. This does not mean that private philanthropy should be debarred from creating institutions, especially since the donor may not be disposed to expend in more fruitful tasks amounts which he is ready to give for the relief of the aged, or those who are suffering from special types of infirmity. In the field of experimental relief for those who have been thought to be incurable, private philanthropy is amply justified. The voluntary transfer, however, of expenditure from relief of those for whom there is no outlook except the possibility of greater comfort, to the relief of those who can be helped effectively, is in the direction of progress, and there should be no hesitation to fill this gap by more liberal appropriations from the public treasury.

In the almshouse at the middle of the nineteenth century were gathered children, insane, feeble-minded, the sick, the aged, and vagrants, with little attempt at classification, and with no facilities for providing specialized care for different classes of inmates. There are some states in which primitive conditions of this kind are still to be found. The devolution of the almshouse proceeds by such regular stages that the character of its population and of its administration are a fair index of the state of public sentiment, and of the degree of enlightenment which the community has attained. The removal of the insane to special hospitals, in which they are looked upon as sick persons, rather than as paupers, and in which there is a large expenditure for the treatment of those whose condition is acute and curable, is one of the early stages in the differentiation of the almshouse population. The cost of the care of the insane is, of course, likely to be greater after this separation has been made because higher professional skill is brought to bear upon their treatment, a more appropriate dietary introduced, a higher degree of comfort maintained, and an environment created favorable for recovery. The knowledge of these improvements will inevitably attract, as it is desirable that it should, persons whose affliction might otherwise be concealed, or for whom at least no suitable treatment would have been provided. Strict investigation of admissions, reinvestigation from time to time, and the prompt discharge of patients who have recovered, or are so far improved as to make further hospital care unnecessary, and the enforcement of payment — in whole or in part — by those who are found to be in position to make such payment, are the means by which the abuse of public hospital relief can be prevented. It is not necessary that any conditions

K

favorable to recovery shall be lacking to keep the growth of the population of the institution in check. Lavish expenditure for unessentials is, of course, to be condemned, but expenditures for the curably insane have been niggardly and inadequate far more frequently than they have been excessive.

The removal of children from the almshouse to separate institutions, or to the care of placing-out agencies, is another step so obvious and so imperative that it is strange to find communities in which it has not yet been taken. The association of dependent children with adult paupers is directly demoralizing, but even if they were kept physically apart, the complete absence in the almshouse of any suitable educational facilities, and the impossibility of providing any of the features of a natural environment for growing children, would of themselves condemn the practice of receiving children into any such institution. So great is the temptation to effect a petty economy, and so ignorant are many local officials charged with the support of the poor, that statutory prohibition of the reception of children into almshouses is justified, and even the enactment of such statutes has accomplished the removal only with difficulty.

The epileptic have also, in several states, ceased to be inmates of the almshouse, and have been removed to special institutions, some of which are conducted on the farm colony plan. The uniform effect of this change, accompanied by a study of the disease and of the more efficient application of approved methods, has been a lessening in the frequency and severity of attacks. For a fair proportion of epileptics the colony becomes a means of self-support. With the sympathy and special attention given within the colony, patients are able to do an amount and kind of work that fully recompenses the state for its outlay on their behalf, although such patients might not be able to care for themselves under the conditions prevailing outside the institution. Feeble-minded and idiotic persons, whether children or adults, are also more humanely cared for in special institutions created for them, and in many institutions improvement in their physical and mental condition can be brought about.

Hope of greatly increasing the number of recoveries has not been to any great extent realized. In New York State a threefold classification has been made : teachable, feeble-minded children being cared for in one institution, feeble-minded women of child-bearing age in another, and unteachable idiots in a third. In the first of these stress is laid upon education, in the others upon custodial care, with, however, the introduction of whatever will make life more endurable, or will lead to the improvement of individuals who may be found to be teachable. The custodial asylum for women has had an appreciable effect in lessening illegitimacy, and especially in preventing the propagation of various forms of degeneracy in which feeble-mindedness is a connecting link from generation to generation.

Connected with the almshouse there is usually a hospital, and in those of larger size a series of hospitals, enabling more acute cases to be separated from those of a chronic kind. Consumptives, mentally disturbed patients who cannot be considered insane, and other special classes may also be treated in special wards or hospitals if their numbers are sufficient to warrant it. There is a disposition to make a more complete separation of hospitals, however, from the almshouse proper, even if they are under the same administration. Those who are patients in the hospital are treated rather with reference to their diseases than as paupers, as the insane, children, and the physically afflicted have already come to be treated according to their respective needs, rather than merely as public charges to be fed and housed at the least possible expense. In a striking paper published in Charities,[1] Homer Folks, Commissioner of Public Charities in New York City, raised the question as to whether, after the elimination of various classes from the almshouse, we have not left, instead of an undistributed residuum, merely a final special class, viz., aged or infirm persons who are, after all, quite as much entitled to be treated with reference to their special needs as any of the various classes that have previously been removed. Mr. Folks shows that the almshouse has

[1] Monthly magazine number, October 3, 1903.

tended to become a strictly voluntary institution ; that vagrants and other able-bodied persons are no longer nominally received in it, but are rather subjects for the discipline of a correctional institution. Municipal lodging-houses and work tests of wood yards, and other means of providing temporary employment for able-bodied, destitute persons, have eliminated still others from the almshouse population. Nearly all those that remain are definitely removed by physical disability from the possibility of self-support ; moreover, we have an instinctive feeling that aged persons, if by reason of destitution they become a public charge, may be treated with a degree of consideration quite different from that properly accorded to the middle-aged, able-bodied, voluntary pauper. The inference to be drawn from these considerations is that the bulk of our almshouse inmates are dependents rather than paupers, using the latter word not in its legal, but in its ordinary, significance. The distinction between dependence and pauperism, as drawn by Mr. Folks, is that dependency carries with it no suggestion of reproach, while pauperism implies a willingness and a desire to receive charitable aid when such aid is not a necessity — a preference for accepting the public bounty rather than for making all reasonable effort for self-support.

In accordance with this idea, Mr. Folks, as Commissioner of Public Charities, changed the name of the almshouse of New York City to The Home for Aged and Infirm, and made a number of changes in the construction of buildings, in the amount and variety of diet, in the character of clothing, and in the introduction of healthful and beneficial employment of inmates, and in the discipline of the institutions under his charge, which were in accordance with the theory above set forth. The only argument which can be advanced against this position, in view of the historical development of the almshouse and other institutions for the care of dependent adults, is that a community, by providing thus liberally and equally for those whose past lives have been creditable, and for those who have a less favorable history, removes a deterrent force from the feet of younger persons who are now choosing their path. This objection has, however, little

real weight.   Life in the almshouse will hardly become
so attractive that a course which leads toward it will
deliberately be chosen for that reason.   Against any
slight effect which a higher standard of physical comfort
in the almshouse may exercise may be brought considerations a thousandfold more weighty and less fanciful.   To
quote again from the paper by Mr. Folks, to which reference has been made, there are " probably in the lives of a
very large proportion of almshouse inmates some chapters
that had better be left unread.   But to what extent, after
all, should this affect our care of them in the few remaining years of their lives ?   Now that the years of activity,
with their opportunities and temptations, their struggles
for existence are over, now that the ability for self-
support is undeniably gone, no matter how, shall we not
recognize them all, if without means and with no relatives able to support, as entitled to a treatment at the
hands of the public which shall be quite different from
that accorded in correctional institutions for able-bodied
vagrants ?   Death is the great leveller, and, as it casts its
shadow before, those who enter it tend to lose the characteristics that have marked certain individuals as different
from others in their social relations.   As, in caring for
children, we take little account of their good or ill
deserts, but only of their needs, may we not follow a
similar course in caring for those in their second childhood ?   Not by any means that the same treatment shall
be measured out for all, but that differences of care shall
be based on present tasks, habits, and capacities, and not
past deserts."

Along, however, with this recognition of the legitimacy
of considerate treatment for the aged and infirm who are
public charges, there must go an equally clear recognition
of the fact that such care is necessarily expensive, judged
by the standard of expenditures for almshouse inmates
which has prevailed.   Not only do the various items of
maintenance become greater, but the cost of service is increased.   Superintendents and subordinates of indifferent
caliber may carry out a routine system of administration,
but to create a pleasant environment and to meet the various needs of individual dependents calls for a high order

of ingenuity, sympathy, and wisdom. The character of the service, the architecture of the buildings, the grouping of patients, and the very language used in conversation between officers and patients, must all bear evidence of the new spirit. It must be understood that those who are in charge of the home for the aged and infirm are no longer dealing primarily with pauperism, but, like the officers of institutions for the care of children, the insane, and the defective, are dealing with dependents. The causes which make for the decrease or increase of pauperism are not under the control of those who are caring for a particular class of dependents, but are much more likely determined by the acts of ordinary citizens who may scarcely be conscious of the existence of such institutions. The attack upon pauperism must be made in the schools, in the churches, in the public press, and at the ballot-box. Those who control admission and discharge from the home for the aged are, it is true, responsible for one among many influences for good and evil. The transfer of the almshouse, by the successive removal of many classes to whom it once gave shelter, and the creation of a well-managed home for the aged and infirm from the remnant, may well be regarded with equanimity by those to whom pauperism appears to be an unmitigated curse.

It is not impossible that we may see arise as a supplement, or as an alternative to the almshouse and the private homes for the aged, a systematic plan for boarding out aged infirm persons, on the plan already in successful operation for boarding dependent children. With careful selection of homes, and competent subsequent supervision, such a plan might succeed admirably. These features would prevent the abuses which led to the abolition of the earlier system of boarding paupers by contract in the earlier half of the nineteenth century.[1]

[1] See p. 284.

CHAPTER XI

FAMILY DESERTION

ONE cause of distress of which we are becoming increasingly aware in recent years, probably because it is increasingly frequent, is the desertion of wife and children by their natural and legally responsible breadwinner. In the first flurry of astonishment at such an extraordinary phenomenon as desertion by heads of families of their voluntarily assumed responsibilities, there was much speculation as to the motives which could have led to it. All the influences which affect human conduct would appear to be arrayed against it. Conjugal and parental love, the sanctions of religion, the good opinion of friends and neighbors, the most elementary sense of responsibility for one's own express and implied enjoyments, the expectation of aid and support from offspring in later life, the present assistance of the wife under ordinary circumstances and her care and comfort in illness or adversity, form a most formidable array of positive motives against vagabondage on the part of a man with wife and children. The economic advantages lie mainly on the same side. The fugitive from justice — in every state the law provides some method, however defective, either criminal or civil, for reaching the deserter — is at a disadvantage in securing and retaining employment, and a knowledge of his failure to care for his own will everywhere outweigh any number of other virtues.

Why then do men abandon their families, and is there a remedy for the evil? Let us consider first a few exceptional cases in order that we place due emphasis upon the fact that they are exceptional, although actual, illustrations of that desertion which leads directly to destitution and to applications for charitable assistance on the part of the deserted family.

An intemperate man whose wife was also intemperate, and whose home was therefore neglected and unattractive, came under the influence of a temperance reformer and was induced to take the pledge. In order that he might the more easily keep it, employment was found for him in the country at a distance from his family and his former companions. He became a sober and industrious laborer, but in the process he gradually formed new associations and tastes, and in the end completely ignored and abandoned both wife and children. Those who are tabulating the causes of distress often glibly put down "intemperance," because it is easier than to analyze the rather complicated conditions of which intemperance is but one. It would be equally faulty, but not more so, to describe the desertion in this instance as due to sobriety. It was, of course, due to other moral defects which were unfortunately not corrected along with the cure of the drink habit.

Another family came under the notice of a charitable society on the desertion of its nominal head. Investigation eventually established the fact that this desertion was a return to his legitimate wife and children of whom the woman that made the application for aid knew nothing. To leave the second family and return to the first was a legal and moral duty; and on the superficial method of tabulating causes, this case of desertion might be described as due to sudden fidelity to the marital relation, although the earlier infidelity of course lies behind it.

The desertion of a Russian Jewess by her Chinese husband is perhaps not so surprising as the fact of their marriage. The desertion of Protestant wives by Catholic husbands, and of Catholic wives by Protestant husbands is a little more common, as might be expected, than desertion by those who are of the same household of faith as their wives. Desertions occur in marriages of mixed nationalities and races, according to some statistics which cover, however, only a few and possibly not representative desertions, somewhat more frequently than in others, although the difference is not sufficient to justify particular emphasis upon such marriages as an explanation.

Lasciviousness accounts for fewer desertions than might be supposed. A close study of over two hundred desertions reveals scarcely a dozen in which the attraction of another woman can positively be said to have led to the desertion. There is a much larger proportion in which the deserter eventually takes up with another woman, who is often ignorant of the previous marriage and supposes herself to be a lawful wife, but in these cases the acquaintance is made subsequent to the desertion, and where this is not so, there is often no reason to suspect a design to form the new alliance as the prevailing motive for desertion.

One deserting husband died of consumption within a few weeks of his departure ; another was mentally unbalanced and finally died as a patient in a hospital for the insane ; another was driven away from home by his wife's rasping tongue and shrewish temper; another, by his wife's bad cooking and general inefficiency in household affairs.

Despondency resulting from physical ailment or from unstable mental equilibrium, incompatibility of temper and lack of judgment in the direction of family and household affairs, may indeed account for many separations and for the otherwise unaccountable failure in some cases to provide for the needs of wife and children.

Since there are *bona fide* cases of these kinds, and since it is natural to generalize from the particular instances encountered in one's personal experience, even if they are few in number, it is not surprising that sermons have been preached and articles written in denunciation of the wives whose frivolity, ignorance, and irritability makes the home repellent to husband and children. It cannot well be denied that there is need for better training both for young men and for young women in the qualities needed for successful and happy domestic life. Candor, however, compels the social student to point out that the typical family deserter is not the discouraged sick man, or the meek " henpecked " unfortunate, or the dyspeptic driven to desperation by indigestible food, or the reformed drinker seeking relief from the associations of his earlier unregenerate days, or the remorseful deserter from an earlier marriage bond seeking to make amends for his misconduct.

Nor does it appear that the deserters who leave their family dependent upon others for support are driven to this step as a rule by dire necessity. They are for the

most part young men [1] and they leave young wives with
but two or three children [2]—more than the mother alone
can well care for and support, but not enough to discourage
any man with self-respect and average working capacity.
Moreover, many of them are skilled workingmen. Their
average earnings when at work are $12 or $15 a week,[3] and
a large proportion are actually employed at the time of
their desertion, or just previous to it.

The only possible conclusion to which one can come
from a study of these cases is that the deserters are without that normal standard of conduct which is accepted by
human society at large, that they are lacking in a sense of
moral responsibility, and that their failure is of a criminal
character which must be dealt with as theft, or the obtaining of money under false pretences, or even, in an extreme
case, as assault and manslaughter are dealt with ; for the
maintenance of helpless women in the throes of childbirth, the lives and welfare of innocent children, are at
stake, and as long as the family is the unit of human society, the obligation to provide for the family must be
recognized voluntarily or compulsorily enforced.

Before leaving the more general aspects of the subject,
it may not be amiss to point out that there is a reciprocal
obligation on the part of the wife and mother not to
abandon the home, and that desertion of husband and
children is by no means unknown. Sons and daughters
who have grown to maturity are, likewise, under obligation
to support infirm or aged parents, and at least a similar
moral obligation may rest upon grandparents and grandchildren.[4]

The words "desertion" and "abandonment" imply
physical absence on the part of the breadwinner. The essence of the evil, however, is not, of course, bodily absence,

---

[1] Of 191 deserters, 48 per cent were under 35, and 68 per cent under 40,
years of age.

[2] The 191 deserters above mentioned left in all 514 children under 14
years of age, an average of 2.69 in each family.

[3] Of 100 deserters whose wages were known, 75 were earning $9 or
more, 15 of them $20 or more. Among 437 families who suffered in
the *General Slocum* disaster, June 15, 1904, there were 63 widows and 10
deserted wives.

[4] The Charter of New York City recognizes a legal obligation to support indigent grandparents or dependent grandchildren.

but rather a failure to provide proper support,— this failure simply being more complete and noticeable in the case of those who both neglect to provide and who are away from home, especially if their whereabouts are unknown.

The causes of desertion or non-support are thus found to be as numerous and as complicated as are any causes of destitution and of crime. The unwillingness of most wives to appear in court and ask for suitable action is very general and is perfectly intelligible. Although there is no complete solution for the problem in legislation, there are great differences in the effectiveness of existing laws in mitigating the evil. An investigation made by the Philadelphia Society for Organizing Charity in 1902 indicates that in two states there was no special law on the subject of desertion and non-support of wife and children; that there were sixteen states in which the only remedy for the wife is an application for divorce; ten in which a civil remedy was provided in the form of a judicial order against the husband to pay a certain sum for the support of his family ; eighteen states in which desertion was a criminal offence, classed as a misdemeanor, and two in which it was classed as a felony. Charitable societies have recently given this subject increased attention, and as a rule have urged the enactment of more severe laws. It has been argued that desertion should be made a felony, partly because this would, by increasing the gravity of the offence and its penalty, naturally decrease the number of offenders, and partly because, as a felon, the criminal would be more readily subject to extradition. While misdemeanants are extraditable as well as felons, the governors of states are usually unwilling to act except in case of felony. Something could doubtless be accomplished by changes in the laws in the directions that have been indicated, and by the use of probation officers. On this subject the following resolutions were adopted by the National Conference of Charities and Correction at Atlanta in 1903 : —

" *Whereas*, The desertion of wife and children by the legal head of the family, with a deliberate purpose of evading their support, has become a serious evil in the United States, entailing not only a great burden upon public and private relief funds, but causing untold suffering to sick women and neglected children, and seriously impairing public health and morals, and

" *Whereas*, Detailed investigation in several states has shown that of all families under the care of private charitable associations, no less than one in ten owe their destitution to this cause, and that the laws in twenty states for the punishment for desertion of a family in destitute circumstances are without effectual sanction, because deserters know that they have only to step over the state line for immunity, and

" *Whereas*, The National Conference of Charities and Correction believes that the application of extradition to this class of family deserters will prove the most effective remedy and deterrent ; therefore, be it

" *Resolved*, that the National Conference of Charities and Correction petition the governors of the different states of the United States to coöperate in checking this growing evil by exercising their powers of extradition, by issuing requests for the return of fugitive deserters whose families are dependent, as well as by honoring requisitions from other states."

The relief problem which is precipitated by desertion may now be considered. Legislation and education will lessen and may in time remove it, but not at once. It was pointed out[1] at a recent conference on the subject of family desertions that the first essential for the charitable visitor is to recognize a case of desertion when he encounters it. For a long time there was no distinction made between the deserted family and that of the widow, or, for that matter, between the family of the real deserter, who has left for good, and that of the " spurious deserter," who has not gone away at all, or who has gone for a brief period in connivance with the wife, in order to facilitate her application for relief. There are husbands, so-called, who desert their wives on the occasion of each childbirth, returning after some weeks to find that medical attendance, nursing, medicines, and supplies have been furnished without expense to them, and even a stock of infants' and

[1] Miss Mary E. Richmond, at a conference in New York, April 29, 1903.

children's clothing which will probably last until the advent of the next infant. There are men — perhaps "so-called" should be added here also — who go away every winter, or at every approach of hard times, or whenever any money comes in — taking the money, of course, with them. The calm reliance on the charity of neighbors and of churches, and of charitable societies, displayed by such deserters, is a tribute to be accepted with a certain misgiving and reflection as to the wisdom of the policy upon which it rests. The spurious deserter, who is in collusion with the begging wife, is far more common than will be thought possible by the inexperienced. He may be living at home, or temporarily lodging elsewhere.

The twenty-fourth annual report of the Philadelphia Society for Organizing Charity identifies and gives illustrations of five classes, as follows: the Chronic Deserter, the Reclaimable Deserter, the Spurious Deserter, the Half-Excusable Deserter, and the Un-Get-At-Able Deserter. The special report on Deserted Wives and Deserting Husbands, published by the Associated Charities of Boston in 1901, contains an analysis of two hundred and thirty-four families known to the district committees and agents of that society. In the discussion of the treatment of these families several distinct policies are described and illustrated. The first is that of reconciliation, which can be sought in only a small proportion of cases, either because the husband's whereabouts cannot be learned or because his character is "so bad that his going is a good riddance." The second remedy tried by the Boston Society is helping the family by providing training or opportunity to earn self-support in their own home without the man's help, securing help from relatives being considered a part of this second remedy. Breaking up the home ; caring for some of the children by charity, in order that the rest of the family may become self-supporting; securing legal separation, followed, if necessary, by such relief as would be provided for a widow with children, are the remaining remedies tried and approved, according to the varying circumstances of the different cases.

The trend of recent legislation is, perhaps, best presented by the provision of a law passed by the Legislature of the state of Illinois in 1903. The first section of this law is as follows : —

" That every person who shall, without good cause, abandon his wife and neglect and refuse to maintain and provide for her, or who shall abandon his or her minor child or children in destitute or necessitous circumstances and wilfully neglect or refuse to maintain and provide for such child or children, shall be deemed guilty of a misdemeanor, and on conviction thereof shall be punished by a fine of not less than one hundred dollars or more than five hundred dollars, or by imprisonment in the county jail, house of correction, or workhouse, not less than one month or more than twelve months, or by both such fine and imprisonment; and should a fine be imposed, it may be directed by the court to be paid in whole or in part to the wife or to the guardian or custodian of the minor child or children; provided that, before the trial (with the consent of the defendant), or after conviction, instead of imposing the punishment hereinbefore provided, or in addition thereto, the court in its discretion having regarded the circumstances and financial ability of the defendant, shall have the power to pass an order, which shall be subject to change by it from time to time, as the circumstances may require, directing the defendant to pay a certain sum weekly for one year to the wife, guardian, or custodian of the minor child or children, and to release the defendant from the custody, on probation, for the space of one year upon his or her entering into a recognizance, with or without sureties, in such sums as the court may direct. The conditions of the recognizance shall be such that if the defendant shall make his or her personal appearance in court whenever ordered to do so within a year, and shall further comply with the terms of the order or of any subsequent modification thereof, then the recognizance shall be void, otherwise of full force and effect. If the court be satisfied by information and due proof, under oath, that at any time during the year the defendant has violated the terms of such order, it may forthwith proceed with the trial of the defendant under the original indictment, or sentence him or her under the original conviction, as the case may be. In a case of forfeiture of a recognizance and enforcement thereof by execution, the sum recovered may, in the discretion of the court, be paid in whole or in part to the wife, guardian, or custodian of the minor child or children."

The second section describes what evidence of marriage and parentage is essential, and provides that the wife shall be a competent witness in any case brought under this act.

A new law in the state of Pennsylvania provides similarly that, "If any husband or father being within the limits of this Commonwealth shall hereafter separate himself from his wife, or from his children, or from wife and children, without reasonable cause, and shall wilfully neglect to maintain his wife or children, such wife or children being destitute, or being dependent, wholly or in part, on their earnings for adequate support, he shall be guilty of a misdemeanor and on conviction thereof be sentenced to imprisonment not exceeding one year, and to pay a fine not exceeding one hundred dollars, or either, or both, at the discretion of the court, such fine, if any, to be paid or applied in whole or in part to the wife or children, as the court may direct."

This law also permits suspended sentence, declares that a wife is a competent witness, and that proof of separation and neglect to support shall be *prima facie* evidence that such separation and neglect are wilful and without reasonable cause on the part of the husband.

CHAPTER XII

ASIDE from the death or desertion of the breadwinner, the three great and constantly recurring causes of destitution are sickness, lack of employment, and drink. These are not the only causes. Industrial inefficiency, dishonesty, or other criminal act, and a number of other causes not easily classified, produce their share of dependent families, but as compared with the three just named even so considerable a cause as inefficiency or lack of training becomes less conspicuous. Industrial displacement and the prevention of disease are considered in other chapters. We must now face more directly the relief problems attributable to drink. It is a conservative estimate that one-fourth of all the cases of destitution with which private relief agencies have to deal are fairly attributable to intemperance. That is to say, in this proportion of cases the death of the breadwinner or the loss of work and the difficulty in securing new employment, or the exhaustion of financial resources, or whatever other reason may be assigned at the time of application, is readily and incontrovertibly traced back to intemperate habits on the part of the applicant himself, or other members of the family whose coöperation is essential to self-support. There are many other instances in which the applicant has been accustomed to a greater or less use of alcoholic beverages, and in a certain proportion of these, if the facts could be fully known, it would be apparent that greater temperance or entire abstinence would have prevented the need for outside assistance, but the same thing might be said with equal truth of other more or less foolish or wasteful habits. The estimate made above includes only the cases in which there is an obvious connection between the use of alcohol and the dependent condition in which the family is found. The question as to how much should be added to cover the cases in which there is only a partial or indirect responsibility is a matter for conjecture, and estimates upon this point are likely to differ according to the standpoint of the one who makes them. It is a matter for conjecture also, and estimates differ here again, as to what other evil consequences, aside from poverty and destitution, are due to drink. That there is an endless train of evils, aside from the burden of pauperism and dependence which it entails, cannot be gainsaid. Insanity, suicide, and death in other forms result from the use of alcohol, in many instances in which no question of relief arises. Cruelty, neglect, and unhappiness result directly from the use of alcohol in families which are by no means near the verge of dependence. Crimes are committed under its stimulus, and demoralizing associations are formed or strengthened under conditions in which the use of alcohol is an important element, and it makes easier the path to vice and the indulgence of every debasing appetite. Certain diseases, such as tuberculosis and pneumonia, are far more likely to attack those who are subject to alcoholism, and it greatly impedes the recovery of those who are attacked. These consequences are not exhausted in the lives of the intemperate themselves, but are bequeathed to posterity in various forms of degeneracy, spiritual and physical.

The extreme position that alcohol acts always as a poison, and that it cannot be taken except with injurious physical effects, is rejected by a preponderance of medical opinion, nor, in spite of the appalling consequences of alcoholism, can one find moral grounds for objecting to the moderate use of alcoholic beverages by those who find that they are physically beneficial or that they are pleasurable and without evil results. The entire prohibition of the manufacture and sale of alcoholic beverages cannot then be justified on the ground that their use is, for all persons, and under all circumstances, physically and morally injurious. Prohibition may, however, be justified on less extreme grounds. If it is established that for a very large proportion of those who use alcohol physical injuries and economic disaster are likely to result, then the community, even if it be

L

admitted that these results do not follow with absolute uniformity, may wisely determine to cast out the active cause of so much distress and disaster. Even if it be only the weak that yield to their appetite and drink to excess, it may still be best, for the sake of those weaker ones, and in the interests of the community of which they are a part, to forego the pleasure and the beneficial results experienced in a few instances. It is quite conceivable that a community made up of perfectly rational human beings, with a due regard for the doctrine of personal liberty and with a just appreciation of the advantages resulting in some instances from the use of alcoholic beverages, when they look out upon the crime and poverty and distress which are chargeable to its use by others, may deliberately decide that the brewery, the still, and the saloon shall not exist, or that whatever alcoholic liquors are produced shall be permitted to be used for medicinal purposes only, on competent medical advice. This has been the attitude of many who have upheld prohibition as a state policy. There are many who hold views by no means extremely puritanical, and who are quite ready to admit that the moderate use of wine does not imply moral obliquity, who are nevertheless convinced that a community in which liquor cannot be obtained is a better place in which to bring up children and a safer place for the average adult. Maine, Iowa, and other states which have made more or less complete experiments with the system of prohibition, have come nearest creating conditions of this kind, but they have not extended throughout any entire state, and it is probably impossible that they should. A law prohibiting the manufacture and sale of alcoholic beverages can be enforced only when a considerable majority of the citizens believe in its principles. It is essentially a law which must rest upon public opinion. Secret and constant violation of the law, which is always possible when a considerable minority reject the principles upon which it rests, and regard the statute as an infraction of their personal liberty, tends to bring all law into contempt, and speedily makes the law in question injurious rather than beneficial. In the greater cities containing a large foreign population accustomed to a very general use of alcoholic beverages, and

containing also a considerable number of more or less reckless and vicious persons who have a craving for alcohol,
prohibition has seldom been in successful operation for any
long period of time.   In rural communities, on the other
hand, and in the smaller cities it has often been entirely
successful, and children have grown to manhood, although
by no means secluded on their own farms or in their own
villages, without having had an opportunity to drink alcoholic beverages at their meals or elsewhere.   If prohibition has proved to be impracticable over so large an area
as a state, it may still have, then, a legitimate place in the
form of local option, and in many states the territory over
which such option may be exercised may be the county or
even a group of counties acting together.

If prohibition be not adopted, either in the form of a
state law or by the exercise of local option in town, city, or
county, the remedy which next suggests itself is the practice of total abstinence by the individual, fortified, it may
be, by a solemn pledge not to partake of alcohol in any
form.   To the pledge of total abstinence it may be objected
that the drunkard who takes it is not likely to keep it, and
that one who has not formed the habit is foolish to bind
himself unnecessarily.   There are many, however, who
have been addicted to the use of alcohol to their own injury and that of others, who take the pledge and keep it,
and there are others, how many it is impossible to calculate,
but certainly vast numbers, who have taken a pledge as
children or in their young manhood and have been deterred
by that pledge from forming habits which would have been
fatal.   It is wrong to extort a promise from one who is not
in position to weigh the evidence, on a distorted and exaggerated presentation of the consequences of the use of
alcohol.   Nor is there occasion for such exaggeration.

The argument for total abstinence based merely on the
chances of injury is quite as valid as that which leads to
the practice of life insurance or many other acts which are
entirely rational and well advised.   Elementary education
in the schools regarding the physical effects of alcohol,
and popular instruction of adults through lectures, through
the press, from the pulpit, and otherwise, are wholly justifiable and vitally essential.   Reform and the taking of a

pledge of abstinence often accompany a religious awakening, and are among the finest fruits of such appeals to the higher nature. The practice of total abstinence may be accompanied by some sacrifice of social pleasures, and it may be that its universal adoption would result in some subtle injury to the progress of the human race, as has been claimed, but it is certain that it would enormously reduce the number of the dependent poor, and that it would make it possible to help effectively many who in their slavery to the drink habit are beyond human aid.

There are many with whom alcoholism is essentially a disease, and unfortunately very often an incurable disease. Life may then come to an early end, or it may be prolonged with periodic debauches at shorter or longer intervals through many years. The unfortunate victim, whatever the circumstances under which the habit was fastened upon him, may become an object of infinite pity in the end. The most heroic attempts for the sake of the family may be in vain, and the most sincere and apparently complete reformation may be succeeded by repeated collapse. For such diseased persons the most skilful medical care is needed, and often confinement, voluntary or involuntary, for a prolonged period. There are various secret remedies, some of which present credible evidence of cures effected by their instrumentality. It is, however, for the medical profession to test these remedies, and resort to them with the aid of relief funds is rarely advisable, and, if at all, only with the knowledge and consent of a reputable physician. The layman may not be in position to appreciate all the details of the code of ethics recognized by the medical profession, but with the position that any remedy or preventive of disease known to a physician must be divulged to his brethren of the medical profession, under penalty that one who fails to do this sacrifices his own professional standing, all the world must agree. Homes for intemperate men—for the reformation of drunkards; special hospitals or sanatoria for the medical treatment of such as desire to be cured of an appetite beyond voluntary control, are essential parts of a general relief system. The most important single step that could be taken for the eradication of the curse of intemperance would be the early recognition of the symptoms of habitual drunkenness, and the sentence of every person who has reached this stage either to a hospital or to the custody of a competent probation officer, until cured.[1] The substitution of this plan for the present utterly useless and absurd fines and short sentences to jail or workhouse would be both humane and scientific. A further step would be the creation of a farm colony, comprising a series of hospitals and institutions for different grades of patients, to which those who need such treatment could be sent, and in which they could be kept until, in the judgment of a competent examining board, they are ready to be restored to their place in society. Within the institution, inmates might, as a rule, during the greater part of their stay be fully self-supporting. This system would be applicable not only to victims of alcohol, but to such as are addicted to opium or other harmful drugs. To this radical policy for the treatment of inebriates, a physician has objected on the ground that it is condemning those who have committed no crime to " experimenters armed with a hyperdermic needle." In reply to this cynical estimate of the present capacity of the medical profession to deal with one of the largest class of those who are undoubtedly afflicted by disease, it is sufficient to point out that insane patients are similarly intrusted to medical " experimenters " and on the whole with good results.

The giving of aid in the homes of those who are addicted to drink is attended by grave dangers. Relief should always be conditioned upon some definite and radical steps toward the curing of the real evil. It cannot be declared at what point attempts to reform the drunkard should be so far abandoned as is involved in a separation of wife and children from one who, through drink, makes himself incapable of caring for them, and yet this point is reached in extreme cases, and the interests of the family require either a temporary or a final breaking up of the home. This may require a prosecution of the husband for non-support, ac-

---

[1] See a paper presented at the Chicago International Conference of Charities and Correction, 1893, by T. D. Crothers, M.D., on the " Problem of Inebriate Pauperism."

companied it may be by cruelty or neglect, or only temporary institutional care of some kind may be needed. Graver still is the situation when it is the mother, or when it is both parents, that are addicted to drink.   Religious influence; the personal influence of some one who will take a genuinely friendly interest in the family; the withholding of relief except on such conditions as will tend to insure sobriety; medical treatment in appropriate cases; and custodial care under reformative and educational influences, are remedies which may be brought to bear somewhat in the order named, keeping always in mind, especially in considering the young, that the real remedies are the strengthening of character and the removal of temptation from those who are weak.

CHAPTER XIII

INDUSTRIAL DISPLACEMENT

LACK of employment, which, at the time of application, is given in the great majority of instances as the reason for being in need, is usually found on inquiry to be due to some personal deficiency in the employee. He has been discharged for intemperance, for inefficiency, for inability to meet the demands upon him, or for some objectionable trait which may or may not have anything to do with his actual efficiency for the particular task upon which he was engaged. In a certain proportion of instances, however, by no means insignificant in the aggregate, destitution is due to lack of employment, which cannot properly be charged to any fault of the employee. Loss of employment, indeed, is a frequent occurrence, and although it does not as a rule result in immediate destitution, it is almost always a matter of very serious consequence to the laborer and his family. The introduction of machinery; changes in methods of industry; a falling off in the demand for particular commodities; disturbances of credit; or the mere substitution of a new management in a particular industrial enterprise, which is either more or less efficient than the old, may have the effect of throwing persons out of work. If they are young and adapt themselves readily to new circumstances, comparatively little harm may result. There may be demand elsewhere for the same kind of work which they have been doing, or they may be able to do something different and thus find employment where there is a demand. The laborer who has had in youth a varied manual training, and who is not readily discouraged, will be less likely to suffer seriously from such enforced changes. The man who has accumulated some savings will also be at a great advantage when forced to look about for new employment.

It is not surprising, however, that where there is a high standard of living, and where rapid and exhausting labor is the rule, industrial changes should come, in some instances, to those who, on account of age and exceptional hardships, cannot readily adjust themselves to the new situation, and who, consequently, become dependent through no exceptional neglect or fault on their own part. At worst their failure to provide for such a situation may indicate a failure to realize the probability of its occurrence, and the expenditures that have been made may all have been for perfectly legitimate and desirable objects. It is under such circumstances that industrial displacement is properly regarded as a real cause of distress. If it is accompanied by intemperance or dishonesty or inefficiency or laziness; or if it is followed by desertion of family or the adoption of any other criminal method of escape from the consequences, those features of the situation must be dealt with on their merits. When, however, there are no such complicating factors, it becomes the more necessary to give assistance in reëstablishing the applicant in some suitable occupation. The first principle to be recognized is that the obligation to find employment, like the obligation to continue suitable employment when one has it, rests primarily upon the applicant himself. It is quite possible to undermine self-reliance by doing gratuitously the things which a self-respecting man will do for himself. The search from one place to another among the establishments in which it would be appropriate to make application for work; the scrutiny of want advertisements; the study of the pages of a business directory; consultation with fellow-workmen in the same branch of industry; and registration in a reputable employment agency, are all means of which use may be made by the man in search of work.

It is true that there are instances in which the most desperate efforts to find employment are unsuccessful; and when week has succeeded week, and month has succeeded month in fruitless efforts, the seeker for employment may become despondent, and by his very lack of success reduced to a physical and mental condition in which further unaided search becomes impossible. Successive failures finally rob the applicant for work even of the power to imagine himself able to succeed, and the most trivial obstacle becomes magnified into one that appears insuperable. Before this condition has been reached the lack of income has often reduced the family to a destitute condition, although the wages of wife or children may have replaced those of the natural breadwinner. When the situation is such that relief must be supplied if employment cannot be provided, and there is nevertheless an able-bodied man in the family, it is obviously both charitable and economical to give a helping hand in the finding of suitable employment as a substitute for relief, or, more accurately, as a means of relief. This may be done through a free employment bureau, or an employment bureau in which payment of registration fee may be deferred until it can be met from wages, or through the payment of registration fee as a gift or loan to the applicant, or through personal solicitation on the applicant's behalf among possible employers. The funds of charitable societies and the energies of their agents and visitors should not be absorbed in performing the services which naturally belong to ordinary business employment agencies, but when the alternative lies between charitable aid and employment, the latter becomes a legitimate choice and this objection disappears.

Reference is here made to individual instances of unemployment arising under normal industrial conditions. In a period of exceptional stress, when large numbers are thrown out of employment simultaneously, there may arise a need for extraordinary relief measures such as are described in the chapter in Part IV on Industrial Distress in New York and Indianapolis in the Winter of 1893–1894. It may be assumed that employment is to be found in ordinary times if there is the ordinary persistence in seeking it, or that the laborer will have enough laid by to tide over any brief period of compulsory idleness. Insurance against the hardships of unemployment may take the form of out-of-work benefits in a trade-union or of deposits in a savings bank. It is incumbent upon relief agencies not to discourage the disposition to make such independent provision for slack times, and not to place at an apparent financial advantage through charitable gifts those who, because of inefficiency, laziness, or other defect, are first laid off when the number of employees is reduced.

A few years ago a careful study of industrial displacement and unemployment, as a cause of distress, was made by Francis H. McLean from the records of the New York Charity Organization Society. The 720 cases selected were those in which lack of employment or insufficient employment was assigned as the chief cause of need among those who applied to the society for the first time in the year ending June 30, 1896. There were in all 924 such cases out of a total of 1884 families known to the society for the first time that year. Of the 720 case records examined it was ascertained that the decisions in 107 instances were subsequently, on fuller knowledge of the families and deliberation by the district committees, reversed, and some other cause of destitution assigned. Mr. McLean found, on examining the records, that the committees were usually right in reversing the earlier decisions, and as a result of this inquiry the Society's method of tabulating these results was modified so that the final official decisions of the district committees were thereafter recorded.

There were eleven cases in which, although application for assistance was made, and there was at the outset apparent need, it was subsequently found that there was really no destitution. These eleven cases, and the 107 in which the decisions of the agents were reversed, were omitted from the classification. Of the remaining 502 it was ascertained that there were 332 cases in which the chief cause of need was unemployment, and 164 in which the displacement was not industrial, while there were 106 cases which were doubtful. Dividing the latter equally between the first two classes, it would appear that 53.3 per cent of the 720 cases examined were genuine cases of unemployment. By this analysis the percentage of cases credited to unemployment is reduced from 49 to 26.1 per cent. In the following table Mr. McLean classifies the causes in detail : —

A. Causes of Displacement — Industrial : —

1. General dulness in business 73
2. Seasonal dulness in trade . . . . . . 58 [1]
3. Insufficient employment 61
4. Inability to earn livelihood in independent business . 26
5. Failure in independent business 14
6. Failure of employers 7
7. Changes in business arrangements . . . . 11 [2]
8. Closing of business houses or factories . . . 11
9. To make room for relative of employer . . . 2
10. Not yet located in new industrial centre . . . 13
11. Crowded out by younger men 5
12. Changes in domestic arrangements on the part of employers 10
13. Dynamic movement in trade . . . . . 3 [3]
14. Direct or indirect result of strike 2
15. Permanent injury to health resulting from practice of regular trade 3
16. Not fitted for place occupied 2
17. Poorly paid employment 1
18. Industrial inefficiency 5
19. Old age 5
20. Physical infirmities 3
21. Miscellaneous 17
                                                        ———
                                                        332

B. Causes of Displacement — Personal : —

1. Shiftlessness 33
2. Intemperance 15
3. Sickness 38
4. Death of member of family 4
5. Accident 12
6. Immorality 2
7. Voluntary displacement 11
8. Quarrel with employers 13
9. Disobedience to orders 3
10. Character weaknesses 20
11. Dishonesty 3
12. Improvidence . . . . 2 [4]
13. General pauperism . . . . 8 [4]
                                                        ———
                                                        164

[1] Logically we should carry our investigation one step farther in these instances, for of course such seasonal depressions come periodically and can be anticipated. Why, then, did these families come to want during any particular depression? But as the number of cases is comparatively small it seems hardly worth while to make the further analysis. It is sufficient to say that in eleven instances intemperance can easily be traced, and sickness in the family in six.

[2] For instance, a firm changing hands, the new proprietors hiring men of their own choice.   [3] Such as the introduction of machinery.

[4] These last two heads do not necessarily indicate displacement at all. It is hard to justify the decisions of the committee in even considering them as unemployment cases.

It was also attempted to ascertain how far the statistics indicate industrial contraction.[1] It is pointed out that in most of the occupations from which applicants for relief come, the dynamic movements are not great; but that there is an actual diminution in the number of men required in particular trades is clearly indicated in a number of instances. Four hundred and seventy-three cases are tabulated for this purpose as follows : —

	Number of Cases	Per Cent
1. Cases of displacement indicating industrial contraction	106	22.4
2. Cases of insufficient, irregular, or poorly paid employment	159	33.6
3. Replacement indicating no character weaknesses	128	27.1
4. Replacement indicating character weaknesses	80	16.9
	473	100

The term "character weakness" of course refers to the person displaced who applies for aid. It appears by the table that simple replacement of one laborer by another is indicated in 44 per cent of the total number of cases. The replacement in a majority of cases proceeded from no character weakness. Of course much of the replacement was due to such causes as sickness, accident, etc.

In enumerating the occupations of the displaced, Mr. McLean calls attention to an element of uncertainty arising from a tendency on the part of applicants to represent themselves as engaged in a slightly higher occupation than that in which they really have been engaged. Thus rough laborers who have assisted artisans become transformed into artisans. From the records, however, the impression is that those who call themselves tradesmen are in fact tradesmen, although often on a meagre scale.

---

[1] It is only "localized" industrial contraction that is here meant. What might, by contrast, be called "sheer" industrial contraction — that is, a reduction in one plant, without any corresponding increase in others. This, however, we have no satisfactory means of determining. The table shows actual contraction in certain industrial plants, which includes an indefinite amount of "sheer" contraction.

TABLE SHOWING OCCUPATIONS

	NUMBER OF CASES	PER CENT
1. Unskilled men (ordinary laborers) . .	78	15.7
2. Unskilled women (cleaners, ordinary wash-ers, etc.)	54	10.9
3. Laundresses and seamstresses ˙ . .	36	7.3
4. Porters, packers, and drivers . . .	41	8.3
5. Stablemen, janitors, elevator and hotel men, etc.	19	3.8
6. Domestic service	33	6.7
7. Tobacco and cigar trades	14	2.8
8. Clothing trades	20	4
9. Building trades	34	6.9
10. Foundry and metal trades	13	2.6
11. Upholstering and furnishing trades . .	9	1.8
12. Mechanical and skilled trades . . .	29	5.9
13. Bakers	4	.8
14. Clerks, bookkeepers, and salesmen . .	25	5.0
15. Shoe and leather trades	7	1.4
16. Printers and compositors	7	1.4
17. Marble and stone workers	12	2.4
18. Furriers	4	.8
19. Professional and semi-professional . .	16[1]	3.2
20. Dressmakers	8	1.6
21. Miscellaneous	33	6.7
	496	100

An analysis of 496 cases by ages gives the following results : —

AGE ANALYSIS

AGE	NUMBER OF CASES	PER CENT
Twenty to twenty-five	33	6.7
Twenty-five to thirty	64	12.9
Thirty to thirty-five	120	24.2
Thirty-five to forty	95	19.2
Forty to forty-five	74	14.9
Forty-five to fifty	47	9.5
Fifty to fifty-five	23	4.6
Fifty-five to sixty	25	5.0
Over sixty	15	3.0
	496	100

[1] Including stenographer, 1; inventor, 1; dentist, 1; journalists, 2.; fresco painter, 1; clarinet player, 1; midwives, 2 · veterinary surgeon, 1; nurses, 4; scene painter, 1; artist, 1.

The next table shows the period elapsing between last regular employment and application to the society for assistance. In some instances families doubtless received aid from other sources before the present application. Most of them, however, appear from the records to have had no previous assistance.

Classifying results according to certain time groups, we find : —

Time from Displacement to Application	Number of Cases	Per Cent
Work (although insufficient) to date .	79 [1]	15.9
Less than three months . . .	185 [2]	37.3
Three to six months	58	11.7
Six to twelve months	32	6.5
One year or over	17	3.4
Uncertain	125 [3]	25.2
	496	100

Mr. McLean presents also a table indicating the length of time covered by the business references given by applicants, this tabulation covering 578 cases.

Time Period Covered by Business References	Ages of Applicants									
	20–30		30–40		40–50		Over 50		Totals	
	No.	Per Cent	No.	Per Cent	No.	Per Cent	No.	Per Cent	No.	Per Cent
Having no references	25	22.7	40	15.9	26	18.4	15	20	106	18.3
Uncertain . . .	22	20	87	34.5	49	34.8	31	41.3	189	32.7
Less than two years	23	20.9	44	17.5	18	12.8	10	13.3	95	16.4
Two to five years	25	22.7	42	16.6	20	14	6	8	93	16.1
Five to ten years	13	11.9	29	11.5	14	10	8	10.7	64	11.1
Ten to twenty years	2	1.8	10	4	14	10	5	6.7	31	5.4
Totals	110	100	252	100	141	100	75	100	578	100

[1] A large number of these were washerwomen and cleaners.
[2] Of these 71 applied during the first month.
[3] Includes a number of men who rely for support upon odd jobs.

The extremes from this table indicate that 18.3 per cent of the applicants whose records were examined have no recorded industrial history, aside from cases of misrepresentation.   There were 32.7 per cent who gave references which could not be verified.   While most of these were fictitious, there were doubtless some who could not be located because of removals or for other reasons.   Those who gave no references and a part of those whose references could not be verified are to a large extent men who live by odd jobs.   For 16.1 per cent on the other hand employment can be traced over periods ranging from two to five years, and for 16.5 per cent over periods ranging from five to twenty years.   More definite information affecting displacement where it involves the greatest hardship is given in the following table, showing for certain selected trade-groups the period covered by business references ending, it will be remembered, in lack of employment, in the majority of instances due entirely to industrial, and not to personal, causes : —

TRADE GROUPS SELECTED	TIME PERIODS COVERED BY BUSINESS REFERENCES (SELECTED)		
	2 to 5 years	5 to 10 years	10 to 20 years
Unskilled men	14	5	5
Unskilled women . . .	3	2	2
Building	6	0	3
Domestic service	7	5	1
Miscellaneous trades . . .	11	7	6
Clothing	5	2	2
Tobacco	3	2	0
Clerks, bookkeepers, etc. .	8	6	1
Porters, packers, and drivers .	25	14	4
Foundry and metal trades . .	11	5	2
Totals	93	48	26

One further point in the industrial history of the applicants is examined, viz., the length of time covered by the last regular employment.   In 130 cases out of 578 previously examined it is impossible from the record to ascertain this period : —

Time covered by Last Regular Employment	Number of Cases	Per Cent
Less than one month	14	3.1
One to four months	61	13.6
Four to six months	16	3.6
Six to twelve months	40	8.9
One to two years	26	5.8
Two to three years	27	6
Three to four years	22	4.9
Four to five years	12	2.7
Five to ten years	34	7.6
Over ten years	17	3.8
Irregular	179	40
	448 [1]	100

Thus 40 per cent of the cases considered appear to have been, temporarily at least, unable to get permanently placed. They were only irregularly employed even when they last had employment. Thirty-eight and eight-tenths per cent, however, had been regularly employed for over a year. Exclusively of the regularly employed, there were 91, or 23.3 per cent, with whom displacement had apparently occurred twice within six months. Some of the seasonal trades are represented in this table, and on the whole it appears to indicate a fair degree of economic stability. It is of interest to add that, of 473 applicants at the time when the inquiry was made, 190, or 40 per cent of all applicants, were satisfactorily returned to industrial activity, either by their own efforts (153 cases), or by the efforts of the society (37 cases). Fifty-one persons, on the other hand, or 10.8 per cent, secured only temporary work in some inferior trade or occupation. Of the 254 persons who secured work of some kind, temporary material relief had been provided in 50 cases, relief and temporary employment in wood yard, laundry, and workrooms in 76 cases; and temporary employment in wood yard, work rooms or laundry in 49 cases; while 109 were advised and directed without material aid.

It is unfortunate that there are not available similar statistics from other societies, or from the same society for other periods, and that there are not accessible statistics

[1] Obtained by subtracting the 130 eliminated from 578.

from trade-unions, employment agencies, and labor bureaus in which unemployment, due to natural causes, is distinguished, as in these tables, from lack of employment due to personal qualities of the employee. It is true that the statistics of charitable societies will naturally afford a very much larger percentage of cases in which employment has been lost through inefficiency or personal defects than would be found in statistics from the other sources named in any period of general unemployment. It is, of course, the least desirable who are first displaced and whose periods of unemployment are longest. To deduct the total number of those who, from the employers' statement, would appear to have been displaced on account of personal deficiencies from the number of the unemployed, would be a misleading method of determining the extent of industrial contraction. These can better be spared than the more efficient or trustworthy laborers, but it does not follow that if all had been equally capable and satisfactory, all could have been retained.

Among the means by which those who are brought to destitution by lack of employment may be replaced in their original or other suitable occupation are : —

I. The use of employment agencies and of newspaper advertisements.

II. Direct appeal to possible employers of labor, and coöperation with the trade-union.

III. The creation of industrial colonies or industries in which, under direction, those who cannot be placed in regular industries may become, to a greater or less extent, self-supporting.

IV. The use of temporary industries, *e.g.* wood yard, broom factory, laundry, workrooms for unskilled, etc., as a work test, as a means of training, and as a substitute for direct relief, and

V. Material relief, duly safeguarded, pending efforts by the applicant and others to secure employment through one or more of the means above enumerated. In ordinary times, this resource will not be required for the able-bodied.

M

CHAPTER XIV

THE relief problem of the American seaboard cities is greatly affected by immigration. The immigrant of the twentieth century offers little resemblance to the colonist of the early days of the republic. The colonist was establishing new outposts of civilization; he was one who was capable of making his way in the face of adverse circumstances; he was influenced by some strong religious or political or economic motive, and felt within himself a daring and strength of character sufficient to overcome the dangers, the loneliness, and the privations of the frontier. Colonization is, in short, one of those differentiating agencies leading to the selection and survival of such as have initiative and exceptional capacity. Immigration, on the other hand, offers a comparatively easy escape from hard conditions. The immigrant is one who follows in a path already made easy. He goes where his friends or relatives have gone, and settles in the spot where they have settled. He yields to the artifices of transportation agents, or may even be assisted by the public authorities of his own community to emigrate for his country's good. Until there is legal interference he comes under a contract to work at occupations and under industrial conditions about which he may be entirely ignorant, thus lending himself readily to a lowering of the standard both of living and of wages. He is scarcely conscious even of the handicap of speaking a foreign language, since he is worked and lodged with others of his own nationality, and under foremen who can speak to him in his own tongue.

The immigrant who goes under tempting circumstances to a place literally prepared for his arrival has, therefore, rather less than the average initiative, independence, and courage, the qualities which are so predominant in the original settlers of a new country. This is, of course, by no means a correct description of all immigrants. There may be little difference between the best immigrant and the best colonist, or even between the majority of immigrants and the majority of colonists. The description applies rather to the marginal colonist and immigrant respectively — to the least efficient class who are nevertheless represented in each in considerable numbers. In the frontier colony the minimum wage-earning capacity and industrial efficiency is necessarily high; in the immigrant it may be very low, and it is with these marginal immigrants that relief agencies have chiefly to deal.

The Immigration Laws of the United States have been framed to some extent explicitly to meet this situation. Not only is it made unlawful for lunatics, feeble-minded persons, and habitual criminals to enter, but those who are " liable to become public charges " are also excluded, and large discretion is necessarily lodged in officials stationed at the various points of entry, in determining whether particular persons are not included in this category. The possession of a stipulated sum of money, or positive assurance from a friend or relative apparently worthy of confidence that the applicant for admission will not become a public charge, is regarded as evidence of eligibility for admission. No such test, however, can effectively bar out all who are on the brink of dependence, and as a matter of fact many immigrants do become public charges, either in their own person or through the commitment of their children to public institutions, within a few years of their arrival.

The assisted ocean passage and the ready employment on arrival, to which reference have been made, although they serve to attract less efficient and intelligent laborers, are advantages which are not to be had for nothing. By excessively long hours, by overcrowded, unsanitary tenements, and by insufficient wages, the immigrant returns full measure of payment for his escape from the struggle for independence and its initial hardships. Initial obstacles have been removed only that the remainder of his days may be exploited to his injury. The liberty which he has bartered he may regain by suffering and toil for himself or for his children, but there will be many who fail, and it is to meet these failures that the relief policy must be framed. The widows and infant children left behind by those who have died from consumption, or who have been killed in factories ; the shiftless, intemperate men and women whose lives have been sapped by their premature employment as children ; ineffective workers who are so because they are illiterate and untrained ; the sick and disabled, whose relatives are in distant lands and are poor, — these, and other types of dependents whom we have already had to consider in other relations, are increased in number and their natural resources for relief are fewer, because of immigration.

Recognition of the family, even in its collateral branches, and the placing of burdens upon those who are blood kindred, is one of the first principles of organized relief. When, however, all inquiries run quickly to the ocean's edge, the chances of any effective recognition of family responsibility are greatly lessened. A vague statement that one's parents or other kindred are in Syria, in Poland, in Southern Italy, or in Ireland, and that they have all that they can do to support themselves, is not easily disproved even if it is not always true. Correspondence with relief agencies throughout the European continent is difficult, and even when it has been established, is often inconclusive because of the different points of view and the differences in language, customs, and standards. When one has lost employment and has but a few acquaintances, and these perhaps hastily formed, it is, of course, more difficult to furnish those evidences of character and fitness which would be available in the native land, but which are not readily imported among the immigrant's assets. It is beyond reasonable expectation also, that when an immigrant has, through old age or infirmity, become a public charge, there should be quite the same degree of tenderness and consideration for him as he might have experienced in a similar adverse fate in the home of his ancestors. I am not apologizing for any indifference to the necessities of those who are in distress, but pointing out that absence from those upon whom they have the strongest claim for the offices prompted by ties of kindred and of intimate association through generations, is a deprivation of that for which there is no ready substitute. This, however, increases rather than lessens the responsibility of those who in public or in private charities administer relief. Those who have been in the country but a short time may wisely be returned to their homes, but others, who may remain after the lapse of years essentially immigrants, may be in distress, and it may be possible to relieve them, or necessary to support them, in their dependent condition. It is not by withholding relief from individuals or from families who may wisely be aided that the evil consequences of unrestricted immigration are to be met. The strengthening of existing laws, by the addition of a clause excluding illiterate adults, and by providing more efficient means for the deportation of those who have been admitted through misrepresentation or fraud, is advisable, and the uniform and equitable administration of existing laws is essential; and in addition voluntary agencies and private citizens may wisely counteract, at the sources of emigration, the misinformation which has been persistently spread abroad. Definite measures are now taken, for example, in Ireland, to check emigration, and these are supported by representative Irishmen whose devotion to the interests of the Irish people, both at home and in America, is unquestionable.[1]

The arguments in favor of unrestricted immigration are that cheap labor is needed in the building of railways and in many other undertakings in which the directive intelligence can be separated from the physical labor required; and that any practical test, such as ability to read or write, possession of a given sum of money, or even a certificate of good character from the place of departure, will operate to exclude many who, under new and favorable conditions, in a new land, might prove to be very useful and entirely self-supporting citizens. While it is true that cheap labor

[1] There is a similar anti-emigration movement in Sweden, and the Italian government has a Bureau of Emigration which aims to discourage the departure of desirable citizens, and permits the United States authorities to examine for the detection of undesirable persons.

may be made profitable from the employer's point of view,
it does not follow that those who are considering the interests of the community as a whole can look with favor
upon it.   The superintendent of a mill which had within
a few years replaced efficient but highly paid American
laborers by Hungarians analyzed the results of the change
in conversation with the author as follows : The new
laborers could do less work in a given time, but they
were willing to work at less wages, and they were willing
to work more hours in the week.   Being less efficient and
having less initiative, it had been necessary to increase the
number of foremen and to pay them somewhat higher
wages, holding them responsible to a greater extent than
before for the correction of mistakes and for driving the
men under them at their maximum capacity.   As the men
worked for longer hours, the machinery was idle for a
smaller part of the time, and the total product was increased
at less expense.   This illustration is not presented as typical.   In many instances the product would doubtless be
diminished rather than increased by such a substitution,
and the cost increased so that the net result would be a
diminution of profits.   Within reasonable limits the general principle is that high-priced labor is economic labor,
the condition being that it shall be as intelligent, as trustworthy, and as efficient as it is well paid.   Nevertheless
the exploitation of cheap labor, as is illustrated in the instance above cited, is not infrequent, and whether in the
long run it is disastrous or beneficial in a given industry,
there is no doubt that for individuals in charge of particular industries at particular times it will offer an opportunity for pecuniary profit and that such an opportunity
will be seized.   With the consequences to the industry in
the long run, the employer of the moment may have little
concern.   It has been asserted that without the immigrant
—without these " lower, dependent-producing grades " of
labor — we could not have an industrial organization.   I
am unable to accept this view, or to agree that it is a matter
of conjecture whether our industrial organizations could
be maintained without them.   There is plenty of experience and ample warrantable analogy for believing that
if it were necessary for American communities to get on

without a large element of illiterate, unskilled, and low-priced labor, they would succeed in doing so ; and would leave no work of vital importance unperformed.

In a nutshell, if the American workman, accustomed to a high standard of living, is confronted with a disagreeable task, he will invent a machine to do it for him. Disagreeable labor, such as is performed by Negroes, by ill-paid Italian laborers, by Chinese coolies, by sweat-shop workers, and by others in a similar grade of development, and such as was formerly performed by Irish immigrants, and, to some extent, by the less efficient and progressive classes of native-born laborers, is performed by human beings only when they can be had cheap. If there is no one willing to work at the wages which can be earned in such occupations, and if the industrial efficiency of the individual worker is such as to justify his employment at higher wages elsewhere, it does not mean — it never has meant — that these industries will be discontinued. It means that they will be performed by machinery or by processes from which the more disagreeable features have been eliminated.

The sweat-shop has never been a necessity of New York City ; but it is a natural product of the presence of large numbers of people who can be worked in sweat-shops. Through organization and legislation the particular trades which were ten years ago, or even five years ago, carried on in sweat-shops, have been largely transferred to decent workshops and factories ; and it is reasonable to believe that the grade of efficiency represented by the sweat-shop would disappear if it were not for the continued supply through immigration of those who have been accustomed to, and will accept, the lower standard ; and who, from the point of view of the individual manufacturer, are more profitable than decent workshops and improved machinery.

The menace of immigration lies not so much in an imaginary channel from European poorhouses to American poorhouses, although there are those who do pass through just such a channel ; but rather in the well-trodden highway which leads from the low-standard laborers of Southern Europe to the lower margin of American industry, which is kept low, not because the immigrant wishes it, but because his standard and efficiency, his physical and mental equipment, are such that he is at the mercy of those who exploit his unskilled labor to their own profit. The unskilled, inefficient, underpaid immigrant may be a source of pecuniary gain to his individual employer, but his presence is an injury to the community.

The effect of utilizing underpaid immigrant labor under conditions which, in order to afford a living at all, make excessive demands upon adult men, and lead irresistibly to the employment of women and children, is directly to increase the number who sooner or later require relief. To produce stray instances or even a goodly number of persons who have struggled through such adverse conditions without becoming dependent upon others, is not to offer evidence to the contrary. The plain tendency is to augment the number of those who break down prematurely; of those who, in advanced years, have made no provision for their own maintenance; of the children whose support must be supplied by others than their own parents; and of those who, meeting with unexpected misfortune of any kind, have no resources except the generosity of strangers.

It is, of course, ports of entry, and preëminently the city of New York, that suffers most from the effects of undesirable immigration. Those who have normal wage-earning capacity, and who do not require the presence of a number of their own nationality about them, may push on to the interior cities and towns, or may find employment at farm labor. Those who remain behind comprise the most and the least ambitious. For the man who can really succeed, there are, perhaps, greater rewards in the greater cities; but those who are least efficient and capable remain, not because it is to their advantage, but because it is easier. They do not know, and they have no means of finding out, what opportunities would be open to them elsewhere, and they shrink from a venture which might prove fatal. Their instinct leads them not to repeat the original mistake of cutting loose from friends and acquaintances, even if these are but of slight value as compared with the more than lifelong ties which have been severed by removal from their original home.

The conditions which arise in the seaboard cities from

ever augmenting immigration call for some revision of the principles of settlement and of transportation.

The principle relating to settlement, inherited from the English Poor Law, and applied with many modifications in the various states, is that so far as public relief is concerned, dependent persons are to be aided in the communities in which they have had a permanent residence, and that if they become dependent elsewhere, they may legitimately be returned to the place in which they last had a permanent residence. The length of time necessary to establish a residence or a settlement varies greatly among the different states. Residence in the county or in the town as against other counties and towns within the state is usually gained or lost in a shorter time than is required to gain or lose residence in the state itself. However necessary or expedient it may be to limit public relief to those who have a settlement established through long-continued residence, it is clearly unwise to adopt the same principle in the administration of private relief, and then to apply it both in public and in private relief in such a way as to lessen the distribution of the immigrant population throughout the entire country.

The argument for liberal immigration laws is based upon the assimilating powers of the American people. If, however, colonies of various nationalities are established at the very point of entry, the opportunities for assimilation are greatly diminished. The inducement for those who speak a different language to acquire knowledge of English is lessened, and there are fewer occupations open to those who are required in any event to learn some new means of livelihood. Either many of those who are still admitted should be excluded by more stringent laws, or there should be developed systematic plans for distributing them to the places where there is need of the labor which they can perform or, if necessary, to establish colonies for the purpose of affording them a home and employment, and an opportunity to make a start under favorable conditions. A temporary landing in New York City, and the spending of a few months in a desperate attempt to gain a footing, is not in any real sense to establish a residence. When one who has had this experience becomes, through loss of employment and inability to find anything to do, dependent, it may be advisable to aid him, and impracticable, for exceptional reasons, to return him to his native country, but the general principle that dependent persons are to be aided where they have a settlement ought not to debar the giving of aid in transportation to another place if the conditions there are known to be more favorable. It is not the general condition of the market for labor that has caused the difficulty, but the limited demand for and the excessive supply of the class of unskilled immigrants, or immigrants whose skill lies in a direction for which there is no demand. In so far as relief is required, the responsibility for it rests undoubtedly upon the community in which the person has become dependent, or the one from which he has come. Those who remain dependent immediately upon transfer to some other place should be returned at the expense of those who have sent them away. Transportation to other places should not be resorted to merely as a means of lessening the demand for relief. Only in so far as there is a reasonable prospect of actual employment in the new community, or a transfer of the burden to those upon whom the dependent person has an immediate personal claim, is the resort to transportation justified, and even this is justified only as a remedy for an unsufferable condition created by immigration and the congestion of an abnormal number of the least efficient immigrants in the cities of their first arrival. It is not then simply a question of money, but a question of assimilating capacity. Either the number to be admitted, therefore, must be greatly reduced, or the burden of assimilation must be far more widely distributed, and in truth there is need of both remedies.

CHAPTER XV

DISCRIMINATION IN RELIEF

THE object of an investigation as a preliminary step in the relief of distress is not primarily to expose imposture, or to enable the brand of " unworthy " or " undeserving " to be placed upon such as do not satisfy the standard of the investigator. The inquiry is rather directed toward the discovery of the root of the trouble in the particular instance, and the discovery of the facts which need to be known in order to enable an intelligent decision to be reached as to the course which should be pursued. Incidentally, it leads to the rejection of fraudulent claims and the correction of any wrong impression which misleading statements by the applicant, whether intentional or unintentional, may have caused. The elimination of fraud, and the selection of those who are legitimate and promising candidates for charitable relief, are fundamental in all rational relief policies. To allow the fear of imposition to paralyze the strong arm of charity is, however, as needless as it is foolish. Independent verification of the applicant's statements ; thorough and businesslike inquiry by trained visitors into the essential facts ; the preservation and the use of records, and a reasonable disposition to profit by experience, afford the safeguards necessary to successful work.

A good investigation demands that each application shall be considered on its merits, without prejudice. The one indispensable qualification of the visitor who is to make the inquiry is an open mind, which will take nothing for granted, but which will also give to every new application the benefit of every reasonable doubt, in spite of any disappointments which may previously have been experienced. The investigation should be neither superficial, leaving essential points neglected on the one hand, nor, on the other, mechanical, carrying out a rigid programme regardless of the purpose for which the particular inquiry is made.   The inquiry should be directed not only toward the immediate decision which is to be reached, but also toward the discovery of real but unrecognized needs. It will naturally vary with the nature of the application, and with the information previously acquired, and will be shaped in each instance to some extent by the particular features which develop as the inquiry proceeds.

The points upon which societies that give relief to the poor in their homes have found that it is desirable, as a rule, to have information, are the following : —

> Surname.
> Residence.
> Husband's first name.
> Wife's first name.
> Age, occupation, and income of each.
> Children's names.
> Age, work or school, and income of each.
> Married children in family.
> Others living with family, and relationship.
> Color or nationality.
> Church relationship.
> How long in United States?
> How long in city or town?
> Number of rooms.
> Rent.
> Apparent cause of need in first instance.
> Married children not living in family.
> Previous residences.
> Relatives.
> References.

The applicant's own statement should ordinarily cover at least the following points : —

> I. Chief breadwinners in the family.
>   Health.
>   Income.
>   Former employers.
> II. Other breadwinners as above.
> III. Expenditures.
>   Debts, and to whom.
>   Articles in pawn.
>   Insurance, name of company.

IV. Sickness in family.
   Physican, treatment, etc.
   V. Relatives and friends able to help, and other possible sources
   of relief.
   VI. Aid asked.
   VII. Aid received.
   VIII. Supplies on hand.
   IX. Miscellaneous. Schools.

Usually long before a complete investigation covering all of the field outlined in the above enumeration has been made, conclusive evidence will have been ascertained as to whether the application is a *bona fide* one, and whether there is a reasonable prospect of that degree of coöperation on the part of the family which will justify serious efforts in their behalf. If the application has not been made in good faith and the statement has been found to be lacking in accuracy and frankness, it may still be advisable to act in the light of the knowledge that has been obtained, and to attempt to exercise disciplinary influences either in lieu of, or as a supplement to, material relief. If, however, the attitude of the family is essentially uncoöperative, and if it is obvious that with the resources at hand no good result can be accomplished, it may be wiser to withdraw entirely and to concentrate attention upon those who are more receptive and more responsive.

The investigation is not merely for the purpose of reaching a decision as to whether relief shall be given or withheld. It is for the further purpose of enabling the amount and kind of relief to be determined, and also to reveal the personal and natural resources from which relief may rightly be obtained. The thorough searching out of those facts in the previous economic history of the family that will lay bare the real cause of the distress is to be insisted upon, in order that genuinely remedial and constructive work may be undertaken from the beginning. What is needed is that the cause, if it is in the nature of the case practicable, shall be removed, and the condition of dependence brought to an end. The investigation cannot be completed at once, but its foundation may be laid thoroughly at the beginning, and information will then be obtained upon many points which it would be more difficult to secure at a later stage. Having thus laid the foundation by a formal and definite attempt to secure all the information obtainable at the outset, full and well-rounded knowledge will come gradually.

It is not alone relief societies and other agencies which have to do with the poor in their homes that have need for the investigator. Institutions for dependent children and adults, hospitals, employment agencies, day nurseries, and other philanthropic enterprises have quite as much need to base their treatment and their selection of beneficiaries upon exact knowledge. There will naturally be differences in the inquiries to be made, for investigation should always be shaped with reference to the need to be met, but the broader principles underlying, for example, an investigation for a charity organization society will require little modification when applied elsewhere.

Investigation is sometimes looked upon as an injustice to the poor, and sometimes as a necessary evil. In its proper place, and with a justifiable occasion, it is neither. Investigation is to be judged relatively to the plans which lie beyond. If the relief which is undertaken is inappropriate in kind and inadequate in amount, the fact that it is given only "after a thorough investigation of each case" serves only to condemn the investigation as heartily as the "relief" to which it leads. Only when it is the purpose, and when it is within the capacity, of the one who investigates to give real help, or to enable real help to be given, is it justified, and then it is not to be regarded either as injustice or as a necessary evil, but as an essential part of a service which is wholly beneficial.

In addition to the danger of imposition at the time of application, there are certain dangers supposed to be inherent in the carrying out of a liberal relief policy. The most important of these is the fear of the demoralizing effect upon growing children. It is thought that any child of average intelligence will be likely to discover that in addition to what is earned by working members of the family there is coming in, weekly or monthly, a certain sum for which no one renders an equivalent. The possibility of such an income, it is feared, again, may become firmly fixed in the mind of the growing child, and the expectation of receiving some similar unearned income may exert an undue influence over his own later conduct.

Close observation of a number of families in receipt of monthly pensions from private charity, over a period of several years, has convinced the writer that this fear is not well grounded. On the contrary, children who learn about the pension may often learn at the same time why it is granted, and get a first useful lesson in the value of the qualities which have induced favorable action on the part of donors. They are apt to come to look upon the pension as an advance or a loan which it will be their own duty to repay, either directly to the source from which it has come or to others who are similarly in need. In a family that has been longer in receipt of such a pension than any other known to the writer, the oldest boy, who has now for two or three years been working in a shop with steadily increasing wages, recently said to his mother, with earnest feeling : "As soon as I have another raise, we can get along without that money from the Society; and as soon as we can spare it, I am going to begin paying them a dollar a month from my wages." This attitude, to which the boy came spontaneously, and not as a result of direct suggestion, is hardly typical. It is, however, the result of a long-continued, close oversight by an efficient visitor and nurse, — the mother being an invalid, — and need not be expected in any case in which an allowance, however liberal, is made in a perfunctory way, without an accompaniment of personal oversight.

A second danger which has been especially encountered in connection with the pension system is the temptation to deceive. If the family's circumstances are changed, if relatives who have previously been in straitened circumstances become able to help, or if for any other reason the pension becomes unnecessary, there is, of course, a temptation to conceal these facts for the sake of securing the continuance of the pension. Perhaps the extreme case is that of a woman who had been receiving a monthly allowance of five dollars, and who continued to receive it for over a year after her re-marriage, the appearance of an infant two months old first suggesting to the visitor that possibly things were not as they had been. In this instance the recipient of the pension went so far as to protest volubly that the child had been left with her by a relative to board, and after this had been disproved and the marriage definitely established, she was still ready to present ample testimony that her financial situation had not been improved by this new alliance, but that quite the contrary effect had been experienced. In another instance, an old couple in receipt of a pension had successfully concealed the existence of the wife's married sister, whose husband was earning a fair income, although not sufficient to enable them to share largely with the dependent couple.

These instances show only the necessity for ordinary caution — or perhaps one should say extraordinary caution. They are likely to occur in the experience of charitable societies that conduct their work in a superficial and perfunctory manner. To avoid the danger of such deception is by no means impossible or even especially difficult. Against the two examples cited can be placed scores of instances in which the idea of deception has never entered the mind of the pensioner, in which every material change of conditions is promptly confided to the visitor or readily discovered in the course of that continuous personal oversight which is essential to the success of the plan.

Close vigilance to insure the elimination of fraud, the detection of imposture, and the removal of the temptation to deceit are often essential in subsequent, as always in the initial, steps, but here again a caution is necessary — that suspicion, the withholding of confidence, and the intrusion of needless precautions against deception are apt to give rise to the very qualities against which such precautions are taken. It is well to expect fair dealing, truthfulness, and candor and thus to make easier the revelation of the better side of those with whom the visitor comes in contact.

CHAPTER XVI

RESTATEMENT AND CONCLUSION

THE charitable impulse has four distinct stages of development : the desire to alleviate obvious and obtrusive distress; the desire to relieve distress adequately ; the desire to restore the dependent if possible to a position of self-support; and finally, the desire to create social conditions in which pauperism is entirely absent.

The impulse itself, in its most primitive, and perhaps most permanent, form, is deeply ingrained in our human nature, and is encountered in all the quarters of the earth. The sight of suffering calls forth, as if by direct reflex action of brain and heart, the impulse to act, to give, to share either of our goods or of our strength to the end that the evident signs of suffering may be obliterated. It is strange how little it takes, however, even in civilized man, to satisfy this original impulse, how slight the obstacle that will suffice to prevent even its crudest expression.

The daintily gloved, well-groomed gentleman who, in summer, will toss a quarter to the mutilated cripple to be rid of his supplications, will, on a cold winter day, when to reach the quarter in an inside pocket means a little more trouble and slight exposure, pass on with a quicker step, stifling his impulse to give by the reflection that organized charity condemns giving to street beggars, anyway. This is the kind of charity which has an open hand but a closed eye, which gives what is demanded to any one who asks, when it involves no sacrifice, but does not earn the blessing promised to him that considereth the poor.

An effective desire to relieve distress, upon which intelligent relief measures may be based, is so closely allied to this original charitable impulse that they may not always be distinguished. The second is a direct development

from the first, showing that the primitive instinct is not
to be condemned, but rather encouraged and trained.   It
follows that carefully planned relief measures may safely
be given a more prominent place in our national and
municipal policies.   One of the chief defects of the charitable system of many American communities, even of
those in which relief is most ample and most elaborately
organized, is that for certain kinds of need the relief is
inadequate in amount and not at all organized.   The desire
to relieve distress — really and sufficiently to relieve — is
of gradual growth.   We naturally develop a relief system, public and private, just as we do an educational
or an industrial system.   We become willing to make
large sacrifices to carry it into effect.   Relief is the means
by which, in a progressive community, the blows of un-
merited misfortune; the crushing burdens of protracted
illness and serious accident; even, at times, and in some
communities, the loss of employment because of industrial
changes through which the community gains but the individual suffers; and, more obviously still than any of these,
the care of orphans and neglected children, may be assumed — when it is right and necessary to assume them —
by the community, either through private agencies established for that purpose, or through public agencies
supported by taxation.   The relief system is the means
of transferring insupportable burdens to a group large
enough to bear them.

Cripples, children who are defective in sight, speech,
or hearing, children who are defective in intellect, should
be discovered and placed under the special care of those
who can, to some extent, build up their defective organs,
or at least care humanely for them in their affliction.   A
keen lookout should be kept in every schoolroom and in
every home for those who need special attention or care,
and who cannot themselves, or whose family cannot, provide it; and no community can be said really to care for
the relief of distress until it is awake to all such needs —
curing the curable while they are curable, and relieving
the incurable in a humane and charitable way.   This does
not by any means uniformly imply care in an institution.
Each class of dependents — each individual who is in

need — must be considered separately, and the best that professional skill and experienced judgment can dictate should be forthcoming. This is, in the long run, an economical policy, but it is to be urged, not because it is economical, but because it is charitable.

The full development of the second stage of the impulse of charity brings us as before into the next. We do not find ourselves seriously relieving distress, without at the same time directing our efforts to the prevention of its recurrence. And yet, as we grow more charitable, as we develop a more fraternal and democratic type of philanthropy, we become increasingly concerned about the permanent welfare of the individuals and families who have appealed to our sympathies. Especially is it true that when able-bodied men and women are found to be asking others for help we become profoundly dissatisfied with mere almsgiving. We are convinced that there is, even in the present — possibly not ideal — organization of society, no reason, at least no irremovable reason, why able-bodied persons should not support themselves and their children. When they are unable to do so, it must be for lack of training, or for some lack of mental discipline, which possibly physical want, actual deprivation for a time of the necessities of life, will alone supply.

The problem is, then, to coöperate with the better elements in such dependent persons — and oftentimes there are in them surprisingly promising elements — in such a way as to make them self-supporting. It may be necessary, in order to avoid misapprehension, to guard against creating the impression that those who are unsuccessful in the economic struggle are necessarily the most unattractive and unlovely of neighbors. It is not necessarily so. It has been pointed out that Esau had really a much more attractive personality than Jacob — that he was unsuspecting, ingenuous, and generous, whereas Jacob, the chosen seed of Israel, left much in these directions to be desired; but it remains true that Jacob had the particular qualities needed in him who was to be the leader of the people. It is so in the contrast between the dependent and the self-supporting. The former may have excellent qualities, but without thrift, without a certain minimum capacity for earning and saving, they go to the wall, and they bring suffering and deprivation upon themselves and their children. If we are interested in their welfare, therefore, we shall strive to implant and to encourage the growth of these economic virtues. Possibly we may not personally value them so highly as other virtues. Patriotism, religion, love of home, generosity, or a thousand other qualities may strike us as more admirable, but in spite of this, if those whom we might help are deficient in the very qualities which bring them self-respect and an independent standing among their fellows, we will strive to supply those particular elementary deficiencies. When relief is required, we will naturally supply work if we can, rather than money or food. When those who ask aid have no trade or vocation, we will see whether training in some suitable direction cannot be given. When they are criminally negligent in failing to provide for their children, we will call upon the criminal law, even if they stoutly protest their affection; for affection that flowers only in neglect is not a trait of extraordinary value. In other words, to sum up this third stage in the development of the charitable impulse, it is a duty to look into the future always, to consider the ultimate as well as the immediate effect of our benevolence — to bear in mind that we shall have constantly in our midst just as many beggars as we are willing to pay for; just as many unnecessary public dependents — human nature and social conditions being what they are — as we are willing to support in a life of vagrancy and dependence. It is an indication of an awakened public conscience, of a developed spirit of charity, when those who desire to help others give effect to that desire in such a way as to eliminate every curable case of dependency, providing liberally for those who need permanent relief and providing efficiently, and, if possible, once for all, for those who can be driven, or encouraged, or lifted out of the slough of dependency.

I have indicated that in the slow genesis of the spirit of fraternity, of democratic philanthropy, of that charity which does not conflict with justice and which alone is true charity, there is still a higher and riper conception of its significance.   There arises at last, in many places and for different reasons, a determination to seek out those social forces that have a downward pull and to destroy them by concerted action.   There arises a realization that it is possible to call into increased activity social forces that are redemptive, regenerative, uplifting in character, and that these will make unnecessary many charitable tasks, and make easier all that remain.   Improved sanitation brings improved health and physical vigor.   Improved housing and public parks lessen the need for hospitals and asylums.   Universal elementary education, manual training, kindergartens, normal schools, professional schools, and the university become actual preventive agencies.   The better care of dependent children helps not only the particular children but the community of which they become members. Intelligent, persistent, social effort to improve the physical and the social environment in which all our lives are cast is thus linked with the most elementary and universal of all the impulses of the human heart, that to help those who need help; and through all its stages — individual effort to relieve distress merely because it is painful; effort to seek out and relieve distress that does not obtrude itself but is known to exist; effort to help people to help themselves, and to strike at the causes of distress in the individual; and effort to strike at the social causes of human suffering — through all its stages there runs the continuous development of this ideal — which is a social ideal — the ideal commonwealth in which there shall be no pauperism and no destitution.

PART II

TYPICAL RELIEF PROBLEMS

TYPICAL RELIEF PROBLEMS

DIGEST OF SEVENTY–FIVE ILLUSTRATIVE CASES

In conclusion, for a more complete understanding of the principles of relief, it will be of advantage to study the details of a number of typical cases. To some of these concrete instances of distress let us then turn, extracting from actual family records as much as is needed to set forth the nature of the problem in each case, and using disguises of name and incidents only as far as is necessary to keep confidences inviolate.[1]

Friedrich, Margaret, widow. Eight or ten years ago there died in New York City from consumption an intelligent and industrious German, who had become an American citizen, leaving a widow and three attractive children. He had supported his family comfortably, but his own illness had exhausted his savings before his death, and the insurance policy, as often happens where indemnity for the loss of a wage-earner is of the greatest possible consequence to the family, did not furnish any such indemnity, but only enough to satisfy the undertaker. Of the three children, one boy was two years of age, the daughter was six, and the first-born eight. We need not speak of those that had died.

If this were the whole story, it would be a simple but typical case of a widow with small children, requiring little, much, or no help, according to her own stock of

---

[1] These records are mainly from the Registration Bureau of the New York Charity Organization Society, and they are used in this manner, with names changed, by special permission of the Society. The Bureau contains also the case records of the New York Association for Improving the Condition of the Poor, and in some instances the families were known to both societies.

physical strength and skill in washing, cleaning, sewing,
or some less common employment by which widows do
from time to time earn their livelihood. Unfortunately,
Mrs. Friedrich had no such physical strength as would be
essential to so difficult, even if not uncommon, an undertaking. Within two years it was known that she had a
cancerous growth which would require the knife, and that,
even if the outcome were favorable, she would probably
remain unfit for hard work.

Mrs. Friedrich had relatives in the old country from
whom she had been cut off by her marriage. She had
humbled herself to ask help in her need after her husband's
death, but they would make no answer. She must depend
on such resources as came to her aid in the new world
where she had married and where she has lived for twenty
years. Her home is on the top floor of a tenement in an
up-town cross street, in a flat which rents for nine dollars
a month, and which, by the tenant's good luck, has an
unobstructed outlook across the North River to the hills
and woods on the New Jersey shore.

The relief problem in this case first presented itself
within a few months after Martin Friedrich's death. What
were its elements? First, that four persons — a mother
with three fatherless children — must be in some way provided for. No one of them could earn anything. Secondly, that the mother was a model mother, as she had
been a model wife. If a pathetic note of complaint was
sometimes heard from her, it was not more frequent or
more depressing than is often heard by the children of the
rich when they listen to the conversation of their parents.
She was affectionate, ambitious for her children, scrupu-
lous in all the art and practice of a trained German house-
wife, and physically just able to keep her own rooms in
order, and to look after the children, except when, for
periods of a few weeks, at intervals of as many years, she
went to a hospital for the surgical treatment of her disease.

The third aspect of the problem is that the usual diligent inquiry as to relatives, husband's former employers,
etc., brought no result except that which has been stated.
Favorable testimony as to the character of Friedrich and
his family was abundant, but there were no springs of

financial revenue in these directions to be opened — or at least none were found.

It is a simple problem on the whole, after all. The mother's ailment is not one that makes her in any way an unfit companion for her children. Her character is such as to make her a peculiarly fit guardian for them. The relief problem now resolves itself into three subordinate problems: a sufficient income to pay rent and all other expenses ; medical or surgical care when needed, and constant oversight by a physician or nurse to relieve unnecessary pain and to advise as to when definite treatment is required; such personal, friendly encouragement as semi-invalids especially need, whether otherwise well-to-do, or poor, and such personal interest in the children as will give them a chance in life when their time comes. The Widows' Society, the German Society, a general relief society, the church of which Mrs. Friedrich is a member, or any private citizen or group of individuals whose interest in this particular need can be secured, might appropriately provide the income required ; or it might come from a combination of two or more of these sources. For it will not do to shrink from the fact that it is no mere dole for a fortnight, or even for a single winter, that is required. About thirty dollars a month, through the summer as well as through the winter, will be needed, and there must be a guarantee that there will be some element of perma-· nence in the arrangement.

What would be the alternatives ? There are, of course, several. The children might be adopted into foster-homes; The sacrifice of maternal affection involved in this plan, under the circumstances here described, condemns it out of hand. The children might be committed to a half-orphan asylum, where their mother could see them at stated times, and the mother herself cared for in a home for incurables — with the tacit understanding that on the mother's death the children should be placed in foster-homes. The objections to this plan are that while, for the community as a whole, it is fully as expensive as to keep the children together, the latter would be deprived of their natural and most suitable guardian, while neither mother nor children would be physically better cared for than is possible at their own modest home.   It is in weighing such considerations as these, that every case must stand strictly upon its own merits, and it is possibly true that in the larger number of instances in which it is necessary to decide, the balance of physical comfort would be on the side of institutions.   So far as Mrs. Friedrich and the children were concerned, however, every advantage, sentimental and real, lay on the side of preserving the exceptionally favorable home life.

It would be possible to send the family back to the mother's childhood home in Germany.   The argument in favor of this course would turn upon the probability of a reconciliation with her relatives.   Her own parents were not living.   Her nearest kin had refused to answer her letters, or to answer letters from others in her behalf. She had married and borne her children in America.   Her ineradicable tenderness for her fatherland, of which there was evidence enough, did not take the form of a desire to return.   To have insisted upon it, against her own inclinations, and in face of the absence of any assurance of aid from her own people on her arrival, would have led either to an obstinate attempt by Mrs. Friedrich to earn her own support, hastening her death, or to an application on her own part to the city authorities to receive her children — great as would have been her regret to take this step.

The final alternative would have been to do nothing — leaving the mother to accept such kindly occasional help as might come from a neighbor; to send her boy out to sell papers long before it should be lawful for him to do so ; to move from month to month instead of paying rent, by the ingenious arrangement which yields such extraordinary returns on the poorest tenement-houses, while costing the tenants only what they have to pay — that is, sometimes, nothing; and, in general, to fall through all those makeshifts of penury by which the recovery of the sick is made impossible, and the rearing of children impossible also.   Of course, this is really no alternative at all, or one to be adopted only in ignorance.

We come back, therefore, to the plan of a regular monthly pension, definitely assured, if possible, for at least a year at a time, and practically assured if there is some one to take this responsibility, for so long a time as outside aid is required — probably until at least two of the children have become wage-earners, or until, on the mother's death, some other disposition is made of such children as have not become self-supporting. I speak of the feasibility of this plan in the particular instance with that confidence which is based on the sure foundation of trial and success.

A pension was provided, and with a single interruption of a few months, during which period Mrs. Friedrich lived on a small legacy from one of the relatives who had refused communication with her during the testator's lifetime, it has been continued through several years. It began at $30 a month, but recently has been much reduced, for twelve dollars a week are now earned by the two older children, both of whom are in positions suited to their abilities and strength, and both of whom remained in school until they were fourteen. There have been the usual vicissitudes of health and spirits in this family, but there have always been friends to whom they could turn. A district nurse has been in weekly attendance on account of Mrs. Friedrich's illness, and she has had the benefit of the most expert surgical skill. Her pension has been supplemented by Thanksgiving and Christmas gifts, she has enjoyed the poor relative's perquisites in discarded clothing from more than one family, but at the same time she has not been pauperized, nor has any one of her three bright and every way promising children. They have weathered the dangers of the street, have done well in school, and are a just source of maternal pride.

A few days before this very writing, Mrs. Friedrich said: "Whatever happens now, I have had the children by me at home these years. And they are good children, and if I were to live now, they could even take care of me. But nothing can change what has been — that we have been together with each other since their father died."

A second case is equally illustrative of an opportunity for justifiable relief, amounting, temporarily, at least, to full support.

Brecken, Margaret, a young woman under thirty years
of age, had been for some years the sole support of herself and her mother. For about two years she had had
"lung trouble," which had made it necessary for her to
give up work for weeks at a time on several occasions.
At the time of our first acquaintance with the family she
had been seriously ill for two or three months, although
her local family physician was still insisting that her complaint was only "bronchial catarrh," and that she would
be able to work again in about two months. The mother,
who had previously done the housework, was also ill; and
although her present acute illness was one from which she
would recover in a fortnight or so, there were indications
of inoperable cancer.

The immediate needs, if these two women, who were
exceptionally intelligent and affectionately devoted, were
to be kept in their little home, were the payment of rent,
the supplying of food and medicines, the daily visit of a
nurse, the services of a physician, and, at least during the
mother's illness, the sending of a woman to do the housework. This is, undoubtedly, a liberal programme, and an
exhaustive one. It would be more economical to secure
admission for each of them to a suitable hospital, but this
would mean separation — and separation, in the judgment
of the nurse, who had become well acquainted with them,
would be an almost unendurable hardship, and would
probably mean the earlier death of both. It might even
be cheaper to care for them together in a good boarding-
house; but so much care is necessary for both that only a
sanatorium would be suitable, and most of the items of
expense, under this plan, would remain.

Inasmuch as the custodians of almost any relief fund
would consider the amount required for support and care
of the family at home prohibitive, while, nevertheless, the
dictates of humanity call for this kind of relief, this is
peculiarly a case for adequate relief from one or more private individuals who can be made thoroughly acquainted
with all the circumstances, and who, having this knowledge, are willing to furnish the relief required. If such
persons are not at hand, the circumstances of this mother
and daughter may wisely be used, without, of course, re-

vealing their identity, to create a knowledge of existing
needs, and to arouse a sentiment which will permit the
need to be supplied in this and similar instances.

Sheehan, Mary, widow of Richard.   This widow was
the mother of four small children, and had been advised
two years ago by her husband's former employers to apply
to the Department of Public Charities for the commitment of her children as public charges.   Richard Sheehan
had worked satisfactorily for them for a period of eighteen
years, and for the two years after his death the family
had been supported mainly by these employers.   The
Commissioner of Public Charities, having discovered that
Mrs. Sheehan was a good mother, that her home had
always been an attractive one, and that she was by no
means desirous of parting with her children, accepted the
offer of a society that the latter assume the responsibility of providing for her in her own home from private
sources, thus preventing the breaking up of the family,
and the commitment of the children as public charges.
The employers, although under no legal responsibility,
since Sheehan's death had occurred from an illness in no
way connected with his employment, agreed to contribute
to the society $100 a year toward the support of the fam-
ily, on condition that this contribution should be unknown
to Mrs. Sheehan.   None of the children is strong, one a
cripple with defective hearing and speech, and the woman
also is in delicate health, so that it has seemed impossible
for her to do anything material toward the support of the
family.

Mrs. Sheehan's parents are living in Ireland with a
married sister, all poor.   She has two brothers in this
country, one of whom is unmarried, and boarded with her
for a time, but he caused only discomfort, and finally, to
her relief, went away.   A married brother living in the
neighborhood, earned twelve dollars a week, and his wife
considered this only sufficient for their own wants.

The crippled child was immediately placed in a hospital
for treatment.   The church to which the woman belonged
agreed to send a weekly supply of groceries, and a weekly
pension was provided of three dollars for clothing and other

incidental expenses in addition to the provision of rent, for which purpose the contribution of the employers was provided. A friendly visitor was also readily enlisted, and through her influence Mrs. Sheehan was induced to have medical treatment, although not as yet to undergo a surgical operation which she is thought by her physician to need.

For a year no member of the family did anything or was able to do anything towards earning an income, but in the second year Mrs. Sheehan undertook to do a small amount of sewing from a society which, during nine months of the year, provides her with work for which she is paid a dollar a week, while in the remaining three months she receives the same amount without an equivalent. Special diet, medicines, tonics, gifts of clothing, extra supplies of fuel, and fresh-air outings have been frequent, for all of which there has been ample gratitude and appreciation.

The little girl after fifteen months in the hospital improved so much physically that it was decided to place her in an institution for the deaf and dumb, where it is thought that she can learn to speak.

Recently the friendly visitor being concerned about the appearance of the oldest child, a girl of eight, took her also to the hospital for examination. The physician declared that the case was not one of deformity but of a lack of proper nutrition, as a result of which her whole body was said to be in an emaciated condition, requiring several months in a restful place in the country, together with a varied, nourishing diet. To this the mother replied that she had been giving the children good, plain food, but that this child, who was very nervous and notional, frequently refused her meals, and asked for articles which were not only beyond her mother to provide, but also likely to be harmful to her. She is also very timid, never playing with other children, and positively refuses to be separated from her mother. Arrangements were therefore made for an extension of a seaside outing for the mother and child, from a fortnight to a full month.

The relief supplied to this family amounted all together to about $350 a year or nearly $30 a month. Although this is almost unprecedented in liberality, the indications are that it is under, rather than over, the amount necessary to maintain a reasonable standard of living. It is of course considerably less than the actual cost of maintaining the four children in institutions, which would be about $800.

The three families described above, although presenting the possible alternatives of institutional care, are, as one may see, more suitably aided at home.

The following is an instance of temporary aid at home, followed by permanent provision. The absence of immediate relatives, physical incapacity and age, all indicate the desirability of admission to an institution, rather than aid in a private apartment. In this instance no difficulty is experienced because of personal faults, eccentricities of temper, or an unfavorable personal record, such as would lessen the disposition of the managers of a private home to receive her.

Where the conditions are all thus favorable, admission to a home can usually be secured within a brief period in any of the larger cities. It does not often happen that the conditions are all so uniformly favorable. Intemperance or other moral defect, the presence of relatives who could aid but will not do so, infirmities of temper, or such complete physical disability as demands an undue amount of personal attention, and various other complications are likely to arise, which increase the difficulties of securing private institutional care. The choice may then arise between the more expensive home for incurables, or admission to a public almshouse. There are, of course, in addition, the alternatives of board in a private family, of living alone with whatever assistance is requisite, or with a relative, or under some exceptional plan such as the circumstances of an individual case may suggest. It will be seen that Mrs. Mahler's husband had made provision for her support, but through misplaced confidence the principal of the sum left to her had been lost.

Mahler, Marie, widow of advanced age. At the death of Mrs. Mahler's husband she received insurance to the amount of $1750, which she intrusted to her landlord, a real

o

estate dealer. He had paid her ten per cent annually on the
loan, but at the time of his death it was found that he had
left no provision for repayment of the principal or to pay
his other debts.   His wife, as long as she could afford it,
cared for Mrs. Mahler, but at the time of the application
to the society it was necessary that some other provision
should be made.   Mrs. Mahler had no living relatives,
and her friends, although willing to do something for her,
could not do what was necessary.   She had partly supported herself by doing embroidery and fancy work, but
her hands were now badly crippled with rheumatism, and
this had become impossible.   She was most anxious to
enter a permanent home.   Her respectability and refinement, and her truthfulness concerning the loss of her
money, were established by sufficient evidence, and arrangements were made with an acquaintance of Mrs.
Mahler's to give her board and necessary care and attention, until she could be placed in a home.   For this she
was to be paid $10 a month, which amount was obtained
from three charitable agencies, all appropriate sources for
the relief of a woman so situated.   Application for admission was made to two appropriate homes, and, after a
delay of eight months, Mrs. Mahler was admitted to one
of these, a part of the money having been contributed by
her friends, and the remainder secured by an appeal in
the newspapers.   Mrs. Mahler was very contented and
happy at the arrangements made for her care, both during
the period of waiting and upon her admission to the home
for the aged.

Another similar solution of the choice presented between
the almshouse and a private home may be of interest,
especially since the choice in this instance was so far determined by the applicant's character.   She was not only
unwilling to become a charge upon the public, but has
shown equal independence in refusing to accept relief
offered her, when she did not need it.   It will be noticed
also that her application was pending for a longer period.

Rahn, Marie, an aged German widow, on being visited,
was offered aid in groceries and clothing, but declined

it, saying that she needed assistance only in the payment of rent. On a previous occasion a private society, to which she had applied and which had aided for three months, referred her to the Department of Public Charities, but she had declined to become a public charge. A little later she made application for admission to a private home, and was doing enough sewing to meet her expenses except for rent. Several individuals were interested, and giving irregular help. These sources of relief were organized on a definite plan, enough being obtained to pay the rent regularly. After living in this manner for nearly two years, she was admitted to the home to which application had been made.

Kennedy, Jane, widow, was referred for aid by a private individual. Mrs. Kennedy was ill, and her children were unwilling to support her. The housekeeper at previous address spoke well of her, as did also her other references. A private citizen had aided Mrs. Kennedy for some years, and the church to which she belonged gave her $2 each month. A son in Chicago sent for his mother to live with him, paying her transportation. A year later, however, Mrs. Kennedy returned to New York, as she and her daughter-in-law could not get along together. Her sons agreed to care for her.

During the next six years Mrs. Kennedy was frequently ill and in need, and again came under the notice of two private societies, which aided her at times. The sons and a married daughter aided irregularly, but offered their mother a home with them, which, however, she declined. Efforts were made to have the children contribute regularly, but these were unsuccessful. The church still continued to aid.

The wife of one of her sons became insane, and he moved to another city, leaving a daughter, by a former marriage, to take care of the children. Another son lost his mind through excessive drinking. For some time a grandson lived with Mrs. Kennedy, and aided her, but she became very eccentric, and efforts were at last made to have her placed in a private home for the aged.

Incompatibility of temperament is frequently regarded

as a cause of distress and is enumerated in some tables classifying such causes. Insanity on the part of two sons, and eccentricity on the part of Mrs. Kennedy herself, indicate an hereditary predisposition toward mental disturbance, and this in itself would not only increase the chances of dependency, but would increase the difficulties of those who, from their relationship or thorough charitable motives, undertook to provide for it. At the same time it cannot be said that Mrs. Kennedy's children met their full obligation, and her application to a private home has less chance of success for this reason.

Duncan, Mary, had been, from a young woman, a successful nurse. About four years before her application for aid, she had been run over by a bicycle and badly crippled, unfitting her for her profession. She had been an inmate of four homes, principally such as are intended for convalescents, but had made a record in these places of being generally disagreeable and cross, and a source of an unusual amount of trouble to matron and attendants — all of which could easily be accounted for by her health and adversity. Admission was secured for her to a home for incurables, after temporary care in one of the convalescent homes in which she had previously resided.

Bacon, William, a Civil War veteran, and his blind wife Mary, afford a typical illustration. William being of English birth, the family first came under notice sixteen years ago by an application to the St. George's Society referred by the latter to the Charity Organization Society for investigation. For the ten succeeding years, the couple remained for the most part self-supporting, temporary employment being secured for the husband at intervals. On one occasion a church asked for information, but when visited the wife said that they were not in need, and that there had evidently been a mistake. Ten months later, however, a private citizen asked that assistance be given them, on the representation that, although the man was employed, his earnings were insufficient to support them. It was said, also, that the couple had formerly received an allowance made by the city toward the support of the blind, but that for some reason this had been discontinued. An application for a government pension had always, thus far, been unsuccessful. A supply of coal was given the family at this time, the first relief that they had been found to need. A year later a physician called attention to the needs of the old couple, the husband being a patient in a public hospital, from which, however, he returned to his home, rather than consent to a transfer to a hospital on the Island. He was not fully recovered, but hopeful and unwilling to break up his home. The church and a relief society, under these circumstances, provided rent, fuel, and food. Further but fruitless efforts were made to secure the government pension ; and, although there was a general feeling that the couple would be better off in a home for the aged, there was final acquiescence in a plan by which a church visitor assumed the responsibility, undertaking to raise what money was needed to supply their needs in their own home.

Trow, Ebenezer, is a man of refinement and education, nearly seventy years of age, a graduate of a college of the highest standing. Twelve years ago he first appeared, asking for employment, which was secured for him in the office of a safe deposit company. Nothing further was heard of him for nine years, when he again applied for work, but expressed anxiety to enter a home. His references agreed in describing him as honest and respectable, but lacking in judgment, and sensitive. There were no relatives living, but private individuals, upon whom he had no special claim, provided for his board temporarily, pending his admission to a home for the aged. In a little less than two years an opening was found for him, his admission fee, with $76 additional, being raised by a college fraternity. Of the surplus, Mr. Trow draws a dollar a month for extras, and after two years' residence in the home seems reasonably content.

Wheeler, Charles, a railway conductor, deserted by his wife, has himself borne a good reputation, and gave evidence of a clean personal history. His two children have been indentured to farmers in the West. For nine months, at the time of his application, he had been living on the earnings of former years, which were then exhausted. Through a newspaper appeal a sum sufficient to pay his entrance fee in a home for the aged was provided; but after his admission he became ill, suffering with nervous prostration and possibly tuberculosis, the latter being the diagnosis of the physician at the home. He was thereupon transferred to a bed in a home for incurables at a special price, for which he shows the most grateful appreciation. The repayment of the entrance fee, which in this case was $150, will be sufficient to pay his board in the home for incurables for about a year.

Burden, Caroline. On account of her husband's intemperance Mrs. Burden felt obliged to leave him thirty years ago. She then had some money, however, and her son remained with her. For six years they lived very comfortably on her own income and her son's wages. At that time her son died, leaving her about $2500. The son's employers took charge of this sum, paying her six per cent interest and taking a kind interest in her business affairs. She opened a store, but on account of illness was forced to give it up. She then met with an accident which made treatment in a hospital for several weeks necessary, and from this accident she never fully recovered. With the occasional help of the son's employer, however, she remained self-supporting, drawing the last of her money about a year before her application for care. She was found to be of good reputation, and to have no relatives in position to aid her. Temporary admission was secured to a country home for the aged, but while there she had several epileptic seizures, on one occasion falling downstairs and dislocating her wrist. It was thought that she was mentally unbalanced, but on examination by experts was pronounced not to need attention and was returned to her friends. Application was made to various homes for the aged without result, and board was finally secured for her in a private family at an expense of ten dollars a month. The sum of $100 for ten months' board was contributed by the son's employer and an application was left pending at a suitable home for admission whenever a vacancy occurred.

The five following cases are not unlike those which have been presented above, but are grouped together for the reason that all of the histories began in the almshouse. As a result of investigation all were removed from the public institution, either to the care of their relatives, or to a private institution.

Brennan, Sophie, was committed to the almshouse, having been found sleeping in doorways and halls and entirely destitute. For a year before this commitment, efforts had been made to induce her three sons, all of whom were railway employees in receipt of good incomes, to support her. They made occasional contributions in this direction, which, however, amounted to little. As a result of correspondence with the local authorities at Albany, where one of the sons lives, his wife appeared at the Department and took charge of her mother-in-law. An agreement was made by which this son should have the assistance of his two brothers in providing for his mother's care.

Rathgaber, Georgiana, had been a public charge for one year, when it was discovered that she was receiving a pension of eight dollars, had one married daughter who was a professional nurse, that a married son with no children had a sufficient income to provide for her, while a second son who was blind, was, like the mother, a public charge.

The daughter, when visited, said that she had taken charge of the sum of $450, left by her father, and had taken two dollars a week from it, for her mother's board. When the amount was exhausted, she sent her mother to the almshouse. The intervention of the corporation counsel's office in this instance brought the children to a realizing sense of their legal obligations, and the mother was removed from the almshouse.

Sampson, C. W., aged 70, was admitted to the almshouse after having served ten days in the workhouse for vagrancy. He was in feeble health, afflicted with cancer of the nose, and his clothing was in tattered condition.

He declared himself homeless. From his statement when admitted to the almshouse, it appeared that he had five children, one son who was a teacher, unmarried, and four married daughters, one of whom was a widow. His wife, Mrs. Sampson, lived with one of these daughters. He has one daughter supported by her husband, who is himself in Austria. A third lives in Brooklyn with her husband, who is a printer, and two children, while the fourth daughter, the widow, had acquired her father's business and was living in a brownstone-front house in Brooklyn.

The children were seen and all refused to contribute to their father's support. His wife, to whom his property had been originally made over, likewise refused to receive him. The corporation counsel was asked to take up the case against them, whereupon representatives of the family agreed to pay three dollars a week to the department of public charities for Mr. Sampson's support, on condition that suit should be withdrawn. This offer was accepted, the fund was allowed to accumulate for a short time in order that there might be enough to supply Mr. Sampson with suitable outfit of clothing. He was then discharged, and is now living upon the amount provided by the family.

Sharp, James, was committed to the almshouse three years ago, and has remained during that time a charge upon the state. A fellow-inmate divulged the fact that this was an assumed name, and gave the superintendent his correct name. This led to an investigation from which it was discovered that Sharp has a wife and children living in the city. One son is the general manager of an important business in Brooklyn, and was desirous of providing for his father. It appeared that he has a mania for getting admitted to institutions under assumed names, making it impossible for the family to locate him.

Nelson, Charlotte, widow of a physician, respected and successful in the practice of his profession. Mrs. Nelson is, however, of a crotchety disposition, scarcely mentally responsible, although adjudged to be not insane. When first known to the society, some years after her husband's death, she had been living at a woman's lodging-house, but had acted queerly, and having no money was asked to leave.   No relatives were found able to assist her, and although persons were found who remembered her husband, there was no one upon whom she had any special claim.   She has one son of a roving, shiftless, and irresponsible character, a musician by occupation, but scarcely able to earn his own support, although full of visionary schemes for caring liberally for himself and his mother. Mrs. Nelson was aided to the extent of $50 in the form of rent and food, but she met with several accidents, and after treatment in a public hospital, as it was not deemed safe for her to be left to herself, she was transferred to the almshouse.

A fortnight later, however, money was obtained through a newspaper appeal for her care in a private institution, where, at the date of this writing, she had remained for two years.   Here she had a private room and special consideration, but was chronically dissatisfied, and was constantly writing, and encouraging her son to write, complaining letters to persons who might possibly be induced to aid her in other ways.

Caspar, Mary.   About eleven years ago, Mrs. Caspar, who was then a widow supporting her old mother, took into her home her sick sister, Mrs. Manning, and her two small children, Julia and Katherine.   Mrs. Manning had a worthless husband and had, for some time, supported herself and children.   Mrs. Caspar was then employed in a restaurant at eight dollars a week, in which place she worked for about ten years, her hours being from 7 A.M. to 4 P.M.   Her work was really done in a cellar kitchen.   It was entered from the restaurant above, and the only ventilation possible was from a window over the stairs.   Mrs. Caspar also did office cleaning from which she earned three dollars a week; and, not satisfied with this double employment, brought home each week some towels to wash.   After an illness of five months, Mrs. Manning died from consumption.   Her husband lived in the neighborhood, but at no time contributed anything toward the support of the family.   He soon after died in one of the public hospitals.

About a year after Mrs. Caspar took in the Manning family, her sister-in-law, Mrs. Stephen, died suddenly, leaving four girls.   One of these was adopted by another sister, but the other three were promptly taken into Mrs. Caspar's family, who retained charge of the two children of her own sister.   Stephen, like Manning, was shiftless and intemperate, giving nothing toward the support of the children, and keeping entirely away from them except when he was in need of a place to sleep.   He also died within a short time from a hemorrhage following an attack of pneumonia.

The oldest of the Stephen children went into the restaurant with her aunt, earning three dollars a week to wait on the cooks.   Here they remained for nearly ten years, until the restaurant went out of business.   As Mrs. Caspar's health was then very much broken she was persuaded to secure a lighter kind of work.

The task of caring for the small children fell upon Julia Manning, and Mrs. Caspar said that the fact that they have all turned out to be such good girls is due to the tender care given them by Julia.   As soon as Julia was old enough she was put to work, but after only a few months her health failed, and it was at this period that the family came under the care of the society.

The youngest of the Stephen family has had hip disease from birth, and has been treated almost continually at an orthopædic hospital.   A brace was purchased for her at a cost of $12, which was paid for by Mrs. Caspar òn the instalment plan at fifty cents a week.   Another of the Stephen children is also delicate, and has had frequent medical care.   There has scarcely been a week during the eleven years in which Mrs. Caspar has not been under expense for doctor's bills, medicines, and other expenses due to illness.   After application for relief was made, something was done to lighten her burden, but it seems insignificant when compared with the heroic efforts made by Mrs. Caspar herself and the children whom she has trained.

Notwithstanding these home burdens, Mrs. Caspar has

always found time to care for a sick neighbor, and to see that the girls attended regularly to their church duties. During the past year Julia, whose health has rapidly failed, has been visited every week by her priest. If there were a possibility of saving her life thereby, she would be sent to a mountain sanatorium, but her aunt, her priest, and her physician are averse to this, in view of the probability that she has but a few weeks to live. Carrie Stephen, the one who was taken in charge by her mother's sister, also has consumption, and is at present in a country sanatorium.

Extraordinary burdens, borne with still more extraordinary fortitude, are set forth in this story of Mary Caspar. The history has its greatest value in the heroic qualities shown by Mrs. Caspar and by the niece whom she reared, and who afterward shared with her the responsibility for the younger children. It exhibits the frightful ravages from pulmonary tuberculosis sometimes witnessed in a single family. The neighborliness of the poor to each other is shown no less conspicuously than the readiness still found, although more rarely under the severe economic conditions of the city, to receive orphaned children and to care for them as if for one's own.

The growth of institutional care for children, and the placing out of children in foster-homes through societies formed for the purpose, has doubtless aided the tendency to hesitate to accept these added responsibilities. On the farm, or in villages, the actual cost in money of an additional child is relatively much less than in the tenement of a great city. When to this is added the possibility of securing ready commitment of the child to an institution, where the physical and religious conditions of training are supposed to be exceptionally favorable, it is not surprising that the natural absorption of orphan and half-orphan children in the community is seriously checked. The case of Mrs. Caspar, and many others that could be cited, show that this absorption does, however, still take place, and of course the majority of such instances do not come under the notice of charitable societies.

Sydney, Philip. A family whose difficulties were so complicated and who offered a problem so nearly unsolvable as to justify description as a desperate case, is that of a colored West Indian, his white wife, and their three children. The first difficulty, which, in a sense, includes most of the others, is that this unfortunate negro is afflicted with leprosy. Four years ago one of his feet was amputated, and his first experience with charitable agencies was as a patient in the hospital where the amputation was performed. Here he was found by a visitor to the public hospitals, who became sufficiently interested in his situation to raise the money with which to purchase for him an artificial foot. It was expected that with this need supplied he would be able to support himself and his family, which at that time consisted only of his wife and a two-year-old child. There was at first some timidity about visiting the family, especially about holding conversation with the leper, but the physicians speedily gave assurance that this was not dangerous ; in spite of which assurance, it may be recorded parenthetically, the clerks in the office of the Health Board developed a mild panic when the leper himself, in response to such assurances, expressed his pleasure and then first made it known to those whom he was addressing that his inquiries related to himself. The best medical opinion which could be obtained was that leprosy, at least in this climate, is not contagious in the ordinary sense, but that, nevertheless, it is communicable, and that risks would be involved if one were to come into physical contact with the leper, especially if one happened to have even a slight open wound, or such opportunity for infection, as, for example, a hangnail.

In the three years after his apparently complete recovery from the surgical operation the family managed to exist with only occasional relief. The mixed marriage and the husband's physical affliction made the securing of any employment a matter of the greatest difficulty, in spite of the health inspector's assurance that he was not a source of very great danger and that the thing for him to do was to get a job. Two more children were born. Throughout these three years at least one member of the family was always an inmate of a public hospital, and for a considerable part of the time two were under care at the same time. The man has more than the average intelligence, is a skilled typewriter, and has not shown reluctance to undertake any employment offered to him. For nearly two years at the date of the present writing he has supported himself from a news-stand and in similar ways, asking for a loan only to establish himself, and, after reverses, to reëstablish himself in a good location.

Although leprosy and the marriage of white with negro are not common, they are only, at the worst, instances of complications that are by no means uncommon. Marriages of mixed nationality, of mixed religion, of mixed social origin, of extreme differences in age, or of extreme differences of temperament, are constantly appearing to increase the difficulties of the charitable agencies, and to complicate what might otherwise be comparatively simple tasks. Tuberculosis and another even more dreaded disease are communicable in about the same degree as leprosy, and introduce problems of a similar kind.

Zed, Albert and Mary. In January, 1892, aid was asked for a family consisting of Mr. Zed, twenty-eight years old, his wife, twenty-six, and two children under three years. The previous September, owing to an accident while at work, Mr. Zed lost one of his eyes, and since then had not contributed to the support of his household. Mrs. Zed, a fringe maker, had utilized such time as she could spare from her children by working at her trade in her rooms. Fellow-workmen took up a collection when Mr. Zed was hurt, but it had been exhausted, and debts for living expenses had accumulated.

The man, while sober and honest, was found lacking in energy and stability, giving up work for trivial reasons, and in his periods of idleness allowing his wife to bear the burden of support. She was delicate physically and never free from the need of tonics. The children were puny, unhealthy, and from their birth required cod liver oil and also alcohol baths. There was ample work for a friendly visitor, the man needing constant urging to his duty and the woman wholesome sympathy and encouragement.

At various times the visitor and her committee placed the children under hospital care, secured the coöperation of societies and individuals, keeping proper nourishment

supplied, and repeatedly found work for Mr. Zed, who
would keep it so short a time that assisting him in that
respect was discouraging and almost hopeless. His wife,
always willing to do her utmost, was hampered by increased
expenses and debts from long illness.

In January, 1893, owing to the fact that Mr. Z. had been
working faithfully and the friendly visitor had kept a
careful watch over them, they were free from debt and had
a little surplus in the savings bank, but in May of that
year he had been idle or only earning small wages, there
had been more illness, and again debts had been incurred.
In September, 1894, one child was buried, and during
the following May and June two died from scarlet fever.

Until October, 1896, constant help was required and
obtained. Permanent work was then secured for him at
thirty dollars per month, which he still retains, having
worked steadily from that time to the present. Mrs.
Zed has worked diligently at her fringe making, debts
have been paid, an honest return made of money loaned
by the friendly visitor in emergencies, and they have bought
a new sewing-machine and other comforts.

Keenan, Frank and Norah. Mrs. Keenan was first aided
in groceries when her husband had injured his ankle.
Eight years later the family was again aided with food and
clothing, references giving a good report. A daughter,
Kate, was placed in a private hospital, where she died, and
Mr. Keenan went back to his old position. The two oldest
children were in Ireland with relatives.

Two years after this Mr. Keenan was ill, and two private
societies and a church aided. Mrs. Keenan secured work
in the workrooms, and diet-kitchen tickets were also given.
Her husband then died, and funeral expenses were met by
friends. The relatives in Ireland refused to receive Mrs.
Keenan, who had steady work and was able to pay her
rent. The next year the family was aided by a society
for the relief of widows. All the children were delicate,
and an effort was made to find work for the mother in
the country. She, however, refused to go. Diet-kitchen
tickets were given frequently, and two of the children
were sent on a fresh-air outing to the country. Here they

were so much loved that the family with whom they stayed wished them to remain, but to this Mrs. Keenan would not consent. A friendly visitor had supervision of the family.

Mrs. Keenan soon afterward secured regular work at a settlement, earning six dollars a week, and as her son Charles also had employment, she notified the society which had aided that she could now manage. Two years later Charles was away for a time, and when he returned found steady work, and had increased wages. His mother was still employed at the settlement, and her daughter, Jane, also had work there.

The following is an instance of effective relief through transportation. It was justifiable in the case of the Bradshaws because they had been but a short time away from their Virginia home, and actually owned a small farm in that state, to which they were returned. The folly and the hardships inherent in the " passing on " system are so serious as to have led both the National Conference of Jewish Charities and the National Conference of Charities and Correction, following the lead of the former, to adopt a set of rules,[1] binding upon the societies adopting them, and a telegraphic code for communication between those who purpose sending dependent persons to another community and their corresponding societies, and to individuals in or near the community to which it is proposed to send them.

Bradshaw, Henry and Florence, were brought to notice by the church which they attended. Mr. and Mrs. Bradshaw had formerly kept a boarding-house in a southern city, but this they had given up as Mrs. Bradshaw was ill with lung trouble, and had come to New York, hoping to better their condition. Before keeping the boarding-house the family had lived on a small farm which they owned in Virginia, and which at this time was rented. Mr. Bradshaw was unable to do heavy work, and failed to get employment of any kind. His wife's health failed, and as all their money was gone, they pawned what jewellery

[1] See Appendix.

they had.   Mrs. Bradshaw's relatives aided as far as they could, and one of her sisters took the two oldest girls.

Through the church and a private society, assistance was given in rent, fuel, and food, and transportation was provided for Mr. Bradshaw, who returned to Virginia. A month later, by a newspaper appeal, enough money was secured to send Mrs. Bradshaw and three of her children to her husband — the two girls remaining with their aunt — and to pay for the transportation of the furniture. Part of the money was also sent to a private society in the city to which they were going, and with this amount groceries were provided for them upon their arrival.   A little later, upon hearing from the family, it was learned that they were all well and happy at their return home.

A typical illustration of the futility of furnishing transportation in ordinary cases, even when such transportation is to the original home of the applicant, is that of the Campbells, who on each of three occasions presented plausible reasons for the giving of aid in transportation to Scotland, but who showed themselves equally irreclaimable in both countries.

Campbell, Peter and Agnes.   Peter was known chiefly on account of the occasional sprees in which he indulged, but the enterprise which really characterized the family was shown by the wife, who was a persistent beggar. Three times the St. Andrew's Society helped the entire family to go to Scotland, but each time Mrs. Campbell returned because there were greater pecuniary returns in this country.   A corresponding society in Glasgow reported that Mrs. Campbell had succeeded in establishing that her husband had been killed by a car in Scotland, and had received $100 damages.   It was after this, however, that the same husband established his reputation for laziness and intemperance in America.   A son Charles inherited his mother's fondness for travel.   He went to Africa, but returned to find humble employment as a messenger at four dollars a week.   The decision of the Society was that the family was entitled to relief in work only.

The writer personally well recalls the circumstances under which the next-mentioned family was first brought to the attention of a charitable agency. It is one of exceedingly few instances to which the word "starvation," just short of its fatal stage, might be truthfully applied. The limbs of the infant, which afterwards died, bore a striking resemblance to the startling pictures published to illustrate the results of Cuban reconcentration, or those which exhibited the conditions of the victims of East India famine. The infant rallied and showed immense improvement within a few days of the beginning of proper nourishment.

The transaction by which Mrs. Donnerwald disposed of her store and fixtures was turned to the advantage of another dependent widow who was the purchaser. The amount of the purchase money was loaned to her, and in her hands the store became a means of self-support. For such ingenuity in adjusting those who are not quite capable of managing their own affairs, there is ample scope in the field of charitable relief. To discover that the keeping of a store which has been a complete failure for the one is exactly the occupation required for another who has made a failure as a laundress, and to bring about a change of callings, is an example of the kind of service which may mean considerably more than a grant of groceries or of money.

Donnerwald, Arnold and Lizette. Mr. Donnerwald had been a saloon-keeper, but was forced out by the high license fee required by a new law, and lost $1000. He then started a restaurant, but this did not pay, and later tried a candy store. He did fairly well at this for a time, but his mind became unbalanced as a result of undue worry and malnutrition. Mrs. Donnerwald at that time was taking in washing, as well as attending to the shop, and all of the family, through lack of proper food, were in poor physical condition. Some little aid was given by a former employer of Mrs. Donnerwald's, but relatives were unable to help, and her husband's children by a former marriage were also poor. The family was favorably spoken of at previous addresses. A private society gave assistance and

P

provided tickets for a diet kitchen, and a little later another society aided to the extent of five dollars.

A purchaser was found from whom Mrs. Donnerwald received forty dollars for the store and fixtures. Fifteen dollars of this amount was used to pay an instalment debt incurred for furniture. A baby who was ill was placed in a hospital, where it remained for five months. Although still very ill, the child was sent home, and died in a few days. Work was found for Mrs. Donnerwald for which she was paid six dollars. Her husband was now in an improved condition, owing to better food, and, as the doctor did not consider him to be dangerous, he was allowed to remain at home. Both the private society and the diet kitchen continued aid for some months, and in the winter fuel also was provided.

A year after the application, Mrs. Donnerwald having secured plenty of work, the family became self-supporting.

The following case furnishes an instance of a deficient income on account of physical incapacity. Refusal of relief in this instance would doubtless have led to the commitment of the children as public charges, while the giving of a moderate amount of assistance, and aid in securing suitable employment, enabled the family to become self-supporting, though not until after Mr. Bowles's death.

Bowles, Thomas and Jane. Mr. Bowles, having been idle for months, unable to secure employment because of exceptional stoutness (weight over 300 pounds), and varicose veins, which prevented his walking or standing continuously, applied to a newspaper for aid. He had been clerk and bookkeeper, and afterward, with what money he had saved, started a cigar store. In this he had failed, losing his capital, and had since pawned everything of value which they had. There was no income whatever, and Mrs. Bowles was near confinement. Aid was provided for several months, and on some occasions money was advanced by individuals who knew the conditions.

Arrangements were made for Mr. Bowles to enter a hospital for treatment. After he left the hospital, he was unable to find suitable employment, and the wife thereupon tried canvassing, but was unsuccessful. Work of a more appropriate kind was found for her subsequently. Just a year after the first application, employment was secured for Mr. Bowles at six dollars, which was later increased to eight and ten.   They were able to redeem many articles from pawn, and the wife finally gave up her work to take care of her three children.   In the autumn, however, the season for the man's employment having ended, he again applied for assistance, and a position was found for him in a public hospital at $10 a month and board, which was afterwards increased to $20. This position he held until his death, eighteen months later, at which time his fellow-employees raised the money for his funeral expenses.   Mrs. Bowles then supported herself and the children by caring for three foundlings, and even at the time of the birth of a fourth child, soon after her husband's death, it was not necessary for her to be aided.

Mrs. Harrigan presents a more complicated problem. She had the unusual, but not absolutely unique, experience of burying two consumptive husbands, and even with the third she did not become independent of charitable resources.   The tuberculosis of the first husband was doubtless aggravated by alcoholism.

Harrigan, George and Annie.   Application was made to a newspaper which referred the family to the society.   It was learned that Mr. Harrigan had been ill with tuberculosis for about six months.   Prior to his illness he had been a "longshoreman," and had saved nothing out of his earnings.   Forty dollars was raised by friends on a raffled watch, and upon this money the family lived for some weeks.   There were two small children, one of whom died a month after the application was made, at which time the man also died.   The family was aided by two private societies, although at previous addresses some intemperance was reported.   The other child, a girl, was placed in an institution for children.

Seven years after the first application the woman again asked for assistance.   She had remarried, and her second husband, John Deering, had supported her until a few months before, when he too was taken ill with tuberculosis. Clothing and other articles had been pawned to supply necessaries, and the family now was in need of food. The societies which had at first aided supplied coal and groceries and milk. Coal was given also by the city. Through a church which had become interested, Mr. Deering was sent to a hospital for consumptives, but remained only a few days, when he returned home, and died a month later. Mabel was brought home from the institution, and temporary employment was secured for Mrs. Deering.

Fifteen months later an application was made by Thomas Brown, who stated that he had married Mrs. Deering; that a month before their marriage he had broken his leg, and since that time had done but little work. Mr. Brown said that he needed clothing in order to secure work. Mrs. Brown was approaching confinement, and the visitor who called gave her advice in regard to a doctor. This advice, however, was not followed, nor were wood-yard tickets given to Mr. Brown used. All references gave unfavorable reports of Mr. Brown. He was considered unreliable and lazy. The closing report is given by the visitor, who had learned from Mabel that she was employed in a factory at four dollars a week, and was living with an aunt. She would, however, give no information concerning her mother.

Braddock, Susan, a widow with two sons, Michael, a cripple, twenty-three years of age, and Charles, a boy of eleven. At the time of application all were homeless. Michael, the cripple, was admitted to a hospital, and the younger boy to an institution for children. Work was offered the mother, but was declined because of small pay. Temporary work was found for Michael after his discharge from the hospital, but the family removed in a short time to an unknown address, and was not heard from for five years.

Mrs. Braddock then applied for assistance again, giving the name of McAndrew. Her second husband had been run over by a wagon, and completely disabled. He had been in a hospital for eleven months, and had not been able to work after his discharge. He had brought suit against the ones who were believed to be responsible for the accident, but had gained nothing. Mrs. McAndrew's younger son, now sixteen years of age, had broken his wrist. It had been improperly set and could not be used, and he could therefore do very little work.

A year later application was again made. Her husband had died soon after the last application, her second son was out of work, they were in arrears for rent, and about to be dispossessed. With assistance in securing temporary employment, the family remained self-supporting for one year, when they were again in arrears for rent and in need of food and clothing. Temporary relief was provided, and work secured for Charles. At the end of another year Charles had become subject to epileptic fits, and Mrs. McAndrew herself was ill, making relief and the attention of a nurse necessary. The epileptic son had fallen while at work, and was badly injured. He was placed in a hospital, and board was secured for the mother, who was now alone.

Two years later the woman applied for assistance in her earlier name of Braddock, which she had resumed on her son's account. She stated that Charles had been cured by a clergyman, but as he was out of work they were in need. Food and temporary employment were supplied, and eleven months afterward the son who had been cured had another seizure, and relief was again required at intervals during the following year, at which time the family moved to an unknown address. There was no record of the elder son, Michael, after the first application.

Illness and accident are sufficient to account for Mrs. Braddock's misfortunes, and no special stress need be laid upon her credulity, and her clergyman's imposition in the matter of the " cure " of her epileptic son.

The cases thus far considered have been those of widows, or of aged persons, or of families in which there was a deficiency in earning capacity, or on account of illness. Somewhat different are those in which the family becomes dependent because of the desertion of the head of the family, or because he is incapacitated by intemperance or shiftlessness or grave moral deficiency of some other kind.

Mrs. Carney, concerning whom we have the following brief record, was herself of immoral character, and her children, instead of being committed for destitution, might more appropriately have been removed by a magistrate for improper guardianship. As there was no official record against her, the application to which reference is made for the return of her children would probably be granted.

Carney, Grace, had two of her children committed to an asylum, on the ground of her husband's desertion, and her own inability to support them, being ill. Mrs. Carney was placed in a private hospital, and after her discharge remained with friends, but before she was well enough to work, or care for her children, she disappeared. She visited them at the asylum, however, and wrote to them frequently, but always used false addresses. She was immoral, and frequently in need of hospital treatment. Mr. Carney, who was an iron-worker earning good wages, could not be found; therefore no action could be brought against him.

Eighteen months after the commitment of the children, Mrs. Carney wrote from another town, saying that she had a good position, and was about to take her children home.

As an illustration of heredity in pauperism, the three following cases may be studied to advantage. It will be recognized that the individuals are by no means all of bad character, and that there are not lacking misfortunes of the kind that prompt charitable neighbors to unquestioned relief giving. It remains true that the development of Mrs. Young's offspring is far from creditable to the community.

Young, Kate, a widow known to the society for the past twenty years. Six years after the first application, Mrs. Young again came to the attention of the society, when she spoke of herself as a widow "many years," although it was known that her husband was living but three years previous. Mrs. Young did sewing occasionally, but lived chiefly by writing begging letters. She was spoken of as untruthful, ungrateful, and intolerant of questions, and in

this respect her two married daughters were like her.   Her
home, however, was always clean, tidy, and comfortable,
and at previous addresses the family was well spoken of.
At the time of application there were four sons at home,
Thomas, James, Alfred, and William.

Thomas was an epileptic, and could not do much work.
Five years later James married, and Alfred, who was ill
with consumption, boarded with him.   No further record
is given of Alfred after the return home, four years later,
or James, who was then a widower with three children.
These children remained with their father only until the
following spring, at which time they went to live with
their maternal grandmother.   William, the fourth son,
was lazy, given to cigarette smoking, and rarely earned
anything.   References given by the sons were found to
be either false or unfavorable.   Nothing definite could be
learned about any relatives, Mrs. Young evading questions
in regard to them.

At various times the family was referred to the society
by private individuals, to whom Mrs. Young had applied,
aid having been given at times by all, and by some of
them for many years.   For six years Mrs. Burn, one of
Mrs. Young's married daughters, and her children, also
lived with her.   The family separated upon the return
home of the married son, James, and the same winter a
society for the aid of widows was found to be assisting
both families.   In addition to the aid given by private
individuals, the family had been helped by two private
societies, had received city coal, and had had sewing from
two other societies, one of which had also aided in other
ways.

Fourteen years after the first application, Thomas, the
epileptic son, died.   Arrangements had been made previously for his admittance to a home for epileptics, but
this his mother had not allowed.   After his death Mrs.
Young applied again to a private individual, who had been
interested, but aid from this source was refused.

A year later Mrs. Young, who was then in poor health,
was referred to the society by a private individual, but
upon a visitor's calling, declined aid, saying that she did
not need it.   Her daughters were living in the same house,

and they had comfortable homes. Mrs. Young was aided occasionally by a private individual and received sewing during the winter, for which she was paid a dollar and a half a week. Threats of arrest for vagrancy were necessary to put an end to the begging letters.

Burn, Annie and John. Mrs. Burn is the daughter of Mrs. Kate Young (see above), and acquaintance was first made with her twenty years ago, at which time she, her mother, and another married sister, all had the reputation of being untruthful and beggars, and the brothers of being lazy. Mr. Burn, who was supposed to be in poor health, but whose ailment was really laziness complicated by intemperance, never remained long at any work. For a time he earned fourteen dollars a week on a street railway, but there he was considered unreliable. His wife did sewing occasionally.

Nine years later Mr. Burn deserted, and his wife with two of her children went to live with her mother, where she posed as a widow, — although Mr. Burn visited her frequently, — while the two oldest children were placed in an institution, where they remained for a year. At the end of that time one of them, Arthur, obtained employment as a hall boy, and, at the same time, Mrs. Burn was aided in securing work as a saleswoman. It was later found that she was filling the position under the assumed name of a cousin, whose excellent references she had used in obtaining the place. Her employers, however, spoke well of her.

Soon afterward Mrs. Burn left her mother's home, upon the return of her brother, who had become a widower, with his children; and a year later Arthur enlisted for war, returning, however, the following year, ill. He reënlisted four months later, and was ordered to the Philippines. His mother made this an occasion for appeal to two private citizens, who aided her. Mrs. Burn's health failing, she left work and was aided in rent and in procuring an elastic stocking. Her daughter Emily was employed in a shop at four dollars a week, and later at six, at which time her mother also had employment at twelve dollars a week, but gave it up soon afterward.

The following year Mrs. Burn was ill, and her mother and married sister, Mrs. Low, lived in the same house with her. Two years after this a private individual was applied to for money in order to give Mrs. Burn a start with a firm in another city. Her daughter Emily had married a farmer in New York State and Mrs. Burn's second son was employed in a New York store.

During the years the family was under notice they were aided frequently by different private societies, among them a society for the aid of widows, which for a winter helped Mrs. Burn, until the fact was discovered that her husband was living. In addition to this assistance many private individuals had aided, some of them for a long period of time.

Holton, Alfred and Frances. Mrs. Holton is the daughter of Kate Young and sister to Annie Burn (see above). Her husband, whose references gave him the reputation of being intemperate and dishonest, although a few years before he had worked steadily and faithfully, had deserted, and under an alias enlisted in the army. A friend who had previously aided referred Mrs. Holton for work. During the next few months many private individuals reported the family, Mrs. Holton having applied to them for aid. Her daughter Lucy was regularly at work, and sewing was given to Mrs. Holton by a society, which insured her a dollar a week. A private individual also aided and gave temporary employment. The opportunity for a fresh-air outing was given to the children, but this was declined.

In the autumn of the same year Lucy secured a position in the millinery department of a dry goods house at seven dollars, and through the assistance of a private citizen and a charitable society the needed outfit of silk waist and skirt were purchased, with the understanding that the money was advanced only as a loan. For three seasons a private society supplied Mrs. Holton with sewing, and at the end of that time, her husband having returned home, the family became self-supporting.

The immediate cause of the dependence in the following case was a loss of employment owing to a change in

industrial conditions. Whether the ultimate responsibility
should be assigned to industrial causes or to family conditions, may well be left to the student, who in either event
will undoubtedly feel a considerable degree of sympathy for
the draughtsman who lost his employment just after finding
himself called upon to provide for four infant children.

Rossi, Attila and Vittoria, an Italian Protestant family,
the parents both under thirty years of age, and four children
comprising two sets of twins, respectively one month and
thirteen months of age. A two-year-old child had died
immediately after their application for assistance. Mr.
Rossi is an intelligent man of refined and delicate appearance, an architectural draughtsman by training, and unfitted for other than clerical work. He had been employed
for over a year with a well-known building firm, which,
however, had closed out the architectural branch of its
business on account of the strike in the building trades,
leaving Mr. Rossi without employment.

When he called at the office he was in a very discouraged
frame of mind, declaring that, even when employed at $12
a week, his income was not sufficient to support his family,
that he must find a place where he could earn at least $14,
and if he could not do this, he would run away and leave
his family. The visitor, who berated him soundly for this
cowardly attitude, was inclined, on calling at his home, if
not to sympathize with it, at least to appreciate more fully
his difficulties. Mrs. Rossi had gone out to search for employment. The husband, who was at home with the children, said that they were taking turns in the hunt for work,
one staying with the children. The one who remained was
kept busy every moment with the four babies, getting their
milk warm, feeding them, and giving them necessary care.
The gas bill was very high, as the gas had to be kept burning almost constantly to keep the milk warm for the babies.
One of the younger twins was quite ill, and had apparently a slender hold on life. Rooms and children were,
however, immaculately clean.

Mrs. Rossi could do shop work without injuring her
health, but was really not strong enough to care for the
four children and do the necessary work at home. The

plan of hiring a woman to look after the children while the wife worked had been tried, but was not a success. A woman who promised well had been engaged at $3 a week and board, but she left at the end of the week saying that the work was too heavy. Mrs. Rossi's people live on the same floor, but they cannot give any assistance. Her aged father and mother are supported by one son and two daughters, all of whom are at work, and the mother is able only to do the necessary housework in her own rooms. They are giving Mr. and Mrs. Rossi meals, but cannot continue to do this.

Mr. Rossi does not wish charity, but the only solution that appears to him possible is to place the four children in some home or institution, so that both he and his wife can work and earn the money to live on, and to pay for their children's board.

Prior to this application the family had twice been referred for assistance by a sympathetic clergyman, but on each occasion Mr. Rossi had been found to be at work, and earning about $12 a week, and with only one set of twins in the family, this had been considered an income on which they should be able to live, notwithstanding instalment-plan debts for furniture and clothing.

Illness enters into the problem presented in the three following cases. A family which has a normal standard of living, will, of course, provide for illness, as well as other contingencies. A question might therefore arise whether illness, any more than old age, may justly be put down as a cause of destitution. It remains true, that when a family is near the margin of self-support, constantly recurring illness contributes the element which appears to justify either public or private relief. In the decision as to whether relief should be from public or private sources, weight may properly be given to any evidence tending to show that, while in position to do so, attempts were made to provide for illness. Much may be said in favor of limiting private charity to those who make reasonable attempts to provide for old age, accident, or illness.

Brady, Frank and Ellen. Mr. Brady applied for assistance, his wife having but a few days before left the hospital after confinement, and being now at home and in need of food. Mr. Brady's references being favorable, a private society aided. A month later Mr. Brady had secured work, and nothing was heard of the family for six years, when Mr. Brady again called. He had worked for a drygoods house for five years, had been ill in a hospital for five weeks, and upon his return to work had found his place filled. For three months he received $6 a week from a sick-benefit fund, and then secured temporary work, which, however, ceased soon afterward. Mrs. Brady had for three months been employed four days a week at a private institution, but was now out of employment. Rent was due and they needed food. The references of both Mr. and Mrs. Brady spoke well of them, and at previous addresses they were favorably considered. A private society again aided, and later a church took charge.

After another year Mr. Brady again applied. He had had no employment during the winter, but they had been aided by a church, which aid, however, was now withdrawn. Wood-yard tickets were offered, but refused on the ground that he was not strong enough for such work. Three months later Mrs. Brady called at the office, saying that they were in great need, and that neither of them had work. Aid was supplied, and work in the laundry for Mrs. Brady. An interval of four months passed before Mrs. Brady was again seen. At this time Mr. Brady was in a hospital, ill with grippe, and she too had been ill, and now had but little work. Aid was secured from a private society, and a diet kitchen supplied nourishing food. Two months after this Mr. Brady made application to another society. They were again out of employment, Mrs. Brady was ill, and they were in need. Groceries were given, and also a wood-yard ticket to Mr. Brady. Soon afterward Mrs. Brady secured employment in a hotel at $14 a month. Her husband had used several tickets at the wood yard, but was now in need of shoes, which were given. Two months later both man and wife were working, and had become self-supporting.

Wilson, Charlotte, a widow, little past middle age, who had supported herself by making artificial flowers and letting furnished rooms. She lost her work at the time of her application, and also her lodgers, two of whom had left owing room rent, and one of them having stolen from her $45 in cash. Mrs. Wilson was anxious to get light work so that she could keep her rooms. She could give no business references, as she had secured her work in artificial flowers through another employee. She had a good reputation, however, at her previous residences, and was favorably considered at the mission which she attended.

It was learned that until she was forty years of age she had been a circus rider, tight-rope walker, and ballet dancer. A personal friend was found who loaned Mrs. Wilson enough money to enable her to move to cheaper rooms, where she secured a lodger, and was given some plain sewing. A few months later she undertook, also, work as chambermaid in a hotel. Six months after her first call she had a fall, resulting in a broken arm. Although she was taken to a hospital, her arm was not properly set, and always troubled her afterwards. Coal, groceries, and delicacies of various kinds were provided during the winter, and in the spring, both of her available rooms being rented, she became self-supporting.

For over a year she continued to keep lodgers and to work as chambermaid, but on account of a change in managers at the hotel she lost her employment, and undertook instead to do some cleaning for her landlord. A slight margin between her earnings and needs was filled in from charitable sources. A year later another small amount of assistance was required, but she then secured temporary work and became janitress at two houses, receiving $8 a month and rent free, but having to pay for some of the heavier work on account of her injured arm. In the winter she had again injured herself slightly, enough to interfere with her work, and groceries and coal were supplied, and temporary employment. In the spring, temporary work being secured again, she became for the time self-supporting.

We have said that private relief may not improperly be made contingent upon provision having been made for the misfortune which causes distress. When destitution is brought about by the desertion of the natural breadwinner of the family, it would seem necessary to waive this condition, since desertion is a crime, which the wife can scarcely be expected to anticipate, and for which the deserting husband will hardly have made provision. Another consideration, however, becomes paramount, and this is a consideration which enters also into every other decision about relief. This is the effect of relief upon others in the community, who are likely to be influenced by the results of desertion. If a man of comparatively weak character, who is having a severe struggle to support his family, and who is on the verge of discouragement, sees that ample provision is made for the family of his neighbor when its head disappears, the idea may well take root in his mind that this is, on the whole, the best way for him also to provide for his own. From actual desertion in a desperate case it is only a short step to temporary desertion in special emergencies, and from this to fraudulent desertion, when, by connivance between husband and wife, it is pretended that he has gone away, when he is, in fact, at home, or in the immediate vicinity.

Camaili, Joseph and Johanna. Mrs. Camaili desired to have two of her children committed, her husband having become infatuated with another woman and deserted. Because of whooping-cough in the family, no institution would accept the children, but a settlement and the church to which the woman belonged provided what assistance was necessary. The man's whereabouts were ascertained in another city, and a visitor in that city persuaded him to return to his family.

Eighteen months later, however, there was another application for commitment, the father having deserted, as it was learned, for the fourth time. His father and mother and sister, however, remained with the deserted wife. It was ascertained that he had gone to the same city in which he had been found before, and from there he sent word that he would like to have his family join him. The public authorities declined to provide transportation, for the reason that a report from the place where he was living indicated that his home was not a desirable one, or suitable for the reception of his children. The family, however, decided later to go on their own account, and nothing has since been heard from him.

Richards, Kate, deserted by her husband. Mrs. Richards came of a respectable family. She has a sister who has aided her, and sons living in the city who would aid if she would come to them, but she is an incorrigible vagrant, apparently unsound of mind, abusive, and intemperate. Her sons had been removed from her custody while young, and sent to foster-homes in the west. She appears frequently at application bureaus, telling incoherent stories, and is often aided with meal tickets, clothing, and lodgings, has often been a guest at the Woman's Hotel of the Salvation Army, and has been an inmate of a workhouse, a home for discharged prisoners, and a home for fallen women. She makes false and irrational statements concerning her family. After irregular dealing with the woman for five or six years, the case was definitely closed as unhelpable with the resources at hand.

Kemp, Anna. When Mrs. Kemp first made application for assistance she and her seven children had been deserted by her husband, who was intemperate and shiftless, whereupon she had come to New York, as she had a brother and sister here who aided to some extent. Five of the children were committed to an institution. Mrs. Kemp then secured day's work, and was able to support herself and her two other children, Edward and Lily.

Three years later Edward was earning three dollars a week, and his mother about six. Efforts were then made to have the children taken out of the institution and cared for at home. But relatives refused to help, and as John's eyes were giving him a great deal of trouble, he and two sisters remained in the institution, and the two others were taken home. Soon afterward John died in the institution. A year later all of the children were at home with the mother, and the family was doing well.

Deserted families afford very serious problems, which, however, are probably not more difficult than those arising in attempts to help the families of intemperate men ; certainly not more difficult than those inherent in attempts to improve the condition of a family in which there is an intemperate mother.   When destitution is caused by drink there are always, of course, other complications — illness, shiftlessness, or inefficiency.   One or many of these symptoms may appear, and whether the principal difficulty be industrial, or physical, or moral, intemperance is likely to enter as a contributory factor in a very large proportion of cases.   Statistics upon the point differ widely.   It is probably true that in one-fourth of the cases brought to the attention of public or private charitable agencies distress is due to the intemperance of the natural breadwinner of the family, and that in fully another one-fourth, drink aggravates a situation which would otherwise easily be remedied.   This would be shown on a full statement of all the facts in the cases already cited.   It is a more prominent element, although again by no means the only one, in the following instances.

Dolan, Thomas and Ann, asked for aid seven years ago, but could not be found when visited, and were not heard of again for four years, when Mrs. Dolan applied for aid in rent, her husband having deserted, and her relatives being unable to help.   At the various places where the family had lived it was found that Mrs. Dolan had supported the family, and that her husband was drunken, lazy, and abusive.   Application was made for the commitment of the children on the ground of destitution, but this was refused by the public authorities, and an order was obtained from court requiring Dolan to support his family.   He was found and returned home, but would not work, and was not prosecuted under the magistrate's order.

Ten months later Dolan was sent to the penitentiary for burglary, remaining for nine months.   On his discharge Mrs. Dolan permitted him to come home, concealing the fact, however, from the church which then was aiding. One child was taken to an eye and ear hospital for treatment, and another was taken care of by friends, while Mrs. Dolan went to an infant asylum for confinement, her husband again deserting the family at this juncture.   After the birth of the child aid was given Mrs. Dolan to take rooms and get her family together. A year later, conditions being practically the same, Dolan frequently deserting his family and failing entirely to support them, and his wife refusing to prosecute seriously, the home was broken up, and the children committed for improper guardianship.

Henderson, William and Myrtle. At the time of their application the family was living in well-furnished and neat rooms, and they were able to give reference from whom a favorable account was obtained. Henderson was inclined to be intemperate but was intelligent and skilful. Relatives were found who, although in moderate circumstances, were willing to help, and the family was left in their care. They remained self-supporting for seven years, at which time special shoes were provided for George, a crippled boy. The father at this time was earning $8 a week.

A year later application was made for the commitment of three children. The cause of the trouble was found to be increased intemperance of the father, who was then idle. Relatives again aided. The Department of Public Charities secured from a magistrate an order requiring Henderson to support his family. He was induced to take a pledge of total abstinence and has kept it. The crippled boy was sent to a state institution for crippled children, and relief was supplied to move the family, and to provide for a month's rent and for necessary clothing. Except for a serious illness from typhoid, the family, in the year that has elapsed since it was decided not to commit the three children as public charges, has been in no serious trouble, and relief has been required only in moderate amount.

Koern, Edward and Elizabeth. Aid was asked originally on account of approaching confinement of Mrs. Koern. They were taken in charge by a church, which during the following year aided frequently, although reporting Mr. Koern as drunken. In the five years following, on account of the illness of the wife and children, the family was aided also by a relief society, Koern's record throughout being that of intemperance and irregularity at work.

Q

Two of the children were placed in an institution by the church, but were taken back by the father. Later, application was made for the commitment of two other children, but it was disapproved. Mrs. Koern has a lame foot which frequently incapacitates her for work. Mr. Koern now began to show improvement, and was earning $15 to $20 a month caring for furnaces. The younger children were placed in a day nursery. Mrs. Koern was treated by a physician and a district nurse, and nourishing food was provided for her. The eldest child was sent regularly to school, and for the last two years of the record Mr. Koern had regular work as watchman on a street railway.

Hardy, Ferdinand, twenty-one years of age, was a driver by occupation, strong, very intemperate, and on that account out of employment, abusive to wife and children. His wife was a year younger, in rather delicate health, but said to be a good mother. Mrs. Hardy had her husband arrested and sentenced to six months for non-support. They had been married for five years, during which time Hardy had never worked more than two or three months at a time. His relatives were abundantly able to help them, but, probably because of earlier discouraging experiences, allowed the family to be dispossessed from their rooms. On being interviewed, however, Hardy's mother promised to assume the care of the family, if her son was released, not otherwise. It was apparently her desire that her son should be rid of his family, but he was not himself inclined to desert them. Mrs. Hardy secured her husband's pardon, the relatives aided them to start in new rooms, and the man went to work. They have two healthy, attractive children, but both parents are of weak character. If they become entirely estranged from their wealthy relatives, or if the latter lose their property, the family is likely to become chronically dependent.

Bruce, Emily, a widow who appeared not to be in need, but who applied for assistance, was found in an apartment of seven rooms, for which the rent was forty-five dollars a month. It developed, however, that Mrs. Bruce had really been living on a sum which she had received on her husband's death from a beneficial society to which he had belonged. She had taken the larger apartment in the expectation of being able to rent rooms, and at the time of the visitor's call two artists were in fact boarding with her, paying together, however, only eight dollars a week for their board. Her sensible suggestion was that if aided to move to rooms at moderate rent, she would be able to support herself and her children as a seamstress, in which occupation she had had experience.

Bonner, Thomas and Cora, an English family, were investigated at the request of a national relief society, to which Mr. Bonner had applied for assistance. References were favorable, except that former employers in London wrote that Mr. Bonner had been discharged for losing time, and it was found that he was addicted to drink. English relatives refused to give assistance. Mr. Bonner continued to drink, and abused his family. Many efforts were made to reform him by friendly visitation from churches and charitable societies, but these efforts were unsuccessful, and about two years after the first application he was placed under arrest for disorderly conduct and abuse of family, and was sentenced for one month. Immediately after his discharge he was sentenced to a second term of six months.

Mrs. Bonner supported the family with little difficulty when he was away, and did not wish to have him return. She was persuaded, however, to receive him again, and he apparently made an effort to reform. In the following year he gave further evidence of this desire by entering a home for intemperate men, but after his discharge again succumbed to his appetite. A son, William, refused to stay at home with his father, who several times reformed and worked well for a time, but each time again fell away.

The friendly visitor, five years after the first application, and three years after any distinctly unfavorable record, reported that the family was doing well, and that Mr. Bonner had remained sober for nine months.

Jones, John and Margaret. John is an able-bodied man of thirty, a printer by trade, and a successful operator on a machine, although not a rapid hand compositor. He had been for ten years in one office, but had left it to better himself, as he supposed, in another city. Not being successful, he had returned, and was out of employment. There were four small children, whom the parents desired to have committed to an institution. The magistrate, to whom application had been made, refused to commit them, on the ground of non-residence. After many conflicting reports and unsuccessful attempts to start the family on a basis of self-support, it was finally ascertained that the difficulty lay with Mrs. Jones. Both man and wife drank, but the wife was the more intemperate. Her rooms were found frequently to be dirty, and the children to be utterly neglected, although at times there would be an improvement, and the children attended a private school irregularly. The family was frequently dispossessed for drunkenness and fighting, and the parents were known to have used vile language before the children.

The man's mother confided to the visitor that the couple were intoxicated when married, although she did not know this until later. The wife had been reared a Catholic, but the husband was of a Protestant family, and it was difficult to ascertain whether the children had been christened at all, and if so, in what faith. The man constantly borrowed small sums of money in various directions and rarely repaid. His mother supplied him with the money necessary for his union fees when he secured employment.

After a little more than two years of persistent effort to reform the parents and to secure fair treatment of the children, the attempt was given up as a failure, and, at a time when the family had been dispossessed and the furniture thrown upon the street, the children were committed to an asylum, and the father placed under an order of court to pay for their maintenance. The family had again, in the meantime, become residents of the city.

We have not yet done with our examples of intemperance. Those that follow illustrate in addition the absence of moral qualities, aside from intemperance, and also illustrate the opportunities which arise for remedial measures in these cases. There are some who are peculiarly gifted for the moral reformation of the intemperate and the vicious, and to all who have this gift one must bid a "God speed" in their efforts. Material relief in such cases as are here described, however, when unaccompanied by discipline, or by extraordinary personal influence, seldom achieves a result in which the donor can take satisfaction.

Byrnes, Sarah and Theophrastus. Through a period of ten years a charitable society attempted to rehabilitate the family of Theophrastus and Sarah Byrnes. This man was a physician, a graduate of a well-known medical college, and had excellent professional qualities. He contracted the morphine habit, however, as result of treatment after an accident, and has gone steadily down hill ever since. He has abandoned his family and is living with another woman (Mrs. R.), but on account of his children his wife will not take action against him. The woman with whom he is maintaining relations at present came from a good family, whose members feel very bitter toward Dr. Byrnes. She had been previously married and has one son, and both mother and son have become victims of the opium habit.

Many efforts have been made, by friends and by physicians, to reform this man. He has been a voluntary inmate of three institutions for treatment, and has been given excellent opportunities for work at his profession — all, however, without success. Both the man and Mrs. R., probably largely because of their use of opium, have become unreliable, dishonest, and dissolute. They have had charitable aid at various times, in the form of groceries, clothing, rent, tickets for night lodgings, etc. — all given as an incentive to influencing them to lead a different life, but without permanent success.

Bender, John and Bridget, had been continually applying for aid in rent, food, and clothing for fourteen years. On one occasion, the wife being in the almshouse, John had asked for shelter of some kind for himself. Their record is bad — laziness on the one side, untruthfulness on the other, and intemperance on both. A nurse made a report that he was suffering from varicose veins and needed an elastic stocking; that he was physically unable to do any work that would require standing; and, moreover, that he was subject to epileptic fits, and was, practically, a physical and nervous wreck. As if to match his condition, Bridget, the wife, had a repulsive eruption on her face, for which, at the time of this report, she was being treated at a public dispensary. Their account of their own past life was confused and unsatisfactory, neither being able to make any statement as to the time and place of their marriage or in regard to their children.

This situation is presented, not as an example of a family that should have relief at home, but as one concerning whom this question will constantly arise, to be decided affirmatively or negatively. It is safe to decide it negatively in such cases, and to take the position that the children should be removed and the parents separated for hospital or permanent institutional care.

Beaumais, Marie. A very different case is that of Marie Beaumais, who is related, by many removes, to a woman of wealth and social position. This distant kinswoman, not so much because of the relationship as because of a personal friendship for this woman's mother, has expressed a willingness to make her a monthly allowance, provided she will cut loose, with her children, from her utterly disreputable and worthless husband. He has done practically nothing, in their ten years of married life, except to squander his wife's small dowry and to live upon her earnings. Even the modest homestead which had belonged to his wife has gone to meet principal and interest of a mortgage indebtedness. She is not physically strong, and, as her means are exhausted, the absence of the allowance would mean the commitment of her children as public charges, and the necessity of supporting herself at service or in some similar manner. With reluctance, therefore, and with many assurances to the visitor that she had, personally, no ill-feeling toward her husband, she consented to a legal separation on the

ground of non-support, and became established in a few
rooms with her children, expecting to earn whatever is
needed for their support over and above the allowance
which was thus secured.

The wisdom of this conditional offer has been questioned, and such a harsh word as " hypocrisy " has been
used to describe Marie's acceptance of the offer, in view
of her husband's not infrequent visits to her and her children in their new quarters, and her own expressions of
continued affection for him ; but her attitude is really
sufficiently straightforward to satisfy the most exacting.
She had no desire to be separated from her husband, she
had no fault to find with him, — at least, to outsiders, —
the legal action was but an empty form to which she
agreed as the only condition upon which an income which
she needed could be secured.

Jay, John and Rachel, applied to a charitable society
twenty years ago, but no necessity for relief was discovered. The same request was made the following year.
Mrs. Jay then said that her husband had deserted her,
which, however, was found to be untrue. The relief
society paid rent and provided groceries. The record
then has a blank of eleven years, which will readily be
filled in by an experienced visitor, by unrecorded applications to individuals, churches, and societies, rewarded
by occasional success. Application was then made to a
church whose visitor offered employment to a grown girl
in the family, which was refused. It is pathetically and
briefly recorded that all aid given had not helped the family.

The housekeeper at the house in which the family had
formerly lived said that they had been dispossessed for
drunkenness of both the man and woman. In this year
the relief society gave relief twice, once a grant being
made at the request of the church. The head of the
family was now ill and needed extra nourishment. He
had, however, patented a window-sash, which a clergyman
arranged to place upon the market.

The following year the family was again reported for
aid, this time by a private citizen to whom they had applied. The husband was ill, a son of working age had

irregular employment, and the daughter to whom employment had previously been offered was out of work. A loan association reported that a loan of $50 had been made twice, the furniture being pledged as security. Both loans had been repaid, but the second under compulsion.

Two years later a third church asked an investigation, the man having died the year before. The housekeeper at a new address said that the family did not pay debts and spent their money for drink; that the boy stole lead pipes from the house and cut up the wardrobes in the apartments for fuel; that the family had lived extravagantly for a time on the man's insurance. Two years later the unpromising boy had regular employment at $10 a week, and therefore the family was left to its own resources.

Drake, Samuel and Sarah. After relief had been given a few times significant facts in the previous career and in the ancestry of this couple began to come to light. It was found that Mrs. Drake's mother had been insane, and that she herself had been led astray by a distant relative, and that the latter was father of the eldest child. He had placed over $500 in a savings bank to her credit. This money, with the earnings of both man and wife, had been squandered by Drake. He was a gambler and was frequently away from home for several days at a time. His mother was living in an apartment house, divorced from her husband, who was also a gambler. Drake's brother had paid the rent of the family through an entire winter on condition that he should not annoy them, but reported that this agreement had been broken and rent was discontinued.

A few years later the family was again brought to notice by the report of a lady interested in rescue work, who said that she had herself brought up Samuel Drake, and that he had much to fight against. At this time aid was given to the family in groceries, clothing, and coal to the value of some $90. Five months later it was necessary for the housekeeper to intervene in a family quarrel, in which the man was beating his wife and using language unfit for the children to hear. In the following month, while Mrs. Drake was out, her husband sold all of the furniture, and the four children were committed to an institution for lack of proper guardianship. One week after this a church had become interested in the family, and reported that the man and his wife, with an infant who had not been committed, were living in a furnished room.

Garrett, John and Catharine, were first brought to notice by the principal of a primary school, who found the children to be in need of shoes. The family was aided frequently by two private citizens, the investigation having shown at the outset a fairly creditable record, although Mrs. Garrett was eccentric, and the eldest boy, Patrick, frequently changed his work. Two daughters were in an institution for children.

Five years later Garrett was ill, but refused hospital treatment. Patrick ran away from home, was found, and sent to a foster-family by the Children's Aid Society. He returned with money supplied by his mother, and was committed to an institution. A relief society had an unsatisfactory experience with the family. Patrick returned home after repeated demands by his mother for his discharge, but was lazy and incorrigible. Mr. Garrett worked irregularly, but the family was inclined to rely on others for all the help that it was possible to get. Mrs. Garrett was admitted to a hospital and had a slight surgical operation.

Ten years after the first application a second son, Andrew, who had become the main breadwinner of the family, was ill. Patrick enlisted in the regular army, and the family had become known to two agencies formed for the purpose of aiding soldiers and sailors. Mrs. Garrett was housekeeper, but quarrelled with the tenants, and the two daughters, who had formerly been in an institution, were at home and working occasionally. The decision with which the record closes records that the family had been aided too much, and would better be left to themselves.

Kelley, Michael and Ann. The record covers a period of nine years with an interval of five years. At the time of the original application the husband was lame as a result of an injury from a railway accident. He then had a reputation for intemperance and abusiveness. He was admitted to a convalescent home, and received necessary surgical care, after which work was found for him on a street railway. The wife worked irregularly at the laundry, a son of working age had employment, and later a daughter went out to domestic service.

On the next application for assistance, a few years later, John, who had previously been employed, was out of work, but refused woodyard tickets. The daughter at service was doing well except that she occasionally went home at night and remained away for a day without notice. The whole family was untruthful.

Next year Mrs. Kelley slipped on the stairs and broke her arm while working for the caretaker of a wealthy man in a house that was otherwise unoccupied during the summer months. Her husband insisted that she should sue the owner, although she had no valid claim, and when she refused, he abused and deserted her. John also refused to support his mother. The owner of the house in which the accident occurred supported Mrs. Kelley until she was able to work.

A few weeks afterward John was found in her rooms intoxicated. Mrs. Kelley had now reached the age limit at which she might have been admitted to a home if otherwise a suitable candidate, but she refused to consider any such suggestion, and in any case she could probably have been sent only to the almshouse. She accepted such employment as was offered her, but was often dispossessed for drunkenness and disturbance of neighbors. Annie gave up domestic service and went to work in a silk factory, at which time the family disappeared from notice and nothing more has been heard of them.

Dunn, Edward and Caroline. When Dunn called at the Application Bureau, at the suggestion of a church, he needed work and general assistance. Investigation showed the family to be drunken, quarrelsome, and shiftless. Their rooms had always been dirty and neglected. Mrs. Dunn had previously been married to a man whom she at first declared to have been killed in a quarrel, but whom she later said that she had sent to the state prison for bigamy. From the prison authorities it was learned that he had been twice committed, once for burglary, and once for perjury. Neither the father nor mother was disposed to work to support the children. One child was at the time living with Mrs. Dunn's mother, who also had a record of dependence under various aliases. The children should have been removed at this time for improper guardianship, but this result was not brought about.

About three years later Mrs. Dunn applied for the commitment of her son, stating that her husband had deserted soon after her former application, and was now living in a suburb with a married daughter. Later he was reported to be an inmate of the almshouse of the county in which the suburb is located. The child who had been with the grandmother died in an institution. The boy for whom she now desired commitment had previously been in the same institution, but was discharged on the ground that his parents could support him, and in the meantime his mother had changed his name to Montmorency. Temporary institutional care was secured for Montmorency in the hope that Mrs. Dunn would enter a hospital for treatment, which she later refused to do. She agreed, however, to the placing out of her child for adoption.

Way, Theodore. Investigation was asked by a private citizen, to whom Mr. Way had written, saying that he had been arrested and was in the "Tombs" awaiting trial. The complaint was that of passing a worthless check, drawn on a bank which was found not to exist. Mr. Way's story was that he had had business relations with persons whom he supposed to be reliable, and had been persuaded to deposit several hundred dollars with them. He later drew upon them for $50, which was obtained without difficulty. He had then given a few checks for small debts to various people, but before these had been heard from he was asked to cash their check for $75. Not having the money he indorsed the check and took it to a liquor dealer, who cashed it. It was this check which had been returned as worthless, and had led to his arrest. Mr. Way claimed also that the city owed him $2000, his bill having been

approved, but not paid.   If he could collect this money
he could pay the liquor dealor, who would then be willing
to withdraw the charge.

At his father's death Mr. Way had inherited a large
sum of money, which he had put into business and lost.
His mother had still some valuable furniture, which had,
however, been in storage for some time, and there was
now danger of losing it, as payments were in arrears.
He had but one near relative, an uncle who was a man
of some prominence in politics and otherwise.   This uncle
would do nothing for Mr. Way, but was induced to provide
board and money for the wife.   A masonic lodge, to which
the man belonged, also contributed for her support, but
would do nothing for Mr. Way.

Six months after the letter had been received, Mr. Way
was tried and found guilty; sentence, however, was suspended, and he was discharged and was not again heard
from.   His wife, for the following year, was supported by
relatives, who made their contributions for this purpose
through the society.

If intemperance and other moral defects can seldom be
remedied by material relief, still less can relief cure a
strain of chronic dependence.   Those to whom begging
presents itself as the easiest solution of any even temporary embarrassment, and who therefore prefer to beg
rather than work, are perhaps of all dependents the most
unresponsive and unhelpable.   While a few illustrative
instances are here grouped together, it must be understood, that by no means all of the individuals in these
families are representatives of the begging class.   Families do not differentiate themselves so completely.   The
beggar is joined together with the drunkard, and the
honest, industrious, and faithful mother may find herself
cursed by a brutal husband or an ungrateful and. worthless son.   The following instances are therefore all the
more typical because they present complications both of
good and of bad qualities, in addition to the strain of pauperism which appears to run through them.

Patrick, John and Anna.   A church worker, several of
whose earlier cases had turned out to be different from

what the worker supposed them to be, but who had excused the misinformation supplied by saying that the families were under the charge of associate workers and not personally known to the one who had referred them, finally wrote as follows in regard to a family for whom a supply of coal was requested : —

"Mr. Patrick is out of work. They were found sorely in need. A respectable couple with a child of four months. Everything has been pawned to get food. Plenty of room for coal. We are furnishing temporary aid in groceries. They have only one quilt on bed for their covering. No blankets. Everything has been pawned. Mrs. Patrick's health is run down so that the baby has not had proper nourishment. It is a worthy case, and I am glad I have the case under my personal supervision and attention. Mr. Patrick, I fear, has consumption. His cough seems suspicious. A bag of coal which I ordered will be sufficient until to-morrow, and I would much appreciate an early delivery of coal to this couple of good habits."

A visitor called at the address given, and Mrs. Patrick repeated the statement made in the letter which had been received. She said that her husband was consumptive and unable to do any work; that she herself has a father and sister living, but that Mr. Patrick has no relatives in the world. Mrs. Patrick was unable to explain why she was receiving aid from a church of a different denomination from that to which she said that she and her husband belonged, and in various ways she impressed the visitor that she had not been entirely straightforward and truthful in her statements. The usual inquiries were made at one or two houses in which the Patricks had formerly lived, and at one of these the housekeeper referred the visitor to a tenant who had lived in the house for some time, and therefore probably knew the Patricks. This woman said that she knew the Patricks well; that Mr. Patrick had lived there with his mother before his marriage; that he had been most brutal in his treatment of his old mother; had beaten her regularly, and was continually bringing into the house disreputable women from the street; that there was another woman living in the neighborhood who claimed to have been married to

Patrick, and that finally he had been requested to leave
the house because of his behavior; that the woman with
whom he was now living, known as Mrs. Patrick, had
been with him only a short time before his removal, but
that in this time he had beaten her frequently, on one
occasion making it necessary for her to call in the police.
This tenant believed that he was not a drinking man, but
that he was thoroughly lazy and worthless; that he was
strong and well and able to work, but that he had always
been able to find some woman who would support him.

Mrs. Patrick's sister, who was next seen, professed to
know nothing at all about Mr. Patrick, but on being questioned as to the identity of a little child in the room, who
called her "auntie," admitted that she had still another
sister, but she asked the visitor not to go to see her, as
she was not on good terms with the Patricks, and might
say something unkind.

The visitor, however, called upon the mother of the
child, in whom she found a woman who was not afraid to
tell the truth, and who knew the facts. She fully confirmed the story of the tenant at the address previously
visited. She declared her brother-in-law to be a strong
young man without a trace of consumption; able to obtain
employment, but unwilling to work; of good appearance
and plausible manner. She informed the visitor that at
the time of her call Patrick had doubtless been concealed
in the adjoining room, and for this reason his wife had
not dared to say anything derogatory about him. Patrick
was further described as a man of very dangerous character, who had frequently threatened to stick a knife into
any one who interfered with him.

The father of Mrs. Patrick and the informant happened
to be in the room at the time of this conversation, and
confirmed everything that his daughter had said, expressing, however, a fear of what Mr. Patrick might do if he
learned that they had told the truth about him. The
visitor thereupon promptly returned to the rooms of the
Patrick family, and questioned Mrs. Patrick again as to
her husband's relatives and his character. Mrs. Patrick
quickly became terrified at this line of questioning; insisted that her husband was a frail, delicate little man,

and that he was not at the time at home.   On being questioned directly as to whether he was not in the next room, listening to the present conversation, she protested that this was not the case, and attempted to prevent the visitor's opening the door to look for herself.   The visitor opened the door, however, into the adjoining room, where Mr. Patrick was found seated on the edge of the bed.   On being addressed by name he sprang to his feet with many oaths, turned violently upon his wife, telling her that he had told her never to tell a lie; denied that he was consumptive; and declared that he was perfectly able to care for his wife and child without charity; that he did not wish charity, and had never asked for it.   He inquired of his wife in a very threatening manner whether he had ever laid a hand on her, and the poor wife, frightened almost to death, replied that he had always been a good, kind husband.

Mr. Patrick was described by the visitor as being well dressed, apparently able bodied, stout and thick set, with no trace of consumption, but with a slight cough, which he himself described as a cigarette cough.

Williams, John and Eliza.   Twenty years ago an investigation was asked by a relief association connected with a church, who felt that the family was becoming dependent.   Williams was a skilled workman able to support his family.   In the following year five agencies asked for information, and it was obvious that Williams, although able to support his family, was quite willing to be supported by outside aid.

Four years later the association which first asked about the family reported that Mrs. Williams was untruthful and unreliable, that it was her habit to appeal to sympathy by showing a sore limb.   Morris, a crippled boy, was the only wage-earner in the family, his father being idle.   The church which had assisted refused further aid, but three years later this church again asked investigation, at which time it was learned that the income of the family, partly from charitable sources, was about $65 a month.

After a lapse of another two years, two more charitable agencies had become interested. The eldest daughter, whose name had not previously been given, had married a theatrical manager, who aided the family at intervals. The children had been taught to ask aid from different sources. The two agencies that had first come into contact with the family had now dropped them entirely, while another relief society reported that the family had actually refused aid from them.

In the following year, a Roman Catholic and a Scotch Presbyterian church reported the family, but Mrs. Williams, when visited, insisted that they were in no need of help. Two years later another and final inquiry came from the relief agency, whose secretary had said, fifteen years before, that she feared that the family was becoming dependent.

Jennings, Charles and Victorine. Mr. Jennings had been a broker in Wall Street, and had failed in business. He came of a family described as very respectable. Mrs. Jennings asked for a loan of $100 to help her husband properly place an invention which he had patented. She would give no definite statement, however, nor any address at which she could be visited. It was later reported that she was going in and out of business offices, probably begging. Nothing more was heard of the family for six years. They were then reported by a private citizen as in need of aid, and they applied also themselves at the society's office. Mr. Jennings's three brothers, on request, provided what relief was necessary. Five years later a church was aiding, although the family was known to them under an assumed name. The patent had been sold for $200. A pension was received by the couple from a home for aged persons, and the church continued its care of the family.

Madison, Henry and Martha. Mr. Madison asked assistance, money brought from Virginia having been exhausted. He states his occupation to be that of writer and genealogist and gives satisfactory references. At previous addresses it was found that they have left a somewhat distinguished impression, in spite of the fact that they have often left their rooms when in arrears for rent, and in spite of the fact that they have five dogs which annoyed the neighbors and destroyed the furniture. Mrs. Madison is very haughty and eccentric, and can be seen only at her entire convenience. She would not see a physician when ill. Both Mr. and Mrs. Madison are of distinguished ancestry — the latter an adopted daughter of a prominent citizen of Baltimore. She took an active part in aiding Confederate soldiers during the war. The family writes begging letters to distant relatives and to persons having some acquaintance with their family, often giving false addresses and assumed names. Aid was given to the family by a relief society, on account of illness.

Hogan, Jane, is a widow with a daughter, actress and playwright, and a son a clerk. Mrs. Hogan called at the suggestion of the editors of a daily newspaper, presenting a letter from a friend in Cincinnati describing the condition of her son Charles, who was ill and in apparent need of his mother's care. On the following day, however, a letter was received indicating that the son was better, and Mrs. Hogan decided not to go to him, but asked assistance in securing employment for herself and daughter.

In a short time the family removed to an unknown address, but appeared again after an interval of eleven years, at which time the son was seeking employment as assistant stage manager, and the daughter Lillian had given up acting, and was then writing plays. She was also an " expert typewriter." She had been cheated out of royalties, and, owing to her brother's illness, all the savings of the family had been expended. The mother had been working as seamstress for actresses, but was unable at the moment to obtain any such work. She could also do plain dressmaking, and asked aid in this direction. The family was paying $25 a month rent, and was dependent upon what was earned from day to day for expenses. This information was set forth in a letter addressed to a lady of large means, who requested investigation, and the statements were corroborated.

Eight months later a similar request was received from another multimillionnaire to whom an application had

R

been made, and on being visited Mrs. Hogan said that for nearly a year she had had almost no income, and her son had been idle for two years, and had been blind, although as a result of an operation he was now able to see a little. Lillian had dramatized two novels, which had secured her an income of $100 a week, although she had had to pay large commissions. Mrs. Hogan was earning five dollars a week making kimonos. She had secured three loans on her furniture, afterwards converted into a single loan of $75. The daughter had also borrowed various sums, $45 to $50 at a time, and $20 worth of clothing had been pawned. Her present request had been for a loan of about $200 from which to repay other creditors, but there was no definite assurance that this loan could be repaid, or that it would leave the family with any adequate means of support.

Mrs. Hogan at this time was described as very quiet and refined in manner, personally attractive, with white hair and delicate appearance. There were a great many pretty ornaments and pictures in the apartment, and the rooms were artistically furnished. There were oranges on the sideboard, and no signs of destitution. At an earlier address it was ascertained that the family had been dispossessed, for the reason that, although they paid the rent promptly, Mrs. Hogan always insisted on many alterations and repairs each time that the rent was paid. Although quiet, and otherwise desirable tenants, they were " fussy."

It was ascertained that the Actor's Fund had not aided the family. A gentleman who had been instrumental in placing Lillian's dramatizations, and who had advanced money to her, was interviewed. This gentleman repudiated the idea that he was in any way charitably inclined, or that he was personally interested in this family. He insisted that it was a good business investment to loan them money. He had found it profitable personally to make advances, and he expected that it would continue to be profitable. At the time of the interview Lillian owed him $95, half of which, however, was secured by royalties. His books showed that $1400 had been paid to her at various times during 1900, in sums ranging from $45 to $95, and in the year following, $700. He had re-

cently been annoyed by receiving long, fulsome letters of
thanks from Mrs. Hogan, not asking for help, but hinting
that they were having a hard time. To these he paid no
attention.

Blockley, Matilda, widow, and her daughter *Victoria*,
have been known through a period of five years. Both
mother and daughter were high tempered, and quarrelled
so frequently and violently that they were often obliged
to move. They begged assistance from all available
sources. The mother refused to do any work, and the
daughter accepted only what pleased her fancy, and retained no position long because of her inefficiency. She
had a fairly good voice, and insisted that means should
be provided for training that she might go upon the oper-
atic stage. She had sung in the chorus of several church
choirs, and claimed to have taken lessons of a prominent
musician, which, however, the latter denied.

Mrs. Blockley admitted that she had relatives in Germany who had sent her money, but refused to give their
addresses. One church worker reported the family as
"first-class beggars," and seven Protestant churches, one
Catholic church, one physician, two daily newspapers, the
Department of Public Charities, and a hospital, had occasion to make inquiries about them. No improvement in
the family was accomplished, and the record closes with
Mrs. Blockley's death.

Doyer, George and Clara. This record covers, with some
intervals, a period of sixteen years. Originally Mr. Doyer
asked assistance in getting work. Inquiry showed that
they were improvident. They were, however, aided by
four different agencies, besides receiving free coal each winter from the city. Seven years after the first application
the family was referred by a private citizen, who had given
them aid. Mr. Doyer was then described by references as
a good workman, although it was found on a closer investigation that he had worked only irregularly, and was
somewhat addicted to drink. One child, said to be blind,
had been treated at a dispensary, and Mrs. Doyer's married sister was aiding the family. The eldest daughter,

who had been in an institution, was brought home to care for the children, while her father and mother worked.

A younger brother and sister were arrested in the following year for selling papers at night. This led to much newspaper publicity and offers of aid for the family from various directions.

A few years later another private citizen reported the family and in the same year Mr. Doyer died, leaving insurance amounting to $1000 or $1500. The blind boy, William, was attending day classes at the blind asylum. Soon afterwards, Mrs. Doyer, whose morality was questioned by her neighbors, married, and her new husband committed suicide within six months.

Two years later, still bearing the name of Doyer, she applied for aid, and it was found that at this time two relief societies and a settlement were interested. The two daughters who have been referred to, now both married, refused to help their mother because of her improper life.

William had been dismissed from the asylum "as not needing special instruction, as he could see, and as he was incorrigible." Mrs. Doyer was offered work in the laundry, but she refused it.

Ringole, Emma, a blind woman, has received the annual pension from the city for eight years, and her parents were known to have received aid for more than twenty. Until the death of Emma's mother one demented brother remained at home with her, and another, also insane, was an inmate of a state hospital. The father, although worthless and intemperate, earned a little as light caretaker in a church.

Seven years after the first indication of dependence a married daughter was giving two dollars a week for the support of the family, while Mrs. Ringole's sister, living in another state, a charitable society, and two benevolent ladies were each giving five dollars a month. Clothing was provided by private individuals.

Emma, besides receiving the blind pension, gave each year a public concert, sending out tickets in advance accompanied by begging letters. The relief society, after aiding for a time, became convinced that relief was prov-

ing harmful to the family. After the mother's death the
letters accompanying the concert tickets continued to say
that the writer was supporting her, as well as the imbecile
brothers, who were in fact in the state hospital. One of
the private donors announced that she had provided for
Emma, and that no more begging letters would be sent,
but they continued uninterruptedly.

Muchmore, William and Sarah. Mrs. Muchmore was
known to a charitable society eighteen years ago, at which
time she was aided with groceries. Later her first husband
died, and she remarried.

The record for the family for the years following is
a series of evictions for non-payment of rent and other
reasons. Mrs. Muchmore had found this a good opportunity to beg, placing herself and children with the furniture in the street, and thereby attracting the sympathy
of passers-by. Mrs. Muchmore's story to such sympathizers was that her husband had deserted, or that he was
looking for work. In reality he was, however, usually
visiting the newspaper offices, enlisting the interest of the
press in the wider publication of their pitiable condition.
Much assistance was received by these methods, and the
family lived well. They were frequently dispossessed for
drunkenness and fighting, as well as for immorality.

Through the intervention of a private society the three
children were committed to an institution. The family
passed under numerous aliases, were known to many
charitable agencies and churches, and were often established in new rooms, and their rent paid. Mr. Muchmore used a few wood-yard tickets, but he was frequently
arrested for assault and disorderly conduct, and at various
times imprisoned. Mrs. Muchmore's father was a begging
pedler, and lived with her. Her sister, who had several
aliases, lived an immoral life, and aided in the general
begging schemes. When Mrs. Muchmore was not dispossessed, she was usually begging in the street with a baby,
often under pretence of selling pencils. Mrs. Muchmore's
grandfather was shiftless, and of no help to the family.

Mrs. Muchmore was finally arrested and committed to
the workhouse for three months. Her husband disap-

peared, in fear of arrest, but later requested news of the
children, when it was found that he had given a false
address.

De Vaudremont, Felix, a political exile, of the French
nobility, had exhausted his means, and was at the
time of application teaching French. He had received
assistance from several private individuals, and now requested aid in securing pupils.

Nine months later the family was referred to a charitable agency by a private citizen who had aided. M. de
Vaudremont had been librarian at a denominational club,
but was dismissed for inefficiency. Two hundred and
fifty dollars had been given him with which to return to
France, but this he had later refused to do. He is
something of a geologist and botanist, and the valuable
collection which he had made in his travels was gradually
disposed of to meet expenses. A son, Henri, was a stamp
and coin expert, and made a little money in this direction,
and also by doing some clerical work, but he was nearly
blind. One daughter, Louise, was blind, and at one time
received the city blind pension, but this had been discontinued, as her father refused treatment for her, whereupon
he had written a letter of protest to the governor of the
state. Another daughter, Madeline, was not allowed to
do any work except to give occasional French lessons, and
any other ambitions of his children were repressed. M. de
Vaudremont insisted upon living in high-priced apartments, and in having his rent supplied by friends and
charitable societies. He had received aid from a national
society, as well as other private societies, a church, and
several private individuals. By some he was thought to
be demented, as his idea was that he was being persecuted.
At one time he had been summoned to court on a charge
of libel made against him by the almoner of a society
which had aided him.

Six years later, when visited, the family had received
money from France, and did not need other assistance.

Blake, Grace. Until she was eighteen years old Grace
Blake lived with her father and mother and sisters in a

little English hamlet. The father was a hard-working
stoker on canal-boats, and the family apparently honest
and decent. When Grace was eighteen, an older sister,
who had married and was living in America, made a visit
to her old home. She found that Grace caused anxiety to her parents on account of her general disobedience and her habit of "being out nights," and offered to
take her back with her to America, in the hope that new
surroundings would have a favorable influence. For six
years Grace made her home with this sister, taking a position at service from time to time, but never staying long in
one place. Finally she stopped going back to the sister or
even writing to her, and the sister, being a poor woman
with four small children, living in a small Long Island town,
lost track of her until she learned from a relief society that
a former employer of Grace's had taken her to the
society.

She was a very small, slight girl, pale and thin, and, to
all appearances, of a childlike innocence. Though twenty-
one years old she looked not more than fifteen. She was
not strong enough to do heavy household work and was
much below the average in intelligence. Her employers
generally found her quiet and docile, but with no memory,
and sometimes in a dazed condition. In her sister's
home and in a home for the friendless, in which she was
placed later, she was stubborn and disobedient, quiet, but
wholly uncontrollable.

Soon after her first application for assistance she became
ill, and found care in a hospital from which she was sent
to a home for girls. She did well here for a few weeks in
the cooking and sewing classes, and in her general conduct, but soon became unmanageable. At the end of five
months she left the home on pretext of going to the society
to which she had applied originally. It was learned later,
through a letter from a probation officer to her sister, that
she was in the workhouse. She had been found in a vacant
lot with a number of men in the middle of the night, and
committed for three months as a disorderly person. At
this point communication with her relatives in England
was established through the offices of the charity organization society nearest the village in which they lived.

The old father and mother were found to be anxious to get Grace back, and a sister contributed toward the expenses of the journey. Arrangements were made with the Salvation Army to look after her when she was discharged, and with a society especially interested in English women and girls to provide for her journey home. The date for sailing was set, but unfortunately she had a serious illness after leaving the workhouse, and was obliged to spend several weeks in hospitals. As soon as she was able to travel, however, the postponed plan was carried out. She was received at the home from which she had run away six months before for a few days of rest and convalescence, a suitable wardrobe was gotten together from several sources, and her sister and a representative of the society saw her on board the boat. The sister also sent $5 to the old father to enable him to meet Grace in Liverpool. Word was received from the English charity organization society referred to above that he had been there to meet the boat and take her home. A letter written after Grace had been at home several weeks states that she is surrounded by kindness, and that although she is sometimes restless she is growing more contented. The case is of interest not only because of the satisfactory outcome considering its difficulties but because of the coöperation required from such a variety of agencies.

Greenwood, Arthur H. Mr. Greenwood, at the age of sixty-eight, with a prosperous early life to look back upon, is unable to support himself and his wife. Gradually he has lost his standing with the stock brokers and bankers who formerly made up his business circle, and for years he has been a curbstone broker of no reputation. According to his relatives he "has at all times burned the candle at both ends" and "has been subject to all vices." He has a physical disability which unfits him for hard work, and he is familiar with nothing outside his old business. He speculates whenever he can get his hands on any money. Recently he was engaged in a transaction of doubtful character which he feared might get him in prison.

Mrs. Greenwood is ten years younger than her husband. She is a nervous, hysterical, dependent woman, with an

attractive manner.   There are two children by a former
marriage.   Both are married and live in towns near by.

When a few weeks ago Mr. Greenwood applied to his
children and other relatives for aid in keeping him out of
prison, the son, the daughter's husband, and a well-to-do
nephew formed themselves into a committee to provide
for his needs.   They are actuated chiefly by family pride
and a desire to protect his children and grandchildren,
rather than any other motive.   They asked a charitable
society to act as their intermediary — investigating the
case to find what ought to be done, and drawing upon
them for the necessary funds, but keeping their identity
secret.   They were ready to undertake permanent responsibility for Mr. Greenwood apart from his wife, but
they did not wish to deal directly with him.

Acquaintance with the Greenwoods, which has developed
since, has brought out the fact that Mrs. Greenwood has a
brother in comfortable circumstances who, to all appearances, would be able to provide for her.   In this family
also there are stories of business reverses, which, as they
are attributed to Mr. Greenwood, have caused strained
relations between the two families.   Because of this
"strong feeling," Mrs. Greenwood's brother has· been
unwilling for the past year to help her and her husband,
but there are indications that he might be persuaded, in
combination with other relatives, to look out for his sister
if she were unencumbered, just as Mr. Greenwood's relatives are willing to provide for him apart from his wife.

The solution, therefore, seems to lie in getting Mr.
Greenwood into a home where he will be properly cared
for, the expense being borne by his relatives, and in throwing the responsibility for Mrs. Greenwood on her relatives.
The obstacle in the way is the opposition of both the persons
chiefly concerned.   They have been married twenty-five
years and object to being separated, and Mr. Greenwood
seems unalterably opposed to entering an institution.

Piper, Bertha.   About two years ago Mrs. Piper asked
to have two of her three children placed in an institution.
It was found that she had been deserted by her second
husband eighteen months before, and that since then she

had supported the family by janitor's work and a little sewing and washing. She was not strong, she had not had nourishing food, the work had been far beyond her powers, and she had finally broken down. She was very loath to part with any of her children, but knew no other way of getting along. Her husband had been intemperate and brutal, and she hoped she would never see him again.

She was sent to the seashore with all the children for two weeks, and came back much improved. For several weeks her rent was paid, and she met the other expenses by washing. Then she decided it would be better to take a janitor's position again, and did so without consulting the society that had been helping her. Here she found again that the work was too hard, and it was discovered that she was keeping her oldest child, a girl of twelve, at home to help her with housework and sewing, and that both were working until late at night. She was persuaded to give up the janitor's work and move into more healthful rooms. Since then she has been vacillating between the two modes of existence — taking a janitor's position only to find that her health would not stand it, and that it forced her to give up her outside work, and then moving into rooms upstairs, relying on washing and days' work, and accepting outside help toward the rent. At each change she takes new heart, and thinks that she will surely be able to get along comfortably by the new arrangement. The little girl goes to school intermittently, and does well when she is sent. The main features in the situation are the woman's unwillingness to be dependent on outside help, except as a last resort, and her heroic efforts to provide for her children.

The three following cases fairly illustrate the difficulties encountered by a widower with children, and by those who would endeavor to help them. The separation of the children from the father after the death of the mother is, as a rule, the easiest and most obvious course, but in some instances, as in the first one cited, it is found practicable to keep the family together.

Avallone, Marcello, who lost his wife two or three weeks after the birth of their last child, upon the advice of friends applied for the commitment of three of his children. He was a stone mason by trade, and earned four dollars a day, but had had only irregular work for some months, and at the time of application it was difficult for him to get work at all. There were six children, including the baby. The eldest boy, Vincenzo, nineteen years of age, was foreman in a tailoring establishment, and earned about eleven dollars a week, from which he contributed $9 a week for household expenses. A sister, Carmela, who was fifteen years of age, looked after the children and helped her father in the care of the house. Angelo, the second boy, was learning tailoring, but received no wage. At the time of application Angelo's age was falsely given, Mr. Avallone having been advised by his friends to make him appear younger in order to simplify commitment.

Fifty dollars of the seventy needed to meet the expense of his wife's funeral had been borrowed from friends, and this they were endeavoring to repay. It was learned from the lessee at a former residence, who spoke highly of the family, that he had offered to take one of Mr. Avallone's children, but to this he had refused his consent. After some conferences and advice, Mr. Avallone gladly consented to keep his home together, and sent the two younger girls, to whom a private society gave suitable clothing, back to school. As the rent was too high, the family was removed to cheaper rooms, and the month-old baby, through the efforts of a charitable society, was placed out at board in a private family.

Schultz, Frederick, whose wife died of cancer a few weeks after the birth of a child, who also died, suffered from locomotor ataxia, and was living at home with one child. He had received treatment at various hospitals, and had spent much money in private treatment, but doctors held out no hope of recovery. His right foot and leg were badly affected, as were also his eyes, particularly the right one. Mr. Schultz had been employed as a grocery clerk, but was now unable to do such work. At one time he had kept a small store, but was unsuccessful, and he finally sold out for about $50. His brother took charge of this sum, together with a little money he had saved, giving to Mr. Schultz whatever was needed. This brother had also aided to some extent from his own means.

When first taken ill Mr. Schultz belonged to a German lodge, which gave him five dollars a week. This was afterward reduced to one, and finally ceased altogether. His father-in-law, who was said to be extremely poor, lived with him for a time, but afterward went to live with his daughter, who is unable to give any assistance to Mr. Schultz. At the time of his wife's death four of the children were committed to an asylum, the youngest girl, aged ten, remaining at home to assist her father and to attend school. Mr. Schultz did washing for a neighbor, earning a dollar a week, and had a roomer who paid another dollar. Some of the furniture he had sold to buy food. A nurse from a private society visited him, and aid was given in various ways. Later he received treatment for his eyes from a specialist, a national society aided, and diet-kitchen tickets were given. Two months after this he was ill with stomach trouble. The national society continued to provide food and also supplied coal. A month after this Mr. Schultz secured temporary work at from fifty to seventy-five cents a week. The church gave clothing and shoes, and coal was supplied by a private agency. Soon afterward he was ill with grippe, and at that time a society provided food, a doctor, and one dollar every other week. The next month Mr. Schultz was ill again, and the nurse, who continued to visit, gave diet-kitchen tickets, vichy, and coal. Later, suffering from abscesses, he was treated at a dispensary. He had no work, and received fifty cents a week and food from the church. Coal was supplied by a private agency, and an individual who had become interested also aided. At this time Mr. Schultz was taking vapor baths at home. A few months later he was much improved in health. His lodger had left, and he was doing some shoe mending, washing, and peddling. The brother, who was a baker, gave bread occasionally, but no other assistance.

Skidmore, Ernest and Alice. The family first came to notice sixteen years ago, at which time Mrs. Skidmore

expected confinement. She refused to go to a hospital
and a doctor was sent by a private agency. Mr. Skidmore
was a bartender, but was idle most of the time. Two
months later the family removed, and Mrs. Skidmore made
application for employment. An offer of work was secured
for her at twelve dollars a month and board but she
refused it. Work was also offered in a laundry, but this,
too, Mrs. Skidmore declined. Two years later Mrs. Skidmore was referred to a private society by an individual
to whom she had applied, and to whom she was known as
a persistent beggar. At this time her husband was working
only in the summer, and during the remainder of the year
lived upon what his wife earned.

Twelve years after this Mr. Skidmore applied for
assistance. His wife had died two years before, and he
was out of work. The eldest son, Thomas, had been
employed in a dry-goods house for seven years, but had
been discharged for mischievous behavior three months
previous to application. The two younger boys were
working, and earned $2.50 a week. A private individual
who had aided the family constantly in various ways, and
had at times given as much as $15 a week, was still called
upon for aid by the youngest boy. Mr. Skidmore suffered
from kidney disease, and was not inclined to work. Employment was secured for Thomas by his father, but he
refused to take it, and spent most of his time at the church
to which he belonged. A month later the family was again
referred by the private individual who had previously aided,
and who was still being annoyed by daily requests for aid
from the youngest boy. Of these requests Mr. Skidmore said he had no knowledge, nor had he received any
of the money, but thought that his son was working. It
was learned that the boy, when employed, had not worked
satisfactorily, had made frequent excuses for absence, and
had been generally unreliable. A few days later he was
arrested for stone throwing.

Two months later Mr. Skidmore died of apoplexy, and
relatives paid the funeral expenses. Thomas secured
employment on Long Island at seven dollars a week, and
John, the second boy, was also employed, at three dollars
a week. All three boarded with relatives on Long Island,

paying six dollars a week each, toward which expense the individual already interested contributed.

Dr. Leffingwell opens his book on Illegitimacy with the following paragraph : —

"Against the background of history, too prominent to escape the observation from which it shrinks, stands a figure, mute, mournful, indescribably sad. It is a girl, holding in her arms the blessing and burden of motherhood, but in whose face one finds no traces of maternal joy and pride. There is scarcely a great writer of fiction who has not somewhere introduced this figure, in the shifting panorama of romance, appealing for pity to a world which never fails to compassionate imaginary woes ; now it is Effie Deans in the Heart of Midlothian, now Fantine, resting by the roadside with Cosette in her arms, or Hester Prynne, pressing little Pearl against the scarlet letter, as she listens from the pillory to the sermon of Mr. Dimmesdale. Who is this woman so pitiable, yet so scorned ? It is the mother of the illegitimate child. By forbidden paths she has attained the grace of maternity, but its glory is for her transfigured into a badge of unutterable shame."

Mrs. Anna T. Wilson, in a discussion on the Care of Foundlings and Illegitimate Children at the International Conference of Charities, in 1893, quoted this paragraph, describing it as both pathetic and prophetic — prophetic of a juster era, when the prototypes of the Cosettes and Fantines of to-day shall have faded altogether from the earth ; pathetic, that it should be necessary to plead the sacredness of all motherhood, the divinity of all children.

Two illustrations, differing widely, although both working out fairly well in the end, may be cited : —

Webster, Clara, was an unmarried mother of twenty-eight years, whose child at the time of application was one month old. For thirteen years Clara had lived as a domestic with a family in the south, where she had gone upon her mother's death when her own home was broken up. The father of her child was a relative of this family, a

man of good standing, who was afterward elected to a high
political office.   As the easiest solution the family sent
the girl north, and here her baby was born in one of the
city's maternity hospitals.   She was then compelled to
seek employment.   Her right hand was deformed, and
this prevented her taking work in which very much use of
the hand would be essential.   A private agency, however,
secured a position for her with her child in the country.
Here she was regarded as "invaluable," for she proved
efficient and faithful during a period in which there was
much illness in the family with whom she lived.   For
nine months she remained in this position, at the end of
which time, her baby being ill, another situation was obtained for her at a convalescent home, where the baby was
admitted as a patient.   From here she removed to a second convalescent home, as the child was still delicate.
After leaving the home a situation was again obtained for
Clara with her child, in which she remained until the following spring, when she returned to the convalescent
home at eight dollars a month.   Here she stayed for the
season, the child improving much in health.   For three
years situations in various places were obtained for her,
all of which she filled in a most satisfactory way.   She
finally obtained a position in the country, in which she
remained for five years.   The family thought much of
her and were fond of the child, and she did her work well.
At the end of the five years she was married to a widower
who lived in the same town, a mechanic of good character,
who has made a happy home for Clara and her child.

Murphy, Kate, also an unmarried mother with a three
months' old child, was rather more difficult to deal with, as
she persistently gave different names and told conflicting
stories each time she visited the office of the private
agency which was trying to place her in a situation.   It
was learned that Kate had already had one or two other
children, of whom she managed to get rid, and it was only
as a last resource, when every effort to discard her baby
had failed, that she made her application.   She was untruthful, difficult to manage, and stubbornly reticent, giving no information whatever in any direction which might

help to facilitate action.   A situation was secured for
her in the country with her child, and although she at
first rebelled against having to leave the city, under the
kindness and good influence of the family with whom she
was placed, she became gradually reconciled to her position and worked faithfully and well, taking every care of
her child.   A year later, owing to a death in the family
which had engaged her, the home was broken up.   Kate
had no difficulty in obtaining another position, three or
four families being anxious to have her, and she finally
went into a doctor's family in a neighboring town, where
she remained working satisfactorily, and her baby doing
well.   The agency which had secured her the first situation has kept in constant touch with her both by correspondence and personal visits, and Kate is duly appreciative
of the opportunity given her.

Information concerning homeless men asking for meals
and lodgings is usually meagre.   The following instances
are typical of those in which some information is obtained.

Davis, James, after unsuccessfully seeking work, and
being homeless, applied for assistance to enable him to
earn enough to release his clothing from pawn.   He was
able to do only light work, as he was not strong, and had
for a short time been a patient in the tuberculosis ward of
a public hospital.   Mr. Davis was provided with meals
and lodgings, and light temporary work as night watchman was secured for him.   This, however, he found to be
trying, owing to bad air and his inability to sleep during
the day.   A few days after his application a college friend
provided him with a ticket for Colorado and a letter
insuring work for him upon his arrival there.

Curran, Patrick, a homeless man, asked assistance in
securing suitable clothing and shoes.   He had obtained
a position as porter in a hotel at $25 a month.   For four
years he had been ill with rheumatism, and this had
interfered with his work.   He had lately, however, received
treatment and was much improved.   Previous to his illness
he had held good positions, and all references spoke well

of him.   The clothing was supplied and meals and lodgings were also given.   After working for two days Mr. Curran was discharged, as the man formerly employed in the position had returned.   Work was secured for him at another hotel with a wage of $30 a month and meals, but this he was forced to give up as he had to work in a badly ventilated basement.   A few days later, having been supplied with meals and lodgings while looking for work, Mr. Curran secured another position where he was paid twenty dollars a month and meals.

Peterson, Horatio, made application upon his return from Florida, where he had been sent by the minister of a church, and where he had found it impossible to get work, none but colored help being employed.   He had formerly worked in a restaurant in New York, the keeper of which, a colored woman, said that he was quarrelsome and could not get along with the other servants.   She also accused him of having stolen $100 with which he had gone to Philadelphia, he continually annoying her after his return.   He had also been employed at one or two private residences, where a favorable opinion was held of him, except that he was considered at times to be mentally unbalanced, and at such times interfered with the other servants.   It was learned that his mother was an inmate of an insane asylum, and that he also had spent some months there.   At one time also he had served a short term in prison.

The following are fairly typical of the great variety of cases arising in an effective enforcement of the laws for the suppression of vagrancy and mendicancy.

Johnson, Dave, is a full-blooded negro, twenty-one years of age, of hardly more than rudimentary intelligence.   He has been known in New York, for two years and a half, as a professional beggar of the "sidewalk" variety.   When a boy, he had lost one leg at the knee as a result of the practice of stealing short rides on trains.   This disability was his most valuable asset in the pursuit of his chosen occupation.

s

Since September, 1901, he has been seven times arrested for vagrancy in New York City, and three times sentenced to six months in the workhouse. It has been found that he has served terms in other cities for shop-lifting and pocket-picking, and once for petit larceny. In different places he has been elevator boy, bootblack, newsboy, driver, and errand boy, and could work well under proper direction, but would not keep at anything steadily. A letter written from the workhouse implies that he found begging profitable, for he says : "When arrested I had but four pennies in my possession, and the officers claimed they had been watching me three hours ; you see easily that this is a falsehood, for if I was begging, I would have had much more money than that."

Attempts to start Johnson in a legitimate business at the end of his terms in the workhouse have failed, and he has become increasingly violent in his threats against the mendicancy officers — and in his deeds. During one of the periods when he was in durance for vagrancy, he stabbed a fellow-prisoner in the knee. Recently, when a mendicancy officer was about to arrest him, he struck the officer with his crutch, stunning him for a moment, and in the scuffle that followed bit his forehead. As a result of this, Johnson has been convicted of assault in the second degree and sent to State's Prison for five years. In pronouncing sentence in this case, the court made use of the following language : —

"You have been convicted upon the testimony of officers assigned to the Charity Organization Society, one of the most useful and deserving organizations of this city. It is their work to investigate those who are in need, and when they find that applicants are in need, to see that relief is supplied. They are also keeping the streets of the city clear of professional beggars, and in this they deserve the utmost sympathy and support of the community. It is not often that their cases come into this high court, but I wish the officers of the society to understand that when this does happen, they will have here every consideration and assistance which it is within our power to give. They inform me that you are a professional beggar; that you have been convicted of vagrancy and other offences ; that you have served a term in the King's County Penitentiary; that while a prisoner recently on Hart's Island, on a charge of vagrancy, you made an assault upon a fellow-prisoner. While their officers, in the proper discharge of their duty, were attempting to arrest you for vagrancy on this occasion, you committed a vicious assault, and it is upon this charge that you have been convicted. If you are to be supported by charity, the place in which you should be supported is the State's Prison, and I have decided to give you the longest sentence which the law permits for your offence. You are sentenced to five years in State's Prison."

Hagerman, James. When James Hagerman was eight years old his mother died, and his father soon married again — a woman whom the boy did not like. He does not say that she mistreated him, but that he stole from her and struck her, and at the mature age of nine left home and began to support himself by begging. A fall which he had when still a small boy resulted in the loss of one leg above the knee. He drifted to New York, where he sold papers and begged, living at a newsboys' lodging-house, until he fell into the hands of the law and was sent to a reformatory for five years. A position in a tailor shop was found for him on his discharge, but he did not keep it long. His employer one day taunted him with his recent experience on the Island and he left. Very soon he was arrested for stealing a truck load of goods, and received a maximum sentence of five years. At Elmira his record was poor, and he was kept there four years and six months, and then transferred to a penitentiary to finish his sentence. After his release from prison he worked for a while at shoemaking, the trade he had learned at Elmira, but soon went back to begging. Before he had been out a year he was sentenced to three months for vagrancy, and within six months after finishing that term to another six months.

Meanwhile he had married a girl of his own class, called Nell, but they soon drifted apart. On the occasion of the latest arrest for vagrancy he made a strong plea for a chance to begin over, and it was given him. After severing connections with Nell, who afterwards went to live

with another man, he had "taken up" with a girl named
Maggie, whose husband was then in jail awaiting trial.
In their circle of acquaintances there is nothing unusual
in these casual relations, but James and Maggie seem
genuinely attached to each other. It was felt that both
had been unfortunate in their surroundings and that, with
a new chance, both might yet lead decent lives. In spite
of James's history he still, at twenty-nine, "makes a favorable impression." He is far from the wretched, cower-
ing creature that is so often the product of a prison career.
He is not only spirited, but good natured and optimistic,
and has a most attractive vein of manliness. Children
are fond of him. He carries with him at all times a German army button which his father used to wear, and he
likes to tell of his father's part in the Franco-Prussian
war. He is rather seriously disabled. Besides lacking
one leg entirely, he has a bullet in one arm, and his remaining leg has been repeatedly broken and operated on.
He is, however, skilful with his hands. He was established by friends in a suitable locality ; he was supplied
with the tools and materials of his trade, and has hung
out his cobbler's sign. He gets some work, and two
cousins who have been discovered help him a little, though
they are themselves poor.

D'Arago, Katharine. For twenty years Madame d'Arago
has been supporting herself by devices of unusual ingenuity and coming, from time to time and by various chances,
to the notice of the Charity Organization Society. In
1886, when she first asked help from the society, it was
found that she had received some assistance from another
source in 1882; she had begun writing begging letters,
and she had pawned the blankets in the house where she
had been staying and "had to leave." At that time she
stated that she had been in America only six months.
The next year it was learned that she had recently finished
a two years' term in the State's Prison to which she had
been sentenced in 1884 for immoral traffic, carried on
under the name of the Countess della Grada, clairvoyant.
Her history, previous to 1884, is difficult to unravel.
With a fair degree of consistency she claimed to be an

Austrian of noble family, and she always said that her husband was an Englishman, and that she expected help from his relatives and her other English friends. In regard to the number of years that she had been in America, however, the date of her husband's death, and the number, ages, and residences of her children, she made hopelessly conflicting statements. It is known that at the time of her consignment to the penitentiary she had a daughter nine years old who was taken in charge by the Society for the Prevention of Cruelty to Children. Ten years later she claimed to have two children, fifteen and thirteen years of age, in an institution in the country. In one of the letters written in 1896 she said that she had married in Rome and had one child living there. She frequently referred vaguely to her "only son," who had died. Generally she said that she had come to America as companion to an English woman, of various names, three or four years before the time of the statement. She was always prodigal of references, which could seldom be traced. When she introduced herself to the Charity Organization Society, she had many foreign letters of recommendation and said that she knew six modern languages and music. Letters are on file written in Italian and German as well as in English. The English is that of a foreigner, and both English and Italian are used in such a way as to indicate that they have been acquired by the "natural method" rather than in the class room. In whatever language she writes she displays a facility of expression, especially in her vituperation against the Charity Organization Society, that might be envied.

The year following her first application, that is, in 1887, she again asked for help, on the ground that she was caring for a dying sister and her children. It was found on investigation that the sister's husband was able to provide for her and that a relief society was aiding. When the sister died, a month later, Madame d'Arago asked for money for the funeral expenses. The request was refused, as the sisters in charge of the hospital where the woman had died were willing to arrange for the burial. This exhausted Madame d'Arago's patience with organized charity, and thenceforward she studied to evade it, and was increasingly chagrined when she found that many of her appeals, even if far afield, led back to the same office. On one occasion she got the money by means of a letter addressed to a prominent citizen, whereupon she wrote a most abusive letter to the society and called on the secretary. In this letter, and several similar ones written later, she exhausts her vocabulary of reviling and insulting epithets.

Although she evidently hoped that she had at that time severed connections with the society, the records give a fairly connected account of her activities since. She seems to have been unable to win confidence, and of late years her first request has frequently been received with suspicion. From institutions, from societies of every religious affiliation, from newspapers, and from individuals of prominence in the city, and, recently because, as she says, "there's no mercy, no charity, for a helpless woman in this big and wealthy city," from citizens of national reputation have come inquiries in regard to this woman.

Her attitude toward any attempt to help her, aside from giving her what she asks for, is best seen in the letters she writes to the visitors. The letters she leaves at her "address," where she can never be seen, to be given to the "Lady Visitor" who "will call again." For these visitors she expresses elsewhere the utmost scorn: "They are such very fancy ladies." "Gentlemen as a rule," she says in one letter, "have more soul and feeling as women"; and in another, "As for those women, I hate them all." "Pray don't go house for house to make me a public charity." "Pray use discretion." "I am so sorry that ye have taken so much trouble to go al around to publish me as a Pauper. I would rather have starve than have such imprudent Young Ladies state my circumstances to the public. Safe your neighbor! especially from public slander. What did you do? Went around to fetch ignorant children to find me? Is this the principle of your employment? Pray safe me further investigation. I prize my peace above your promises." In the same letter an interesting note is supplied by her report of the distress of the family with which she was living at the moment.

In 1889 she asked for help at a convent on the ground that she secured converts to the Roman Catholic faith.

She took with her a man — apparently a German — for whom she tried to get assistance. This is the first recorded instance of the practice she later developed into a profession, of acting as an agent for her unfortunate acquaintances. A few years later she seems to have turned to proselyting in another direction, for she was writing to a Protestant clergyman : " I would wish God would help me to raise an Italian chapel and school in East New York in the Episcopal Faith. I could canvass two hundred to three hundred Italians together with their children who now go to no religious worship." In a later communication she assures him : " I am able to unite forty families and more than two hundred Italians, to join a more intelligent religion."

For most of the time since 1893 she has lived among the Italians, getting a lodging and meals wherever she could, in return for services rendered to them. It has rarely been possible to find her " home," as the address she gives is generally a bank, a bakery, or a saloon, where she receives her mail and meets her clients. She says that at one time she was at service in Brooklyn. For a while she lived at a Salvation Army lodging-house under the name of Bertha Klein, but generally she has kept to the Italian colony in which she was found in 1893. In 1894 she was living with an aged Italian to whom she referred in terms of respect as the Reverend Doctor, and apparently conducting a saloon for the Italians of the neighborhood, advertising a bureau of information where she gave general advice and carried on the business of notary, commissioner of deeds, and railway agent.

The list of occupations in which she has been engaged is long. According to her own account she has been — as occasion demanded — travelling companion, teacher of languages and music, translator, interpreter for the policemen on the block, book canvasser, seamstress, maid, nurse, typewriter, factory hand, cook, general servant in a boarding-house (where she was obliged to " peal al potatoes for twenty boarders ") and " Missionary with the family of Rev. Dr. W. in Rome and the Orient." Her most constant source of revenue, however, has been derived from the profession she developed for herself. She made herself acquainted with the workings of many charitable agencies in the city, especially institutions for children, and advised her friends where to apply for aid whenever they wanted it. If her clients succeeded in getting what they asked for, she would accept a fee from them; if not, she would write to the society to which they had applied, saying that they were "bad" and needed nothing. Her specialty was placing out children. She got children into institutions for a consideration of $10 or $15 apiece. She also secured the release of the child from the institution, when that was desired, for $10. Unfortunately for her prosperity, her second application to an institution was apt to arouse suspicion and start an investigation. She also found homes for children in families. This was accomplished through advertisements in the Italian papers, one of which reads: "A poor woman of the province of C——, left a widow with three children, six months, four and six years old, seeks a family which will care for them. They are healthy and very pretty. Address by letter, Mrs. d'Arago, at number 315 Margaret Street." The address given was a saloon kept by a German, who said he allowed her to receive her mail there and meet her applicants, and often gave her something to eat, because she was "so kind to little children who have nobody." As late as 1903 she was still procuring "working papers" for children. When one mother for whom she had performed this service refused to give her as much money as she demanded, she told the little girl's employer that she had tuberculosis and thus brought about her dismissal. Another way in which she used her good offices is revealed in one of her letters asking for money. In enumerating her troubles and misfortunes she says, "And I got an Italian woman out of prison and for reward — she did not pay me."

Several letters addressed by her to the Bureau of Dependent Children seem to indicate that she used her wits against her enemies as vigorously as in behalf of her friends. These letters contain notes on families who have children in institutions, but who, she asserts, are perfectly able to provide for them at home. "Italians," she writes, "import children Daily and get them in Homes; parents who have children in Homes keep Groceries and Beer

saloons; husband works at shovel, — and I will send you
a list next week — Hundreds I know." The promised
list tells how mothers " dress in fine style," and the family
has " fine whiskey, beer, and wines," and lives " luxuri-
antly " while " the City has to pay " for the maintenance
of their children. In regard to one family she is particularly vehement. She writes four pages about them, giving
details of their circumstances and advising as to the best
method of approach in order to confirm her statements ;
for, she says, " All I can help to get you good cases I will,
but you yourself must find out Points to confirm yourself."
The methods of investigation she recommends suggest
that she studied to some purpose the ways of " those
fancy Ladies " who annoyed her so often. These letters
to the Bureau of Dependent Children may be one of her
devices for getting children restored to their parents at
the parents' request. The fact, however, that they were
written while she was living in the Salvation Army lodging-house, as Bertha Klein, point rather to another explanation, — that she took this way of revenging herself
on clients who had not come up to all her demands in the
way of pay. In either case it is entirely possible that she
had helped to place the very children under discussion.

From time to time, in the course of these twenty years,
Madame d'Arago has apparently become discouraged and
thought of Europe with longing. Twice, it is known, she
has obtained money avowedly for a return to Italy or to
England, but she has used it for other purposes. She has
been at times found in wretched surroundings and sick,
as her appeals had stated, but she will never give any
information or allow any investigation of her circumstances. In the last ten years she seems to have become
intemperate, and she has at least once been arrested in a
street fight. On the other hand, there has been no evidence, since the first years, of the kind of immorality with
which she was then charged. In spite of her cleverness
of a certain kind, her ingenuity, and her fund of information in certain directions, she has never been prosperous.
It is clear that life has been hard for her and that she has
suffered much. Not the least pathetic note in her history
is that she seems to have had no friends — to have lived a

stranger among the people she knew so well. There is every evidence that her statement, " I never tell nobody anything of my trouble or suffering," is literally true as applied to her daily associates, though she made notable exceptions to the rule in asking for help from men and women far removed. There is a ring of sincerity in her lament to one of these latter, " These are not my nation."

PART III

HISTORICAL SURVEY

CHAPTER I

THE REFORM OF THE ENGLISH POOR LAW

INASMUCH as the reform of the English Poor Law in 1834 has exercised a unique influence upon all subsequent discussions of the policy of public relief, it is interesting to inquire whether the circumstances under which this reform was brought about were such as to warrant the conclusions ordinarily drawn from it.

The famous report of the Commission of 1832, upon which the reform was based, is a masterpiece of painstaking investigation. It happens also that the history of the English Poor Law has been written by one of the three commissioners charged with the administration of the new law, so that our current interpretation of earlier and later English history is colored by the very views that controlled the reformers of that period.[1]

In a word, the dominating idea of the reform of 1834, which has remained in almost unquestioned supremacy in England and America, is that the lax administration of relief was responsible for the deplorable prevalence of pauperism at that time; and that this is the chief source of danger from which even now the poor must at all hazards be protected. It is curious that not only writers on the poor law,[2] but even economists[3] and historians, in

[1] Nicholls : "History of the English Poor Law."

[2] In thirty years the dependent population, called into existence by the facilities of relief, brought the country to the verge of ruin. — Mackay: "The English Poor." This volume, however, has the merit of discussing the problem of pauperism as an integral part of the social and economic history of the people.

[3] Compare, for example, the description of "the operations of the English Poor Law" in Hadley's "Economics," pp. 53–55. The paragraph on this subject is a part of an admirable discussion of economic responsibility.

referring to this subject, have usually treated it as an entirely detached episode, and yet nothing could be more futile than to attempt to estimate it without reference to the stirring events of the generation in which it occurred. The report of the various commissions and parliamentary committees appointed to inquire into the conditions of particular classes of laborers is perhaps a more authentic and instructive source of information than the report of the Poor Law Commission itself, for the very reason that the attention of the investigators in these other inquiries was not fixed to such an extent upon particular evils and upon the search for their remedy.[1]

At the time when the new commissioners undertook to reform the administration of the Poor Law, England had been at peace for about twenty years. The nation had been partially relieved from the crushing burden of war taxes.[2] The collapse of prices and the violent readjustment made necessary by the close of the Napoleonic wars caused, it is true, severe industrial distress.[3] Within ten years, however, the freedom of commerce from the war embargoes, and the return of capital to the investments and occupations of peace, showed their natural effect. The relations between England and her colonies were greatly altered by the removal of restrictions upon colonial commerce; and treaties were made with Prussia, Denmark, and other European countries, which were most beneficial.[4] The exclusive commercial powers of the East

---

[1] For example: Reports of the Central Board of his Majesty's Commissioners who inquired into the employment of children in factories, 1833.

Report on Enclosures, 1808.

Report of the Select Committee on the State of the Coal Trade, 1830.

Report of the Select Committee on Manufactures, Commerce, and Shipping, 1833.

[2] Early in the present century the Imperial taxes — for the greater part war taxes — amounted to one-fifth of the whole income of the country, whereas now they are not more than one-twentieth, and even of this a great part is spent on education and other benefits which government did not then afford. — Marshall: "Principles of Economics," p. 233.

[3] Never was the United Kingdom in a more parlous state than when the crowning triumph of Wellington placed it at the head of the nation. — Rose: "The Rise of Democracy," p. 15.

[4] Cunningham: "Growth of English Industry and Commerce in Modern Times," p. 593.

India Company were abolished, introducing a régime of free competition in the commerce of the East. Steam power was applied to navigation.[1] The conclusions embodied in the report of the Bullion Committee had been accepted, specie payments had been resumed, and the currency had thus been placed upon a stable basis.[2]

The industrial revolution was complete, the new factory system having replaced the old system of domestic manufactures. The temporary distress caused by the loss of by-occupations for agricultural laborers had passed away, and the national industries had adjusted themselves to the new conditions. Agriculture itself had also undergone a revolution by which the modern system had replaced that which had prevailed with slight changes for centuries. By drainage, fertilization, and the better means of communication, the productiveness of the land had been vastly increased at the very time when the division of labor had been brought about so that those who remained on the farm devoted their energies entirely to farm labor.[3]

In this process individuals undoubtedly suffered, but the nation at large greatly gained.[4] The wasteful system of common holdings had disappeared. The enclosures which

[1] The expansion which has taken place in our foreign commerce was not so much due to the breaking down of [the] old monopolies as to the improvements in the physical means of communication. — Cunningham : "Growth of English Industry and Commerce in Modern Times," p. 596.

[2] How great an effect a change of this kind in the monetary standard of value may have is sufficiently obvious to American students of the period since 1897.

[3] Cunningham : "Growth of English Industry and Commerce in Modern Times," p. 657.

[4] If things were very bad in 1821, they had begun to recover during the next decade, as the Parliamentary Committee of 1833 reported that the general condition of the agricultural laborer in full employment was better than at any former period, and that his money wages gave him a greater command over the comforts of life. — Cunningham : "Growth of English Industry and Commerce in Modern Times," p. 652. Compare with this Marshall's account of the conditions at the beginning of the century : The eighteenth century wore on to its close and the next century began ; year by year the condition of the working classes in England became more gloomy. An astonishing series of bad harvests, a most exhausting war, a change in the methods of industry that dislocated old ties, combined with an injudicious poor law to bring the working classes into the greatest misery they have ever suffered, at all events since the beginning of trustworthy records of English social history. — "Principles of Economics," p. 233.

took place at the end of the eighteenth century and at the
beginning of the nineteenth, while depriving the poor of
rights which they had enjoyed, permitted the introduction
of a more rational use of land, offering great contrasts to
the enclosures which had been so fiercely denounced in
the sixteenth century, and as a result of which grazing as
a rule replaced tillage.[1]

Other changes were made in the first third of the nineteenth century, which, although of a different character,
still exercised a marked influence upon the character of
large elements of the population. In spite of the severe
law against combinations of workingmen the trade-union
movement then made its successful struggle for existence.
Ten years before the Poor Law Commission entered upon
its duties Parliament had passed a bill to repeal all the
combination laws and to legalize trade societies. While
the immediate effect of this repeal was the organization of
a large number of unions, frequent strikes and serious
disturbances, this effect again was temporary; and by the
time which especially concerns us the trade-union movement had become a means of strengthening the position of
the laborer and increasing his wages, and especially had
become a recognized means of preventing the possibility
of shifting to wages the temporary burdens of hard times.[2]
It had been anticipated by those who had been most active
in carrying this reform that the repeal of the laws against
combinations, and the consequent stopping of the perse-
cutions which such laws had made possible, would result
in the virtual disappearance of trade-unions. It was felt
that these had existed only because of oppression and that
they would fall to pieces with the introduction of equality
before the law. Such forecasts were not fulfilled. The
trade-union movement did, perhaps, occupy less exclusively

[1] Cunningham : "Growth of English Industry and Commerce in
Modern Times," p. 487.

[2] The labor question may be said to have come into public view
simultaneously with the repeal, between sixty and seventy years ago, of
the Combination Laws which had made it an offence for laboring men to
unite for the purpose of procuring by joint action, through peaceful means,
an augmentation of their wages. From this point progress began. — Gladstone, quoted in Wallas's " Life of Francis Place." Chapter viii of this
Life gives an excellent account of Place's relation to this repeal. The
subject is more generally treated in Webb's " History of Trade Unionism."

than in the period immediately preceding the attention of the leaders of the working people, but if so, this was only because it became merged in larger social and political agitations of the period, in which the trade combinations played an important part.[1]

If it were our purpose to trace the intellectual and moral forces which resulted in the great national awakening which may be said to have culminated in the reform bills of the thirties, rather than the actual changes in the laws and the industrial system, it would be necessary to study the socialistic movement of which Robert Owen was the apostle.   Inasmuch as his specific proposals failed it is only necessary to call attention to the enthusiasm and the enlightenment resulting from his crusade, which permeated more or less completely the whole movement for larger freedom and constructive reform.   His demonstration that the great distress from which particular classes suffered was " a new economic phenomenon, the inevitable result of unfettered competition and irresponsible ownership of a means of production," [2] contributed to the partial allevi-ation of those evils by Parliament, and made easier the adoption of less radical and more practicable remedies.

It would also be essential, in a full account of the forces which gave shape to the ideas and policies of the period, to include the contribution of Malthus and other political economists, and to trace the rise of the Manchester or *laissez-faire* school and its influence upon legislation. Such inquiries would be aside from our present purpose, closely related as they are.   Even within the field of actual reform it is necessary to pass over such important although minor events as the fight for a free press and cheap news-papers, a movement popular among the poor, and the organization of the metropolitan police force of London, which, although as unpopular as the other was popular, was likewise in the long run beneficial.

It was in this period that the criminal law was thoroughly reformed under the leadership of Sir Robert Peel, the death penalty being abolished for many offences, over three hundred acts relating to the criminal law

[1] Webb : "The History of Trade Unionism," chapters ii and iii.
[2] *Ibid.*, p. 143.

T

having been wholly or partially repealed, and the remainder codified into a consistent and intelligible system.[1]

Catholic emancipation, while of greater importance in Ireland than in England, was, nevertheless, a significant change for a large element of the population in both countries. The removal of the disabilities under which Roman Catholics labored, by which it became possible for them to enter the universities and to hold high office in the state, was only an indication of a radical change for the better in the political and social status of those who professed that faith. Other dissenters from the established church shared in the liberal movement in a manner which added to their standing in the community and gave them increased reason for looking upon themselves as citizens and equal sharers in the social and industrial life.

A humanitarian movement totally unprecedented in volume and intensity swept over the face of England in the thirty years under review. It brought about the beginning of the factory acts, the restriction of child labor,[2] the protection of pauper apprentices, and the agitation against slavery in the colonies and in foreign countries, as well as the organization of private societies for the amelioration of the condition of the poor. In the text-books of history attention is largely focussed, so far as this period is concerned, on the enormous political revolution, although it was brought about without the violence accompanying similar political changes in France and other countries.[3] In the brief twenty years between the close of the Peninsular War and the reform of the English Poor Law the political control of England passed completely from the aristocracy to the middle classes. The suffrage was placed upon a new basis, parliamentary representation was wholly reformed, and even the great

[1] J. R. Thursfield : "Life of Peel," in English Statesmen Series.

[2] It is now admitted that the legislation for the factories has worked almost entirely beneficent results. None of the evils anticipated from it have come to pass. Almost all the good it proposed to do has been realized. — McCarthy : "The Epoch of Reform," p. 96.

[3] Some of the grievances under which the English people suffered before this Epoch of Reform were severe enough to have warranted an attempt at revolution if no other means of relief seemed attainable, and if that desperate remedy had some chance of success. — McCarthy : "Epoch of Reform," Introduction, p. vi.

leaders of the earlier period retained their positions and their influence only in so far as they frankly accepted the new situation and acted upon the idea that the change which had been made was not even to be questioned.

Such then were some of the more important changes in this period so marvellously productive of change and progress. The balance of power shifted from the country to the town, from the landed interests to the industrial and commercial interests, from the aristocracy to the middle classes. The development of the factory system, the introduction of labor-saving devices, the introduction of steamships, the repeal of taxation, the division of labor, the introduction of elementary education, the better protection of children and of operatives engaged in dangerous occupations, and the increased dignity which are inseparably associated with political and religious freedom, all combined to elevate the position of the average citizen, to increase the national dividend, and to give to the producer, as compared with the unproductive classes, an increased share in the national product. If in the whole history of England a golden moment were to be chosen in which to discontinue relief extended from the public funds to large numbers of people, it would have been in the exact period in which the Poor Law Commission had the opportunity to test their ideas of the advantages of strict administration. It is not improbable that if the relief given so lavishly before the industrial and social changes had been made, or even after they had begun, but before the country had adjusted itself to the new conditions, had been withdrawn earlier, the results would have been different and that the unpopularity gained by the Commissioners even as it was would have been greatly increased.[1]

[1] The transition was made with little warning, and without any preliminary training in thrift, but at a time when wheat was plentiful and cheap. When soon afterwards there were crop failures and high prices, there were bitter complaints, especially from Lancashire and other northern counties in which the abuses of the old system had been much less serious than in southern counties. From these counties it was the taxpayers rather than the poor that testified to the excellence of the law. In a later period the resentment of the working population was strongly exhibited. Rose, in his volume on the " Rise of Democracy," says that " ' physical force ' chartism gained its strength from the popular hatred against the Poor Law."

Is it not probable that the great improvements which are
supposed to have resulted from the stricter administration
of the Poor Law may have been due instead in large part,
in so far as they were changes in personal character, to
the other causes that have been outlined — causes which
it will be noticed are not economic alone, but to a large
extent educational, social, and moral? If we can imagine
the history of the English poor between 1820 and 1850
without the intervention of the Poor Law, either in its more
liberal or in its stricter administration, is it not probable
that the changes occurring in the occupations and habits
of the people would have been virtually what they were
in fact?[1] In other words, has not the part which was
played by the Poor Law in its more lax form and the effect
of the introduction of the more severe standards been
greatly exaggerated? When we compare this single
influence with those which even in their bearing on the
welfare of the poor alone are of such greater sweep and
magnitude, it becomes obvious, not indeed that a lax
administration of the Poor Law can be defended but
that it is an error to give disproportionate emphasis to its
effect upon the welfare and character of the laboring
population. The change from an agricultural to an industrial community might rather be regarded as making
possible an improvement in Poor-Law administration, although the new problems caused by the increased population of the towns are many and serious. England was
saved from pauperization, revolution, and other unforeseen
disasters, not by deciding to distribute less relief or by
deciding that the able-bodied poor, if assisted at all, should
be assisted only in the workhouse, wise as these decisions
were, but by the rise of religious and political liberty,
by introducing in advance of other countries modern
forms of agriculture and industry, by developing her commerce and trade, by the adoption of a more nearly democratic organization of society, and by listening to the voice

[1] Private relief is often far better than public relief. Cunningham
records that in 1819 and in 1826, when there was a great deal of distress
among the Scottish weavers, large relief funds were started to which the
wealthy contributed more largely than they would have done in England
where the Poor Law was so abundant. See Cunningham : " Growth of
English Industry and Commerce in Modern Times," p. 638.

of humane and public-spirited counsels. The lessening of the poor rates was made practicable by and was not the principal cause of the progress of the period.

The reform of the English Poor Law is found to be merely one step in a series of related changes occurring in a particular epoch, and under exceptional circumstances not likely to be renewed. It requires historical interpretation, and is as far as possible from universal precedent. The laxity and demoralization to which attention has so frequently been called, is not to be looked upon merely as an exhibition of human nature certain to be made whenever relief is offered on easy terms, even though it may readily be granted that the offer of relief upon easy terms is dangerous and reprehensible. The abnormal relief-giving may even to some extent be ascribed to greater actual need, caused in turn by the war taxes, the primitive methods of agriculture, industry, and commerce, and other unreformed features of the English social life of the period. The present plea is that the naïve interpretation of the relation between pauperism and the Poor-Law administration should be discarded, and that if that experience is to be utilized, it should be studied in its entirety, due weight being given to such other causes as have been known to be operating to form the habits and determine the character of the people. The causes of poverty are diverse and elusive and it is always profitable to examine them in a new light.

In the following chapters an outline is given of the methods by which American communities have dealt with their relief problems. It must be confessed that they have shown comparatively little originality or independent development, although exceptions should be made in favor of the movement inaugurated by Robert M. Hartley in 1842,[1] the state boards of charities,[2] originating in Massachusetts in 1863, the widening scope of the charity organization societies in recent years, and the liberal emergency relief measures which have usually been adopted at times of extraordinary disasters.[3]

[1] See chapter on private outdoor relief.
[2] See "Supervision and Education in Charity," by Dr. J. R. Brackett. Macmillan, 1903.   [3] See Part IV.

CHAPTER II

PUBLIC OUTDOOR RELIEF IN AMERICA[1]

AMERICA has suffered comparatively little from pauperism, vagrancy, and those forms of crime and disorder that are produced by extreme want. There are individual instances in every community of persons who have made an economic failure of their lives; there are instances in many communities of large numbers who are subjected to great hardships in their daily toil; but complete failure, resulting in dependence upon others for the necessities of life, is more exceptional than among savage tribes or among advanced civilization elsewhere, and even those who are taxed most severely in their daily work by long hours and hard conditions receive a return for their work which enables them to live at a higher standard than do manual laborers of other countries. Brutal and squalid as are the conditions which we meet occasionally in city tenements, there is no widespread or general condition of squalor or brutishness which can be regarded as typical or permanent. Or if in a particular neighborhood the conditions appear to remain permanently bad, it is nevertheless found that the individuals making up the community are constantly changing and passing out of the unfavorable environment.

---

[1] From this brief sketch has been omitted any account of the almshouse system, and the history of the various methods of caring for dependent children outside their own families, these two subjects having been treated by Robert W. Hebberd and Homer Folks respectively in a series of historical studies, published in the Charities Review, 1899–1900, to which the author contributed an account of the care of the poor in their homes by public and private agencies. This account is republished in the present chapter and that immediately following. Mr. Folks's contribution has been republished under the title Dependent, Delinquent, and Neglected Children. Macmillan, 1902.

Except in a few cities, the number of the destitute has been small. Except in recent years, neither chronic lack of employment nor low wages have been a serious factor in the lives of any considerable number of people. It is still true that for the average workingman and his family there is no recognized need of assistance, even in sickness or in old age. Both on the farm and in town the laborer supports himself. He borrows at times to meet temporary needs; he gets into debt, it may be, at the grocer's and the butcher's; and he fails sometimes to pay the rent; but he cheerfully pays enough more for rent, meat, and groceries at other times to make up for such delinquencies. He nearly always carries a small amount of an expensive kind of life insurance, and he organizes readily benefit societies and trade-unions with benefit features, both of which, it may be said in passing, need better legal safeguards than have yet been generally provided.

Americans are not economical — in a sense they are not thrifty. They are generous to a fault, and they have little patience with petty saving devices. Their labor, however, is unusually productive; thus their margin for saving is large, and unremitting hard work is more common than in other countries. Still more characteristic is a readiness to adopt new methods. Economies of production are as much the rule as is the absence of economies in consumption. It is natural to use tools and machinery. The inclination to discover short cuts, to combine in such a way as to save labor, to invent more economical processes, is found everywhere.

If, therefore, Americans are not by nature saving or thrifty, they are still capitalists in that they naturally use machinery and saving devices, and methods of industry which enable an ounce of muscular energy to accomplish the greatest possible result. The essence of capital is not accumulated wealth, but rather the ability to apply brains to industry in such a way as to make human labor productive, and in this sense capital is more abundant in America than elsewhere.

Widows with children expect to earn a living, besides giving the children such care as the standards of life demand. Widowers with small children have more trouble, but a daughter sometimes becomes a sufficiently competent housekeeper at a tender age, and remarriage is of course, as with young widows, the rule. Desertion by the nominal head of the family becomes alarmingly common in the cities, but it is surprising how often the deserted wife and mother finds herself practically better off when relieved of the worthless husband's presence, and how often the real calamity is his return after more prosperous days have set in for the family which he had abandoned.

Thousands of street waifs, abandoned or runaway boys and girls, have been poured into Western and Southern country homes through the channel of charitable agencies, without apparently exhausting the capacity of those distant communities ; and of late it has been found that immediately about, and even in, the cities of the seaboard there is much absorbing capacity of the same kind. This is not merely an instance of effective organized charity, but is also an illustration of the surplus means which enable so many workingmen to assume additional burdens.

It must not be supposed that the true pauper type is absent. In every part of the country there exists a certain number of families who are dependent because of mental and physical deficiencies, and America has followed the policy of Great Britain and some other countries in supporting this class in part by a system of public relief in their own homes.

The fundamental peculiarities of American social conditions to which reference has been made must be borne constantly in mind in the study of the prevailing system of providing care and relief for needy families.   If the attention is fixed solely upon the machinery of relief, and it is assumed that the liability of falling into destitution is approximately the same as in European countries, it will appear that there has been a lamentable failure to organize the relief system upon a definite basis, a failure to bring about a clear distribution between public and private agencies, and, among the former, between local and central administrations.   It will also appear that the systems of the several states differ widely, that there has been a lack of responsible public oversight, and that official statistics are incomplete and unreliable. There is much justification, as it is, for such criticism. It is reasonable, however, to temper its force by the recollection that the most important feature of the whole situation in this country is not the wisdom or unwisdom of public outdoor relief, not the rival merits of organized and individual charity, not the function of the churches in relief work, not the formation of various schemes of industrial relief, but the very general absence of any serious need of relief in any form, except that which relatives and neighbors give in response to personal claims, which it would be an impertinence to register, or to discuss as elements of a relief system.[1]

Through the whole of the past century there has prevailed a system of public outdoor relief, usually administered through local overseers of the poor from funds provided by taxation. In the Southern states neither this system nor any general provision for the destitute was found to be so necessary as in other parts of the country, for the reason that negro slaves, who occupied the lowest place in the social and industrial organization, were in all cases a charge upon their owners, when unable to support themselves, rather than upon the community. There are still several Southern cities, among which may be named Baltimore, Washington, St. Louis, New Orleans, Atlanta,

---

[1] It is scarcely necessary to cite evidence of a fact so obvious to students of comparative social conditions during the past century. It may be interesting, however, to quote the observations of the two most acute and competent judges from across the sea, whose remarks refer to periods nearly half a century apart: —

America then exhibits in her social state an extraordinary phenomenon. Men are there seen on a greater equality in point of fortune and intellect, or, in other words, more equal in their strength than in any other country of the world, or in any age of which history has preserved the remembrance. — De Tocqueville: "Democracy in America."

Little outdoor relief is given, though in most states the relieving authority may at his or their discretion bestow it, and pauperism is not, and has never been, a serious malady, except in some five or six great cities where it is now vigorously combated by volunteer organizations largely composed of ladies. — Bryce : "The American Commonwealth."

To those may be added the testimony of an earlier writer than De Tocqueville : There are no tithes, no poor rates, no excise, no heavy internal taxes, no commercial monopolies. . . . I never saw a beggar in any part of the United States ; nor was I ever asked for charity but once — and that was by an Irishman. — From "An Excursion through the United States and Canada, during the years 1822-3." By an English Gentleman. London, 1824.

and Savannah, in which little or no outdoor relief is extended. There are also a few Northern cities, notably New York, Philadelphia, and San Francisco, in which no outdoor relief is given ; but these are regarded as distinct exceptions even within the states of which they are a part ; and the absence of outdoor relief in those cities is to be attributed to special and local causes. Buffalo, Pittsburg and Los Angeles, located in the same states respectively as the three cities just named, all have a liberal if not lavish expenditure from the public treasury for the relief of the poor in their homes.

As far as the public relief of distress is concerned we must perhaps accept the dictum of Amos G. Warner that the almshouse is the fundamental institution in American poor relief. This has not always been the case, however. Whether even now the almshouse or the alternative of a public grant at home is the residual and ultimate resource depends very much upon the personal characteristics of the responsible public officials. From one point of view the almshouse may be said to care for "all the abjectly destitute not otherwise provided for." Often, however, local authorities have received into the almshouse but a small fraction of the public dependents — those who are absolutely homeless and helpless — leaving to be helped in their own homes all who can maintain, even with partial or entire public support, the pretence of a home. Outdoor relief under such circumstances becomes the real residual resource rather than the almshouse, the latter being little more than a hospital ward. Historically outdoor relief antedates the almshouse in nearly all the states. This is not because the almshouse system was unknown to the founders of the more recently settled commonwealths, but because at first there is so little pauperism that an almshouse or even a "poor farm" seems unnecessary, and the almshouse has often arisen as the result of a reform movement due to excessive relief and its attendant evils.

There has been no period within the century when the system of public outdoor relief has gone unchallenged. In the first quarter prominent landmarks in the discussion of the subject are the report to the General Court of Massachusetts in 1821 by Josiah Quincy, President of Harvard

College,[1] and the searching report to the New York Legislature by J. N. Yates, Secretary of State, in 1824.[2] In the second quarter more attention was given to temperance agitation than to charitable reforms, but many private relief societies of various types were founded, and finally one of the most valiant of the temperance agitators evolved from his study of intemperance and its consequences and from his experience with collateral social problems a plan for the oldest of those associations for improving the condition of the poor which have since under various names grown and multiplied until they must be regarded as a most important factor in the private organized relief of the poor in their own homes.

In the third quarter of the century eleven state boards of charities were created, one of whose chief functions has been to introduce greater discrimination into the disbursement of relief, both outdoor and institutional ; while entirely within the period since the beginning of the final quarter has fallen the origin and growth of the one hundred and fifty-four charity organization societies[3] which have most energetically combated the abuse, and usually the practice in any form, of public outdoor relief.

The Quincy report of 1821 on the Pauper Laws of Massachusetts is a brief and scholarly essay upon the general subject of public relief of the poor. It is based upon an investigation of the practice and opinions of local overseers, and appendices are given showing the number of paupers from each town from which returns are received, the aggregate number for 162 towns being 4340. The total population of these towns at the time of the report was 287,437, while the whole number of inhabitants of the state at the time was 472,000. A proportionate number of paupers in towns not reporting would have made the total somewhat over 7000. The average estimate of the expenses for the support of children and adults was $52 a year, or $364,000 per year for the 7000 paupers. The sta-

---

[1] Now very rare. Its text, however, is reprinted from a copy in the Boston Public Library in Charities for September 30, 1899.

[2] Also rare.   Reprinted by the New York State Board of Charities in the annual report for 1900.

[3] Sometimes called bureaus of charities, or associated charities.

tistical information given with the report is meagre, and the
Committee contented itself for the most part with a general survey of the situation, drawing its conclusions regarding necessary reforms as much from the discussions then
current in England as from the results of their own local
inquiries.   It is pointed out that if the increase in the payments out of the state treasury be taken as evidence of a
corresponding increase in the pauper burden of Massachusetts, then there had been in Massachusetts in the twenty
years preceding the report an increase greater than in that
for the corresponding period in Great Britain.   Without
pretending to assert that this is a true criterion, the committee considered itself justified in concluding that the
pernicious consequences of the existing system are palpa-
ble, " that they are increasing, and that they imperiously
call for the interference of the legislature in some manner,
equally prompt and efficacious."

The system thus condemned included not merely provision for the poor by supplies in money, or articles at the
homes of the poor and provision by almshouses, but also in
some towns provision for the poor by letting them out to
the lowest bidder, in families at large, within the town ;
and in other towns, by letting them to the lowest bidder,
together, that is, all to one person.

The auction system as applied to single families is condemned as extravagant and as applicable only to very small
towns.   The overseers of one town are quoted as admit-
ting that the average expense, which was about $1.30 per
head per week, was large, but added that " the poor being
sometimes boarded with those who are in want themselves,
it is not lost to the town."   By printing this quotation in
italics President Quincy indicated his appreciation of the
more serious objection to the plan of which the overseers
seem to have been unconscious.

Auction of the entire number of paupers to the lowest
bidder, while it partakes of the character of the preceding system, is less expensive and has the merit that it is
" an approximation of the method of supporting them in a
poorhouse."   In Massachusetts and in other states this
method of caring for the poor actually led in many towns
and counties to the establishment of houses of industry.

As to the provision by outdoor relief given in the homes of the poor, the committee declares that the evidence from the towns of the commonwealth coincides with the general experience of England in condemning this system, both on the ground of expense and on the ground of its effect upon the character of the poor.   Upon the whole the committee reached the five following conclusions : —

I. That of all modes of providing for the poor, the most wasteful, the most expensive, and most injurious to their morals and destructive to their industrious habits is that of supply in their own families.

II. That the most economical mode is that of almshouses having the character of workhouses or houses of industry, in which work is provided for every degree of ability in the pauper, and thus the able poor made to provide, partially at least, for their own support, and also the support or, at least, the comfort of the impotent poor.

III. That of all modes of employing the labor of the pauper, agriculture affords the best, the most healthy, and the most certainly profitable ; the poor being thus enabled to raise always at least their own provisions.

IV. That the success of these establishments depends upon their being placed under the superintendence of a board of overseers, constituted of the most substantial and intelligent inhabitants of the vicinity.

V. That of all causes of pauperism, intemperance in the use of spirituous liquors is the most powerful and universal.

The committee did not recommend immediate legislation, but suggested that the results of its investigation be communicated to the several towns and that steps should be taken looking forward to the eventual placing of the whole subject of poor relief in the commonwealth under the regular and annual superintendence of the legislature.

The Yates report was more exhaustive and has far more historical value, since it contains not merely the facts regarding almshouse and outdoor relief in the counties, and to a large extent even in the towns of the state of New York, but also a considerable amount of information regarding the relief systems of other states.

The first part of the report exhibits the number of paupers in the several cities, towns, and counties in this state; the sums of money expended for their maintenance ; the sums expended for the costs and fees of justices, overseers of the poor, and constables, in the examination and removal of paupers, and in other incidental services ; the number of paupers removed; the ratio of paupers in each county; the ratio of taxation imposed upon each county for the maintenance and relief of the poor; the amount of taxes raised for that purpose in the several counties for the preceding six years ; and extracts of letters from mayors of cities, supervisors and clerks of counties, overseers of the poor of towns, and from other sources entitled to credit, showing the management, general success and effect of the various local experiments in the state for the support of the poor, either by towns or in poorhouses.

The second part exhibits a digest of the poor laws of most of the states of the Union with extracts from official letters and documents showing the operation and effect of those laws, together with a view of the state of pauperism in Europe, and brief extracts from works of American and European writers, illustrative of the evils of pauperism and suggesting plans for their amelioration and removal. The report distinguishes two classes: the permanent poor, or those who are regularly supported during the whole year at the public expense; and the occasional, or temporary poor, or those who receive occasional relief during a part of the year, chiefly in the autumn and winter.

In the first class at the time of the report there were in New York State 6896; in the second class, 15,215. Of the permanent paupers there were 446 idiots and lunatics ; 287 blind ; 928 aged and infirm ; 797 lame or in a confirmed state of ill health and totally incapacitated. There were 2604 children under fourteen years of age, and 1789 paupers of both sexes, all of whom, though not in the vigor of life, may yet be considered capable of earning their existence if proper labor were assigned, and suitable means to induce them to perform it, and whose labor might produce at least $150,000 annually.

Two-thirds of all the permanent pauperism and more than one-half of the occasional pauperism is attributed to intemperance.

The counties bordering on the ocean and on the Hudson River, having somewhat more than one-third of the population, provided more than one-half of all the paupers. The city of New York alone maintained one-fourth of all the permanent poor. Mr. Yates considered it hardly necessary to explain the cause of this great disparity, but to the modern student it is interesting that he found it in the dense population of that city, and of the large villages and towns, which from their convenient situation for navigation and commerce, allure to their haunts and recesses the idle and dissolute of every description. " Populous places," he says, " have at all times been burthened with a larger proportion of paupers than places where a thin or scattered population is found."

Comparing New York with other states as to the burden of pauperism, it is found that in New York there is one permanent pauper for every 220 souls; in Massachusetts one for every 68; in Connecticut one for every 150 ; in New Hampshire one for every 100 ; in Delaware one for every 227 ; in Pennsylvania one for every 265; in Illinois (then a new state) no paupers were as yet supported at the public expense.

In the towns and villages where there are no almshouses the poor are disposed of by the overseers in three ways :

I. The overseers farm them out at stipulated prices to contractors who are willing to receive and keep them on condition of getting what labor they can out of the paupers.

II. The poor are sold at auction — the meaning of which is that he who will support them for the lowest price becomes their keeper; and it often happens, of course, that the keeper is himself almost a pauper before he purchases, and adopts this mode in order not to fall a burden upon the town. Thus he and another miserable human being barely subsist upon what would hardly comfortably maintain himself alone — a species of economy much boasted of by some of our town officers and purchasers of paupers ; or,

III. Relief is afforded to the poor at their own habitations.

The expense for physicians and nurses, in attending paupers in towns where there are no poorhouses, forms a prominent article in the amount of taxation. Pauperism and disease, except in an almshouse, are generally found to be associated, and hence it is that this item of expense is so much complained of in the towns just alluded to.

After a full examination of the pauper system and its various provisions and results, two problems are presented for the consideration of the legislature : —

I. Ought the whole system to be abolished, and the support of the poor left altogether to the voluntary contribution of the charitable and humane ?   Or,

II. If the system ought not to be abolished, is it susceptible of improvement, and in what mode can the improvement best be effected ?

The report notes that men of great literary requirements and profound political research have opposed all compulsory provision for the poor, but considers that the fact that every state in the Union and many European governments have a code of laws for the relief and maintenance of the poor is no slight proof that the total absence of a pauper system would be inconsistent with a humane, liberal, and enlightened policy.

Proceeding to the second question, the proposition is said to be very generally admitted that our poor laws were defective in principle and mischievous in practice, and that under the imposing and charitable aspect of affording relief exclusively to the poor and infirm, they frequently invited the able-bodied vagrant to partake of the same bounty. Full and satisfactory details are quoted from the Society for the Prevention of Pauperism in the City of New York and by writers of letters, from which extracts are given of the gross abuses which have grown out of these laws. The general conclusions were : —

I. That the existing laws led to litigation of the most expensive and hurtful kind, exhausting nearly one-ninth of the funds intended for the relief of the poor, and leading to harsh removals of many human beings, like felons, from no other fault than poverty.

II. That the poor when farmed out or sold were frequently treated with barbarity and neglect.

III. That the education and morals of the children of paupers — except in almshouses — were almost wholly neglected.   They grew up in filth, idleness, ignorance, and disease, and many became early candidates for the prison or the grave.   The evidence on this head was regarded as too voluminous even for reference.

IV.   That there was no adequate provision for the employment of the poor throughout the state.   Idleness very generally generates vice, dissipation, disease, and crime.

V.   That the poor laws had come to encourage the sturdy beggar and profligate vagrant.   Overseers not unfrequently granted relief without sufficient examination into the circumstances or the ability of the party claiming it.

VI.   That the laws also held out encouragement to the successful practice of street begging.

VII.   That idiots and lunatics did not receive sufficient care and attention in towns where no suitable asylums for their reception were established.

In general, there was shown to be an evident want of economy in the disbursement of the public funds; and it was demonstrated that the law of settlement was a fruitful source of litigation and difficulty.

The report aimed at specific reforms which, in a word, were to be accomplished by restricting outdoor relief and establishing houses of industry.   The worthy poor were to be relieved in an almshouse, where children were to be received and properly educated, and, in a workhouse or house of correction conducted in coöperation with the almshouse, compulsory employment was to be given to the idle.

A bill was prepared embodying these aims to accompany the report.   Two of its prominent features were held to be entitled to much consideration : —

I.   It would relieve the poor with greater humanity and emphatically with more economy than under the existing poor laws.

II.   It would provide employment for the idle and compel them to labor, and in consequence put an end to the practice of street begging.

The plan submitted proposed : —

I.   That one or more houses of employment in each county, with a farm of sufficient extent be connected with each institution ; the paupers there to be maintained and

U

employed at the expense of the respective counties in some helpful labor, chiefly agricultural, their children to be carefully instructed and at suitable ages to be put out at some useful business or trade.

II. That each house of employment be connected with a workhouse or penitentiary for the reception and discipline of sturdy beggars and vagrants.

III. That the excise duties be increased and a tax laid upon the owners of distilleries of whiskey and other ardent spirits to compose a fund for the relief of the poor.

IV. That one year's residence in a county constitute a settlement except in certain specified cases.

V. That no male person in health with the use of all his faculties and between the ages of eighteen and fifty years be placed upon the pauper list or be maintained at the public expense.

VI. That severe penalties be inflicted upon those who bring to or leave in a county paupers not legally chargeable to it.

VII. That street begging be entirely prohibited, beggars of this description to be instantly sent to the workhouse; and that magistrates be subject to indictment and punishment for any neglect of this duty, and grand juries specially charged to inquire into such neglects and to present such offenders.

Referring to comparative statistics of the bureau of pauperism in different states, some of which we have already quoted, it is pointed out that in Rhode Island and Virginia the number of paupers is less than in New York and in Pennsylvania, and that in Delaware, Rhode Island, and Virginia, where the poorhouse system has prevailed for the greatest length of time and to the greatest extent, the burden of pauperism and the expense which it entails are less than in any state in which that system has been more recently or partially introduced.

A few additional items of information may profitably be culled from the appendices : the total expense of the city and county of New York for relief to the outdoor poor for the year preceding the report was $10,000, while the amount expended for paupers in the almshouse was $50,908.27 ; for maniacs in the asylum, $3332 ; and for vagrants in the Bridewell and penitentiary, $5321.26, making a total of $74,561.53.

The families assisted as outdoor poor are stated by the commissioners to be composed chiefly of Irish immigrants, as are also the vagrants sent to the Bridewell and penitentiary. " In fact, we are literally overrun with this description of paupers."

The following sentiments from the pen of S. Allen, Esq., at that time mayor of New York, are enlightening as to the prevailing views on the causes of pauperism. The reader should not fail to notice the easy transition from one cause to another when a practical remedy is to be suggested.

" Idleness and a total inattention to frugality are among the principal sources of pauperism. There is a natural propensity in men to inaction, and therefore it is that so many of those who are compelled to depend upon their own exertions for subsistence become paupers. Every man, however, has a principle within himself which, if not destroyed by mental or vicious causes, urges him to the full exertion of his faculties for the prevention of this catastrophe. A definition of this principle may be given in two sentences, to wit, the desire for fame and independence, and the conscious feeling of shame and fear of want. . . .

" These evils may, in a measure, be remedied and a gradual decrease of pauperism (produced by the inordinate use of spirituous liquors) effected. The article ought to be rendered more inaccessible to consumers by an increase in its price. . . . In addition to this no able-bodied person ought to be permitted to receive the public bounty by the way of alms, and in all cases where it is practicable the building of poorhouses ought to be discouraged."

The Society for the Suppression of Pauperism, in its annual reports for the years from 1818 to 1824, as might be expected, strikes somewhat deeper ground, and lays down a programme of reform and educational improvement such as was scarcely to be surpassed later by the associations for improving the condition of the poor and the charity organization societies.

The causes of pauperism are enumerated as follows : —

I. Ignorance.
II. Idleness.

III. Intemperance and drinking.
IV. The want of economy.
V. Imprudent and hasty marriages.
VI. Lotteries.
VII. Pawnbroker.
VIII. Houses of ill fame.
IX. Gambling-houses; and
X. The numerous charitable institutions of the city.

Some of the remedies suggested are : to divide the city into small districts, each district to have two or three visitors to visit the indigent, etc.; to establish savings banks, benefit societies, life insurances, etc.; to refuse support to paupers who have not gained a settlement ; to procure an entire prohibition of street begging; to aid in giving employment to those who cannot procure it, by establishing houses of employment, or by supplying materials for domestic labor ; to open places of public worship in the outer wards ; to promote Sunday-schools ; to devise a plan by which all spontaneous charities may flow into one channel ; to procure the abolition of the great number of shops in which spirituous liquors are sold by license.

"The managers recommend the practice of abstaining from giving money to beggars who usually appropriate what they get to increase the profits and the business of the dram seller." [1]

In its very first report, that for the year 1818, there is an even more positive enunciation of the modern idea.

"Let the moral sense be awakened and the moral influence be established in the minds of the improvident, the unfortunate, and the depraved. Let them be approached with kindness and an ingenuous concern for their welfare ; inspire them with self-respect and encourage their industry and economy ; in short, enlighten their minds and teach them to take care of themselves. Those are the methods of doing them real and permanent good and relieving the community from the pecuniary exactions, the multiplied exactions and threatening dangers of which they are the authors." [2]

[1] Fourth Annual Report, 1821.
[2] First Annual Report of the Society for the Prevention of Pauperism in the city of New York, 1818.

The managers of this society do not hesitate to arraign unwise philanthropy even more explicitly than by including the charitable institutions among the causes of pauperism. They ascribe the evil of its increase " to the same cause, in this city as in England, viz., to the provision made for the relief and maintenance of the poor. Pauperism has increased among us in a ratio as great as was ever witnessed in this country. The alternative proposed may appear extravagant, but it is believed that genuine humanity and benevolence to the poor themselves would dictate the abolition of our pauper system. . . . In this city it is extremely rare to find an industrious and virtuous person wanting the necessaries or comforts of life."

Both in Massachusetts and in New York good results followed the agitation of which the Quincy and the Yates reports are respectively the most conspicuous symptoms. Greater discrimination came to be practised and a relatively larger part of the public relief was provided in county or local institutions which were more under the public scrutiny. The abundance of free land in Western territories and the opportunities for employment for all able-bodied persons continued to relieve any real pressure of population, and accordingly there was little temptation to public officials to make easy the way to a life of dependence upon the public bounty.

The abolition of public outdoor relief in New York City, except in medicines to the sick, an annual cash disbursement to the blind, and the distribution of free coal in the winter, occurred on December 20, 1875, by adoption by the commissioners of charities and correction of a resolution that the experiment be made of giving the necessities of life to the outdoor poor instead of money or orders on grocery stores. A week later it was resolved to visit all applicants for relief within forty-eight hours after application, and it was officially announced that the department disclaimed all intention of aiding the unworthy poor. Again, on January 10, 1876, it was proposed to visit all applicants for coal. From this time forward the department gave coal only, the previous appropriations for general relief having been reduced by the board of estimate and apportionment.

It is a curious view that the necessities of life consist wholly of coal and do not include food, shelter, or clothing. It is also interesting that one of the three commissioners in office at the time this action was taken, after twenty years, although still employed in the Department of Public Charities, and at the time in a prominent position, was entirely unable to recollect the circumstances under which the change was made, asserting when questioned on the subject that it must have been made by the "reform administration" of 1873; nor has the writer been able to find other persons who recall any particular agitation of the subject at the date when this action was taken. No opposition seems to have developed, and during the quarter of a century in which the city has distributed no kind of outdoor relief except coal and the pension to the blind, there has been, so far as can be ascertained, no desire on the part of the officials of the Department of Charities to go back to the early system; while doubts have frequently been expressed both by "reformers" and by "politicians" as to whether the distribution of coal was of any special value. This anomaly was ended by the charter of 1897 which created the Greater New York by the consolidation of Brooklyn and other municipalities with the old city of New York. Under the charter public outdoor relief is prohibited except that to the blind.

Brooklyn. — The steps by which public outdoor relief was discontinued in Brooklyn are of special interest, since, in what was then the city and is now the borough, the change was more complete, the distribution of fuel being discontinued at the same time. The statistics of outdoor relief for Brooklyn show, from the years 1872 to 1877 inclusive, an increase of over 100 per cent in the number of beneficiaries annually receiving help. The average expenditure by the city per year for these six years was $114,943.72, which includes the cost of administering the relief, this expense amounting to 40 per cent of the total. An average of 39,109 persons were relieved each year. These facts became, in the year 1876, a matter of public comment and aroused general criticism of the existing system. The officers of relief themselves agreed that the system in its form at that time was pernicious, and that the only way of preventing a further increase in the number of pauper claimants on the city was the establishment of a system of thorough visitation. Such a system by paid officials had been in partial operation previous to this time, but had been abolished because of unsatisfactory results. At the time under discussion the poor were required merely to come to the office of the commissioners and affirm under oath that they needed the relief for which they applied.

At the instigation of the State Charities Aid Association a meeting was called in May, 1876, for the purpose of inaugurating a movement for volunteer visitation by private citizens of all applicants for public relief during the ensuing winter. As a result of this meeting an organization was formed for the purpose of thus assisting the commissioners of charities. When this association was in position to offer its services, the attention of the commissioners of charities was officially called to its existence and an offer was made to visit all applicants for relief during the winter of 1876-1877. The commissioners did not seem to appreciate the offer, and for a time threw serious obstacles in the way of the execution of the plan. Finally, under pressure of public opinion, they accepted the offer and a visitation committee of between two hundred and three hundred visitors was set at the work of investigation.

The results of these investigations convinced the visitors that many of the families applying for relief were doing it habitually from year to year, not because of actual need, but because their neighbors were receiving help, and because they considered it their right. As a result of a discussion held at the end of this winter resolutions were passed expressing disapproval of the existing system and suggesting to the commissioners that outdoor relief be abolished, by stages if necessary, but entirely within a year or two. It was recommended that for the winter of 1877-1878 the poor be relieved with coal only, and that at the end of this year even that could be discontinued.

The commissioners of charities were unwilling to adopt the plan proposed, and to the surprise of the visiting committee, who had volunteered their services for the coming winter, completely ignored their offer, and proceeded to make plans for the distribution of relief under a system arranged by themselves, of which the public was not given information. The visiting committee brought the matter before the county board of supervisors, who, having the sole right to vote appropriations for the supplies needed by the commissioners of charities, exercised over the distribution of relief a controlling influence which the commissioners of charities could not ignore. The supervisors, who were at this time in sympathy with public sentiment, accepted the recommendations of the visitation committee, and voted to supply coal only. The commissioners of charities objected to this, and the movement was left in an indeterminate state at the close of the year 1877.

In the new board of supervisors for 1878 a majority appeared to be in favor of a return to the old system. The reforms proposed were disregarded; resolutions were passed supporting the commissioners of charities in their plan to distribute relief as in former years, both provisions and coal; and the efforts of the visitation committee seemed to have been completely overthrown.

It was already known to the committee, through previous investigation, that the distribution of outdoor relief to able-bodied paupers in Brooklyn was not, in fact, authorized by the state legislation relating to the subject. The question now arose as to whether this fact should be brought up, and a complete stop in all outdoor relief be forced upon the supervisors and commissioners of charities, or whether they should be allowed to go on without restraint in the old way. There seemed to be no possibility of a middle course. It was decided after deliberation that, while the cutting off of both coal and provisions might entail temporary suffering among the poor, it was yet better to bring the matter to this sharp issue than to allow a resumption of the former methods. The question was therefore brought to a legal issue. The supervisors consulted their attorney, and found that the whole system of outdoor relief as in vogue for years past was entirely illegal, as far as it related to able-bodied paupers. This, of course, overthrew the entire system in a moment.[1]

[1] It is necessary to add, however, that the city until 1899 made small annual appropriations to certain relief societies engaged in the care of the poor in their homes. This anomalous policy was then discontinued on the recommendation of the city controller.

To the surprise of those interested in the private relief agencies of the city, no increasing demand for aid resulted. The winter passed favorably, and no exceptional suffering seemed to have appeared. The statistics of the following years, appended below, show this to be an actual fact. Not only was there no additional demand on private relief agencies, but the almshouses of the county did not become overcrowded, as was anticipated. In short, nowhere along the whole line of relief agencies was there found an increased demand upon their resources. On the contrary, the figures show a steady decrease in the years following 1878. Part of this decrease is due undoubtedly to the general improvement in business prosperity succeeding the crisis of 1873, which now began to take full effect. Still, the statistics seem to indicate that the abolition of outdoor relief in Brooklyn resulted in a real improvement of the status of the very poor. Aside from these figures, so far has public sentiment supported the conviction which they express that, for the twenty years intervening between 1878 and the present, not once has there been any agitation in Kings County for the resumption of outdoor relief.

	POPULATION	OUTDOOR RELIEF, PERSONS AIDED	INDOOR RELIEF, PERSONS AIDED	COST OF OUTDOOR RELIEF	AMOUNT DISTRIBUTED BY THE ASSOCIATION FOR IMPROVING THE CONDITION OF THE POOR
1870	396,000	38,170	8,542	$163,437	$21,851
1871	414,000	35,658	9,234	141,208	22,011
1872	432,000	22,863	8,999	95,771	21,821
1873	450,000	25,033	7,487	100,555	22,211
1874	468,000	30,411	7,343	134,935	23,466
1875	485,000	35,850	7,923	116,967	24,336
1876	501,000	44,208	9,155	98,815	23,000
1877	518,000	46,330	9,268	141,137	20,818
1878	534,000	46,093	9,706	57,054	18,824
1879	551,000	stopped	10,231	stopped	16,640
1880	557,000		8,736		14,774
1881	584,000		10,347		17,716
1882	601,000		11,121		18,050
1883	619,000		11,678		22,246
1884	639,000		11,190		19,061

Washington. — In Washington the only public outdoor relief has been that distributed through the police department. There are no officials connected with the charitable administration of the District of Columbia exactly corresponding to the charities commissioners, overseers of the poor, or similar officials in other cities. The position of superintendent of charities was created on August 6, 1890, "for the purpose of securing more equitable and efficient expenditure of the several sums appropriated for charities." All appropriations for charitable purposes were expended under his general direction, and in conformity with a system or plan formulated by him, subject to the approval of the commissioners of the district, but the relief of destitute persons in their own homes was not made a part of the duty of the superintendent or of his subordinates. In 1900 a board of charities was created to discharge the duties formerly devolving on the superintendent. A lump sum has usually been appropriated by Congress "for relief of the poor." For the fiscal year ending June 30, 1897, this amount was $13,000. It was distributed by the commissioners of the District of Columbia, in accordance with the recommendation of the superintendent of charities, as follows: —

For physicians to the poor	$7,200
For medicines and printing prescriptions for the physicians to the poor	3,400
For the woman's dispensary	500
For the aged women's home	300
For coffins for the indigent dead	300
For emergency relief of cases investigated through the police department on order of the commissioners of the District of Columbia, on recommendation of the superintendent of charities, to be distributed in provisions, fuel, or clothing through the police	1,300
Total,	$13,000

The only part of this expenditure which corresponds with ordinary public outdoor relief is the $1300 designated for emergency relief through the police department. This allowance from the public treasury was usually considerably increased by private donations. In the winter of 1894–1895 the citizens' relief committee, which consists of private citizens acting upon invitation of the commissioners, gave through the police department $6284.26, one-fourth of the total amount disbursed by the relief committee in that year.

After much discussion of the relative advantage and disadvantage of this method of relief, on January 15, 1898, was adopted the following order by the Commissioners of the District.

"*Ordered :* That allotments for relief of the poor, such as have been heretofore distributed through the metropolitan police force, shall hereafter be distributed through the Associated Charities under the direction of the central relief committee."

Four days earlier by a special order the commissioners had transferred one thousand dollars ($1000), the unallotted balance of the current appropriation of the thirteen hundred dollars ($1300) referred to above, to the central relief committee, so that since the beginning of 1898 police distribution of public relief has been a thing of the past. The sole reason for this change, according to the chief of police and the commissioner who has the police department especially in charge, is that the work of investigating and relieving destitute families is not a police duty, does not properly belong to the police department, and seriously interferes with the legitimate work of the police department. Other than these purely negative objections have been urged by others, but the reason assigned is that which actuated the board. It is understood that in the police force itself the distribution was naturally looked upon with some favor in view of the opportunity which it gave to win friends, and to remove whatever unpopularity might attach to the ordinary work of enforcing laws. It is obvious that whatever objections there are to public outdoor relief are intensified in this particular system. Outdoor relief by police officers not only tends to demoralize its recipients, but obscures the clear conception of duty which is essential to guardians of the peace.

Baltimore. — In Baltimore the police was formerly employed, as in Washington, to aid destitute families. No part of the money used for this purpose came, however, from the public treasury. Newspapers and private citizens supplied the funds. On January 12, 1898, representatives of the principal relief agencies of the cities petitioned the board of police commissioners to discourage as far as possible the sending of money and supplies to the poor. A letter was received in reply to the petition, giving the position of the board as follows : —

". . . That the large increase in the area of the city, in the number of buildings therein, and in its population, has imposed upon the police department so much additional work that it is very desirable that it should be relieved as far as possible of all services other than those which are strictly police duties, and I am directed by the board to advise you that while it will not refuse to accept and distribute such contributions as may be made by our citizens, we very much prefer, for the reason above given, now that the organized charities of the city have so perfected their organizations and enlarged their facilities as to be able to handle all contributions to advantage, that those who have heretofore asked the police department to dispense their contributions should send them instead to some one or more of the organized charities of Baltimore, a number of which you represent."

The new charter of the city of Baltimore in 1898 reorganized its charitable administration. It made no change, however, in the long-established policy of the city confining public relief to that given in the almshouse or in private institutions, but, on the contrary, by its terms expressly prohibits adult outdoor relief.

Philadelphia. — Philadelphia, unlike Washington and Baltimore, has been familiar with the system of public outdoor relief, though it was discontinued there after the corresponding change which has been described in Brooklyn. Its abolition in Philadelphia is thus described by Charles D. Kellogg, who aided in the establishment of the Philadelphia Society for Organizing Charity, and who soon succeeded his brother, Rev. D. O. Kellogg, as secretary : —

On January 18, 1878, several gentlemen connected with the soup houses and some of the other relief agencies of Philadelphia met informally to consult concerning means by which all the charities of the city "might be protected from the countless impositions practised upon them." A

general meeting of managers and trustees of charitable
enterprises of the city was called. At that meeting a
committee embracing representatives of all the leading
charities of the city was appointed to consider and report
on the whole subject. The committee included Joshua L.
Baily, Rudolph Blankenburg, Philip C. Garrett, Thomas S.
Harrison, William W. Justice, Charles Spencer, and James
A. Wright, who a few years later were members of the
famous committee of one hundred, which did much at that
time to stem the tide of political corruption.

The committee's report was laid before a general meeting of citizens on June 13 of the same year. One of the
reasons given by them for a radical reform in the general
administration of all relief agencies was the inefficiency
and corruption which pervaded the city outdoor relief
as distributed by the official visitors of the guardians of
the poor. "The public has but slight acquaintance with
their work and no sympathy for it. They are regarded
with more or less distrust which is often based on ignorance
and makes no allowance for the peculiar legal embarrass-
ments they encounter, such as their obligation to provide
for all who come to them without visible means of support.
The best of the officials intrusted with the management
of the system would, we are assured, be glad to find the
people of the city showing some sense of responsibility for
their work, and helping to set them free from such a legal
subjection to imposture by a complete system of voluntary
visitation and inquiry."

The committee proposed the organization of a society to
be called "The Philadelphia Society for Organizing Charitable Relief and Repressing Mendicancy," which should
constitute a central agency, through which all the public
and private charities of the city might work for mutual
protection, economy, and efficiency. This somewhat formidable and impressive action created much anxiety and
corresponding opposition among the political dispensers
of the official relief from the city treasury, who resented
interference with so profitable an instrument of political
patronage ; and professional politicians began to devise
means to strangle the reform at its birth. To crush the pre-
tensions of the new society — that by a better adjustment

and coördination of all public and private charity, the claims and needs of the dependent classes could be more adequately and economically met — it leaked out that it was, in the following year (1879), determined by its enemies to suspend the twelve paid visitors, who were the dispensers of the $50,000 to $75,000 previously appropriated annually to the overseers of the poor for outdoor relief, and taking the new-born enterprise at its word, to throw upon it the whole burden of relieving those who for years had applied to the city for coal, groceries, etc., and had received doles from the visitors. The new society began in November, 1878, and the following year the city's winter budget cut off all customary provision for the city outdoor relief, and citizens were requested to refer all applicants for relief, not otherwise provided for, to the new society, which bravely undertook the burden. It was urged that such a change would increase the suffering among the poor, would swamp the voluntary relief societies, and, by filling the almshouse to overflowing, would increase the expenses of the indoor departments of the guardians of the poor far beyond the amount which would be saved by abolishing the outdoor relief.

The results may thus be summarized. When the first winter was passed, and its work was reviewed, it was found that the number of applicants heretofore receiving city relief, and applying to the new as well as to the older relief societies, was, after the first sixty days, too small for computation ; that the general relief societies discovered no appreciable increase of the demands upon them ; and that the almshouse population had diminished to such an extent that the expenses of the overseers were reduced by $23,900. The total saving in the first ten years after, as compared with the ten years before, the abolition of outdoor relief was an average of $99,652 a year, notwithstanding the city's rapid increase in population ; and the fourth annual report of the Society for Organizing Charity noted a marked decrease of vagrancy and street begging apparent throughout the city.

Other accounts differ from that given by Mr. Kellogg in assigning the necessity for economizing as the chief rea-

son for the change of system, but, whatever the motive, it
is clear that the change was not made at the direct request
of the society, or as the result of sentiment against outdoor relief created by direct agitation. Whatever the
causes that brought about the discontinuance of outdoor
relief, the past twenty-five years have witnessed a complete
acquiescence in the present plan. In the severe winter
of 1894 a large relief fund was collected under the direction of the voluntary "mayor's committee." There was,
however, no proposition in the city councils to reëstablish
outdoor relief, and the Department of Charities and Correction would have been quick to oppose any such proposition if it had been made. There has been no distribution
of relief funds through the police department since 1894,
when a small sum contributed by private citizens was
placed in its hands.

Boston. — In the city of Boston the discussion on the subject of outdoor relief reached an acute stage in the year
1888, when a committee of the board of overseers of the
poor visited Brooklyn, New York, Philadelphia, Baltimore,
and Washington to confer with persons interested in public and private charity on the subject. All of these cities
had been without any general system of outdoor relief for
at least ten years. In a pamphlet published by the board,
the committee reports its observations in the cities visited
and its conclusion that a change from the system then in
vogue in Boston to that of any of the cities visited would
be a change for the worse. Special prominence is given to
that part of the report which deals with Brooklyn. Stress
is laid upon the large amount annually donated from the
public treasury to private charitable institutions, including
a payment of from $110,000 to $140,000 per year for the
board of children. This system was believed by the committee to be much more harmful than outdoor relief as
managed in Boston. The committee also points out that
the principal private relief society gave on an average but
$1.54 a year to a family, of which one-fourth came from
the public purse. The committee makes the pertinent
suggestion that if the contention of the critic of outdoor
relief is valid, that the $10 or $12 provided by the overseers of the poor could be discontinued without injury, it

would be equally possible for the poor of Brooklyn to do without the $1.54 supplied by the private society, and that if only this amount stands between them and independence, it would be very desirable for Brooklyn to give up private relief entirely. Arguing the matter more seriously the committee thinks that the amount provided is not sufficient to prevent suffering, and that in many instances families are broken up unnecessarily, while a large amount of individual aid is probably given with little or no investigation.

Alfred T. White, in letters published in Lend-a-Hand, contested the last point, quoting testimony to the effect that alms were asked less frequently than before outdoor relief was discontinued. Mr. White also insists that there is no connection between the number of dependent children and outdoor relief, or that if there is any, the relation of the system of public outdoor relief to dependency is similar to that which it bears to adult indoor relief; *i.e.* to augment the amount of dependency in both forms. Benjamin Pettee, secretary of the board of overseers, replied to Mr. White's first letter, but made no reply to the fuller presentation of statistics and opinions contained in Mr. White's second letter, dated March 7, 1889.

One of the final paragraphs of the Boston report of 1888 should be quoted in full, as it contains a prophecy which singularly failed of fulfilment, as shown by the experience of Philadelphia in 1894 : —

" It may be that no great suffering will ensue under the present system in Philadelphia, but your committee fear that, if funds are short now in good times, a panic like that of 1873 would make it absolutely necessary for the public funds to be drawn upon; it would work like a two-edged sword, reducing the means of those who usually support the private societies, and largely increasing the number of needy ones. In Boston the cases aided in the years succeeding 1873 were nearly double the number aided now, although, in the fifteen years, the population has increased about one-third."

If the report of the Boston overseers did not fully convince the residents of Brooklyn, Philadelphia, and other cities that they had made a mistake in abolishing outdoor relief, it seems to have had a quieting effect on any agitation toward the same end at home, and in the period since the report was published there appears not to have developed any very general sentiment against outdoor relief. Several of the active workers in the Associated Charities, if not converted from their earlier faith, have at least come to acquiesce in the present system as not likely soon to be radically changed. Some have gone farther, and doubt whether Dr. F. H. Wines[1] may not be right in pronouncing opposition to outdoor relief a "fad" and insisting that the whole question is one of administration. Certainly the administration of relief is excellently conducted by the board of overseers and its efficient secretary. Among the recent members of the board are the wife of a governor of the state and two presidents of district conferences of the Associated Charities.

Benjamin Pettee, who has served the board of overseers as secretary for over thirty years, is a vigorous advocate of public outdoor relief, and may be said to represent the views of the majority of the board in maintaining the general position taken by the special committee in 1888. The arguments in favor of outdoor relief urged by Mr. Pettee are, first, that it avoids the necessity for breaking up families and substituting institutional care of children for the more natural oversight of parents; second, that it may be made adequate and uniform, and that its burdens are fairly distributed, while private relief is spasmodic, rests entirely upon charitably disposed persons, and may fail entirely because of shrinking income at the very time when destitution is greatest and the need of relief most pressing.

In reply to the argument most frequently urged by opponents of outdoor relief, that a sense of the right to relief overcomes the natural sense of disgrace in receiving help, the secretary urges that this objection applies equally to relief funds in the hands of private societies. Applicants feel that they have a right to such relief, since it was contributed to relieve destitution and was not a gift to particular families. Mr. Pettee thinks that in cities which have no public outdoor relief there is more begging,[2] and that

---

[1] Similar views have been expressed by F. B. Sanborn and others.
[2] The author is convinced that the contrary is the case.

x

there are, in fact, many families in need of relief who do not get it. It is admitted, however, that there are no statistics and no carefully recorded observations that will enable us to decide whether or not this is correct. When asked whether, if public outdoor relief were discontinued in Boston, a large majority of the families who are now being aided would not be able to take care of themselves, Mr. Pettee frankly admits that many of the families could do so, but insists that it is very questionable indeed whether it is advisable that they should be compelled to do without the assistance that is now given. The diminished income would, he thinks, result in deprivation of necessary food, shelter, and clothing. Since it is largely widows with small children who would thus suffer, Mr. Pettee insists that the probability of their being able to get along without the relief which they now obtain is not a sufficient reason for abolishing it. A safeguard against the undue increase of public outdoor relief is found in the universal repugnance to being classed as paupers. Many persons who would strive to maintain their independence as against public aid are less unwilling to apply at the office of private societies, and the road to pauperism is thus made easier by the private relief societies than by the system of outdoor relief.

Such are the arguments in favor of the present system. It is admitted that a lax and inefficient system of administration may result in widespread demoralization, and that under the best conditions it is difficult to avoid political influence both in the actual distribution of relief and in the appointment of overseers and visitors. There is some difference of opinion as to the extent to which politics enters into the present distribution of relief in Boston, but a conservative judgment, based upon interviews with persons competent to testify, is that the political element is not entirely absent, and there are clear indications that the overseers are oftentimes not so strict in the application of their principles as is required by the welfare of the families concerned. The following table shows that there has been a considerable diminution in the amount of relief distributed relatively to the population and a still more marked decrease in the number of families

aided, resulting in an increase during the decade ending
1890 of 70 per cent in the amount of money given to
each family aided : —

OUTDOOR RELIEF, BOSTON

The amounts given do not include what was paid other cities and
towns for relief of Boston poor living therein or amounts expended
for burials.

YEAR ENDING	AMOUNT	FAMILIES IN BOSTON	AVERAGE	POPULATION
Apr. 30, 1877	$80,341.89	6,627	$12.12	341,919 (1875)
" 1878	66,926.66	5,586		
" 1879	59,975.64	5,317		
" 1880	56,777.36	4,277	13.28	362,839
" 1881	57,178.35	4,397		
" 1882	57,563.26	3,999	14.39	
" 1883	58,117.67	3,953		
" 1884	60,475.00	3,854		
" 1885	64,292.96	4,132	15.55	390,393
" 1886	57,876.57	3,459		
" 1887	56,508.63	3,028	18.66	
" 1888	58,397.70	2,953	19.78	
" 1889	60,719.80	2,752		
" 1890	56,414.96	2,509	22.48	448,477
Dec. 31, 1890, 8 mo.	36,509.06	1,837		
Jan. 31, 1892, 13 mo.	59,451.59	2,578		
" 1893	55,144.04	2,440	22.60	
" 1894	63,479.38	3,632		
" 1895	75,900.47	4,006	18.95	496,920
" 1896	71,326.00	3,196		
" 1897	67,821.41	2,998		
" 1898	68,289.13	3,076	22.20	
" 1899	71,386.67	3,394	21.03	
" 1900	64,502.45	2,863	22.53	560,892
" 1901	63,298.30	2,707	23.38	
" 1902	64,391.41	2,637	24.42	
" 1903	63,499.14	2,420	26.24	
" 1904	70,041.91	2,346	29.86	

Opposition to outdoor relief in Boston has by no means
disappeared. In one district the Associated Charities
regularly relieve the overseers of the care of all families
residing within the district who apply to the society for
aid. This plan works admirably. The secretary of the
board of overseers says that complaints are rare, and when

they are made are found on investigation to be without foundation. Miss Zilpha D. Smith, who was for many years general secretary of the Associated Charities, and others who have watched closely the operations of the system, are uncompromising opponents. It has even been suggested that the improved administration may have been a misfortune, since it has not removed the fundamental evil, while it has removed some of the arguments which were found to be effective in other cities. This, however, is obviously a partisan view as it can hardly have been a mistake to improve the constitution of the board. There is constantly in progress an education of individual overseers in the principles that should govern the relief of destitution and this in itself is a valuable result.

The overseers of the poor do not have charge of the almshouse or other charitable institutions, but only of the care of the poor in their own homes. This introduces peculiar difficulties, since, if outdoor relief is refused, there is no certainty of admission to the almshouse, the latter being dependent upon the discretion of a separate board. The overseers, however, may impose any conditions on the receipt of outdoor relief, and excellent use has been made of a wood yard, which is maintained by the overseers for the double purpose of employing able-bodied men whose families are in receipt of outdoor relief and providing an opportunity for homeless men to earn shelter and meals in the adjoining wayfarers' lodge.

The position of those who desire to abolish outdoor relief is briefly as follows : —

No manipulation of relief funds, however ingenious and complete, can do much except incidentally to improve the condition of the poor. Incidentally, by being ever at hand to prevent men from experiencing the results of their own actions and interfering between cause and effect, both private and public relief exert an enormous influence on the character of the poor — often an evil influence. The system of relief, however, may be made educational, inculcating thrift, prudence, and self-restraint, reënforcing the natural instincts of self-preservation. It is very much more difficult to make public relief serve this purpose than private relief. Discrimination is difficult on the part of public authorities, and there is an almost irresistible tendency to increase the amount disbursed, and an even more pronounced tendency to increase the number of recipients. The abolition of outdoor relief does not increase destitution, since a large proportion of those who are at present receiving aid will be found not to require help, but will develop resources of their own. Those who remain may be adequately dealt with by the organized and individual benevolence of the city. If relief from the taxes should be confined to that given in institutions, every one, good or bad, would know that when he reached the end of his means he could find shelter, food, and clothing, all the necessaries of life, in the almshouse; and since he would be sure of finding them there only, where at best life is unattractive, he would be stimulated to supply these necessaries for himself when possible. Relatives also would be led to do more for those unable to support themselves. Private societies and individuals could then confine their relief to the exceptional families where past thrift or the expectation of self-support in the near future makes interference by private philanthropy desirable.

The chief argument against outdoor relief, however, is that from experience. The five leading cities of the seaboard, New York, Brooklyn, Philadelphia, Baltimore, and Washington, counting Brooklyn as a separate city, have found it possible to care for their poor without outdoor relief, and, it would appear, without serious disadvantages. In Western cities, while there have been fewer successful attempts to abolish entirely such relief, stricter administration, and a decrease in the total amount disbursed, have been found to be advantageous.[1] In the cities which have tried both plans the number of persons in the almshouses is diminished when there is no outdoor relief, and there is no noticeable increase in the amount of alms given by private individuals or relief agencies.

In common with the other colonies, Massachusetts inherited from England the general system of poor relief which prevailed in that country in the last century. The present Massachusetts poor law recognizes, as does the

---

[1] The experience of Indianapolis in this direction is especially instructive.

English law, "a right to relief." The language is as follows: —

"Every city and town shall relieve and support all poor and indigent persons lawfully settled therein whenever they stand in need thereof. The overseers of the poor shall have the care and oversight of all such poor and indigent persons so long as they remain at the charge of their respective cities and towns, and shall see that they are suitably relieved, supported, and employed, either in the workhouse or almshouse, or in such other manner as the city or town directs, or otherwise at the discretion of said overseers."

The words in which Thomas Mackay sums up the objections to public outdoor relief are more severe than should be applied in some American communities, although they are amply illustrated in others: —

"From a variety of causes — the general sentimentality of the times, the ignorance of local administrators, the pressure of a population which does not contribute to, but hopes to share in, the general largesse, the corruption of politicians who regard the poor rate as a mere electioneering fund — the poor law, as administered throughout the greater part of the country, is simply a disaster to the best interests of the poorer classes, and succeeds in maintaining a head of pauperism which, though it continues to decrease, is still a disgrace to the intelligence of the country. The system multiplies the number and perpetuates the poverty of the poor."

The objections which to the writer appear conclusive against the distribution of outdoor relief from the public treasury may be summarized as follows: —

I. Under modern conditions private philanthropy is a safer, more stable, and more generous source of supply than taxation. Experience does not seem to confirm the fear that private relief is untrustworthy in times of special distress. It is when there is well-founded conviction of exceptional distress that the purse-strings of the charitable are most freely loosened, and to assume that it will be otherwise is to doubt the most fundamental and the most general of all human instincts. It is not the ordinary taxpayer alone, but the millionnaire also, who holds the

key to the immediately available surplus from which our
universities, our art galleries, our libraries, and our relief
funds of various kinds are to be enriched. There are undoubtedly sources of taxation which may be drawn upon
more fully for the public good, and to these public hospitals, almshouses, and other institutions should look for
their share — proportionate to their needs.

II. A salient fact is, secondly, that private charity is
not very likely to undertake to do what the public does,
even if imperfectly. As a means then, of encouraging
and leaving the field clear for private initiative, as a means
of preventing any confusion of thought on the part of the
public as to what is and what is not done by the state or
its subdivisions, as a means of marking off clearly the
functions of private relief and public relief — those who
do not believe in public outdoor relief would draw a sharp
line between the two. We would ask the state to care, in
appropriate institutions, for those who are recognized as
needing institutional care — those who can be dealt with
in large classes — especially the defective and the insane,
the sick, and again especially those who have contagious
diseases, or diseases dangerous to the community.

III. Miss M. E. Richmond has suggested that the state
should care for those for whom control as well as support
is required; and this again would lead us to leave outdoor
relief to private initiative. Of course it would not follow
that the entire burden of support and training for these
designated classes should necessarily be taken over by the
public authorities. Private philanthropy might do a part
of this also, and should have the right to do what it will
and can. It would be necessary for the state to act in so
far as private funds are not supplied. There would then
be left, however, exclusively for private individuals and
voluntary associations all material assistance required in
the homes of the poor.

IV. This is appropriate, for it is a more delicate
ministry, one requiring greater personal interest, and a more
patient study of the varying elements of each particular
problem. If the family life is to be maintained, and if the
income is not sufficient to do it, the deficit should not be
made up mechanically — as to some extent it must be, if

public officials are to do it — but with infinite pains, with personal sympathy, with temperate consideration of the earning capacity of members of the family, such as a private donor or the visitor of a private society is more likely to show. It is clear that there must be a division of work somewhere, if we are to get the full coöperation of both. However much more than this private philanthropy may do, we shall do well to leave strictly to private charity the giving of all the assistance required to supplement wages, to aid families temporarily disabled by the death or illness of the breadwinner, to supplement the earnings of a mother who is a widow and responsible for the rearing of children, and other similar forms of relief, simply for the reason that private charity has naturally, or certainly may have, more elasticity, more freedom from arbitrary restrictions, and a higher standard of trained professional service.

V. A public fund is subjected to more demands which should be resisted, but which it is difficult even for the most upright and conscientious officials to resist. They come from politicians, but not from them alone. Missionaries, church visitors, clergymen, school-teachers, and even agents of charitable societies have been known to fall into the habits of sending lists of families, and it is a rare overseer or official that will not think it advisable to make some show of doing something when such indorsements arrive. Such requests are often entirely reasonable, and they are not infrequently addressed, as it is right they should be, to private agencies as well. In the degree, however, to which the fund becomes impersonal, and its expenditure dissociated from its source, these demands are likely to become the principal factor in the decisions as to what shall be done — rather than the real needs and the best interests of the family concerned. This impersonal character and this distance between the donor and the one who comes into contact with the family is most complete in the case of public outdoor relief; and the difficulty of its judicious administration, therefore, other things being equal, is greatest.

VI. Even if, finally, there were no inherent fatal objections to the system of public outdoor relief, as we have tried to show that there is, we should still counsel against any agitation for its introduction in New York, Philadelphia, Baltimore, or Washington, because the amount of money which the city seems willing to expend for the care of its dependents in the support of the institutions for which the city is now responsible is inadequate.   There has not been a year in the last twenty years when the appropriations in New York City for food, fuel, clothing, and other supplies in the almshouse and hospitals were as large as they should be.   The same thing, in perhaps a less degree, is true of other cities.   Certainly it would be folly to introduce a demand for an appropriation for outdoor relief, which would probably work injury, when the funds set aside for indoor relief are not sufficient for the actual needs of the aged, the defective, and the sick.

CHAPTER III

IT is now time to consider the part which has been taken by private charity in the relief of the poor in their homes.

With the rise of more populous towns in the early half of the century, and the consequent increase of the number of families for whom special relief of one kind or another seemed necessary, there sprang up naturally a number of private charitable agencies, each, as a rule, giving special attention to some particular class of needs. Among these were some intended for particular nationalities ; as, for example, the German Society of New York, organized in 1787, similar societies in Baltimore in 1817 and in Boston in 1847, the French Benevolent Society of New York, organized in 1809, and that of Boston in 1854, the Scots Charitable Society in Boston in 1657, St. Andrew's Society of New York, founded in 1756, and one of the same name in Baltimore in 1806. Others, however, were intended for widows or for other particular classes of dependents. The Widows Society in Boston was started in 1816, and in the year following there was organized the Boston Fatherless and Widows Society, both intended primarily for Protestants. The Society for the Relief of Poor Widows with Small Children in New York City was organized in 1798. In Boston numerous special trust funds are still administered by the overseers of the poor, some of which date from the last century, although others have been added in recent years. By the year 1840 there were over thirty relief-giving societies in the city of New York. These associations were instituted " on the prin-

---

[1] For the sake of completeness several paragraphs are reproduced in the latter part of the present chapter from the author's earlier and more elementary " Practice of Charity."

ciple of providing for particular classes of the indigent, which united moral objects with the relief of physical want." [1]

An informally constituted committee in the winter of 1842–1843 made a careful examination of the situation, the results of which, in the form of conclusions, were stated by the committee as follows : —

" *First.* That the want of *discrimination in giving relief* was a fundamental and very prevalent defect in most of these schemes of charity. They had no adequate arrangement by which it was possible to learn the character and condition of applicants. Of course no sound judgment could be exercised in distributing aid ; and the societies being subjected to constant imposition, large sums were so misapplied as to create more want than they relieved.

" *Second.* The societies were found to act *independently of each other*, which was another very fruitful source of evil. For as there was no concert of action or reciprocation of intelligence between them, they were ignorant of each other's operations; and artful mendicants so turned this ignorance to their own advantage as often to obtain assistance from many of the societies at the same time without detection. The most undeserving consequently received the largest amount of assistance, and were thus encouraged in dissolute and improvident habits; while the better class of the needy not only obtained less aid, but often far less than their necessities required and the benevolent would have bestowed, provided such a knowledge of their character and circumstances had been possessed which a better system would have conferred.

" *Third.* They made no adequate provision for *personal intercourse* with the *recipients of alms* at their dwellings, nor for such sympathy and counsel as would tend to encourage industrious and virtuous habits, and foster among them a spirit of self-dependence. In short, the final and prospective end of all true charity was generally unattained by them, inasmuch as, in addition to other defects, they failed to provide for the permanent physical and moral improvement of those their alms relieved.

[1] First Annual Report of the Association for Improving the Condition of the Poor, p. 14.

"*Fourth.* The inquiries of the committee also embraced the *legal provision for the poor*, which resulted in the conviction that no form of charity which has not especial reference to the removal of the causes of pauperism can fail to increase its amount; and it appeared equally certain that no such provision could embrace all the objects of private benevolence or supersede its efforts; and after the laws had done their utmost an immense work would remain unaccomplished, which could not be effected by isolated individual exertions."

The agent of the committee, Robert M. Hartley, visited Boston, Philadelphia, Baltimore, and other cities, and by correspondence in this country and abroad attempted to gather information that would be of use in inaugurating a better plan. It appears, however, that he considered these visits entirely profitless, and that the system which he subsequently put into operation was elaborated from his own ideas.[1]

The New York Association for Improving the Condition of the Poor deserves special attention, not only because its foundation marks an epoch in the creation of valuable literature on the subject of preventive charity, but because in the practical details of organization it formed a model upon which many similar associations in America and Europe have been formed. It is an interesting coincidence that the foundation of this Association and the appearance of its early reports, discussing with much vigor and insight the principles underlying the new movement, should have taken place just in the middle of the century, and that within the five years following there were published a number of extremely valuable reports, tracts, declarations of principles, and suggestions for visitors, of exactly the kind that would be most likely to prove useful to other societies desiring to take similar action. In the language of Mr. Hartley's biographer: —

"The design of the association was to advance the social, moral, and material interests of large masses of the community by a united effort embracing the whole city, through the operation of a system which, so far as possi-

---

[1] Memorial of Robert M. Hartley, p. 187.

ble, would provide for existing difficulties, avoid unknown evils, and secure beneficent results. It contemplated escaping the evils inseparable from isolated and independent exertions, through the united and concerted action of a general organization, hoping thus to diminish the chances of imposition, to ascertain the exact amount of charity each individual received, and to secure its judicious distribution. Moral means were also to be employed, from the fact that no other would be adequate to produce the results which the condition of the indigent required. It contemplated, likewise, preventive rather than remedial measures. It was primarily and directly to discountenance indiscriminate almsgiving; to visit the poor at their homes, to give them counsel, to assist them when practicable in obtaining employment, to inspire them with self-respect and self-reliance, to inculcate habits of economy, industry, and temperance, and, whenever absolutely necessary, to provide such relief as should be suited to their wants. Such was the platform upon which the association proposed to build, and such were the aims it thoughtfully set before it."

The following clear and definite rules were laid down for the guidance of visitors: —

I. To regard each applicant for relief as entitled to charity until a careful examination proves the contrary.

II. To give relief only after a personal investigation of each case by visitation and inquiry.

III. To relieve no one excepting through the visitor of the section in which he lives.

IV. To give necessary articles, and only what is immediately necessary.

V. To give what is least susceptible of abuse.

VI. To give only in small quantities in proportion to immediate need, and of coarser quality than might be procured by labor, except in cases of sickness.

VII. To give assistance at the right moment; not to prolong it beyond the duration of the necessity which calls for it; but to extend, restrict, and modify relief according to that necessity.

VIII. To require of each beneficiary abstinence from intoxicating liquors as a drink; of such as have young children of proper age, that they be kept at school, except unavoidable circumstances prevent, and to apprentice those of suitable years to some trade, or send them to service. The design being to make the poor a party to their own improvement and elevation, the wilful violation or disregard of these rules shall debar them from further relief.

IX. To give no relief to recent immigrants having claims on the Commissioners of Immigration, except in urgent cases for two or three days, or until that department can be informed of such cases, when the responsibility of this association toward them shall cease.

X. To give no aid to persons who, from infirmity, imbecility, old age, or any other cause, are likely to continue unable to earn their own support, and consequently to be permanently dependent, except in extreme cases for two or three days, or until they can be referred to the governors of the almshouse.

XI. To discontinue relieving all who manifest a purpose to depend on alms rather than on their own exertions for support, and whose further maintenance would be incompatible with their good and the objects of the institution.

XII. To give to those having claims on other charities a card directing them thereto, which indicates thereon why such relief was refused by the association; also a card, a duplicate thereof, which the member should require the applicant to produce when he affirms that the association has denied him relief.

It will be seen that the association did not undertake to aid those who were entirely and permanently dependent nor, unless in very exceptional circumstances, those who were permanently but not entirely dependent and who were in receipt of public outdoor relief. There seems to have been disappointment in the operation of the twelfth rule, since in an address by the secretary to visitors in the year 1847 he was compelled to admit that "unfortunately, as our own experience will attest, though there are numerous charitable organizations in the city, few have been found of much practical use to this association." This was regarded as proof that the association was filling a place in the systematic charities of the city which

was filled by no other, but was not to be regarded as a
reason for abandoning the practice of refusing to give
assistance to those who were clearly the proper beneficiaries of other existing agencies. More interesting, however, is the confident belief of the secretary that after
excluding permanent paupers and dependents properly belonging to other agencies, fifteen thousand persons in New
York City remain in whole or in part dependent for subsistence upon gratuitous relief, and that each of these "has
a distinct mark set upon him by Providence or his own
character, which mark clearly indicates the department to
which he legitimately belongs, or the source from which he
should derive relief." The mark which visitors of the
association were asked to recognize as indicating their
own poor was the possibility of elevating the moral and
physical condition of the applicant. Those who could not
be elevated were not to have relief. Furthermore visitors
were to bear in mind that there were practical limits to
the amount of care and attention which they could give,
and the constitution was interpreted to allow relief only
to those whose moral and physical condition will be improved by the amount of relief and attention which the
visitor in the proper discharge of his duties is able to
bestow. As if to emphasize the importance of this discrimination visitors are told that "their recollections will
confirm the declaration that every exposition of our objects which has been given to the public, whether in the
visitors' manual, the annual reports, or other documents,
enforces and illustrates these as the fundamental objects
of the association."

In sharp contrast with this class were to be placed those
bearing the "corporation mark,"—that is, those who should
be helped by the public authorities in the almshouse or
otherwise. The association refused to dignify public support by calling it charity, and did not hesitate to say that
the present system of outdoor almshouse relief is one of
the most productive sources of pauperism in the city.
The association enrolled a large number of volunteer visitors who became not only its almoners, but also its agents
in the work of personally improving the moral and physical condition of the families with which it had to do, and

remonstrance was often necessary to prevent the visitors from relaxing efforts at moral reform, and calling in the discredited system of relying entirely upon almsgiving. The visitor is constantly enjoined that it is his duty to send all who bear the mark of the corporation to the alms-house commissioner for relief, when the responsibility of the association toward such families ceases.

Although the association was aware of the danger of allowing its energies to be absorbed by outside special enterprises and refrained from undertaking certain reforms to which they would have been inclined, they were nevertheless active in several directions besides the supplying of material relief. Most important among these was the agitation for improved dwellings, the first fruit of which was the "Report of the Committee on the Sanitary Condition of the Laboring Classes of the City of New York with Remedial Suggestions," published in 1853. This report contained definite recommendations for legislative action, as well as an appeal to capitalists and owners of real estate to embrace the opportunity before them and to take advantage "of the singular privilege of becoming benefactors of the poor with pecuniary advantage to themselves." It appeared that most of the new tenement-houses were on so contracted and penurious a scale, that they were actually inferior to many of the old buildings whose places they supplied, that vice and pauperism were perpetuated by such causes, the almshouse and prisons supplied with recruits, and the city burdened with taxes for the support of dependents. In conclusion the report denies that the more strict legislation recommended would interfere with the rights of property-holders or with the rights of tenants ; emphasizes the educational influence of more sanitary regulations upon the laboring classes, and expresses the belief that many of the laboring classes are more alive to their privileges than has been generally supposed, and that, so far from thwarting endeavors to promote their health and cleanliness, they will render every possible assistance, for they will discover that their own best interests are promoted by all those measures which are calculated to improve their sanitary condition.

The association inaugurated the plan of collecting cast-off clothing for distribution among the poor and also of providing for the wise distribution of broken victuals by registering the names of such residents as were willing to give only to families sent by the association. The plan of loaning stoves was in force for several years. There were repeated efforts to repress vagrancy and street begging, and the educational work of the association extended to the circulation of tracts containing directions about food and drink and their preparation, and warning against intemperance and other vices. Many thousand copies of a twelve-page pamphlet entitled " The Economist " were circulated, and Poor Richard's famous brochure, " The Way to Wealth," was also published as a tract by the association with, however, several appended extracts from Proverbs and Ecclesiastes calculated to supply what was regarded as a want of religious feeling and sentiment in the original. After careful examination of the recommendations for and against an employment bureau, it was decided in 1850 not to enter upon this field but to continue the policy of urging removal to the country upon all those who were unable to find employment in the city.[1]

The association in the sixty years of its existence has taken an active part in many useful reforms and social improvements, and has been instrumental in organizing a large number of charitable institutions and societies for special objects not included within its own original scope.

In several other cities relief associations were started within a few years after the foundation of the New York association. The Baltimore Association for Improving the Condition of the Poor dates from 1849, the Boston Provident Association from 1851, and the Chicago Relief and Aid Society from the autumn of 1857. Although the Chicago society adopted a different name, it was undoubtedly indebted for many of its leading features directly, or through the influence of other societies which had copied the plan, to the New York Association for Improving the Condition of the Poor. This is shown most clearly in the general rules of the society which follow at most points the rules of the parent organization. At first

---

[1] Over forty years later, however, the association for a period of five years conducted an employment bureau. See p. 336.

volunteer visitors were employed by the Chicago Relief and Aid Society, but this was soon found unsatisfactory and paid visitors were employed. A division of the city into districts was, however, continued in Chicago and in Baltimore, while in New York City both the territorial subdivision into districts and the employment of volunteer visitors were eventually discontinued.

Among the originators of the Provident Association of Boston were Rev. Dr. Ephraim Peabody and the Hon. Robert C. Winthrop. The territorial limits established at the outset have never been extended. Its principal objects, as stated in a brief paper by Mr. Edward Frothingham, the present general agent,[1] were to endeavor to elevate the character and improve the condition of the poor, and to suppress street begging. The city was divided into twelve districts and these were subdivided into one hundred and seventy sections; each section having its volunteer visitor whose business it was to visit, investigate, and, if necessary, to relieve all families who were referred to them by subscribers through whose contributions the association was supported.

With the early annual reports was published a directory containing a list of the streets of the city and carefully prepared directions to both subscribers and visitors. The latter, of whom there were at no time over one hundred, were expected to send monthly reports of their experiences to the general agent at the central office. After 1880 this system was changed. The volunteer visitors were found difficult to control; many lacked judgment; most of them were extravagant; and they often neglected to forward their monthly reports. Captain A. G. Goodwin, who was for twenty years the general agent, used to say that the visitors often gave him more trouble than the applicants. So the volunteers were gradually allowed to drop off, their places being filled by paid visitors. At the present time the visiting and aiding the poor is entirely in the hands of trained agents who make visiting their business and do nothing else. The wisdom of changing the volunteer system to paid experts is thought to be demonstrated by

[1] "One of Boston's Great Charities," in the Prospect Union Review for March 6, 1895.

the saving to the association of many thousands of dollars. The worthy poor are said to be better cared for, and a check is given to imposition and fraud, formerly so prevalent. The association has in its service three of these paid visitors, each assigned to a particular district.

Mr. Frothingham considers that experience has proved beyond question that great relief agencies like the overseers of the poor (who have charge of public outdoor relief in Massachusetts) and the Provident Association can do their work far more expeditiously, economically, and safely with a small body of trained visitors than through a large number of inexperienced volunteers. The conclusion, however, does not apply to a society like the Associated Charities, in the prosecution of whose work volunteer visitors are, he thinks, indispensable.

In the year 1871 the Chicago Relief and Aid Society had an experience such as has probably never fallen to the lot of any other organized charity of Europe or America. This was the task of receiving and disbursing within a period of about six months the sum of about $5,000,000 for the relief of sufferers from the Chicago fire. An account of the manner in which this trust was discharged is given in a separate chapter.

It is unnecessary to trace the beneficent and multifarious activities of the special and general relief societies of various types organized in recent years. Scarcely any city is without such private societies, and sometimes they are subsidized from the public treasury. Moreover, the churches engage to a greater or less extent in relief work, their funds for this purpose being placed either in the hands of paid visitors or of special church officers, such as deacons, although it not infrequently happens that it is thought best to organize a special committee or society within the church to discharge this duty. The Protestant churches have not passed beyond this somewhat unorganized stage, nor have they usually reached the conclusion which would be the most sensible, and of which there are some striking examples, viz., to withdraw entirely from the province of material relief.

The Roman Catholic church has developed within the past forty years a network of societies of laymen which have greatly simplified and improved the charitable activity of that church so far as it has to do with the care and relief of needy families. The Society of St. Vincent de Paul owes allegiance to the Council-General in Paris, but with the exception of ninety-two conferences in the three councils of Brooklyn, St. Louis, and New Orleans, the conferences in the United States are under the direction of what is known as the Superior Council of New York. There were in 1902 four hundred and twenty-eight distinct conferences with an active membership of 6979. Their receipts and disbursements for relief were about $180,000. While this is only a small part of the total amount given by the Catholic church and its members to destitute families, it is of importance because of the comparatively progressive and enlightened manner in which the society is administered, and because it is supplemented by the volunteer personal service of the active members of the society who pledge themselves to visit and to give religious and moral oversight to those under its care.

Extraordinary conditions in the Jewish communities of the chief centres of population, arising from the heavy immigration from eastern Europe, have made necessary liberal provision for the needs of destitute Hebrews. Of recent years the distribution of this relief has been systematized, and in some instances greatly increased in amount. In several cities various societies have been consolidated into an organization known as the United Hebrew Charities, or the Federation of Jewish Charities. The United Hebrew Charities of New York has four constituent societies and seventeen coöperating societies and sisterhoods. It maintains an employment bureau, a medical and obstetrical service, provides regular monthly stipends aggregating in 1903 about $35,000, occasional relief in money to the amount of nearly $80,000 ; transportation to about $17,500; clothing, shoes, furniture, tools, etc., about $8000 ; fuel, about $3000. The cost of the medical service is a little under $4000, and that of burials nearly $3000. The total expenditures of the United Hebrew Charities for the five years ending September 30, 1903, were : 1899, $136,439.75; 1900, $145,734.72; 1901, $155,602.64; 1902, $175,046.40; and 1903, $206,148.74.

Many of the recently arrived immigrants do not apply for relief but for tools for their respective trades. These are to a large extent persons who, when economic conditions are favorable, eventually become self-supporting.

In the summer of 1899 a careful study was made by the manager of the United Hebrew Charities of the city of New York of one thousand applicants who originally asked for assistance in the fall of 1894. This investigation showed that 60 per cent did not apply after that year ; 73 per cent did not apply after 1895, 80 per cent after 1896, 85 per cent after 1897, and 93 per cent after 1898 — leaving 7 per cent of the original number still being assisted during the year 1899. Of one hundred cases investigated, 12 per cent were found to be self-supporting, 22 per cent had removed from New York City, having been assisted originally with transportation, and 66 per cent could not be found and were doubtless to a large extent self-supporting. These figures demonstrate both the exceptional conditions under which Hebrew families have been compelled to ask for assistance and the absence of a pauperizing effect in the aid given.

Perhaps the earliest Protestant church charity which became permanent is the Boston " Quarterly Charity Lecture," formed in 1720 by a few persons who held quarterly meetings on Sunday evenings for benevolent purposes at which some member was invited to preach.[1] On March 6, 1720, Cotton Mather gave the first of these lectures of which there is a record. The meeting is now held annually. The collections made at this lecture and the income from two endowed funds, yielding from $1500 to $1800 annually, are distributed equally among four Congregational churches who dispense them according to the prevailing custom of the charitable organization of each church.

The proportion of destitute families among adherents of the Roman Catholic and the Jewish faiths is larger than among the membership of Protestant churches. To a large extent, however, the Protestant churches have aided families whose connection with the church is a very shad-

---

[1] Chapter on "Charities of Boston," by George Silsbee Hale, in " Memorial History of Boston," p. 660.

owy one, consisting oftentimes merely of the attendance
of children upon the Sunday-school or even proximity of
residence.

St. George's Protestant Episcopal church in the city of
New York disbursed a poor fund in the year ending April
1, 1899, amounting to $2400, besides which $159 was subscribed for Thanksgiving dinners for the poor ; a guild and
employment society gave work through the winter to forty
women who were paid $733.15 ; the Helping Hand Society
aided in providing hand sewing, as a result of which eight
hundred and fifty-two garments were made by beneficiaries,
and over $400 additional was paid in wages and in the form
of dry goods and groceries ; a Seaside Cottage for summer
excursionists, accommodating forty resident guests and
from one to two hundred day excursionists at a time, was
maintained for thirteen weeks at a total expense of
$3295.62, all of which was contributed in the Easter Sun-
day collection.   The chief items in the disbursement of the
poor fund proper were : to pensioners, $420; to the sick,
$411.28; to the poor direct, through the clergy and deacon-
esses, $325 ; medicine, $180.86 ; orthopædic and other
appliances, $80.75; groceries, $738.84 (of this amount,
however, $302.50 represents sales at low prices, and only
the balance, $436.34, donations) ; coal, $48.35 ; meals and
lodgings, $3.70 ; rent, $19 ; shoes, $48.65.   This amount
was obtained chiefly from communion alms in amounts
varying from $11.36 in September to $202.01 in January.
The number of families to whom groceries were given during the year was one hundred and sixty-six, and about an
equal number made regular purchases.

In Trinity Church of New York City and its eight chapels the appropriations for the poor, exclusive of those for
the maintenance of hospitals in which the parish is interested, amounted to $5850.61.   Of this over $1000 was for
burials, and $631 for medical services to the poor of one
of the chapels.

St. Bartholomew's parish, while disbursing a poor fund
of smaller amount, has an even larger number of special
enterprises for the elevation and improvement of the poor.
The poor fund for the year ending November 1, 1899,
amounted to $1725.27, of which sum $200.22 was from

loans returned by beneficiaries. Except the sum of $227.35 this amount may be said to have been expended in the charitable relief of needy families, though it was for a variety of purposes, including nursing and medical aid, clothing, funerals, rents, cash loans, and payments of fees in the Employment Bureau maintained by the same parish. Besides the poor fund the parish disbursed through its visitor $416 in the form of pensions, paid wages, etc., in a tailor shop amounting to $1632.74, enabling the shop to give away or sell at moderate prices 1248 garments. There was disbursed in fresh-air work $2000, and smaller sums in other special ways. This church maintains also a Penny Provident Fund in which there are 2648 depositors who saved in the current year the sum of $1844.82.

It would be difficult to find a more frank and eloquent confession of the perplexities involved in church relief than is contained in the two following paragraphs from the report of one of the assistant ministers of this parish : —

" The never ending stream of applicants for help in some form or other — sometimes in the way of employment, oftentimes in the way of direct and material aid in circumstances of poverty, sickness, and want — is a disheartening feature. It never seems to grow any less. All we do only relieves. All that is done everywhere by all churches and charitable agencies only seems to touch the surface and help temporarily. We do not seem to cure and remove the trouble. Here and there a case occurs probably where the good effect is permanent, but the trouble is deep seated. It is both acute and chronic and may be expected, I suppose, to be always with us. It would be easier and lighter for us, however, — less depressing and more endurable, — if it were not for the tinge of unworthiness and imposture which runs so freely through it, leaving one often at a loss how to deal with it and exposing one to the charge, on the one hand, of being 'soft' and 'an easy mark' for fraud, or, on the other hand, of being hard hearted, unsympathetic, and unchristian.

"One wonders sometimes whether there may not be a measure of truth in the latter charge, such is the damaging effect of the frequent contact with the revelations of human nature's weakness and wickedness, and one is sometimes compelled to acknowledge the truth of the former charge by the actual results of an attempt to be charitable."

These are three of the churches in which the amounts contributed for the purpose of helping the poor in their own homes are probably larger than in other Protestant churches, and they are therefore not typical, either in amount or in kind, of the average work done by the churches as such.

Inquiry has been made concerning one prosperous and active Presbyterian church in the city of Philadelphia whose membership, while it does not contain a large number of the poor, does embrace an unusually large number of citizens who are leaders in educational, social, and philanthropic activities.   It is reported that the total relief fund does not exceed $300 or $400 and that this is largely in the form of loans which are repaid.   Whether the money is loaned or given it is chiefly used for the purchase of fuel in winter.   There are no regular pensioners.

A Methodist Episcopal church, whose membership embraces a large number of families of very limited means, disburses relief in a year amounting to $250.   This is given to five families, three of whom are on the regular list, while the remaining two are intermittent recipients.   Except in an unusual emergency this church never gives more than one dollar per week per family, and with one exception this aid is given only after work of equivalent value has been performed.   The exception is in the case of a cripple who is the support of an invalid mother.   The work which she does making buttonholes on vests consumes so much of her time and strength that the church does not feel justified in asking her to do any work for the one dollar a week given to her.   Save in the case just mentioned the beneficiaries are all widows with small children.   Four of the five are members of the congregation; the other has no church connection.

These two churches would not include the giving of Thanksgiving and Christmas dinners in their statement of relief disbursed, as these are intended as social courtesies rather than as relief ; they are frequently given to families which have not reached the point of needing relief, and generally in such a way as not to reveal the source of the

donation. The pastors and officials of many churches
would now disavow any intention of making the church a
relief agency, and the churches are becoming solicitous that
their own members as well as possible applicants who are
not communicants shall understand that the churches do not
exist primarily for this purpose. It is their policy to report
original applications for relief from outsiders to the charitable societies, and, as far as their own members are concerned, to anticipate destitution by persuading those who
are likely to become dependent to make use of agencies for
saving, or otherwise to prevent the need for outside help.

Here and there throughout the country particular parishes or congregations will be found which are compelled to
give a considerable amount of relief, and which as a result
of experience have adopted modern methods of relief, but
there are no general statistics of the amounts given by the
various congregations of any of the Protestant churches,
and there is nothing like a uniform system in general use
in the entire body of churches of any one of the great
Protestant denominations.

A few pastors have taken the advanced but entirely ten-
able position that the churches are intended only for worship and for religious fellowship, not for the supply of
material needs. The relief fund has given way to outside
or affiliated agencies for the promotion of thrift, temperance, and education. Other churches, such as those already
described, without going so far as to abolish relief, have
introduced discrimination and personal service as its allies,
have enlisted volunteer corps of workers, where necessary
have employed professional visitors, and have willingly
exchanged information with other churches and with relief
societies regarding families who may be known to others
besides themselves. To a large extent, however, the
churches and religious societies pursue an antiquated and
short-sighted policy, giving relief from sentimental motives
without personal knowledge of its effect upon those who
receive it, and oftentimes in the hope that possible converts
may be attracted through this means. This criticism
applies with peculiar force to missions, to posts of the Salvation Army, Church Army, Volunteers, and other organizations which aim to reach the outcast and the neglected,

and is defended on the ground that in no other way can they gain the attention and the confidence of those whom they would rescue. The most encouraging aspect of the system, or lack of system, among the churches in their care of needy families, is that there is everywhere dissatisfaction with the results, and if there is also unwillingness to adopt better methods because of a traditional feeling that they are necessarily bound up with harshness and an uncharitable spirit, this should prove to be only a transitional stage, to be succeeded either by associated and intelligent sympathy and progressive relief methods, or by a division of work with relief societies.

Besides the churches and the general relief societies there are numerous agencies for the care and relief of needy families which rest upon a national or special basis. Some of these, as has been explained, date from the eighteenth or the beginning of the nineteenth century. Others, however, have been founded recently. Their benefits are sometimes restricted to members and their families, with only such response to appeals from outsiders as would be given by any mutual benefit society not intended for general relief. Others, deriving their financial support from membership fees and the contributions of the charitable, are intended to aid families of a particular nationality or belonging to a specified class. An illustration of the latter is the Armenian Benevolent Association of Boston, formed for the purpose of helping Armenians within ten miles of Boston, securing employment, caring for the sick, and giving material aid to the needy. As illustrations of the former may be mentioned the Beneficial Association of the Maryland Line, with headquarters in Baltimore, which, besides being a mutual benefit association of ex-Confederate soldiers, also relieves the needs of sick and destitute families of ex-Confederates in Maryland and aids to bury the dead; and the Italian Benevolent Society of New York, which, although stating its general objects to be for the relief of sick and needy Italians, to improve their moral and physical condition, to assist immigrants and to form colonies in different parts of the country, finds it necessary in practice to limit its benefits, to a large extent, to its own members and their friends.

In New York City nearly every nationality is represented by a society which, as a rule, aids residents, provides transportation in suitable cases for those who seek to return to their own homes, and to some extent aids recent immigrants to find employment. In Boston there are fourteen relief agencies for various nationalities, besides seventy-six mutual benefit societies for special races or nationalities with headquarters in New York. Most notable among agencies of this kind is the Baron de Hirsch Fund, which is amply endowed and does not depend upon current contributions. The object of this fund is to Americanize and assimilate the immigrants by teaching them to become good citizens and to prevent, by all proper means, their congregating in large cities. It furnishes mechanics with tools; teaches easily acquired trades or the knowledge of the use of tools; pays entrance fees into trade-unions, loans small sums in exceptional cases to help to self-support, but does not give direct charitable relief. It does, however, provide transportation to points where it is absolutely known there is a market for the particular kind of laborers to be sent. It establishes day and night schools for children and adults, when the local authorities and private organizations have failed to make such provision, wherein are taught the elementary branches of English, including a knowledge of the Constitution of the United States and the inculcation of improved sanitary habits.

Private charity does not embody itself completely in relief societies. Organized agencies are likely to absorb attention in a historical survey, since it is possible to trace them. It must never be forgotten, however, that the aid extended to those in distress secretly by private individuals is of vast amount in the aggregate, although the fact that it is left unrecorded leaves it largely outside the field of the student of past or current relief societies.[1]

[1] There is, there can be, no record of the work and gifts of generous stewards of the abundance which has rewarded lives of labor; of men whom the living recall, the steady stream of whose annual beneficence was a king's ransom, of those whom the living know, whose annual gifts are an ample fortune; or of the "honorable women," whose lives are full of good deeds and almsgiving. It seems only an injustice to the living and the dead of a community, which has had and still has such men

Only a small part of the gifts made for charitable purposes, munificent in the aggregate, are recorded in any permanent way. Donations for material relief have not been so frequent within the present century as in earlier centuries, partly for the reason that gifts for direct relief, rigidly controlled by the donor's stipulations, were apt to have an injurious effect, and partly because endowments for educational purposes, such as schools and libraries, were found to be far more useful. Aside from donations of large sums by wealthy individuals there remains, however, a large field for individual help. Indeed, it is a question whether the unmeasured but certainly large amount of neighborly assistance given in the tenement-houses of the city, precisely as in a New England village or in a frontier settlement, does not rank first of all among the means for the alleviation of distress. The proverbial kindness of the poor to the poor finds ample illustration in the congested quarters of the city, even though physical proximity there counts least in the feeling of responsibility for neighbors. One of the most interesting generalizations made by Charles Booth is that, while all classes in London give largely in charity, the poorest people give the most in proportion to what they have. This is equally true in American communities. What the housekeeper and the fellow-tenants do for the temporary relief of those whose income is cut off by accident, sickness, or misfortune, must be given a large place in any statement of the relief system.

Such assistance as this has many advantages over that given by organized societies. There is little probability of imposition, of excessive relief, or of relief that is ill adapted to its purpose, such as is common in the wholesale distribution made by public officials and which sometimes shows

and women among its members, to attempt a record necessarily so imperfect. — GEORGE SILSBEE HALE: "Memorial History of Boston."

In a footnote to the above passage, the author quotes from the diary and correspondence of Amos Lawrence an estimate that between 1807 and 1829 this private citizen of Boston expended in systematic charity for the benefit of his fellowmen some $7,000,000; and says: "It is hardly necessary to add that this sum was much greater in value then than now, and that large fortunes are both larger and more numerous; but it may be added that the living rival this munificence and exceed it in amount. We are forbidden to name the living, and it is impossible to name all those who are entitled to honor as examples of charity among the dead."

itself in the work of private agencies. We have no method comparable to that of Dr. Chalmers in throwing the responsibility for relief entirely upon the private resources of immediate neighbors, and such a plan might prove inadequate, but as an element in the instinctive and unorganized methods by which the community distributes among its members the shock of unexpected want, unofficial neighborly assistance is always to be given a liberal recognition.

Allied with this, although upon a somewhat different basis, may be placed the professional services of physicians in the charity work of which some falls to the share of every physician, and the information and advice given by lawyers who untangle many a snarl and protect from many a villany without compensation; assistance given by church members and pastors individually to their own poor, no mention of which appears upon the official records of the church; credit extended with little or no hope of payment by retail dealers, who may be nearly as poor as their customers; forbearance of landlords in the matter of rents; the advance of wages before they are earned, by employers; and the various other kinds of assistance analogous to these. They are but one step removed from that neighborly charity which gives because of personal acquaintance. It may be said that these are professional or business relations, rather than personal, yet the underlying motive is similar. The impulse is a charitable one, and if in some instances it is a professional rather than a charitable spirit, it is a magnanimous, altruistic, professional spirit springing from the same qualities that give rise to neighborliness, friendship, and charity. It is wholly unmeasured and immeasurable in amount. It is not to be denied that it is sometimes ill advised and unfortunate in its results. It is, however, fundamental, sound, and sensible as a feature in the relief of distress. It is one of those elastic and elusive, but necessary, social forces which supplement organized schemes and insure needed assistance where, from ignorance of the necessity or from a failure on the part of those who are in trouble to act in what might be considered the rational manner, the more systematic plans might miscarry. It is therefore a creditable as well as a considerable element in the relief system, and it is not the least of its advantages that it gives peculiar scope for the development of those qualities in the individuals which eventually provide organized charity as well as individual assistance. In America such charity is spontaneous in all professions and callings, and among persons of all grades of income.

It might not seem amiss to enumerate in this connection as an agency for the relief of needy families those means of self-protection from the evil results of sickness, accident, and death which rest upon a business basis, such as benefit societies, benefit features of labor organizations, fraternal associations, insurance societies, and clubs of various kinds. They are not, however, charities, although they are of the greatest possible service in making charity in its lower forms unnecessary. If such preventive organizations covered the whole field of industry and if personal thrift were developed to the point at which laborers did their own saving instead of paying large sums to others to do their saving for them, the need for providing relief would almost disappear, as the number of needy families would be so small that relatives or neighbors would easily be found to care for them. There would still be room for both the kinds of charity to which reference has last been made, but they could be exercised to a considerable extent in higher spheres. Instead of providing fuel, clothing, and shelter, they would give increased opportunities for social, educational, and industrial advancement, and would only in rare instances need to provide the necessaries of life for those who are unable to supply their own wants. Plans of insurance and self-help are not a part of a system of relief, but they are not to be overlooked as welcome alternatives.

There remains a class of special agencies which have to do with the care and relief of needy families, but which do not administer material relief in the ordinary sense. Illustrations of these are : —

I. The free employment agencies, and agencies which, while making a reasonable charge for the services rendered, do this in such a way as to make it possible for one who is without means to take advantage of their facilities, making payment after employment has been secured and wages received.

II. Day nurseries, kindergartens, and manual training or industrial schools, which, either without compensation or at moderate prices, relieve working women of the care of their children during the hours when they are employed.

III. Agencies for the promotion of thrift, which provide easy means of saving small amounts, thus lessening the temptation to extravagance, and making the way easy for the safe investment of small sums.

IV. Dispensaries, which afford medical and surgical treatment and medicines either free or at small charge, treatment being given at the dispensary, or, when necessary, by visits at the home of the patients made by dispensary physicians.

The free employment agencies have sprung in part from the desire to substitute normal employment both for relief and for artificially created work, and in part from the discovery of outrageous abuses practised upon those needing employment by some of the ordinary commercial agencies, which take advantage of the necessity of the poor to compel them to accept exorbitant terms. As far as the first of these two objects is concerned, the free bureaus have had very limited success. In order to win the confidence of employers, they are under the necessity of recommending only competent persons who can provide satisfactory references, but such persons can ordinarily find employment themselves. The natural result is that the lists of persons who are really placed in positions do not, to any very great extent, overlap the lists of the beneficiaries of relief societies. The natural beneficiary of the free employment agencies is in a slightly higher class industrially than the beneficiary of public or private relief agencies. Nevertheless, both the free employment agency and those which aid with the understanding that payment may be made after employment is secured, render an important service, and constitute an element in the general system of aiding those who are in distress which cannot be neglected. One of the oldest of these agencies is the Industrial Aid Society for the Pre-

vention of Pauperism, which has been in existence in the
city of Boston since 1835.   It conducts a free employment
bureau, places men and women, boys and girls, singly and
in families, for every variety of work, transient and permanent, in city and in country.   In the winter it employs
men in cleaning ice and snow from the railroads, streets,
and yards.   It also pursues the policy of sending to factory towns families with several children over fourteen
years of age.

The most instructive experiment of this kind was that of
the New York Employment Society, which grew out of the
unusual distress of the winter of 1893–1894.   The society
was incorporated under the above name and later merged in
the Cooper Union Labor Bureau, conducted for five years
as a department of the New York Association for Improving the Condition of the Poor, and discontinued on September 30, 1900, after the establishment of a Free State
Employment Bureau, and a general improvement in business conditions, resulting in a decrease in the number of
unemployed.

The principles laid down by this agency were that no
man should be registered who had not been at least six
months in the state.   It was not the intention that benevolent funds should be allowed to attract the unemployed
from the country or from other cities.   Evidences of
competency were also demanded.   It was felt to be in-
admissible that the inefficient should be pushed ahead of
capable men by the special efforts of the bureau, although
there might perhaps be no objection to the practice on the
part of personal friends, missionaries, and visitors of supplementing individual efforts of inefficient, shiftless men
in the hope of gradually transforming and developing
the qualities in which they were deficient.   Investigation
of moral character was also held to be essential.   Even competent workmen, if addicted to drink, gambling, or other
evil habits, were not to be aided by the bureau, and,
finally, married men with families, or those having others
dependent upon them, were given preference over single
men.   Were there sufficient work for all who were willing
and competent and of good character, this principle would
be void, but during periods of industrial depression, when

there are several applicants for every vacant position, a discrimination was believed to be legitimate.

Although the committee in charge of the bureau did not think it advisable to continue it under improved business conditions, and in competition with free labor advertisements in daily papers, with the Free State Labor Bureau, and with commercial agencies, — which on a business basis aggressively canvassed and advertised for available positions for employment, — they remained of the opinion that the free labor bureau is an important factor in philanthropic work. If such a bureau is to be operated privately, it would, in the opinion of the committee which had gained this experience, better be conducted by a society organized for the particular purpose, rather than by one engaged in general relief work. The two reasons urged for this belief are, that many men whom the bureau would be especially designed to help would not avail themselves of its opportunities on account of the tinge of charity resulting from its connection with a relief society, and that employers are likely to assume that lower wages can be paid, because those who come to the bureau are evidently in urgent need of work. To the first of these objections it may be replied that the fact that the bureau is conducted independently does not lessen its charitable character, assuming that it is operated from philanthropic motives; and to the second, that a relief society would obviously be doing less than its duty if it enabled employers to obtain workmen at less than current wages, although it must be admitted that such societies have not been free from criticism in this respect. It is true, as has already been pointed out, that those who can properly be placed by a free employment bureau are not as a rule the persons who are legitimately under the care of relief agencies, and there would, therefore, seem to be no adequate reason for conducting the two as parts of one institution.

In the five years ending September 30, 1900, the bureau registered and investigated the references of 23,485 men and boys. Forty-five per cent of these had satisfactory references; 25 per cent had unsatisfactory references; and 21 per cent were unknown by those to whom they had referred. Of the men whose references were satisfactory,

z

75 per cent, or 9595, were placed, at an average expense of $2.08.

Upon a somewhat different plan is the free employment bureau of the Society of St. Vincent de Paul, conducted by the Particular Council of New York. Its unique feature is that it has grown out of the needs of the conferences established in the various parishes of the church with which the society is affiliated. Comparatively few of the men for whom positions are found apply directly at the bureau, most of them being men who are known to the visitors of the society to be in need of employment because of application for assistance in other ways. On the other hand the positions to be found are made known to the bureau by members of the society, who are asked to report to the bureau vacancies among their own employees, in business houses, retail stores, etc. This plan enables the bureau to avoid the expense and disadvantages of public advertising, and gives reliable information regarding both applicants and positions.

The records of the free employment bureau of the United Hebrew Charities of the same city show that in a period of twenty-four years work was procured for 65,774 persons, although these figures would probably be somewhat reduced if the statistical methods which were later introduced in the bureau had been in vogue during the entire period.

Several states maintain free employment agencies. That of Illinois is typical, its law having gone into effect on August 1, 1899. Under this law the managers of employment agencies for hire are required to pay a license of $200 per annum, and to give a bond of $1000. Members of local unions were largely instrumental in securing the new law. The manner of conducting the free employment agencies is specifically provided, and it is expected that the work will be carried on throughout the state systematically. Superintendents of local bureaus are required to report on Thursday of each week to the state bureau of labor statistics the number of applications for positions and for help during the preceding week, and also the unfilled applications remaining on the books at the beginning of the week. The secretary of labor statistics is to print each week lists showing separately and in combination the lists received from each office, and is to mail this list to each agency. A copy of these lists is also to be mailed to the factory and mine inspectors of the state. It is the duty of the various superintendents to place themselves in communication with the principal manufacturers, merchants, and other employers of labor, in order that the coöperation of employers and labor may be obtained. To this end the superintendents are authorized to advertise in the daily papers such situations as they can fill, and they may advertise in a general way for the coöperation of large contractors and employers, in trade journals or other publications which may reach such employers. The sum of $400 per annum is allowed the superintendent for advertising purposes.

The day nursery in its simplest form is a home in which the children may be left during the day in order to relieve the mother.[1] This is a comparatively new form of assistance, but it has speedily become popular, and its usefulness is unquestionable. Two objects have been kept in view by the managers of day nurseries: First, to provide care for children who would otherwise be homeless or without proper care through the day because the mother is necessarily employed; second, to enable mothers who otherwise must stay at home to accept employment, thus obviating the necessity for relief. It has already become reasonably clear that indiscriminate aid in the form of care for children in day nurseries is nearly as objectionable as any other indiscriminate relief. To enable the mother to work when the father is lazy or shiftless or incompetent is sometimes to incur direct responsibility for perpetuating bad family conditions. To receive children whose mothers are not employed, but who find it difficult otherwise to keep their children from the street, seems like a natural and praiseworthy course, but experienced workers come to refuse to do this, on the ground that it removes the chief incentives for better accommodations at home. To receive children whose

---

[1] "The Scope of Day Nursery Work," Mary H. Dewey, Proceedings of National Conference of Charities and Correction, 1897, p. 105.

mother works from a mere whim or desire to have a little more in the way of dress or furniture is a doubtful policy.[1] The somewhat striking discovery was made by the managers of one day nursery that by providing practically free care for the children of certain colored waiters they were enabling them to work for the well-to-do students of a great university at wages which, except for the wife's earnings, could not have supported the family.

Such are the economic and social problems which are beginning to complicate the day nursery, as, indeed, they affect all charitable work. They are not incapable of solution. Here, as in other forms of child-saving work, a snare lies before those who hope " to save the child," disregarding the other members of the family. The family must be considered as a whole. Neither the child nor the adult can be dealt with separately. The managers of the day nursery who are actuated by a desire to be of real service to the families whose children are received must in each instance face the question as to whether the family is a proper one to receive this particular form of assistance — whether the result in this particular instance is likely on the whole to be beneficial. It will often happen, as in the case of needy widows with small children, homeless children, children of sick mothers or of mothers who are obliged to work because of sick fathers, that the day nursery is a distinct blessing, offering self-help — which is always, when practicable, the best kind of help. The introduction to the family which is always given by caring for the children in a day nursery can nearly always be followed up with advantage by the matron or the managers. By suggestion and encouragement the attempt may be made to increase the sense of responsibility on the part of the parents, and aid may be given in building up a healthy, prudent family life.[2]

The kindergarten and the manual training or industrial school as educational agencies are an important part of the system of public education. They are referred to here

---

[1] " Day Nursery Work," Miss M. H. Burgess, National Conference of Charities and Correction, 1894, p. 424.

[2] " Boston Charities Directory," p. 68, description of free day nurseries supported by Mrs. Quincy A. Shaw.

incidentally, because to some extent they perform a service similar to that of the day nurseries, caring for children who would otherwise demand the time of the mother who has had to become the breadwinner. The child-saving committee of the twenty-fourth National Conference of Charities and Correction took the ground that the day nursery, kindergarten, and manual training school are aids to child saving which ought not to be dependent upon fitful benevolence, but which should be placed in alignment with common schools, for the protection and culture of child life, and the aid of those who toil for the support of humble homes. Public sentiment would generally support this proposition as far as it relates to the second and third of these classes, but the day nursery would still be held in all parts of the country to be a suitable object for private benevolence, rather than an institution for public maintenance and control. The day nursery is frequently associated with a social settlement, a church, or a charitable society, but it is as frequently established independently, and there is now a federation of day nurseries which is national in its scope.

A systematic effort to promote small savings was inaugurated by the Charity Organization Society of Newport, in the year 1880. Discovering that many of the poor who applied to them for relief during the winter had exactly the same income as others who lived comfortably throughout the year through better management and greater providence, the society secured the services of four women who volunteered to call every week from house to house to collect the small sums that these people could afford to lay by.[1] This society has continued its work since that time, increasing the number of its visitors to fourteen. In the year 1903 the sum of $13,922.40 was collected. The total amount deposited with the society during its twenty-four years of operation is over $75,000. In estimating the value of this work a recent report of the society says : " There is the encouragement of habits of economy, foresight, and thrift among the small wage-earners of our community; there is the prevention of

---

[1] " The Savings Society," by Anna Townsend Scribner, National Conference of Charities and Correction, 1887, p. 143.

Y

hardship and partial dependence on charity which would be consequent upon a winter of enforced idleness or uncertain employment ; for the most of the saving is done in the summer months when the facilities for money making are increased, and the most of the withdrawals of savings come in the winter when those who secure labor during our season [1] are thrown out of work at its finish. There is the personal contact of our poor with the savings collectors, a contact which almost always ripens into a friendship affording opportunity for advice, comfort, and helpful suggestion in household administration."

In such a city as Newport, where there are great seasonal fluctuations in the amount of employment, and where the lavishness of the rich, at the times of their temporary residence, tends to pauperize the poor, there is special need of an aggressive counter influence such as is exerted by a vigorously prosecuted scheme for the encouragement of small savings.

From this beginning the system of small savings has extended throughout the country. Two such societies were formed in Boston in 1887 and 1890 respectively. The Penny Provident Fund of the Charity Organization Society of the city of New York was organized in 1888, and now collects annually about $100,000 from over 100,000 depositors. The committee of the fund announce distinctly that it is not a savings bank, but aims to do what savings banks do not do — to invite savings of small sums, less than one dollar, from adults as well as children. Deposits of one cent and upward are receipted for by stamps attached to a stamp card given to each depositor, analogous to the postal savings system of England. When a sufficient sum has thus been saved, depositors are encouraged to open an account in a savings bank where interest can be earned.

The work of charity organization societies and bureaus of charities is to a large extent educational, and although private agencies themselves, they have the aspect of bureaus of information about charitable work of every description. Besides these functions, however, they have an exceedingly important part to play in the immediate

[1] As a summer resort.

task of relieving distress, and for this reason it will be advisable to include here some account of their origin and method of work. It is true that this involves the somewhat thankless task of doing again what has already been well done. The report of the committee on charity organization in cities at the National Conference of Charities and Correction in 1880, presented by Oscar C. McCulloch, the history of charity organization in the United States, submitted by Charles D. Kellogg as chairman of the same committee at the National Conference of 1893, the chapter on the organization of charities in Warner's " American Charities " ; Miss Mary E. Richmond's article, " What is charity organization ? " in the Charities Review for January, 1900 ; and the attempt made by the present writer, as chairman of the committee on the organization of charity, to ascertain what changes, if any, have taken place in the ideals and fundamental objects of such societies within the twenty years of their history, the results of which were embodied in the report to the National Conference of Charities and Correction of 1899, cover the ground somewhat fully, not to say repeatedly. Especially valuable is Mr. Kellogg's report in tracing the conditions which prevailed at the period, now twenty-five years past, when the charity organization movement took its rise in this country ; the several independent but nearly simultaneous beginnings in Philadelphia, New York City, Buffalo, Newport, Cincinnati, Brooklyn, and Indianapolis ; and finally, the various methods of organization adopted, and the lines of development in the different societies.

The resolution adopted by the State Board of Charities of New York on October 11, 1881, describes a condition of affairs which was more favorable than that to be found in other communities, rather than less so. The preamble and resolution were as follows : —

" *Whereas*, There are in the city of New York a large number of independent societies engaged in teaching and relieving the poor of the city in their own homes ; and

" *Whereas*, There is at present no system of coöperation by which these societies can receive definite mutual information in regard to each other ; and

" *Whereas,* Without some such system it is impossible
that much of their effort should not be wasted, and even
do harm by encouraging pauperism and imposture; therefore,

" *Resolved,* That the commissioners of New York City
are hereby appointed a committee to take such steps as
they may deem wise to inaugurate a system of mutual
help and coöperation between such societies."

Before this time, as has been shown, there had been two
distinctly progressive movements in the organization of
private relief, one at the beginning of the nineteenth century, or earlier, for the establishment of relief societies,
which were to take the place of indiscriminate almsgiving
by individuals, and which were to increase the funds available for supplying the needs of particular classes which
were thought to have been neglected. This movement
has continued intermittently to the present time, and every
year sees the formation of new societies and funds. The
second was the formation of associations for improving
the condition of the poor, whose functions were not to be
confined to relief, although they absorbed in many instances older and smaller societies. As the name indicates, their founders expected that these associations would
promote benevolent enterprises of various kinds, and they
were not to deal in relief at all except in so far as this
could be made a lever for the permanent elevation of those
to whom it was given. To improve the condition of the
poor, as far as is consistent with this aim, was their object.
The particular business and objects of these associations,
as stated in the incorporation of the one first formed, are
the elevation of the physical and moral condition of the
indigent, and, as far as is compatible with these objects,
the relief of their necessities.

Unfortunately these objects were seldom kept as clearly
in view as they were at the time when the first societies
were founded. At the end of the seventies they had become for the most part simply relief societies, and often
their administration of relief had fallen into routine
methods, and was far from contributing as much as it
should to the elevation of the physical and moral condition of the indigent. There were then in many cities,

under various names, voluntary general relief societies, professedly ready to undertake any sort of human task within their ability.[1] Little use was made of volunteer friendly visitors, and consequently organized relief, if it accomplished its purpose of aiding the destitute, did not educate the charitable public in intelligent and discriminating relief methods. Public outdoor relief was in many places lavish, and its administration careless, extravagant, and, in some instances, corrupt. There were no adequate safeguards against deception, no common registration of relief to prevent duplication, and private almsgiving, while it was profuse in meeting the obvious distress, was admittedly and wholly inadequate in meeting situations which require generous financial contributions, and long-continued and persistent personal attention. To meet these recognized evils, and the lack of coöperation to which reference is made in the resolution of the New York State Board of Charities already quoted, the plan which had been successfully in operation in London was proposed by those who were considering possible remedies.

The essential features of the movement, which distinguish it, not because they were novel ideas, but because they were worked out for the first time consistently and because the societies have clung to them with steadily increasing faith in their potency, are investigation, registration, coöperation, adequate relief, and volunteer personal service. In the hands of the charity organization societies, investigation has come to mean something much more than it had meant for those who proclaimed the necessity for discriminating between the deserving and the undeserving. Investigation is not solely or even primarily for the purpose of thwarting the expectations of impostors. It is not even merely a device for preventing the waste of charity upon unworthy objects in order that it may be used for those who are really in need. Investigation is rather an instrument for intelligent treatment of distress. It is analogous to the diagnosis of the physician, who does not attempt to treat a

---

[1] Report of the Committee on History of Charity Organization, Charles D. Kellogg, National Conference of Charities and Correction, 1893.

serious malady from a glance at its superficial indications, but who carefully inquires into hidden and early manifestations of the disease and seeks to know as much as possible of the complicating influences with which he must reckon in effecting a cure. Investigation, therefore, while it should never be inconsiderate or blundering or heartless, must be painstaking, conscientious, and honest. It will exclude irrelevant gossip, but will embrace a close scrutiny of the exact facts, its aim being not to enable the investigating agent to affix a label of worthy or unworthy, but to determine what help can be given, from what source it should come, and how these agencies may be brought into definite and hearty coöperation.

This kind of investigation has been developed in the work of the charity organization societies. Its possibilities have been only gradually unfolded. They are realized only gradually in the experience of individual workers. Investigations made at the outset, even by one who has thoroughly grasped the principles involved, are certain to appear to himself, in the light of later experience, to be either superficial and inadequate, or crude, mechanical, and unnecessarily elaborate. A bad investigation may be either too full or too meagre, or it may be neither.

The investigation is made, not for its own sake, but as a necessary step in the careful and adequate remedy of the defects or misfortunes that have brought the applicant to seek relief. In the majority of cases, however, if the investigation is wise and complete, it will reveal personal sources and facts which will enable the situation to be met without calling in outside aid, and in this way, in a large proportion of instances, investigation might be said to become a substitute for relief. One of the oldest and best-managed general relief societies has recently designated one visitor, who has unusual qualifications for this kind of work, to attempt to meet every case assigned to her by personal work, investigation, and the following up of clews suggested by the investigation, without disbursing any material relief whatever. It is confidently believed that she will succeed, although the number of families in her charge will necessarily be much smaller than if she were authorized to pursue the usual method of investigating superficially and giving material relief where it seems to be needed.

The second fundamental characteristic of the charity organization societies is their insistence upon coöperation. By this is meant not merely agreement among various societies and organized agencies upon general plans of coöperation, but rather coöperation in dealing with individual cases of distress upon the basis of facts ascertained by investigation. It involves, in other words, acceptance of the plan of relief which is calculated to remedy the defects or to supply the deficiencies that have been discovered. This may mean that each of the coöperating individuals or societies shall supplement the efforts of the others by contributing a part of the money or work needed ; or it may mean that they will agree to a division of work, each leaving to the other a part for which its facilities are adapted ; or it may mean a division of the cases to be dealt with, each agreeing to leave entirely to the other certain classes of individuals or families whose needs are to be studied and adequately met by the agency to which they are assigned.

One of the simplest forms of coöperation is that between the church and the relief agency, secured by either directly from the other in the case of a given family, or secured by the agent of the charity organization society from both. In this coöperation material needs should be supplied by the relief agency, and the church should provide the necessary spiritual oversight and the necessary formative influences for the children, and, if necessary, reformative influences for older members of the family. It sometimes happens that the family has no need of reformation, that it contains within itself all the necessary resources for education and training, while the financial income alone is lacking or insufficient. Even under such circumstances the companionship of new friends may not be amiss ; consolation in sickness or trouble, encouragement in periods of unusual difficulties, enlargement of social opportunities, may all be entirely appropriate.

This involves therefore the most agreeable form of that volunteer personal service to which reference has been made as a prominent feature of the charity organization societies. The character of this service is very different from that performed by the old-fashioned volunteer almoner who has been so largely displaced by the trained visitor. The old almoner went about armed with a little note book in which he wrote down what groceries and how much fuel would be needed in the ensuing month, or made an entry that no groceries or fuel would be needed. These books were checked off at a central office and the requisitions honored if they were deemed reasonable and the state of the treasury permitted. The whole plan was calculated to fix the idea of material relief in the visitor's mind to the exclusion of every other idea. In the newer societies which make use of both district agent and friendly visitor, the latter is sent upon very difficult errands, — errands which she can perform better than a professional worker, — and it is understood that relief questions are in the hands of the agent.

One illustration of the kind of work which falls to the friendly visitor has been cited, but in most cases, besides this agreeable and comparatively easy form of friendly visiting, there will be a need for the performance of sterner tasks. Habits of intemperance, shiftlessness, and foolish expenditure will need to be broken up. Downright ignorance and stupidity will need to be overcome. It is necessary to give wise counsel concerning employment, and to suggest readjustment of domestic arrangements. Such suggestion and instruction from one who has succeeded in life, proffered to those who are less successful, might easily become an impertinence and would ordinarily be resented, except from those who are already on an intimate footing. Application for assistance, however, when made either to an individual stranger or at the bureau of a relief agency, is in itself a confession of complete or partial failure in the industrial struggle, and, although it may be accompanied by no personal fault, it opens the door for demanding complete confidence as to all the circumstances which have caused such partial or complete failure. Such application is ordinarily made for the first time only at some crisis in life which makes confidence easy, sweeping away the ordinary barriers of reserve. The friendly visitor, whether supplied by the church or directly by the charity organization society, must appreciate the value of such opportunities and utilize them to gain an insight into the source of the new neighbor's troubles, laying here the foundations for helpful personal relations which are to be continued until the causes of dependence have been removed, if they are removable, or until the plan for supplying any necessary deficiency shall have been thoroughly worked out and put into successful operation.

The working out of such a plan, involving, as we have seen, investigation and coöperation — of which one element should always be friendly personal interest and another oftentimes temporary or continuous material relief — the working out of such a plan and carrying it through with the aid of the friendly visitor, of the relief agency, and, not least, of the family or individual to be helped — the working out of a definite plan for meeting the precise difficulties to be overcome, and the long-continued personal oversight which such a plan involves, is what is meant by the organization of charity, and it is the peculiar task of the charity organization societies, or of the relief societies and individuals who do their work on behalf of the needy in accordance with the principles of organized charity.

One axiom upon which it has been necessary to insist far more strongly than to reasonable people would seem necessary is that relief must be efficient and adequate. Indiscriminate almsgiving, practised through the centuries, seems to have obscured certain elementary and extremely obvious truths. That giving money or the necessities of life, without return, to persons who are leading vicious and useless lives, is, in effect, manufacturing vice and degradation; that it is a travesty upon the name of charity to give a dollar which, by barely sustaining life for a short time, outside a suitable institution, will frustrate the efforts which friends already interested in the beneficiary are making to induce him to accept decent shelter and provision of the necessaries of life within such an institution; that the giving or withholding of relief should be decided primarily with reference to its probable effect upon the one to whom it is given, and that relief should not be given which is directly harmful, in the vain hope that it will in some way promote the personal salvation of the one who gives; and, finally, that charity remains a duty even though one may have made many mistakes in its ministrations, are among these elementary truths.

It is far easier to drop into slipshod methods of administration than to maintain a high standard of real efficiency. It is easier to decide to give half a ton of coal to all of the "deserving" families making application for it than to deal intelligently with each family, giving in some instances, when it is right to do so, several tons of coal, and in other instances merely a bucketful, until other and really adequate means are found of relieving the real or apparent distress, and in still others, where it may be done without too much danger, leaving the applicants to learn by personal privation the necessity for saving, from even a meagre income, sufficient for the purchase of fuel and of other necessaries. When the city gives a pension of $50 a year to all of the indigent blind who have resided in it for two years, it affords a shining example of inadequate relief. The indigent blind can no more be thrown into a general class and treated in a wholesale manner than can the indigent who have lost one eye or those who have failed in the management of fruit-stands. The principle upon which the charity organization societies insist is that relief should be adequate in amount, however large the number of persons or agencies that must unite to provide it, that it must be adapted to its purpose, not consisting, for example, of broken food, if the need is for a shovel to enable one to take work ; that the miserable habit of finding petty excuses for acceding to the wishes of the applicant against the real judgment of the one who makes the decision, must be absolutely abandoned. A case record which fell into the hands of the writer recently tells the story of four generations of dependency caused directly by the character of the persons constituting the three generations which had reached maturity. An agent to whom these facts were or should have been known, calling at the request of some citizen who had referred the case, gave groceries upon the first visit, entering upon the record "Family seems unworthy. Gave groceries because family lives in basement and father attempts to provide otherwise." There was no explanation of what "otherwise" meant, but it could truthfully mean only otherwise than by honest labor; and the action of the visitor is another instance of inadequate relief.

The charity organization societies are not exempt from the danger of demoralization. They are liable to precisely the same danger as relief societies, associations for improving the condition of the poor, and individual citizens who desire to be charitable. Investigation may become with them, as with others, a perfunctory and meaningless thing. For coöperation, in the proper sense of that term, there may be substituted an easy acquiescence in suggestions made by other societies or agencies, whether sensible or not. Relief for which these societies are responsible may become routine, inadequate, and inefficient. If the best societies have kept free to a considerable extent from these dangers, and have constantly renewed the high standards and the intelligent methods which at the beginning, as we have seen, have characterized other movements for the better organization of charity as well as their own, this happy result is due, in a very large measure, to the single fact that they have not, as a rule, directly disbursed relief from a fund previously accumulated, but have, instead, obtained their relief, case by case, as it is needed for individual families. Emergent, or interim, relief must of course be available at a moment's notice, but much the greater part of the relief required may be obtained and held in trust for the family or the individual who needs it. As an investigating and relief obtaining agency, it is constantly necessary for the charity organization society to justify its decisions to others to secure their assent and to win their approval. As an agency for promoting coöperation, it is necessary for the society to appeal strongly and convincingly to all branches of the charitable public. It has little temptation to become sentimental, and its work can be kept upon a basis of broad common sense, honest dealing with facts at first hand, maintaining a due proportion between various kinds of charitable needs, and shunning those forms of charitable activity which win easy but fleeting popularity. Even those who are not attracted by the ideal of the charity organization societies, because they do not fully understand it, nevertheless pay a tribute to their insistence upon high standards, to their thoroughness of method, and to their uncompromising refusal to applaud enterprises which are called charitable, and in which their promoters have great faith, unless they are really of advantage to the poor.

Of course such a position as this in the community is not, in the long run, an unenviable or even an unpopular one. In some of the older cities it is noticeable that many who were once hostile to the charity organization societies have become cordial, that attacks upon them have become less frequent, while in many of the cities in which societies have recently been formed they have escaped the misunderstandings and controversies which had seemed inevitable.

The controversies have, however, not always arisen from a misapprehension of the objects and methods of the societies. Pursuant to their aim of bringing about a better organization of the charitable work of the community, they have often encountered antiquated, mismanaged, and, in some instances, wholly dishonest, so-called charities, and it has been a part of their duty to expose these false claimants upon the generosity of the public. Unfortunately, very respectable citizens, who have carelessly allowed their names to be used in connection with enterprises about which they knew little or nothing, have sometimes been affected by these exposures, and while there are instances in which they have immediately joined in the attempt to correct abuses and punish serious offenders, there are other instances in which they have been led by personal resentment to attack the agency which is responsible for allowing the facts to be known, rather than the evils in question.

Besides the enemies which have arisen in this manner, there are many excellent people who are unable to agree with the decision reached by the societies in regard to the treatment of particular cases of destitution in which they are personally interested. They are disappointed that some other course has not been followed, and they refuse to credit the sincerity of the society in its different view, or they even neglect to ascertain what the divergent view really is. In any given case, the representatives of the society may form a mistaken judgment, and the one who feels that he has a grievance against the society may be entirely in the right as to the course which should have been taken. It is, however, probable that the number of persons who from disappointment or resentment at the action taken, or at a failure to act, may finally become considerably greater than the number of mistakes made by the society would warrant, and a few discontented citizens may easily establish a general public opinion unfavorable to the methods and practice of the society. All this is to be obviated only by tact in explaining the reasons for the particular decision made and a perfect readiness to discuss the questions involved with any who have a legitimate interest in them. Coupled with this, however, there should be, and to an increasing extent there is in fact, a persistent and reiterated emphasis upon the constructive and positive sides of the work of the charity organization societies, and repeated demonstration of the actual value of the results obtained in individual instances.

A special service rendered by the charity organization societies is the provision of a central registration of the relief work of such societies, churches, and individuals as voluntarily make use of the bureau established for this purpose. No community has succeeded in obtaining a complete registration of what is done for the destitute, but in many instances all the important organized charities regularly report to the bureau, and receive in return information as to what is done by the other agencies for families in whom they are interested.

Even if there are not formal reports from the relief societies, the registration bureau of an active charity organization society gradually accumulates the information that is of value concerning nearly all of the families asking for relief, and almost certainly concerning those who are known to two or more relief agencies. This information is obtained in the course of the investigations made by the society when application is made at its own office or to individuals, churches, and societies who request an investigation by the society. The ideal plan, however, is undoubtedly for the registration bureau to receive this

2 A

information directly from the relief agencies, with the understanding that it is confidential and is to be imparted only to those having a legitimate interest.

Attention may be called finally to a very important distinction between the charity organization societies and other organized relief agencies, and in this connection the experience of the Boston Provident Association, the New York Association for Improving the Condition of the Poor, and the Chicago Relief and Aid Society in the matter of volunteer visitors may be recalled. In each case volunteer visitors were formerly employed, and in each case, as a means of promoting efficiency in the disbursement of relief, such volunteer service was discontinued. The charity organization societies, however, have increased rather than diminished the proportion of their work that is done by unpaid volunteer workers. It is difficult to conceive a successful charity organization society working on any other plan. This is not only because of the difference in the character of the work done by the volunteer visitors of the older and the newer societies, but mainly because the object of the latter is nothing else than the organization of charity ; in other words, the education and training of the charitably disposed individual, the men and women who are willing to give either time or money, or both, for the relief of distress. The charity organization society undertakes a more difficult task than the direct relief of distress. This is to insure that the limited amount of charitable work which any one society may perform shall be done in such a way as to train the volunteer who coöperates in doing it. It is not too much to say that the chief aim of the charity organization society is to improve the charitable methods of the general public. Its aim is to help the poor, but to do this by persuasive teaching, and, so far as public opinion can accomplish the result, by compelling the pastor the church worker, the business and professional man, the volunteer of every description, to help the poor in wiser and more effective ways. This is fundamentally for the sake of the poor, and not for the sake of adding to the comfort or well-being of the well-to-do, though the latter are affected incidentally, in that their charitable donations

are made to accomplish more real good, and they are
afforded the satisfaction which always accompanies work
intelligently performed. The distinction made by Mr.
Frothingham is therefore entirely sound.[1] A provident
association whose sole aim is to help the poor directly
should rely upon professional agents. An associated charities whose chief aim is educational must have its corps of
friendly visitors and must win the coöperation of those
who do not in any formal way enroll themselves as workers of the society. Whether it does this or not is one
of the tests of its success. There are many different
kinds of work which friendly visitors may do, in all of
which the training that is desired may be secured.

What has been said will indicate the natural division
of work between an association for improving the condition of the poor and a charity organization society if both
exist in the same city. To the former will naturally belong the relief of the necessities of the poor so far as is
consistent with the improvement of their condition, and
within its scope will also lie numerous forms of beneficent
activity determined by the social needs of the time and
limited only by the financial resources intrusted to the
association by the community, and by the capacity for
management shown by those who direct its policy. Such
an association may properly investigate its own applications for relief, or may adopt some method of coöperation
with the charity organization society by which the latter
will do this work. The charity organization society, however, should seek no monopoly of investigations,[2] and if
the decision as to treatment rests upon the association
for improving the condition of the poor, there are distinct advantages in having its investigations made by its
own agents. The task of the charity organization society
will be to maintain a registration bureau ; to investigate
all applications for assistance made at its office or referred
to it by others ; to form a plan for the adequate treatment of each case ; to secure the necessary coöperation,
moral, educational, and financial, in carrying this plan

[1] See p. 323.
[2] Richmond, " What is Charity Organization ? " Charities Review,
Vol. IX, p. 496.

into operation; to organize relief in individual cases when relief should come from various sources personal to the applicant or otherwise ; and finally, by the employment of the spare hours of all who are willing to do any amount of charitable work, gradually to improve the character of all charitable work done in the community. This is more difficult, and in many instances far more discouraging work than that of disbursing relief. It is for this reason that a wise worker has said that charity organization is not a work to which any man should put his hand unless he is prepared to give to it some measure of devotion ; that it is hard work, requiring time and thought and patience and judgment. It is absolutely necessary work, and the merit of the charity organization societies is that they have not merely talked about it, but have provided a practicable and definite plan by which it can be, and by which in a large number of communities it has been, in a very notable degree, performed.

It will not be necessary to describe the form of government and of organization prevailing in the various societies,[1] but there is one feature characteristic of all except the smaller societies which is of special importance. This is the district committee through which the constructive work of the society on behalf of the families is done. In the smaller societies, where it is not necessary to divide the territory to be covered into districts, there is, nevertheless, usually a committee whose functions are identical with the district committee of the larger societies. The functions of such a committee cannot be better described than in the following paragraphs from the pen of Mrs. Charles Russell Lowell, upon whose initiative the New York society was founded, and who has contributed more to the theory and to the practice of organized charity than any one else in America : —

"The reason for the formation of 'district committees' is to arouse a local interest in the work and to break up the great city into what Dr. Chalmers calls 'manageable portions of the civic territory,' because these smaller divisions appeal more strongly to the imagination of the worker

[1] See, however, Appendix I, Constitution of a charity organization society.

than the whole can possibly do.   To quote Dr. Chalmers
again, 'There is a very great difference in respect to its
practical influence between a task that is indefinite and a
task that is clearly seen to be overtakeable.   The one has
the effect to paralyze, the other to quicken exertion.'

"The first condition of an ideal district committee is,
then, that it should have a domain not too large in which
to work.   Further, that it should be composed of residents in that domain[1] who unite together to take charge
of its public interests and to help such poor persons as are
found, after inquiry, to need help.   Its special functions
are to destroy pauperism within the boundaries of the
district, and also to concern itself with all measures that
will make the lives of persons not paupers, but suffering
from poverty, more bearable.

"In dealing with individual cases of pauperism and of
poverty, the main characteristic of its work is that it endeavors to find adequate relief for each person — that is,
that it seeks to cure, and not to alleviate merely, the distress that appeals to it for aid, and as almost all distress
of the kind that does appeal to strangers for aid is of a
kind that has its cause in some defect of character, the
building up of character is (or ought to be) one of the
first objects of a district committee in all its relations with
individuals.   It is because this character building is the
distinctive feature of the committee's dealings with individuals that what are called 'friendly visitors' are of such
tremendous importance, for it is only individuals who can
influence individuals.   There cannot be the slightest taint
of mechanicalism or officialism in this work, and for every
miserable, weak, hopeless person or family there ought
to be a helping, strong, wise person to undertake their
education."[2]

---

[1] While residence in the district is desirable it is possible, as Mrs. Lowell's own district in New York City abundantly demonstrates, to have a
very effective committee composed partly and even mainly of those who
become personally interested in the territory but have their homes elsewhere.

[2] New York Charity Organization Society, Seventeenth Annual Report.

PART IV

RELIEF IN DISASTERS

CHAPTER I

THE CHICAGO FIRE

FORTUNATELY for students of relief measures, the Chicago Relief and Aid Society was constituted the almoner of the fund of some $5,000,000 contributed to alleviate the sufferings of those who were rendered homeless and destitute by the disastrous fire of October 8 and 9 of 1871. Three years later the society issued a voluminous report of the manner in which this trust had been discharged. The society did not, in making this report, overlook the possibility that the experiences of the Chicago fire and its relief fund might be of value in the case of similar calamities in the future.

In 1871 the population of the city was about one-third of a million. To some extent, at that time, the small, insecure wooden buildings which had sufficed for the city's needs in the thirty-four years since it had been incorporated had been removed, and more pretentious permanent buildings were rapidly being constructed. The wooden and inflammable buildings, however, existed side by side with the new ones, giving to the city "a unique and, in some instances, a most grotesque appearance"; nor were the newer buildings by any means fire proof, even in the loose and inaccurate sense in which that term is commonly applied. From the wooden tenements where the fire started it swept into the central quarter of the city, and thence into the heart of the section which contained the more substantial residences. The streets were soon filled "with an indescribable mass of fugitives," and the night of October 8 is remembered by those who witnessed it "as a picture of appalling horror, distinct in its outlines, weird in its dark shadings, but utterly incapable of verbal representation." One hundred and ninety-four acres were burned over in the west division of the city, where the fire originated, and 500 buildings were destroyed, inhabited by about 2500 persons, chiefly of limited means. In the south division the burned area comprised 460 acres, including the business centre of the city. "All the wholesale stores of considerable magnitude, the daily and weekly newspaper offices, the principal hotels, the public halls and places of amusement, the great railroad depots, and a large number of the most splendid residences, and, in short, the great bulk of the wealth and the chief interests of the city were located in this district. In this division alone there were 3650 buildings destroyed, which included 1600 stores, 28 hotels, 60 manufacturing establishments, principally of clothing, boots and shoes, and jewellery, and the homes of about 22,000 people." [1]

"In the north division 1870 acres were burned over, destroying 13,300 buildings, the homes of 75,000 people, about 600 stores, and 100 manufacturing establishments. This area contained about 73 miles of streets, 18,000 buildings, and the homes of 100,000 people." [2]

The total area destroyed by the fire contained the homes of 100,000 people, the value of the property destroyed being estimated at $192.000,000, after allowing a salvage of $4,000,000 in foundations and available material for rebuilding. This was about one-third of the total value of property in the city, real and personal, taxed and untaxed. About 300 persons perished in the flames.

Residents of the south side who were made homeless by the fire were, for the most part, received by their neighbors; those on the north side spent the first night on the sands of the lake shore, in the small parks, and on the adjoining prairie, comparatively few finding shelter. On the west side those who were left homeless were, to a large extent, sheltered in the churches and schoolhouses, although some of these also spent the night on the prairies northwest of the city. Many were without food for two days. The "greatest terror of all," however, was the separation of families. It was not until October 12, four

---

[1] Report of Chicago Relief and Aid Society, 1874, p. 9.
[2] *Ibid.*, p. 10.

days after the beginning of the fire, and the third day after
the fire itself was over, that the temporary relief committee was able to say that "from reports from all parts of
the city, it is believed that every person rendered homeless by the fire was placed under shelter and supplied with
food last night."

The mayor appealed to neighboring cities for fire en-
gines and for bread to feed the homeless and destitute.
At 3 P.M. on October 9 the following proclamation was
issued : [1] —

"WHEREAS, In the providence of God, to whose will we humbly
submit, a terrible calamity has befallen our city, which demands of us
our best efforts for the preservation of order and the relief of suffering : —
    "*Be it known*, that the faith and credit of the city of Chicago
are hereby pledged for the necessary expenses for the relief of the
suffering.
    "Public order will be preserved.   The police and special police now
being appointed will be responsible for the maintenance of the peace
and the protection of property.
    "All officers and men of the Fire Department and Health Depart-
ment will act as special policemen without further notice.
    "The Mayor and Comptroller will give vouchers for all supplies
furnished by the different relief committees.
    "The headquarters of the City Government will be at the Congre-
gational Church, corner of West Washington and Ann Streets.
    "All persons are warned against any act tending to endanger prop-
erty.   Persons caught in any depredation will be immediately arrested.
    "With the help of God, order and peace and private property will
be preserved.
    "The City Government and the committee of citizens pledge them-
selves to the community to protect them, and prepare the way for a
restoration of public and private welfare.
    "It is believed that the fire has spent its force, and all will soon be
well.
                    "R. B. MASON, *Mayor.*
                    "GEORGE TAYLOR, *Comptroller.*
                        " (By R. B. Mason.)
                    "CHARLES C. P. HOLDEN, *President Common Council.*
                    "T. B. BROWN, *President Board of Police.*
"October 9, 1871, 3 P.M."

On the following day the price of bread was fixed by
ordinance at eight cents per loaf of twelve ounces, and at

[1] Report of the Chicago Relief and Aid Society, pp. 15, 16.

the same rate for all loaves of less or greater weight. A penalty of $10 was fixed for any attempt to sell bread within the limits of the city at any other rate, and it was announced that any hackman, expressman, drayman, or teamster charging more than the regular fare would have his license forfeited. Saloons were ordered to be closed every day for one week at 9 P.M. under a penalty of forfeiture of license. Five hundred citizens for each of the police districts were sworn in as special policemen and the military were invested with full police power. A special relief committee was appointed on October 11, and it was directed that contributions of money should be delivered to the city treasurer, who would receipt and hold such contributions as a special relief fund. Railroad passes from the city were to be issued under direction of this committee.

Two days earlier, before the fire had yet been brought under control, the Lieutenant-General of the Army telegraphed to the Secretary of War that he had ordered rations from St. Louis, tents from Jeffersonville, and two companies of infantry from Omaha to be sent to Chicago. To a later telegram from General Sheridan the Secretary of War replied on October 10 : —

" WASHINGTON, October 10.

" LIEUTENANT-GENERAL SHERIDAN, Chicago : —

"I agree with you that the fire is a national calamity ; the sufferers have the sincere sympathy of the nation. Officers at the depots of St. Louis, Jeffersonville, and elsewhere, have been ordered to forward supplies liberally and promptly.

" WM. W. BELKNAP,
" *Secretary of War.*"

On October 11 the mayor, by official proclamation, intrusted the preservation of good order and peace to General Sheridan, and instructed the police to act in conjunction with him, the intent being to preserve the peace of the city without interfering with the functions of the city government. On the same day the powers granted to the special police for a period of three days were revoked. On the following day, October 12, General Sheridan was able to report to the mayor that no case of disorder or outbreak had been reported, that no authenticated report of any attempt at incendiarism had reached him, and five days later a similar official report was made, declaring that newspaper accounts of violence and disorder were without the slightest foundation. Military aid was discontinued and the Lieutenant-General, relieved of the special responsibility imposed upon him on October 23, and the various companies of infantry which had successively been brought to the city for special duty, were transferred to their respective stations on October 24, or less than two weeks after the fire occurred.

On October 10 the governor of Illinois convened the legislature in special session, declaring that the calamity that had overtaken Chicago, depriving many thousands of the residents of the city of their homes and rendering them destitute, destroying many millions of dollars in value of property, disturbing the business of the people, deranging the finances of the city, and interrupting the operation of the laws, constituted an extraordinary occasion within the meaning of the constitution authorizing such action on the part of the governor. The legislature in this proclamation was asked : —

I. To appropriate such sum or sums of money, or adopt such other legislative measures as may be thought judicious, necessary, or proper, for the relief of the people of the city of Chicago.

II. To make provision, by amending the revenue laws or otherwise, for the proper and just assessment and collection of taxes within the city of Chicago.

III. To enact such other laws and to adopt such other measures as may be necessary for the relief of the city of Chicago and the people of said city, and for the execution and enforcement of the laws of the state.

The governors of Wisconsin, in which state forest fires were at the time spreading desolation, Michigan, Iowa, Missouri, Ohio, and New York issued proclamations calling for liberal private relief. Jay Gould, on behalf of the Erie Railroad, and William K. Vanderbilt, on behalf of the New York Central Railroad, offered to carry forward supplies, and similar offers were soon received from all directions.

The capital city of Illinois on October 9 appropriated $10,000 to relieve the distress in Chicago. Committees from Boston, New York, St. Louis, Philadelphia, and other cities were upon the ground immediately after the fire, rendering assistance to the local relief committee, informing their respective cities of the extraordinary distress and of the particular needs to be supplied.

As might have been anticipated, the residents of the city lost no time in initiating emergency relief measures. On the afternoon of the second day of the fire a number of city officers and prominent citizens met in a Congregational church for consultation regarding the public welfare in the emergency. A call was then issued for a meeting at the same place in the evening.

This meeting was attended by the mayor, commissioners of the police and fire departments, and other city officials, by thirteen members of the board of aldermen and a large number of prominent citizens. The mayor in calling the meeting to order stated that its object was to inaugurate some plan for concert of action by the authorities and the citizens, to furnish immediate succor to the large number of people who had been rendered homeless and destitute, and who "to save their lives had been driven far out into the open country north and west of the city limits, where they were compelled to remain without shelter, food, and in many cases without clothing, until assistance was taken to them"; also "to take charge of and distribute the relief which he was advised was being collected in other cities."[1]

A committee, consisting of the mayor and two aldermen for each of the three divisions of the city, was appointed to act as a general relief committee. This committee met at the same place on the following morning, selected the church in which the meetings had been held as headquarters of the committee, and remained there in continuous session for several days. The following sub-committees were appointed : —

1. In charge of receiving supplies at the railroad stations and sending them to depots for storage and distribution.

[1] Record of proceedings of the General Relief Committee.

2. In charge of transportation and the distribution of supplies from depot to church and school building committees in various portions of the city.

3. In charge of distribution of relief.

4. In charge of supplying water to church and school building committees.

5. In charge of railroad passes to destitute persons wishing to leave the city.

6. In charge of hospitals and medical supplies.

7. In charge of providing barracks for shelter.

The third of these sub-committees, on distribution of relief, consisted of a gentleman who represented the Chicago Relief and Aid Society ; the sixth consisted of two physicians. Suitable notices were printed for the information of the public, one of which, addressed to the homeless, announced that all the public school buildings as well as churches were to be opened for the shelter of persons who could not find other accommodations ; when food was not to be found at such buildings it would be provided by the committee on application to headquarters. The president of the board of trade was authorized to receive and distribute supplies under the control and upon the order of the committee ; and was also authorized to hire or press into service, if necessary, a sufficient number of teams to handle such supplies. By October 12 it was officially estimated that about seventy thousand persons had been relieved by the aid of this committee. On that date a proposition was submitted from the Chicago Relief and Aid Society that the said society should take full charge of the receipt and distribution of all supplies throughout the entire city. After full discussion, a resolution carrying this plan into effect was adopted. The resolution was as follows : —

"*Resolved*, as the sense of this meeting, that the organization of the Chicago Relief and Aid Society be adopted as the means of distributing the food and supplies received for the suffering, and that the present Relief Committee appointed Monday night last, together with the Mayor, Comptroller, City Treasurer and two other aldermen from each division of the city, to be selected by the Mayor and the President of the Chicago Relief and Aid Society, be added to the direction of said society."

At the same meeting the following circular letter was sent to each local committee in charge of relief distribution : —

"Committees at school buildings and churches, in charge of distributing food, clothing, and bedding to persons rendered homeless and destitute by the great fire, are directed to limit the issue of supplies to the absolute daily necessities (not always the wants) of persons applying for, and entitled to, aid, pending the completion of a larger organization and a more thorough system for the distribution of relief. The Committee respectfully urge upon such Committees the great importance of strictly observing this rule, so that the generous contributions we are now receiving may not be diverted from the purpose for which they are needed, and which was intended by the donors."

The relief committee discontinued all official action on the evening of Saturday, October 14, referring all matters relating to its work after that date to the Executive Committee of the Chicago Relief and Aid Society. The mayor had issued the following proclamation the day before, Friday, October 13 : —

"I have deemed it best for the interest of the city to turn over to the Chicago Relief and Aid Society all contributions for the suffering people of this city. This Society is an incorporated and old established organization, having possessed for many years the entire confidence of our community, and.is familiar with the work to be done. The regular force of this Society is inadequate to this immense work, but they will rapidly enlarge and extend the same by adding prominent citizens to the respective committees, and I call upon all citizens to aid this organization in every possible way.

"I also confer upon them a continuance of the same power heretofore exercised by the Citizens' Committee, namely, the power to impress teams and labor, and to procure quarters, so far as may be necessary, for the transportation and distribution of contributions, and care of the sick and disabled. General Sheridan desires this arrangement, and has promised to coöperate with the Association. It will be seen that every precaution has been taken in regard to the disposition of contributions."

This society had been incorporated in 1857, its objects being stated in the act of incorporation as follows : —

"The objects of this corporation shall be strictly of an eleemosynary nature: they shall be to provide a permanent, efficient, and practical mode of administering and distributing the private charities of the city of Chicago; to examine and establish the necessary means for obtaining full and reliable information of the condition and wants of the poor of said city, and putting into practical and efficient operation the best system of relieving and preventing want and pauperism therein." [1]

The acceptance of the trust by the society was made known to the public through an associated press despatch containing directions regarding contributions, an appeal for the continuance of such contributions, a preference expressed for money rather than contributions in kind, and a definite announcement that no more cooked or perishable food was needed at that time.[2]   In order that there might be no confusion, the mayor added to the previous announcements a signed statement in the public press of October 19 that the mayor and the citizens' relief committee had turned over all contributions to the Chicago Relief and Aid Society, and that aside from that society there was no other authorized to receive contributions for general distribution. "There are many special societies," added the mayor, "as well as individuals, to whom special donations have been directed. These are doing an excellent work and cannot be dispensed with. Our object is to direct attention to the fact that there is no conflict in the work, and that contributions for the general fund should come to this association." [3]

The society found it necessary at the same time to publish a statement, requesting all newspapers at home and abroad to give circulation to it, as follows : —

"The response to the sufferings of our stricken citizens was so spontaneous and universal, that money, clothing, and provisions were sent not only to the authorities of our city, but to many individuals, some of which, owing to the derangement of all business, may have miscarried.

"To the end that these unparalleled contributions may be preserved, judiciously applied, and sacredly accounted for, we ask all persons and committees everywhere to send to this society duplicate statements, so far as possible, of all articles and especially of sums of money sent for our aid, together with the name of the person or society to whom sent.

"A complete record of the sources of these contributions, together with the history of their expenditure, will be preserved for future publication."

[1] Act of Incorporation of Chicago Relief and Aid Society.
[2] Report of Chicago Relief and Aid Society, 1874, p. 135.
[3] *Ibid.*, p. 136.

2 B

New committees were now appointed to replace those which had previously been authorized by the citizens' committee. Of the present list, one was on employment, to provide labor for able-bodied applicants; another on reception and correspondence, to receive and answer despatches and letters. The chairman of each of the new committees was authorized to add as many citizens to his committee as he chose, making the committee as large as the magnitude of the work might require, he himself being responsible for its doings. All persons engaged in relief work were requested "to stop hasty distributions, and to give applications as much examination as possible, to the end that we may not waste the generous aid pouring in, as the work of relief is not for a week, or a month, but for the whole of the coming winter, and to a great extent for even a longer period."[1]

This plan remained in force subsequently with the exception that at the following annual meeting of the society an executive committee was chosen by the board of directors from their own number, and invested with power to transact all business subject to the supervision of the board.[2] The members of the executive committee with one or two exceptions gave their entire time to the work during the winter of 1871–1872, and without any financial compensation for such service. During the early weeks of the winter the committee gave the entire day to the work of the various departments, holding nightly meetings at which reports from all departments were received, plans for the following day considered, necessary changes in the methods made, so that a picture of the situation was thus constantly in the minds of its members.[3]

On February 1, 1872, the following announcement was made through the Associated Press : —

"The continued donations since our last report, together with the twenty days of mild weather in January, enable us to say that the resources of the Chicago Relief and Aid Society will meet the wants of the present winter. By resources we mean not only what we have actually received, but various sums of which we have been advised, such as the New York Chamber of Commerce Fund, and the subscrip-

[1] Report of Chicago Relief and Aid Society, 1874, p. 138.
[2] *Ibid.*, p. 138. [3] *Ibid.*, p. 139.

tions of several cities delayed by negotiation of bonds and other causes, which sums, we presume, will be subject to our order when needed. We regard it as a duty to make this announcement the earliest day that it could be made with reasonable assurance of its correctness. We can also say that there will be enough to make temporary provision for our charitable institutions whose resources were cut off by the fire. A careful examination of their affairs is now being made by a committee appointed for that purpose. In our next report, to be published in February, mention will be made of all contributions, both of money and articles, so far as information can be had of the same. Everything received by this Society will be acknowledged, and we ask all other societies of Chicago to send us an account of their receipts. But, as much was given out by various agencies in the first days after the fire without record, we also request all societies and committees elsewhere to send us an account of their donations not mentioned in our next report, to the end that in a still further and final report proper acknowledgement may be made of the entire contributions to our people." [1]

After the confusion and disorder of the first few days after the fire, during which period food was given to all who asked it,[2] an attempt was made to reduce the work of relief to a system for the sake of economy in the ways and means, to secure to the real sufferers the needed aid, to detect and defeat imposition, and to aid in establishing order by withholding encouragement to idleness.

The first step was to divide the city into five large districts of as nearly equal proportion as possible. These districts were subdivided at first into thirteen smaller districts, but these boundary lines were rearranged from time to time as the work contracted. Each district was given a superintendent who acted under the direction of the general superintendent, and the smaller sub-districts were in charge of a subsuperintendent with supervision over his immediate depot of supplies. At first about ninety men and women were employed to assist each superintendent, some of whom aided in the distribution, while others visited those whose names were registered, and sought out sufferers who needed aid but did not know where to find it. As soon as practicable a registration was made of each applicant, after which "none were allowed to take supplies from the depot without full entry of name, residence, condition, and other circumstances which would

---

[1] Report of Chicago Relief and Aid Society, 1874, pp. 139, 140.
[2] *Ibid.*, p. 141.

identify the applicant." [1] The visitor was to keep himself constantly informed as to all the persons thus entered in his district, and to make periodical returns at the office. " He was to learn by observation and inquiry the exact condition of the registered; whether they were well or ill; whether they were idle or industrious; whether they were voluntarily idle, in which case they were peremptorily cut off from aid; whether they were entitled to entire or only partial support; whether they had other means of support than public bounty; and, in short, any circumstances in relation to their condition, or habits, or character, which would be a guide as to the care which should be given them at the stations. There a ledger account was opened with each of them, in which appeared the returns of the visitors, the supplies given, with their dates, and when they were cut off, if discontinued, and the reasons why." [2]

The districts were frequently visited by a general inspector, and a committee on complaints was always ready at headquarters to listen to complaints of neglect or improper treatment, and to provide for their correction if found on inquiry to have been well founded. [3]

The report published by the society contains detailed statistics of the number of families aided in each district from about November 11, on which date 12,765 families were receiving aid. According to the records, the total number of different families that were aided from October, 1871, to May, 1873, was 39,242. Assuming an average of four in each family the total number of persons was thus over 150,000. In the month of January, 1872, accounts were opened with 6385 new families, in February with 2417, in March with 1522, and through the remainder of the year with from 100 to 300 a month, according to the season. [4]

At first, as has been indicated, food was given indiscriminately and in uncertain quantities. Later it was reduced to fixed rations, given at intervals of two or three days, and finally of a week. At first bread and crackers were supplied, the latter being entirely contributions from abroad. After families had been supplied with stoves,

---

[1] Report of Chicago Relief and Aid Society, 1874, pp. 142, 143.
[2] *Ibid.*, p. 143.   [3] *Ibid.*, p. 143.   [4] *Ibid.*, p. 149.

flour was supplied at a greatly diminished expense. Coffee
or tea was given as the applicant preferred, but tea, which
was the cheaper, was usually chosen.[1]

The following is an exhibit of the amount and cost of
one week's rations for two adults and three children :[2] —

3 pounds of pork, at 5½ cents	$.16½
6 pounds of beef, at 5 cents	.30
14 pounds of flour, at 3 cents	.42
1¼ pecks of potatoes, at 20 cents	.25
¼ pound of tea, at 80 cents	.20
1½ pounds of sugar, at 11 cents	.16½
1½ pounds of rice at 8 cents; or 3½ pounds of beans at 3¾ cents	.12
1¼ pounds of soap, at 7 cents	.09
1½ pounds of dried apples, at 8 cents	.12
3 pounds of fresh beef, at 5 cents	.15
Total	$1.98
If bread, at 4 cents per pound, was used instead of flour, the cost was increased	$.42
If crackers at 7 cents per pound	1.05
If 1½ pounds of coffee instead of tea	.17

An ample supply of bituminous coal and special consideration from the many companies and railways enabled
the committee to supply fuel at a weekly cost of $1.12½,
making the cost of food and fuel for each family $3.10¼.
The demand for fuel being constant and next in importance to that for food, a large depot of coal was kept in
reserve for emergencies in case of interruption to railroad
transportation by snowfalls and other causes during the
winter.[3]

The need for clothing was "incessant and immense."
Large supplies had been sent forward, but these were
chiefly of second-hand summer clothing and answered only
a temporary, although good, purpose. The necessity for
substituting better and warmer garments was imperative.
It was discovered that "the markets of this country could
not supply the demand for blankets alone. Piece goods
were in many instances given out in measured quantity to
applicants to make up for themselves. In this work great
assistance was rendered by such associations of ladies as the

---

[1] Report of Chicago Relief and Aid Society, 1874, p. 150.
[2] *Ibid.*, p. 151.   [3] *Ibid.*, p. 152.

Ladies' Relief and Aid Society; the Ladies' Industrial Aid Society of St. John's Church; the Ladies' Christian Union; the Ladies' Society of Park Avenue Church; and the Ladies' Society of the Home of the Friendless. All of these societies employed a large number of sewing women, thrown out of employment by the fire, in making up garments, bed comforters, bed-ticks, and other articles, from piece goods supplied by the Relief Committee, to be returned, thus manufactured, to the several depots for distribution." [1]

Associated with the purchasing committee were experienced and responsible merchants whose "operations extended to all parts of this country and of England." For this committee a large clerical force and a thorough organization were required. The government, through General Sheridan, furnished 7000 blankets and 5000 complete sets of underclothes.

As early as October 24 instructions were issued to superintendents, assistants, and visitors in the service of the society to the effect that "not a single dollar be expended for persons able to provide for themselves, no matter how strongly their claim may be urged by themselves or others. Every carpenter or mason can now earn from three to four dollars per day, every laborer two dollars, every half-grown boy one dollar, every woman capable of doing household work from two to three dollars per week and her board, either in the city or country. Clerks, and persons unaccustomed to outdoor labor, if they cannot find such employment as they have been accustomed to, must take such as is offered or leave the city. Any man, single woman, or boy, able to work, and unemployed at this time, is so from choice and not from necessity. You will, therefore, at once commence the work of reëxamination of the cases of all persons who have been visited and recorded upon your books, and will give no aid to any families who are capable of earning their own support, if fully employed (except it be to supply some needed articles of clothing, bedding, or furniture which their earnings will not enable them to procure,

---

[1] Report of Chicago Relief and Aid Society, 1874, p. 152.

and at the same time meet their ordinary expenses of food
and fuel).

"No aid should be rendered to persons possessed of
property, either personal or real, from which they might,
by reasonable exertions, procure the means to supply their
wants, nor to those who have friends able to relieve them.

"Our aid must be held sacred for the aged, infirm,
widows, and orphans, and to supply to families those actual
necessaries of life, which, with the best exertions on their
part, they are unable to procure by their labor.   You will
intrust this work of reëxamination to your most judicious
and intelligent visitors, who will act conscientiously and
fearlessly in the discharge of their duties."[1] On the same
day definite instructions were added on the following
points : —

"In the distribution of supplies, give uncooked instead
of cooked food to all families provided with stoves — flour
instead of bread, etc.

"The Shelter Committee furnish all families for whom
they provide houses and barracks, with stove, bedstead,
and mattress, and no issue of those articles to such families
will be necessary on your part.

"Superintendents of Districts and Subdistricts will so
keep an account of their disbursements as to give a correct
report to me at the end of each week, the number of
families aided during the week, and the amount, in gross,
of supplies distributed.

"Superintendents will also ascertain and report, as early
as possible, the amount of furniture, number of stoves,
amount of common crockery, etc., which will be needed in
their respective districts.

"Superintendents will also organize their working force
as early as possible, retaining upon their force those who
have proved themselves the most efficient and capable
in the discharge of their duties, reducing the number of
paid employees to the smallest number consistent with the
efficient performance of the work of their districts.

"No person in the employ of the Society will be allowed
to receive for his own use any supplies of any kind what-

[1] Report of Chicago Relief and Aid Society, 1874, pp. 158, 159.

ever, except it be through the ordinary channels of relief, and recorded on the books of the office in which he is employed.

" In all cases of applicants moving into your district from another, you will, before giving any relief, ascertain, by inquiry at the office of the district from which they came, if they had been aided in that district, and to what extent.

" In the issue of supplies you will discriminate according to the health and condition of the family, furnishing to the aged, infirm, and delicate supplies not ordinarily furnished to those in robust health." [1]

On April 1 the work of the society was consolidated in the central office, and it was announced that " Only the sick, aged, and infirm, and poor widows with dependent children will be regarded as subjects for relief. There will be no further issue of stoves, furniture, bedding, nor clothing.

" No further appropriations will be made for buildings or anything pertaining to improvement of property or payment of ground rent." [2]

The difficulties of storing and distributing supplies were increased by the fact that the principal railroad depots had been destroyed by the fire. Between October 11 and October 16, 330 car-loads of goods were received. Coming free of freight charges, they were without way-bills or invoices and necessarily to be unloaded from side-tracks at remote points of the city. They were instantly opened, and their contents sent without record or count wherever they were supposed to be most needed. General Sheridan had taken possession of two large ware-houses which were soon afterwards turned over to a committee, and later three stores, a church, and a skating-rink were occupied as storehouses and points of distribution. [3]

In accordance with the principle of concentration, these general storehouses were afterwards reduced to two, the skating-rink in the west division of the city and a church in the south. The latter was also the headquarters of the special bureau to which reference will be made below.

[1] Report of Chicago Relief and Aid Society, 1874, pp. 159, 160.
[2] *Ibid.*, p. 161.   [3] *Ibid.*, p. 176.

When this was abandoned, the skating-rink remained the sole depot for all articles except vegetables. These were stored in a large frost-proof building built for the purpose, and in two large cellars.[1]

During the early weeks expenditures for transportation were heavy. The committee which was in charge of this transportation also took charge of the special task of providing passes for the large number of persons who wished to leave Chicago and were without the means of doing so. At first passes were issued by this committee, which were honored by the different railways. After a few weeks the committee gave only recommendations for passes which were usually accepted by the roads. At a still later period half-fare tickets were issued upon the recommendation of the chairman of the committee — an arrangement which is generally in force in ordinary times, the recommendation of one or more recognized agencies being accepted by the railways in each city. Between October 13, 1871, and the end of the month 2766 passes were issued good for 6017 persons. By May 1, 1873, these numbers had been increased by about one thousand respectively.

Perhaps the most exceptional feature of the relief problem presented by the fire was the necessity for providing shelter at the beginning of the winter months for a total population of from 35,000 to 40,000 persons. The suburbs of the city were so few in number and for the most part so distant, that only a few of those who were homeless found immediate shelter in them. The churches and schoolhouses which were at first thrown open were "unsuitable, and at best temporary resting places."[2]

The temporary barracks constructed by the Citizens' Committee were open to grave objections as the homes for the winter of a large number of people. It was felt that "so large a number brought into promiscuous and involuntary association would almost certainly engender disease and promote idleness, disorder, and vice, and be dangerous to themselves and to the neighborhood in which they might be placed. Such buildings could only be put up by sufferance upon land to which the occupants could obtain no title,

[1] Report of Chicago Relief and Aid Society, 1874, p. 177.
[2] *Ibid.*, p. 183.

could have no interest in improving, and from which they would undoubtedly be removed in the spring, if not sooner, by the actual owners." It was therefore decided to erect small houses, or rather in most instances to supply the materials from which heads of families might erect their own. The total cost of the houses when simply furnished was $125, and nearly 8000 of these houses were built or the material provided by the Shelter Committee. More than 5000 of them had been erected by the middle of November. It was estimated that the actual rental value of these houses was about $10 a month, and as the cost of the houses exclusive of furniture was $100, the rental for ten months would cover the cost of construction. In no case, however, was rent charged to occupants.[1]

Besides the isolated houses there were in different sections of the city four barracks, in which were lodged one thousand families mainly of the class who had not hitherto lived in houses of their own, but in rooms in tenement-houses. In these barracks each family had two separate rooms, and they were furnished in precisely the same way as the separate houses. As the number of those cared for in one place did not exceed 1250, and these were under the constant and careful supervision of medical and police superintendents, their health and sanitary condition was as good as that which they had experienced in their own homes, if not better. Only one death occurred in the barracks during the first month.

At the same time the provision of separate houses was a much more satisfactory arrangement, and is in fact one of the best instances of emergency relief which has been devised under similar circumstances. To replace a house which had been owned or rented with the essential furnishings was practically to take the place of fire insurance, and the relief provided in this way for 8000 families is the most conspicuous instance on record of the positive efficacy of adequate and well-managed relief in enabling those who have suffered from such a calamity speedily to regain practical self-support.

Of equal interest, although perhaps less striking — since

[1] Report of Chicago Relief and Aid Society, 1874, p. 189.

each case stands more or less on its own basis, making it
more difficult to form a comprehensive survey — was the
work of the Special Relief Committee.

In the course of the thirty years since the Chicago fire,
it has come to be perceived that practically all relief is
special relief, and that there are few instances in which a
close and sympathetic scrutiny of the actual circumstances
will not suggest some deviation from conventional and
routine relief methods.   Even now, however, the United
Hebrew Charities of New York City, one of the largest
relief agencies, expends a considerable sum annually in
" special relief " of unusual kinds, and it was a progressive
and enlightened spirit that prompted the attempt to discover the exceptional cases in which money rather than
relief in kind was advisable, and in which it would be
advisable to aid in the " purchase of tools, machinery,
furniture, fixtures, or professional books, which are necessary for engaging in any business which has a sufficiently
assured prospect of providing a support for the applicant
and his family." [1]

Within the eighteen months from the beginning of its
work the Special Committee expended $437,458.09, of
which $6371.80 was for rent, $10,742 for tools, $138,855.26
for sewing-machines, and $281,389.03 for other special
forms of relief.[2]   By arrangements made with most of the
sewing-machine companies, persons who were deemed entitled to such aid were allowed a discount of 40 per cent
from regular retail prices.   In the greater proportion of
such cases the committee advanced to sewing-machine
companies the sum of $20 toward such purchase, leaving
the applicant to pay the remainder, which, on a $70 ma-
chine, amounted to $22, and for the payment of which a
liberal credit was granted by the companies.   When the
circumstances were such as to render it expedient, the
entire price of the machine, less the agreed discount, was
paid by the committee, and subsequently three of the companies made a discount of 50 per cent when the committee paid for the machine.   In all instances the applicant

[1] Report of Chicago Relief and Aid Society, 1874, p. 199.
[2] *Ibid.*, p. 201.

selected the kind of machine desired.[1] In the judgment of the committee this form of relief was productive of great good. "It rendered a large number of worthy and industrious sewing women, whose means of subsistence had been wholly destroyed by the fire, at once self-supporting."

The relief effected by this committee was varied. "Carpenters, masons, tinners, bookbinders, locksmiths, tailors, shoemakers, and workers in almost every branch of mechanical industry, were supplied with tools ; machinery of various kinds was furnished ; surgeons, dentists, and engineers were supplied with the instruments of their respective callings. Many persons were aided with furniture and means to open boarding-houses.

"The aim of the committee in this class of cases was, by aiding the applicant with the needful tools and appliances for prosecuting some kind of business or industrial pursuit, to enable him, at the earliest practicable period, to obtain a support, and relieve him from the necessity of any further application for assistance.

"The relief thus afforded extended to a class in our community, who, while they were the severest sufferers by the fire, had hitherto received less than any other from the relief funds.

"Money which simply placed in the applicant's possession the means of earning his own support could be received without humiliation and without injury; and the machinery and appliances which were thus purchased were not lost, but constituted lasting additions to the productive industry of the community."[2]

As rapidly as possible the same degree of system and efficiency was introduced into the provision for the sick and disabled, as was shown in other departments, emergency and necessarily crude devices being supplanted, as changed circumstances permitted, by definite arrangements with suitably equipped hospitals, the establishment of dispensaries, and the adoption of sanitary measures to prevent epidemics.

[1] Report of the Chicago Relief and Aid Society, 1874, p. 200. This probably refers to the make and not the quality of the machine.
[2] Report of Chicago Relief and Aid Society, 1874, p. 201.

Although after the fire there was no lack of employment, particularly of unskilled labor, it was nevertheless thought prudent to establish an employment bureau, which was of service in connection with the work of the Special Committee, the Committee on Transportation, and in other ways. The bureau did not undertake to find employment for women, although coöperating societies gave abundant employment to seamstresses.[1]

A special contribution of $50,000 was sent to the mayor of Chicago by A. T. Stewart on October 10. As it was the desire of the donor that it should be mainly devoted to the aid of self-supporting women and widows and children, it remained untouched until November 15, although a committee had earlier been appointed, in part by the donor himself and in part by the Relief and Aid Society. When the distribution of this fund was taken up, "records of the several distributing districts were examined to ascertain approximately the number of applicants of the classes designated that might be reasonably expected to apply for aid from this fund.

"It was thus ascertained that the percentage of widows and single women dependent upon their own exertions for support who had been burned out was about 34 per cent."

The committee fixed $100 as the maximum to be given in any one case, which amount was afterward increased to $200.[2]

The society itself continued disbursements to the same class through the same committee from the month of March, 1872, until the expenditures amounted to $95,100.

There were 915 approved applicants for relief from the Stewart Fund of $50,000, and 808 for relief from an additional $45,100. Of the persons aided, 651 were single women, 1989 widows, and there were 3215 children.

[1] Report of Chicago Relief and Aid Society, 1874, pp. 272, 273.
[2] *Ibid.*, p. 282.

CHAPTER II

THE JOHNSTOWN FLOOD

In the afternoon of the last day of May, 1889, occurred the Johnstown Flood, resulting in the loss of between 2000 and 3000 lives and the destruction in the Conemaugh Valley, in western Pennsylvania, of property valued at $12,000,000. The bursting of a dam released a body of water of about 700 acres, sixty or seventy feet deep, causing death and suffering unequalled even by the Chicago fire — although there have been several disasters in which the loss of material property was greater. The chairman of the Citizens' Relief Committee of Pittsburg uses the following language : [1] —

"In the morning there stood hundreds of substantial and beautiful houses, streets of warehouses filled with merchandise, hotels, churches, schools, and factories ; when night came there was but a plain of gravel and mud, splintered fragments of houses, scattered piles of bricks, masses of massive machinery torn from their beds in the factories and lying in shapeless piles of ruin, scattered and broken household furnishings, costly merchandise, and thousands of corpses buried in mud and water. In one short and terrible hour more than 1600 houses, filled with men, women, and children, were wrecked and ruined."

The city of Johnstown, situated seventy-five miles east of Pittsburg, is the site of one of the most important iron and steel industries of Pennsylvania, and is described, even at the time of the flood, as one of the busiest towns of the busiest of states. From 5000 to 7000 men were employed, chiefly in iron and steel industries, with all

[1] William McCreery : Report of Citizens Relief Committee of Pittsburg.

382

the indications of good wages, thrift, and regularity of work.

The bursting of the dam, although attributed at the time, by many, to carelessness, appears to have been due to the unprecedented and long-continued rains, which resulted not only in this disaster but also in the destruction of a heavy railroad bridge between Harrisburg and Altoona, and in floods in various other parts of Pennsylvania and adjoining states, from which there was even greater loss of property than in Johnstown.

The flood destroyed the bridges and a large part of the city, depositing, where the houses had stood, a vast amount of wreckage of all sorts containing the bodies of human beings and animals. The survivors found refuge in the houses left standing upon the bluffs and higher ground on either side of the flood, thus being separated from each other. As soon as the waters had subsided, on Saturday, June 1, a meeting of survivors was held in a tavern which had escaped the flood, and committees were appointed on finance, on supplies, on police, on the care of the dead, and on other departments of work which appeared to require attention. The first effective step, however, in the relief of the stricken community was taken by the Johnstown Relief Corps, organized by the Pittsburg Relief Committee, under the personal direction of James B. Scott, one of the most capable business men of Pittsburg, who later became a member of the Flood Commission. This corps of volunteers, within twenty-four hours of the disaster, started for Johnstown with a railway train filled with provisions. Full discretion had been given to Mr. Scott and his associates, and every assurance that whatever requisitions were made on the relief committee would be honored. Members of the relief corps, consisting largely of men unused to manual labor, carried these provisions over a rough and dangerous path of nearly a mile, as it was known that the flood had destroyed all food supplies in the valley, and neither wagons nor trains could reach a nearer point.

No previous calamity, with the exception of the Chicago fire, and incidental features of the great Civil War, had

made greater demands upon the sympathy and charity of
the nation. Subscriptions were immediately opened in
all communities. Early on Saturday morning, June 1,
the citizens of Pittsburg and Allegheny assembled to consider what action should be taken, and upon the relief
committee appointed at this meeting fell subsequently a
large part of the responsibility for relief.

A meeting of representative citizens, called in Washington by President Harrison, was typical of the clearness
with which the need of relief was everywhere recognized,
and the spirit of " impatient benevolence " with which the
people acted. " In such meetings as we have here," said
the President, " and other like gatherings that are taking
place in all cities of this land, we have the only rays of
hope and light in the general gloom. When such a calam-
itous visitation falls upon any section of our country, we
can do no more than put about the dark picture the golden
border of love and charity. It is in such fires as these
that the brotherhood of man is welded.

" And where is sympathy and help more appropriate
than here in the national capital? I am glad to say that
early this morning, from a city not long ago visited with
pestilence, not long ago itself appealing to the charitable
people of the whole land for relief, — the city of Jacksonville, Florida, — there came the ebb of that tide of charity
which flowed toward it in the time of its need, in a telegram from the Sanitary Relief Association, authorizing
me to draw upon them for $2000 for the relief of the
Pennsylvania sufferers."

Such contributions, remnants of some earlier relief fund,
are a not uncommon incident of new relief funds. One
of the first contributions made to the Martinique relief
of 1902 was from a fund formed to aid the sufferers from
a fire in Jacksonville, Florida, the same city from which
the subscription to Johnstown had come thirteen years
before.

The Pennsylvania Railroad, the Baltimore and Ohio
Railroad, and the Western Union Telegraph Company,
although themselves severe sufferers, placed their entire
service at the disposal of the Pittsburg committee, and
later at the d'sposal of those who were responsible for the

administration of relief from other sources. One million of dollars, in money, clothing, provisions, and other necessaries, was received and disbursed for the direct aid of Johnstown by the Pittsburg committee.

On June 3 a proclamation was issued by James A. Beaver, governor of Pennsylvania, to the people of the United States, in which he gave official assurance that newspaper reports as to the loss of life and property had not been exaggerated, although, as it afterwards appeared, the estimate which Governor Beaver incorporated into his proclamation proved, both as to the loss of life and as to the loss of property, to be about twice as great as had actually occurred. This is not surprising, in view of the difficulty, not only of establishing communication, but of estimating the extent of the loss, even on the ground. The proclamation, after acknowledging hearty and generous offers of help from the President, governors of states, mayors of cities, individuals, committees, and private and municipal corporations, ended with the assurance that contributions would be used carefully and judiciously and in such a manner as to bring them to the immediate and direct relief of those families for whose benefit they were intended.

Subscription lists were opened everywhere and in a great variety of ways. Material contributions from individuals and local committees were soon concentrated at four different points: at Harrisburg, under the personal control of the governor; at Philadelphia, under the Permanent Relief Committee of that city; at Pittsburg, under the Citizens' Relief Committee; and at New York, under a relief committee. There were, however, other committees at other points acting independently of one another, and there was no common knowledge of disbursements and appropriations. To avoid the confusion certain to ensue from this situation, there was appointed, on the eleventh day of June, the so-called Flood Relief Commission, consisting of ten gentlemen, representing the various principal committees previously formed, and, as far as possible, the direction and control of all relief work throughout the entire flooded district was concentrated in the state commission.

2 c

The Flood Commission consisted of the following:
Edwin H. Fitler, Thomas Dolan, John Y. Huber, Robert
C. Ogden, and Francis B. Reeves, from the Philadelphia
Relief Committee; James B. Scott, Reuben Miller, and
S. S. Marvin, from the Pittsburg Relief Committee;
H. H. Cummin, of Williamsport, as a representative of
the flooded districts in the eastern part of the state, and
John Fulton, of Johnstown, as representing the Cone-
maugh Valley. The last named, however, was unable to
serve, and although attempts were made to supply a sub-
stitute from Johnstown, they were unsuccessful. J. B.
Kremer, of Carlisle, Pennsylvania, was made secretary of
the commission.

At a public meeting held Tuesday, June 4, the whole
conduct of affairs had been placed in the hands of Mr.
Scott, and the responsibility remained upon him for a
period of eight days — June 4 to 12 — until the Pittsburg Committee was relieved; and at the same meeting,
committees had been appointed, in many instances the
appointments being identical with those made in the town-
meeting three days before. During the administration of
Mr. Scott large sums of money were expended from the
funds sent to the Pittsburg Relief Committee (over
$200,000), not only in the purchase of food and clothing,
but in establishing communication between the different
parts of the city, in the search for and burial of the dead,
in the cremation of the large number of bodies of domestic
animals scattered through the valley, and in other measures of relief.[1] From 6000 to 7000 persons were employed
at this time, and 30,000 persons were receiving relief.

It was found that the only constitutional method by
which the assistance of the state, as such, could be given,
was through the state board of health. There was ample
warrant for action by this body, as the conditions were a
serious menace to the health, not only of the immediate,
but of the surrounding, communities, constituting a public
nuisance, with which the local authorities were, of course,
wholly unable to cope, and which was not formally declared by the state board of health to be abated until

---

[1] Report of secretary of Flood Relief Commission, p. 20.

October 12. The clearing of the waterways, and the removal of débris from the streets were, therefore, intrusted to the state board of health, which body, however, was represented, after the retirement of Mr. Scott from active direction on June 12, by Adjutant-General Hastings, who, both as the representative of the military affairs of the state, and as the representative of the governor in carrying out the plan and purpose of the state board of health, assumed full control and formal charge of all local operations. General Hastings also assumed charge of the relief work of the Flood Commission, summoning to his assistance for this purpose commissary officers of the National Guard. Under General Hastings the administration department of the Quartermaster-General assumed charge of the work connected with transportation, the erection of buildings, including storage houses, the purchase of coffins, and other similar duties. The department of public safety was intrusted with the preservation of order, and the protection of property ; the medical department, with the care of the sick and injured, and the proper burial of the dead ; the bureau of information, with the securing of a record of the dead, with means for their identification, and with answering the inquiries from all parts of the world ; the department of valuables, with the care of property which was found, and its restoration to the rightful owner. The officers in charge of these departments, being on military duty, received their regular pay from the state, but expenditures for the wages of employees and for supplies were made by the commission. The commission was represented at Johnstown by General Hastings until July 2, when Judge H. H. Cummin, a member of the commission, went to Johnstown as its executive officer. After a very brief service, however, he became ill, and died on August 11, after which time the commission was represented only by its secretary.

In the first days of June, after the temporary appointment of the local Johnstown committee, as many as possible of the able-bodied survivors were set at work, clearing away débris, under the pledges made by representatives of the Cambria Company and the Johnson Company, that they would be paid for their labor. Stores were also ordered forward by the chairman of the temporary committee. The survivors, who in the midst of their personal afflictions and physical sufferings, undertook to do what they could for themselves, were entirely ignorant of what was being done in their behalf elsewhere, as all telegraphic and railway communication had been destroyed. Even the municipalities had for the time being disappeared. There was no recognized municipal authority, and no suitable place in which a council meeting could have been held. For a time the only authority in most of the nine shattered boroughs affected by the flood was the Police Committee appointed at the town-meeting, and those who had been commissioned to act as police officers. When the sheriff reached Johnstown he was induced to deputize the men who had just been appointed on police duty, thus legalizing their position, although there had been little disposition to dispute their word.[1]

Among the committees appointed by Mr. Scott immediately after his arrival was a Finance Committee, the necessity for which, at that time, arose from the fact that money had already begun to arrive in considerable sums, consigned to various citizens who happened to be known to the donors. Even before railroad connections had been established, money, as well as food and clothing, was brought by private messengers. Such funds were, for the most part, turned over to the Finance Committee, as were other like contributions received later by citizens of standing. The Finance Committee proved to be of great importance in the relief work at Johnstown. It was originally constituted of six citizens, the president of the National Bank, the solicitor of the Cambria Company, the editor of a daily paper, the cashier of the Savings Bank, and two other gentlemen connected with banking insti-

---

[1] For information concerning what occurred in Johnstown prior to the beginning of the operations of the Flood Commission, and concerning the part taken by the Finance Committee, the author is indebted chiefly to Cyrus Elder, solicitor of the Cambria Iron Company, a survivor of the flood, and a gentleman who, from a long residence in Johnstown, before and after the disaster, was able to give valuable personal testimony, not only upon the events of the flood itself, but upon the subsequent effect of the relief measures adopted. Mr. Elder was secretary of the Finance Committee.

tutions.   To this Finance Committee moneys were sent
directly from all parts of the country, and from the funds
in their hands not only was the first cash distribution
made, but there were also appropriations for urgent public
uses, such as the restoration of the bridges and the reorganization and equipment of the fire companies.

During the weeks of greatest distress and confusion the
unanimity of the people in regard to public questions submitted to their determination in town-meeting was very
marked.   There was everywhere a spirit of helpfulness
and acquiescence in the decisions reached by the director
and committees.   Those who had anything gave freely to
those in need, and there was no trace of jealousy, or of
opposition to the temporary authorities.   The unanimous
approval of the action of the Finance Committee in voting
large sums for bridges and other public works is an instance in point, this action of the town-meeting virtually,
as they well knew, voting out of the pockets of individuals money which had been contributed for relief.   There
were frequent meetings at which there would sometimes be
only a small group, embracing most of those who had first
met on the day after the flood.   Later there were larger
assemblages, although probably not more than two hundred.   Any one who desired attended and participated in
the meeting.   The Finance Committee worked throughout
in harmony with the Flood Commission, and took an active
part in the later and larger distribution of cash made by
authority of the commission.   The Finance Committee
appointed several sub-committees.   The most important of
these, which indeed rendered extraordinary service, was
the Board of Inquiry, suggested by Tom L. Johnson,
who came to Johnstown as the representative of Cleveland
donors.   He was intrusted with a large sum of money,
part of which he turned over to the Finance Committee,
and part of which he applied directly.   The Board of
Inquiry was appointed for the special purpose of making
a carefully verified statement of losses incurred by individuals and families, and also of deaths from the flood.

The first problem was, of course, the supply of food.
In addition to the purchases made by the committee in
Johnstown, Pittsburg, and Philadelphia, immense quanti-

ties of provisions were donated and sent forward from all
parts of the country.   By the afternoon of Saturday, the
day after the flood, sufficient food was at hand, and although
there was some difficulty in distributing it because of the
absence of means of communication, there was no time
when there was reason to fear a famine.   Storage depots
were established at convenient points on the railroads, and
from these supplies were sent to the distributing stations
in different parts of the valley.   At the maximum there
were eighteen of these stations.   From them daily reports
were received of the number requiring assistance and the
kinds of supplies needed.   The valley was divided into
districts ;   residents were enrolled and furnished with
order cards available only at the station nearest to them,
the cards being cancelled with each supply of provisions
received.   It was necessary to furnish food, not only to
sufferers from the flood, but to employees and volunteer
workers.   The largest number who received food daily
from the commissary was about 30,000, this number being
gradually reduced until July 2, when it was about 10,000.
Six days later this had been reduced 50 per cent, and on
July 20 all were dropped from the rolls except widows,
orphan children, working girls who had not yet secured
employment, and the aged and the sick.   On October 5
there remained on the list 464 persons, on which day
supplies were issued for ten days, and the last commissary
depot was closed.   Wearing apparel was also purchased
in large quantities by the various relief committees, and
was contributed in kind from all directions.   Depots were
opened for distribution.   Referring to these depots the
secretary of the Flood Commission says that they " were
managed with much judgment, but the distribution was
attended with many difficulties and the result was not as
satisfactory as was desirable.   However, the supply was
unlimited and as it was given out without stint, clothing, as well as food, it can safely be said that the poor of
that city, or of any other city, have never been so abundantly supplied."
    This admission, that the result was unsatisfactory, natu-
rally raises some question as to whether they were really
" managed with much judgment," and upon this point the

evidence of L. S. Emery, Secretary of the Associated Charities of Washington, D.C., is of interest. Mr. Emery accompanied the supplies sent from that city, and arrived in Johnstown on June 7, just one week after the flood had occurred. He gives the following account of the manner of distribution then in force : —

"Two windows were set apart, from which clothing and shoes were being thrown out over the heads of the crowd, and those having the longest arms and stoutest backs seemed to be getting most of it, without regard as to who they were, or the suitableness of the garments thrown out. I paused to observe this for a few minutes, and then passed along to the window and the door where the groceries were being doled out. Here, too, was a crowd of persons with baskets, and as a basket was reached out, it would be filled without any note as to who they were, and the recipient would pass along. I drew up close to the crowd and heard several citizens remark, ' Well, look there, any one can get those goods,' and so it seemed to be, if they were strong enough to stand the crowd and the tedious waiting. Some women stood aloof from the crowd crying, and when asked what the matter was, replied that they could not stand that crowd and could get nothing. Some said they had been waiting since morning to get an opportunity to get up to the door or window to get something to carry away to eat.

"I then went to the headquarters of the Relief Committee and introduced myself to the chairman by the presentation of my certificate or credentials, and spoke to Mr. Scott about the manner of distribution as I had observed it. He would not listen to any suggestion touching a change in the plan of distribution. I then went to one of the local committee and laid the matter before him, and he agreed that there ought to be some system about it.

"I then, with his consent, conferred with active, local sub-committee men, and agreed with them to inaugurate a system by placing one man on one side of the door or window to record the person coming for assistance and the goods received, and a man on the other side to deal out what was required, seeing to it that the sufferers from the flood received the goods, or that they went into proper hands. As they were citizens of the place, they could judge properly. On Saturday, the next day after my arrival, that plan was adopted, and the crowd that had assembled around each of these places early in the morning, as soon as they discovered that a system or check upon the delivery had been inaugurated, began to disappear, and the people for whom the goods were intended began to receive them." [1]

To Mr. Emery, whose statement has just been quoted, the committee assigned the duty of distributing several car-loads of new cooking stoves and ranges immediately after they had been received. He reports that in less than thirty-six hours one hundred and thirty of these stoves had been delivered to *bona fide* sufferers in Johnstown and the suburban boroughs having a certificate from a well-known resident that they were actual sufferers. A record was made of where they lived when the flood occurred, where they were at the time the stove was taken, and where it was to be delivered. A receipt was required in each case. Even at this time Mr. Emery was satisfied that there was on hand a surplus of clothing, enough to clothe all the survivors of the flood for years, and an abundance of provisions. The militia, under a competent leader, were in control, and in hearty coöperation with the citizens in the distribution of relief as well as the reclamation of the city. The presence of bayonets in Johnstown appeared, to this observer, a necessity to good order and safety, not on account of the surviving residents, but on account of the temporary laborers and the plunderers from other places.

The clothing depots were closed on August 17, the remaining articles being sorted and packed away for distribution on the approach of winter, and in October, instead of reorganizing a force for their distribution, they were placed in the warehouse of the Red Cross Association. A large remaining supply, which had been stored in Philadelphia, was later sent for distribution to the Union Benevolent Society and the Children's Aid Society of Johnstown.

Estimates as to the value of supplies of all kinds dis-

[1] Eighth Annual Report of Associated Charities of the District of Columbia, pp. 16, 17.

tributed between June 1 and July 1 vary from $500,000 to over $1,000,000. Over a thousand car-loads of goods were brought to Johnstown by the railways, in addition to the supplies carried by the express companies.

For many survivors shelter was a need as pressing as that of food and clothing. The overcrowding, resulting from the reception of those whose houses had been destroyed into the homes of those who lived on higher ground, soon became objectionable. Governor Foraker, of Ohio, forwarded a large number of tents, which, with others sent from the state arsenal at Harrisburg, were placed at the disposal of the people. This means of shelter, however, was not popular. The tents were used more by strangers who were taking part in the work of relief, than by the citizens, and it was recognized that some substantial kind of shelter was essential. At the same time the condition of the valley was such as to prevent the erection of permanent buildings. There was a heavy deposit of earth, containing both animal and vegetable matter, which must eventually be removed, and over this an accumulation of débris, so that it was possible only to erect temporary structures on the hillside, and on properties which had not been directly within the limits of the waters.

Thereupon seven hundred and ten portable houses were provided, of three different varieties. The Chicago Relief Committee supplied one hundred of these, purchasing them from their own funds, and on June 21 the Flood Commission contracted with the dealers for a hundred more of the same variety. A price was fixed for each house, less than its actual cost, and this price was charged against those to whom the houses were supplied, with the understanding that the amount would be deducted in the later apportionment of relief. The cheapest, known as "Oklahomas," were of one room, 10 × 20 feet in size, and were purchased in sections easily put together. The price charged for these houses was $75. Another style, known as the "Ready Made House," was 16 × 24 feet in size, and was divided by a partition into two rooms. Its price was $175. One hundred of these were purchased at the same time with one hundred "Oklahomas" bought by the commission. Neither one of these types of buildings satisfied the people, and it was not until a considerable reduction had been made in the price that families were found willing to accept them. Plans were prepared for a fourroomed, two-story house, 16 × 24 feet in size, which, while not finished for permanent occupancy, could easily be completed, or could be used as an addition to a more pretentious building. Four hundred of these houses, the price of which had been fixed at $260, were purchased by the commission. It was made a condition of the purchase, with which the builders readily complied, that in the employment of laborers, citizens of Johnstown should have preference over all others. The demand for labor, however, was greater than the supply, and the larger part of the work was done by men from a distance.

One of the first actions of General Hastings was to attempt to restore the ordinary municipal activities of the various boroughs. The surviving municipal officers were sought out, and municipalities were reorganized. In the interregnum there had been a voluntary submission, on the part of the whole population, to the emergency authorities. Order was well maintained, and no crimes were committed. As soon as practicable, surviving municipal officials resumed their vocations, and vacancies were filled by appointment until regular elections could be held. To the student of civil government this deliberate restoration of municipal activities was a very interesting phenomenon. To the student of economics the restoration of 'the ordinary commercial and business activities of the city is of equal interest. General Hastings, with the consent of the municipal authorities, took possession of part of the public square, and upon one of its fronts erected blocks of buildings available for business uses. The Finance Committee, to whose custody these buildings were then turned over, allotted rooms in them to business men upon application from those who desired to use them. Merchants in the cities had been ready to furnish stocks of goods, in many instances on easy terms, but there had been a lack of storerooms, and of places to locate them. The permission to use the public square for business purposes was limited to eighteen months. The funds for the erection of buildings were supplied by the Flood Commission. Forty-two stores were opened on the first floors of these buildings, and upper floors were occupied as business offices. Thus the wheels of general business were set in motion, and the objections made to the erection of these buildings from the funds of the commission were found to be not well grounded. Nothing could have been more effective in restoring ordinary industrial and business life in the community.

By the end of June great dissatisfaction began to be felt in Johnstown because of what appeared, to the survivors and their friends, to be unreasonable delay in the distribution of the relief funds which were known to have been sent to the Flood Commission. The Finance Committee thereupon resolved to make a distribution of cash from the funds in its possession, although this was a deviation from the policy which had been adopted when the committee was organized on June 6. A resolution had then been adopted to the following effect : —

"That the employment and payment of labor to remove the inconceivable amount of débris, in which were buried thousands of human bodies, and carcasses of animals, and in restoring the streams to their natural channels, is of first importance to us, and it is also a matter of national concern, as, if this is not fully effected, the tainted waters may carry pestilence into the regions through which they pass. This will involve an expense of which no approximate estimate can be made."

It was also recognized, however, that the survivors of the flood were then, and for some time must be, wholly dependent upon issues to them of food and clothing, and that the method of distributing money to the living should receive grave consideration, and it was then suggested that another committee should be appointed for this purpose, composed in part of citizens of Johnstown, and in part of members appointed by the governors of states, and chambers of commerce of cities from which contributions had been received, or in such other ways as would give the committee a national character, and would "assure the country that its most generous charity will be judiciously and fully applied to the relief of the victims of our unprecedented calamity." It was evident that, even at this time, the constitution and the relief policies of the commission did not meet with the entire approval of the Finance Committee, which, being entirely local in composition, thoroughly understood the situation, and was in immediate personal touch with all its phases. On June 24 the Finance Committee adopted this resolution : —

" WHEREAS, this Committee has expected that the State Commission, which has control of a large amount of money contributed for the relief of the sufferers by the Flood, would adopt a plan of distribution for the same, and proceed with this work, and its failure to do so has cast upon this Committee the duty of taking such action itself as will at least afford partial relief of the prevailing distress, therefore

" *Resolved :* That the resolution of this Committee, adopted June 6, defining the powers of this Committee, is hereby modified in so far as it is in conflict with the resolution following :

" *Resolved :* That a sufficient number of offices shall be opened in each district which has suffered with the Flood, in charge of competent persons, and that the names of families and places of residence of all sufferers shall be registered by the head of the family, when there is a surviving head, and other survivors being registered individually, the present place of residence being stated when known, this being done for the purpose of enabling the Committee to distribute the funds in their hands.

" *Resolved :* That it shall also be the duty of the persons in charge of registration to make a record of the names of all persons lost by the Flood.

" *Resolved :* That the money in the hands of this Committee for distribution, shall be prorated equally among the surviving sufferers by the Flood, as soon as the registration is complete."

The distribution made under these resolutions was accomplished on July 8, and, being on a per capita basis, came to be known as "head-money" distribution. The sum of $10 was paid to each person who had in any way suffered loss by the flood, without regard to the amount of his loss, or the necessities of the recipients. Payments were made to heads of families, and although the records of the commission do not show the entire number of persons who were aided at this time, it is known that 4616 families or single persons received allowance, and that the total amount disbursed was $148,890. At about the same time a distribution of some $5200 was made by the mayor of the city of St. Louis in person, this having been the request of the donors of his fund, and a further distribution of $16,929.30 was made by representatives of the

New York World. A number of those who participated in this first distribution disappeared thereafter from the records of relief agencies, no further applications being received from them. In some instances the amount received under the per capita distribution was equal to, or in excess of, the loss that had been sustained by the recipient.

On July 8 it is recorded in the minutes of the Finance Committee that the Board of Inquiry, to which reference has been made, had completed its reports, and had made a classified list of sufferers by the flood. At the same meeting it was announced that an important meeting of the Flood Commission would be held at Cresson a few days later, and the Finance Committee thereupon determined to recommend an immediate cash distribution of the sum of $500,000. Members of the Finance Committee had received an intimation, prior to the Cresson meeting, that the state commission would not soon, or possibly not at all, make any distribution of money to the flood sufferers. It was the intention to make a contract for an enormous supply of winter clothing and provisions, and to erect a large storehouse to be filled with them, and to issue these, under the auspices of the commission, to those who applied. This was in early July, and winter six months distant. To assume that such a population as that which had made up the city of Johnstown would, six months after even so terrible a calamity as that of the flood, be dependent upon weekly rations of food and clothing, handed out to them in kind, and that they could not be trusted to make a better use of any money which had been contributed for their benefit, appears now, to the student, to have been the height of absurdity. To the local workers, who were acquainted with Johnstown, this was evident at the time when the scheme was under discussion. The committee appeared before the Flood Commission at the Cresson meeting, and in the most earnest and energetic manner combated the proposed plan, expressing what the character of the Johnstown population was; that it had been an industrial community, largely composed of the higher class of skilled workmen; that the people who had lost their homes were the owners of those homes; had themselves erected them from the savings of their own industry and thrift; and that it would not be less than shameful to adopt any measures that would discredit them, or tend, as a long-continued issue of weekly supplies would certainly tend, to pauperize them. After the withdrawal of the Finance Committee the Flood Commission, in executive session, decided to make a tentative distribution of half a million dollars, as had been recommended by the Johnstown Committee.

It is probable that the administration of relief would have been more efficient, and that avoidable delays would have been prevented, if from the beginning a larger responsibility had been given to those who were upon the ground. The idea embodied in the Flood Commission was unobjectionable, if its members could have taken up a temporary residence in Johnstown, or if it had limited itself to the question of a broad general policy, and had intrusted a larger discretion to the Finance Committee, or some other responsible local body. It was clearly a disadvantage that the important decisions, even as to details, had to be made by the Flood Commission which, after Judge Cummin's death, was represented at Johnstown only by its secretary; and that representations of the Finance Committee, and of local committees, were acted upon but tardily, and after what appeared to them unwarrantable and inexcusable delays.

For the purposes of the first distribution made by the commission, the Conemaugh Valley was divided into eighteen districts, each ward of the city of Johnstown and each of the outlying boroughs constituting a district. Blanks were prepared and the sufferers from the flood in the several districts each gave a statement of the loss sustained, value of property remaining, and names and ages of dependent members of the family. For each district a local committee was appointed, whose duty it was to investigate these statements, and the estimate of the district committee as to the loss sustained by the family was entered on the blank, which was then handed over to the Board of Inquiry. From the data thus obtained the board classified the applicants for relief. The secretary of the Flood Commission reports that these blanks showed evidence of conscientious, careful work on the part of some of the committees, and of haste and carelessness on the part of others.[1] The blanks did not even furnish a correct list of the drowned, as statements were taken from different members of the family, and one who had been lost might variously be described as father, mother, sister, or brother, no clear and consistent statement having been required. Eventually, however, the Board of Inquiry completed its list of claimants and grouped them into classes. In the first three classes were placed those who required relief, without reference to the amount of their property loss, the most necessitous in Class I, and those who would require least relief, apart from indemnity for property losses, in Class III, Class II containing those who were midway between Classes I and III. In the last three classes were placed those who were less dependent, who had suffered from the flood, and whose property losses were considered in qualifying decisions as to the amount of relief to be granted. Reimbursement for property losses was not contemplated, but it was considered that after full provision had been made for those who were absolutely dependent, property losses, such as the loss of homes, shops, stores, factories, workshops, etc., might be considered as an element of distress, and a ground for relief. In this distribution, which amounted in the aggregate to $416,472, no payments were made to Class VI. To the others graduated payments were made as follows: —

To those in Class I	$600
To those in Class II	400
To those in Class III	200
To those in Class IV	125
To those in Class V	80

In making this classification the Board of Inquiry took into account the general condition and circumstances of the family; the resources, if any, which were left to them; the health of members of the family; the loss of wage-earners; the age of the remaining breadwinner and the extent of the losses sustained by the family. It was de-

[1] Report of Flood Relief Commission, p. 41.

sired to avoid making special cases, and to provide a classification which would fairly cover all cases. It was hoped that donors and beneficiaries would understand that relief was applied to all as members of a class, rather than as individuals, and that each one was placed, after careful consideration, in the particular class of which the other members were in the same circumstances as himself. If, in a particular instance, some one received a little too much, or another too little, the class, as a whole, nevertheless would have been fairly treated, and no one would have a right to complain of such slight injustice as would be an unavoidable incident of the operation of any general rule. Definite standards were also set for any reclassification, and a definite reason demanded for transferring a person from one class to another.

The commission's first distribution extended through some six weeks. It was found necessary, on account of delays on the part of some of the claimants, to fix a date, August 3, after which orders which had not been presented would be carried forward and paid with the amount awarded at the final distribution. It was found that many persons, after receiving the amount apportioned to them under this distribution, were satisfied, and made no further demands. A few orders were issued, and payments made to persons who later were found not to have been entitled to help. In some cases these amounts were refunded, but in one case, to which reference is made by the secretary, it was not possible to recover the amount.[1]

On September 13 an appropriation of $1,600,000 was made for the final distribution. This distribution was made on the basis recommended by the Finance Committee of Johnstown, a fixed average sum being paid to each person in the first three classes, and a percentage of losses in varying proportions to those in the last three classes. It was at first estimated that there could be paid to persons in Class I an average of $1200, in Class II, $900, and in Class III, $500, and that to persons in Class IV an average of 30 per cent of their losses could be reimbursed, and in Class V an average of 10 per cent. This scheme was drawn up by Cyrus Elder and John H. Brown,

[1] Report of Flood Relief Commission, p. 43.

a special committee appointed jointly by the Finance Committee and the Board of Inquiry for the express purpose of preparing a statement of the principle which should govern the final distribution of the fund for the relief of flood sufferers, and their report was adopted by Francis B. Reeves and Robert C. Ogden, a committee of the Flood Commission. This statement, after suggesting that the amount distributed to persons in Class I be fixed at $1200, proposed further, "that this be not a uniform rate, but that a certain definite sum be paid, for example, to the dependent widow who has lost her husband by the flood, and a further sum for each child under the age of sixteen years, the latter sum to vary in accordance with the age of the child, the total in all cases to be paid to the mother, except in those few instances which might exist where she is known to be unfit or incapable of discharging the trust. The allotment to orphans having no parent was to be paid into the Johnstown Savings Bank, subject to the order of a legally appointed guardian approved by a joint committee of the local Finance Committee and the Board of Inquiry." The second class consisted mainly of widows without dependents, or with families who were helpful rather than a burden, and the third class of women not made widows by the flood, who had incurred small property loss, but who were capable of self-support. The $500 allotted to them might, it was thought, serve as the capital for some small business.

At a meeting of the commission on October 22 the instructions for distribution were somewhat modified, although payments to widows had begun on the plan previously adopted on October 9, and it was determined that when property losses were considered, to persons in the more dependent class should be given the following sums:—

To those whose losses were not exceeding $500, not more than $400.

To those whose losses were over $500, and not exceeding $1000, not more than $600.

To those whose losses were over $1000 and not exceeding $2000, not more than $800.

To those whose losses were over $2000, a pro-rata proportion of the amount remaining of the appropriation

2 D

made to the class, but no person to receive more than
$6000.

To those in the less dependent classes were to be paid : —

To those whose losses were not exceeding $500, not
more than $200.

To those whose losses were over $500, and not exceed-
ing $1000, not more than $350.

To those whose losses were over $1000, a pro-rata pro-
portion of the amount remaining of the appropriation
made to the class, but no person to receive more than
$2500.

Among the unpublished documents which reveal the
difficulties in carrying into execution the plans decided
upon by the Flood Commission, the Board of Inquiry
and the Finance Committee, is a very interesting letter
written by the secretary of the Finance Committee on
October 21, protesting vigorously against the exercise of
personal discretion on the part of the secretary of the
commission in altering awards made by the Board of
Inquiry without consultation with the board.   In this
letter the principle is most clearly enunciated and fully
amplified, that general rules must be laid down by the
Flood Commission, and that no employee should be allowed to adopt new principles of classification or to make
special cases ; that, on the contrary, it was the function
of the executive to see that the principles laid down by
the Flood Commission were correctly applied, and to
bring to their notice any error or oversight that might
be discovered.   The necessity of avoiding even the possibility of scandals and of the introduction of the element
of favoritism was insisted upon, and the great advantage
of a simple method of distribution as nearly as possible
reduced to a mere arithmetical computation.   This, of
course, assumed that the classification, and any necessary
reclassification of individual claimants, had been conscientiously and accurately made.   The writer of this letter
incorporated another eloquent plea for immediate distribution.   " The end of delays," he says, " has now been
reached.   A single day, or a single hour's delay is now
unjustifiable, and the payment of the fund must begin." [1]

1 Cyrus Elder to John H. Brown.

The last regular payments in the final distribution were made on November 14, although in special instances the checks were issued at later dates. Payment having been completed, another review of all the claimants was made, with a view of equalizing the amounts given to sufferers under like circumstances, and additional checks were sent to a number of persons.

In the final distribution the average amount paid to widows was about $1500. The number of women made widows by the flood was 124, and the amount received by them was $183,281, in addition to which there was set aside for their children a sum which amounted to $108,500. For the care of children made orphans by the flood, it was decided to make an arrangement with the Girard Life Insurance and Annuity Company of Philadelphia, by which they agreed to allow interest compounded annually, and received a sum which, with these accretions, would permit to be paid to each orphan the sum of $50 annually until the age of sixteen, these payments being made through the First National Bank of Johnstown. The amount required for this purpose was $119,616.88.[1]

In this account of the relief work at Johnstown no adequate reference has been made to the aid rendered by special agencies, such as the Red Cross, the Children's Aid Society of Western Pennsylvania, the Grand Army of the Republic, and others whose participation was less conspicuous. The writer has wished to set forth rather those who were primarily responsible for relief and for administration, and to avoid the confusion which would result from attempting to apportion to the various voluntary agencies complete credit for the assistance which each rendered. In any similar situation which, unfortunately, may arise in the future, it is not the part taken by these auxiliary agencies, important as they are, that it will be of primary importance to understand, but the plans devised, the methods employed, the mistakes made, and the difficulties overcome by such bodies as the Flood Commission, the Finance Committee, the Board of Inquiry, and the informally constituted town-meeting which assembled in bewilderment and sorrow on the day following the flood.

[1] Report of Flood Relief Commission, p. 45.

The commission received the following sums : —

Contributions through Governor Beaver . . .	$1,236,146.45
Through the Permanent Relief Committee of Philadelphia	600,000.00
Through the Pittsburg Relief Committee . . .	560,000.00
Through the New York Relief Committee . . .	510,199.85
Total	$2,906,346.30

The total cash contributions disbursed by the commission and by other relief agencies, so far as the secretary of the commission had obtained information at the time of his report, June 23, 1890, amounted to $4,116,801.48.

The commission expended for the relief of those who had suffered from floods in the state of Pennsylvania, elsewhere than in the Conemaugh Valley, $246,475.26, and for sufferers in the Conemaugh Valley, including expense of distribution, $2,592,936.68. The itemized statement of expenditures in the Conemaugh Valley is given by the auditors of the commission as follows : —

For supplies	$61,533.86
For labor	43,931.11
For buildings, rent and labor on buildings . . .	179,033.87
For burial of the dead and for the removal of the dead to "Grand View," including the purchase of the plot and the appropriations made for improving the ground and for purchasing headstones . . .	30,485.41
For the transportation of flood sufferers . . .	17,176.16
For freight, express charges, and telegrams . . .	10,128.14
For printing and stationery	694.01
Expenses of offices at Johnstown	7,774.00
Attorney's fees	98.97
Expenses of the First National Bank, Johnstown, connected with the distributions	750.42
Special sums as designated by the donors . . .	2,071.85
Distribution of sums specially appropriated by the Commission	2,675.00
Paid to committee the amount appropriated for a hospital	40,000.00
Paid to committee the amount appropriated as an "Orphan Fund"	119,616.88
Cash, "First Distribution"	416,472.00
Cash, "Final Distribution"	1,660,495.00
Total expenditures in the Conemaugh Valley .	$2,592,936.68

CHAPTER III

FIRE AND FLOOD IN PATERSON

In Paterson, New Jersey, in February and March, 1902, with an interval of less than a month, occurred two of the most serious disasters which any of the smaller cities has been called upon to face. The first of these was a fire which destroyed the principal business district of the city, including banks, stores, library and municipal offices, and several blocks of the residence district of the working people. The weight of this calamity fell upon some six hundred families who were neither in prosperous nor in straitened circumstances. Before the life of the community had resumed its normal character an unprecedented freshet in the Passaic River flooded the city, greatly damaging the mills, costing a loss of several lives, and throwing several thousand people temporarily out of employment.

On the initiative of the Rev. David Stuart Hamilton, rector of St. Paul's Protestant Episcopal Church, a citizens' meeting was held, at which a fire relief committee was organized with Mr. Hamilton as chairman, and it was understood that the Charity League, a small society which was the forerunner of the Charity Organization Society formed a year after the fire, would also coöperate. At the meeting of citizens it was decided that relief funds should be concentrated, and an appeal was made in the name of the Central Relief Committee. A fund of $34,217.58 was raised from citizens of Paterson. The offer of a New York newspaper to establish and maintain a relief station was declined, with all other offers of outside assistance, of which several were received.

An indication of the confusion and lack of appreciation of the real situation, which are not unusual in emergencies of this kind, was the sending of several quarts of milk and large quantities of bread to the armory, to the embarrassment of the committee responsible for their distribution, in view of the fact that only twelve persons came to that building for shelter. With the exception of these twelve and a few who were taken to hospitals and other public institutions, all of the burned-out families were received, so far as immediate shelter was concerned, into the homes of their friends and neighbors. It was estimated that two thousand individuals were made homeless. The district in which the houses that were burned were located included several blocks of small wooden houses closely built, and in some parts thickly populated. They were occupied by American, German, Irish, Italian, and Polish families, most of whom worked in the silk-mills and dye-houses. There were also some small traders, — fruit dealers, tailors, barbers, etc. For the most part they were hard-working, respectable people, living under fairly comfortable conditions, but there were few who had insurance or even modest bank accounts.

On the morning following the fire St. Paul's Parish House, which had been designated as a relief station, was filled with victims of the disaster and with workers of the committee. The burned-out families who had not required shelter soon began to realize that they did require nearly everything else. Rows of dejected families sat along the walls of the parish room, and pitiful stories, often in unintelligible English, were poured into the ears of the members of the committee. There was little opportunity for consideration, and only gradually was a system of looking into the needs of applicants worked out. At the beginning the distribution of clothing occupied the chief attention of the committee. On a blank prepared for the purpose the name of each applicant was taken down with the address, occupation, etc. Detectives were employed to expose any fraudulent claims. While an investigation was being made, the applicant was sent to secure rooms, the committee promising to pay rent for a month or a half month as seemed necessary. When an entry of this action and of the inquiry had been made the record passed to the chairman of the Charity League's committee for signature. Her assistant stamped and numbered the record, wrote out the relief orders, and finally filed and indexed the record for reference. The following is a typical order for a family consisting of man and wife (without children), who had lost all their possessions.

I. Order for rent for one month, $8.

II. Order for furniture to include one double bed, spring and mattress, one pair of double blankets, one comfortable, two pillows, one kitchen table, two chairs, one rocking chair, one oilcloth (for table), one chest of drawers, one small mirror, two window-shades.

III. For one cooking stove.

IV. For one-half ton of coal.

V. For groceries to the amount of $1.50.

VI. For meat to the amount of $2.

VII. For crockery and kitchen utensils; also for one lamp, clock, and laundry articles.

VIII. For four sheets and four pillow-cases. Four sets of underclothing. For woman's clothing to the amount of $5. For man's suit of clothes and hat to the amount of $10. For two pairs of shoes.

Arrangements were made with various dealers to honor these orders, and the relief trade was distributed as widely as possible. This distribution of the trade was appreciated by merchants, but was the cause of considerable additional trouble for the committee. The variety in the articles supplied by various dealers, and the difference in quality and in price, gave rise to no little ill feeling, and the clamorous complaints made by some families who felt themselves aggrieved, and who were accompanied in their visits of complaint by all their relatives and friends, introduced an element of embarrassment which, although trifling in itself, is an illustration of the endless complications against which committees in undertaking relief work of this kind should provide. Relief orders were given out from the parish house in this manner for about three weeks, at the end of which time a complete change of method was made, the territory covered by the fire being divided into districts and a chairman appointed for each district. Each chairman was expected, as intelligently as possible and with close personal oversight, to supply all of the needs of the families. The amount spent upon any one family, unless there were exceptional features, was not to exceed $50. At the end of another fortnight the district chairmen reported their families in general able to care for themselves, and asked for their own dismissal.

On the very day following this welcome request came the disastrous flood to which reference has been made. The fire committee was transformed into a flood relief committee, and the centre of operations was transferred from the parish house to the armory. The methods which had been employed were continued except that all investigations were now made by a man employed for that purpose. The victims of the flood included a large element of Negroes, Italians, and Polish Jews, in much less favorable economic circumstances, and concerning whom it was more difficult to secure reliable information than in the case of those who had suffered from the fire. For nearly a week several hundred persons were housed in the armory, but at the end of that time they returned to their homes, which, when they were driven out, had been from three to eight feet under water. The assistance given was mainly in clothing, floor covering, and coal, and in restocking small business enterprises. There were a few families that encountered both disasters. The expenditures for emergency relief from February 12 to April 21, 1902, were as follows:—

Shoes	$797.28
China and glass ware	1828.24
Coal and wood	1073.36
Dry goods and clothing	4480.28
Groceries and drugs	1597.82
Rents and board	2536.00
Stores, etc.	2837.43
Furniture, carpets, and sewing-machines	9811.05
Wages and incidentals	300.08
Relief given in cash	8956.09
Total	$34,217.63

Shortly after these trying experiences in Paterson in emergency relief there was formed a charity organization society. At the very outset the efficiency of the new society was put to a severe test by a third disaster similar

to the second of those already described. The second
flood was occasioned by a fall of fifteen inches of rain on
October 8 and 9, 1903, as a result of which about 500 persons needed to be sheltered and fed for several days, and
over 800 families required subsequent assistance. The
first step in the relief of the flood sufferers was a statement issued by the mayor, turning over to the Charity
Organization Society the responsibility for relief, after a
conference, at which the Rev. David Stuart Hamilton,
who had been chairman of the Fire and Flood Committee of 1902, and Otto W. Davis, secretary of the Charity
Organization Society, were present. In Apollo Hall, which
was opened for the refugees on the first night, there were
sheltered and fed between 400 and 500 persons. On the
following day, when it was apparent that the hall would
not be large enough for the purpose, the armory was
secured by authority of the governor. Officers and members of the Fifth Regiment rendered valuable assistance
in handling the tumultuous crowd, composed chiefly of
excited foreigners. About 500 were accommodated in
the armory for several days, but at the end of a week
the numbers had decreased sufficiently to permit the
armory to be closed, and the few remaining families were
temporarily housed elsewhere until they found a place to
begin housekeeping. The work of giving relief to families in their homes was, from the beginning, separated
from the work of providing food and shelter for the
homeless, and the former was placed under the immediate
care of the agent of the society.

In the week following the flood about 800 applications
were received at the office. Friends of the society, including some of those who had had experience in the
former relief work, gave the agent their cordial support
and assistance. The statements of the applicants were
taken, and each application was investigated before aid
was granted other than that which they might secure at
the armory. As there were no trained investigators it
was attempted to do this work with the assistance of a
number of collectors in the service of the Gas Company,
who were idle on account of the flood and whose services
the company kindly offered. Although these men showed

every disposition to give the best assistance in their power their chief service was to demonstrate the need of trained investigators. When the committee attempted to decide from their reports what relief should be granted, they were really unable to do so, the collectors having been unable to see the essential facts or properly to record them. Three trained visitors were then secured from the organized charities and with their assistance the relief was immediately placed upon a better basis.

A large Hebrew population was affected by the flood, and the Hebrews appointed a special committee to assist in raising funds, and also placed at the disposal of the society an intelligent man to assist in investigating among their own people. The work of raising funds was intrusted to a special finance committee composed of representative business men. The newspapers opened subscription lists. No general outside appeal was made, although this was discussed. Instead of this business men of the city were requested to send to other business firms outside, with whom they had dealings and who might be expected to have special interest in the welfare of Paterson, a request for a contribution. In this way a considerable sum of money was realized, the final amount from all sources being $22,894.26. The president of the society, James W. Cooke, gave all his time for two weeks to the direction of the relief work. At first the plan followed the year before — of giving orders for specified articles of furniture, clothing, etc. — was tried, but it was soon discovered that some of the people affected by the flood would be able to make the same amount of money go farther than the representatives of the society. They could, for example, buy a second-hand stove for one-third of what the society would have to pay for a new one, and with a second-hand stove they were as well off as before the flood. The ordering of specified articles was, accordingly, given up, except where it was thought that money would not be spent properly, and $15,000, out of a total of $19,000 disbursed in relief, was given in cash. The following is a complete statement of disbursements. The balance of $2500 was deposited in a Trust Company for use in future emergency relief work.

House furnishings, including clothing and shoes	. .	$3,167.83
Emergency relief at armory	. . . . . .	713.48
Cash payments to flood sufferers	. . . . .	15,450.51
Orders for coal and groceries and sundries	. . .	329.10
Administration account	. . . .	718.06
Balance in bank	. . . .	2,515.28
		$22,894.26

Aside from the temporary shelter of homeless persons, the total number of applications received was 859, of which 716 were from families, eighty-seven from single men, and fifty-six from women living alone. Relief in the form of cash was given to 640 families; clothing and groceries only to thirty-six families. Loans were made in five instances, cash relief having also been supplied in two of these. One hundred and eighty applications were rejected.

CHAPTER IV

INDUSTRIAL DISTRESS IN NEW YORK AND INDIANAPOLIS, WINTER OF 1893–1894

ELSEWHERE in this volume industrial displacement has been discussed as a cause of distress under ordinary economic conditions. The hard times accompanying and succeeding periods of commercial and industrial depression not infrequently present an emergency relief problem comparable to those experienced after disasters of fire and flood. There are, of course, certain particulars in which distress due to hard times resembles ordinary dependence, due to illness or personal misfortune, rather than that which results from extraordinary disasters. It can be predicted with reasonable certainty that within the life history of the individual more than one economic cycle is likely to be completed with its recurrence of prosperity, inflation crisis, depression, and slow recovery. But, inasmuch as such a degree of foresight is not always found even among business men, it is not surprising that industrial depression does, in fact, find the mass of the working people quite unprepared. Those who are thrown out of employment and have no adequate reserve savings are in very much the position of such as have suddenly lost their homes and their employment as a result of hurricane, flood, or fire. The chief manufacturing centres of the United States passed through such a period of exceptional distress in the winter of 1893–94.

As typical of the most effective methods of dealing with such situations we may consider the East Side Relief Work Committee of New York City and the Commercial Club Relief Committee of Indianapolis. The former worked in the heart of the tenement-house population of the most populous city, the latter in a representative Western

city of moderate size.   One expended $118,000, the other
$18,000.   Both were fortunate in the executive capacity
of their organizers and in having early reached a position
of substantial control of the situation.   In both instances
there is available a carefully prepared statement of the
essential features of the relief measures undertaken by
the committee, the former having been contributed to the
Charities Review for May, 1894, by Mrs. Charles Russell
Lowell, and the latter having been embodied in a report
of the committee, of which H. H. Hanna was chairman.

The East Side Relief Work Committee was organized
as a temporary body to relieve temporary physical distress,
but its members were, with few exceptions, representatives
of permanent bodies organized to do permanent moral and
spiritual work in the same locality, and in this fact Mrs.
Lowell finds the special value of the committee as a relief
agency.[1]   The committee included two churches, two
chapels, two settlements, two educational agencies, a conference of the Society of St. Vincent de Paul, and a district
committee of the Charity Organization Society.   All but
two of these were situated between East Broadway and
Eighth Street, east of the Bowery.   Residents from other
parts of the city later joined the committee, but the organization continued local.   A contribution of $1000 from
Hon. Seth Low, President of Columbia College, enabled
the committee to make all its preliminary arrangements
before publishing any appeal for funds, and on December
21 a meeting was called at which three committees were
appointed to assume the financial burden.

The East Side Relief Work Committee was to be left
free to carry out its plans without being trammelled by
considerations of ways and means.   Even as the work
progressed further the committee refrained from advertising its plans, but supplied work tickets to trade-unions,
churches, etc., who were requested to give them to persons
known to them to be heads of families in need of relief.
By this means the attracting of unmanageable crowds and
the raising of false hopes were largely obviated.   No food

---

[1] Charities Review, Volume III, p. 323.   The subsequent statement is
condensed from Mrs. Lowell's account.

stations were opened, and the committee did not assume
responsibility for general relief but only for giving employment to able-bodied men and women, chiefly the former.
After consultation with the street-cleaning commissioner,
who stated that the appropriation allowed to his department was not sufficient to enable him to apply the "block
system" of cleaning to the streets in the tenement-house
districts of the East Side, it was decided to put men at
street sweeping at one dollar a day for seven hours' work.
The commissioner promised that no man should be laid
off from the regular street-cleaning force because of this
extra supply of sweepers, and also agreed to have all street
sweepings removed by city carts.   The funds of the committee were, therefore, devoted to the payment of wages,
no other expense falling upon the committee except for
brooms and for supervision.

At the maximum the number of men employed in street
cleaning was 887, including 25 foremen, seven clerks, and
one superintendent.   Between November 30, 1893, and
April 30, 1894, the committee paid at the rate of one dollar
a day for 57,049½ days' work.   At least 3290 different
men were employed in this period.   Each man had a certain
section to keep clean — in some cases one block, in others
two — and he was required to do his work as thoroughly
and faithfully as if he had been working for a private
employer.   Each of the seven districts was subdivided
into three or four sections with a foreman for each section.
Each foreman superintended about thirty men and made
from five to seven rounds per day.

From a census of the previous occupations of 681 men
who were working on the streets on February 21, it was
found that nearly every trade was represented.   Only one-
fourth of the men were unskilled laborers who would, in
ordinary times, do outdoor work.   The rest were men with
special trades.

A second form of employment was necessary to relieve
the distress among those usually employed in the clothing
trades.   In order to meet their needs four tailor shops were
opened, the product at first being used for the relief of
the cyclone sufferers of South Carolina, partly in order to
avoid any possible interference with what remained of the

regular tailoring trade. Sixty to seventy cents a day was
paid in these shops for eight hours' work, and, in addition,
a lunch of coffee and bread was supplied at the noon hour.
The first shop was opened on December 4, with four men,
and it was filled to its utmost capacity before December
20. Between the latter date and January 12, three additional shops were opened, and at the maximum 220 tailors
and about thirty women were employed. Later the pay
was raised to four dollars for five days' work, the shops
being closed on Saturday as well as Sunday for the reason
that nearly all of the beneficiaries were Hebrews. Tickets
were distributed by eleven of the unions of the clothing
trade, eleven societies and churches, and a few individuals.
In all about 1000 individuals were given work, none for
less than one week, many for six or eight weeks.

Of the 708 men and 94 women employed after January
25, there were sixty-two who were single and without dependents, these being discharged at the expiration of one
week. The remainder had 2775 dependents to support
besides earning their own living. It was found that
among those who were employed in the tailor shops 162
had been more than ten years in America, 234 more than
five and less than ten years, and only fifty-four one year
or less. At the time when they began to work in the
shops of the committee, 166 had been out of work more
than nine months, 382 more than six months and less than
nine, and only eight so short a time as one month. Among
them were eleven men whose regular wages had been $20
a week, 239 who usually received from $12 to $18 a week,
and only seventy-four whose regular wages were five
dollars or less.

Besides the work done in the tailor shops, sewing and
knitting, and mat and quilt making was furnished to women
in their homes. Four hundred and thirty-three individuals were employed in this manner, an average of 122
being at work for a period of sixteen weeks. As in the
case of the shops, this work was given only to holders of
tickets, and the tickets were distributed by twenty-nine
churches, seven societies, and thirteen individuals.

After February 8 shipments to Charleston were discontinued and the product of the shops and of the women's

sewing was given to the various societies and churches for
distribution.   Thirty-three hundred and eighty-five garments — men's and boys' clothing — had been sent to the
South, and in the three months from February to April inclusive 13,261 articles, including men's and boys' overcoats,
suits and shirts, girls' and women's dresses, etc., were sent
to thirty-seven different churches and societies.   Twenty-
two tailors were employed for three weeks after the shops
were closed to finish material already cut.

Toward the end of January, the pressure for work tickets
having constantly increased, a new, and as it proved, very
useful branch of work was undertaken, viz., the white-
washing of tenement-houses.   The president of the board
of health on February 12 addressed a letter to the sanitation bureau of the committee strongly commending the
plan, and suggesting the application of a coat of lime to
the surface of rooms, halls, courts, alleys, and halls of
tenement-houses, and especially to the walls and ceilings
of cellars and light shafts.   In the first tenement-house
which was thus renovated, the work was done by six men
and a foreman, and half the cost of the material used was
contributed by the owner.   Later, from the cellar of this
same house, fifty barrels of refuse were removed, and
carted away at the owner's expense.   The largest number
employed at any one time in this work was 491.   The
method of work, as described by Mrs. Lowell, was as
follows : —

To canvass a street, every tenement-house in it was
visited, and the name of the landlord secured.   When the
landlord lived in the house, as in many instances, his permission was secured, if possible, to whitewash the rooms
that had been kalsomined.   Permission was also obtained
to remove refuse from the cellars, and to scrub paint
where it was necessary, the board of health having stated
that the cleaning of the paint is as healthful as whitewash-
ing the rooms.   Having canvassed the street, a clerk was
sent to the landlords living out of the district to secure
their permission.   A few of them paid for the material.

After securing the consent of the landlord, a foreman
was sent with a force of cellar cleaners to all the cellars
where work was to be done, to prepare them for the white-

washing. The street-cleaning commissioner carted away most of the cellar refuse, and gave permission to dump all in the public scows. The scrubbers followed the white-washers, and after them a woman, employed to talk to the tenants whose rooms had been renovated, to see if the improvements could not be made permanent by care on their part. This proved to be a very satisfactory feature of the work. In addition to the sub-committee, an advisory board of visitors inspected the work, made suggestions to the board, and assumed in part the responsibility for the men and their work, besides auditing the books regularly.

Permission to renovate property was at first hard to get, but after the quality of the work could be inspected and the beneficial effect observed owners were, as a rule, glad to have the work done. Seven hundred houses, comprising 3000 rooms, 800 halls, 500 cellars, 250 shops, stables, lofts, yards, alleys, etc., were whitewashed, and in addition to this work 3485 barrels of refuse, largely dirt, but including 39 of iron, and 154 of rags and bones, besides dead dogs, cats, and rats, were taken out of 550 cellars. Besides this, 2500 halls and 2200 rooms were cleaned and scrubbed.

In the period for which statistics were prepared by the committee 1153 individuals were employed in this work, representing more than 70 different trades and 27 nationalities. They had 461 other persons dependent upon them.

The committee prepared and sent to clergymen and charitable organizations a special circular inviting their coöperation in paying the wages of men engaged in sanitation work, and from those who responded to this circular, paying for work tickets to be distributed by themselves, $2644 was received. Expenditures in the three kinds of work undertaken by the committee were as follows: —

For street sweeping	$65,738.14
For tailoring and sewing at home . .	25,364.43
For whitewashing, etc.	22,424.44

The following tables will show the details of these expenditures: —

2 E

I. STREET SWEEPING

BROOMS AND SHOVELS	LABOR AND SUPERVISION	RENTS	INCIDENTALS — (POSTAGE, PRINTING, STATIONERY, FUEL, GAS, HORSE FOR SUPERINTENDENT, ETC.)
$2272.25	$62,346.37	$500	$619.52

II. TAILORING AND SEWING AT HOME

RENT	FURNITURE AND RENT OF MACHINES [1]	COAL AND LUNCH	MATERIAL	CUTTING BUTTON-HOLES AND SUNDRIES	SUPERVISION	LABOR
$365	$667.38	$423.11	$5945.33	$314.43	$1036.87	$16,612.31

III. SANITARY WHITEWASHING, ETC.

MATERIALS	INCIDENTALS	SUPERVISION [2]	LABOR
$1501.63	$363.06	$1001.99	$19,557.76

IV. GENERAL SUMMARY

GENERAL EXPENSES OF MANAGEMENT	STREET SWEEPING	TAILOR SHOPS AND SEWING	SANITATION BUREAU	MISSIONS AND SOCIETIES	TOTAL
$385.62	$65,738.14	$25,364.43	$22,424.44	$3179.09	$117,091.72

The notable features of the work were that laborers were not attracted from other parts of the city, nor from places outside the city, this having been avoided by not

[1] Seventy-five machines were hired, and six lent by the United Hebrew Charities.

[2] Men applying with tickets, when found competent, were taken on as regular employees and put in positions of responsibility.

allowing work to be in any way advertised, and by the giving of employment only to men and women who presented tickets. The pay for work was in money, the amounts received in wages going directly into the natural currents of trade in the neighborhood, and thus relieving, at least to a slight extent, the distress of retail dealers. The demoralizing physical and moral results of long-continued idleness were obviated in the case of five thousand men and women, to whom work was given. The work undertaken was all of a useful character, and was so managed as to interfere in the slightest possible degree with normal employment. At the close of this work the committee adopted the following declaration : —

" The East Side Relief Work Committee desires to place on record its conviction that the methods by which it has been able to alleviate the distress prevailing on the East Side during the past winter, however necessary and useful in an emergency, should be adopted only under abnormal conditions, such as have existed in New York for nine months.

"When industry and trade are natural, the only safe course for the working people is to accommodate themselves to their circumstances, or to change them by their own action. The efforts of philanthropists to compensate, by artificial means, for irregularity of work or low wages can only result in mischief.

"The Committee makes this declaration lest its efforts, undertaken at a time when for thousands there was no work either in this city or elsewhere, and the people were consequently powerless to help themselves, should be used as an argument in favor of the same methods of relief in normal times, when there is work to be done, and what is needed is individual effort to find it, or concerted effort to make it worth doing ; but the Committee does not wish to be understood except as approving labor tests and educational work, which are entirely distinct in their nature and effects from relief work."

In the report of the Commercial Club Relief Committee of Indianapolis to the directors of the club, regret is expressed that there had not been available a knowledge of the experience of others in dealing with like conditions. The committee's own work was reviewed somewhat minutely in the hope that the record might have value in the future for those upon whom similar tasks should fall, and because the work done by the committee had been especially commended by those who had had an opportunity to compare the measures adopted in various cities.

The movement which resulted in the formation of the committee began with a series of public meetings " of idle men whose express purpose was to attract public attention to the need, then rapidly becoming more and more distressing, of working people who had been out of employment for several months." [1]   At one of these public meetings a committee was appointed to appear before the directors of the Commercial Club, and a special committee was appointed as a result of this appeal.   This special committee submitted its report to the directors on November 14, emphasizing the idea that relief should be given in a way that would enable recipients to earn it ; that as a first step there should be an appeal to citizens to give employment wherever they could, however little it might be.   The methods suggested were : —

I. Registration of unemployed.

II. Efforts to secure temporary employment for them through public contracts and such work as could be provided by citizens.

III. Leniency toward worthy persons known to be unable to meet their obligations for rent, to building associations, etc.

IV. Protection to home laborers from an influx of outside workingmen seeking employment.

V. The establishment, when it became necessary, of a place where substantial food could be bought at a nominal price.

The report was concurred in by the directors of the club, a public meeting of the unemployed, and the mayor. The special committee was continued as a permanent committee to carry out the recommendations which had been made.   The committee held daily sessions, and at the out-

[1] Report of Relief for the Unemployed in Indianapolis, 1893–1894, from which report the present account is condensed.

set much time was consumed in "explanations to interested persons who had mistaken ideas, and conferences with representatives of the unemployed, whose misunderstandings needed to be dispelled." There was later a series of public meetings, conducted by men who were not identified with the beginning of the movement on the part of the destitute unemployed, and whose efforts were directed to creating dissatisfaction and ill feeling; but, although annoying, these meetings had little perceptible effect.

At first it was announced that contributions for relief were not desired, and efforts were directed mainly to procuring employment. In the meantime, the committee representing the unemployed, chosen at one of their public meetings, had undertaken to provide relief until the permanent committee could take up the work. They were, however, asked to discontinue this when arrangements had been made by the permanent committee for the relief of destitution through the agency of the Charity Organization Society. The report of the committee says that "in asking the society to temporarily take up this part of the work the committee desired that the ability of the organized agencies for the relief of distress should be tested before proceeding with other plans. The usual methods of charity work were not applied to the unemployed class who were referred to them." All cases of need which were thereafter reported were looked after by the Charity Organization Society, which expended about $4000 in such emergency relief. The committee pledged itself to reimburse the treasury of the society, so that it would not be without funds to carry on its usual charitable work during the remainder of the year. This enabled the committee to supply food where necessary, without making an immediate public appeal for that purpose. Any effort to raise funds by benefits on a percentage basis was discouraged.

Four days after receiving instructions to proceed to carry out the plan which had been outlined, the committee opened an employment bureau in the basement of the Commercial Club building. It was the intention to make registration in this bureau a basis of the further work of the committee, and an application for employment was regarded as having some significance of worthiness as well as of need. Applicants at the Charity Organization Society, who had not registered at the bureau, were sent there to give some evidence of willingness to work before relief was given; and, on the other hand, the bureau referred to the society those who, in registering, stated that they were in immediate need. In the first month between fifty and sixty registered on an average each day. Temporary employment was procured for about one-fifth of this number. The relief afforded in this way, although not less than was anticipated, was inadequate. It was demonstrated, among other things, that the "dependent class was largely composed of persons who were the first to be discharged when labor was not required, and the last to be employed when it was needed." While the need of relief was thus being demonstrated, steps were taken to arrest tramps and to send them to the workhouse under the vagrancy law, where a stone pile was provided as a means of furnishing work. Gradually, as the public began to realize the extent to which they were being imposed upon by tramps pretending to be unemployed men in need, the enforcement of the law became more strict. The mayor and board of public works promised assistance in requiring the speedy construction of sewers, the repairing of streets, etc., but on account of unfavorable weather and other reasons little relief was experienced from this source.

By the latter part of December the number of persons who were being supplied with food by the Society had increased to more than three thousand. It was felt that an appeal for funds could no longer be safely deferred, and on December 15 a statement was issued that by the end of the month there would probably be four thousand persons dependent upon the public for their food. A printed appeal by the committee, together with a typewritten letter by the chairman, was sent to every person in the city whose name appeared in the list of commercial agencies, and it was also sent to a large number of citizens whose names were found in the city directory. A force of from ten to fifteen typewriters was engaged for several days and nights in getting out letters signed by the chairman. In response to this appeal voluntary subscriptions amounting to some $6000 were received. There was then appointed a citizens' finance committee to conduct a further canvass, and this committee called to its assistance many private citizens. About $13,000 was obtained in this canvass, many of these subscriptions being payable in instalments continuing until the first of April. Subscriptions were obtained from employees of firms, including in some instances the firm members, amounting to $4765.85. The payments of these subscriptions were to be deducted from the weekly pay-roll.

A food market was opened on the last day of the year, at which time the Charity Organization Society was supplying food to nearly a thousand families, representing about four thousand persons. The society's available funds were then exhausted and those who had been supplied with food were thereupon referred to the food market, the secretary of the society certifying that, "according to the best obtainable information, they were residents of Indianapolis who belonged to the unemployed class, and were entitled to the credit offered to persons in need." Account-books were issued to applicants at the market, providing for entries of the charges for supplies, with the date of issue, and containing a certificate of the worthiness of the applicant, as ascertained by inquiry, showing his address and the number in his family. It also contained a copy of an agreement which the applicants were required to sign, pledging themselves to pay on demand such sums as might become due from them, or, whenever called upon to do so by the committee, to perform such work as might be required of them at $12\frac{1}{2}$ cents per hour, to be applied to the payment of their indebtedness for supplies. This was to be the rate of pay for common labor only; if skilled work should be required, it was agreed that a special rate of pay would be allowed. This book was intended to serve the purpose of keeping the debtor advised as to the status of his account, and to impress him with the business spirit of the dealings with him. The food market was located at a point convenient to the headquarters of the committee. It was organized in two different departments, one devoted to registration and investigation, the other to the issuance of supplies. The managers of its two departments were coördinate in authority, and both were under the direction of the relief committee, to whom they made daily reports. A corps of visitors was employed to investigate applications, a report from the visitor being required within twenty-four hours. The daily average number of cases reported by each visitor was about eight, and a sufficient force was employed to keep up with the work. It was the duty of the visitor to ascertain as accurately as possible the facts regarding the citizenship and need of the applicant. This information was obtained from neighbors, from shopkeepers with whom the applicant had traded, and by personal interview and observation at the home of the applicant. The last employer, the landlord, and those to whom references were made, were also interviewed in many cases.

If the written reports which were made on each case contained no information decidedly unfavorable or suggestive of doubt as to the citizenship or need of the applicant, credit at the food market was granted, in evidence of which an account-book was issued to the applicant, containing a certificate signed by the manager of the registration and investigation department. When the applicant became the possessor of an account-book his name was entered in various books of record with a number corresponding in all of them for convenience of reference. When the applicant passed from the registration bureau to the food market he was given a numbered check if there were many persons waiting, and when this number was reached his check was taken up, his book examined, and the manager asked such questions as appeared to him advisable, when there was any reason to doubt the good faith of the applicant. At a later stage, when the arrangements for requiring work had been completed, a card was given directing the applicant to report to the street commissioner for work, the performance of which would entitle him to credit. When the applicant had satisfactory credits for the performance of labor, he was given an order by the manager of the food depot for a week's ration for the number shown by his book to belong to his family. This order

was presented to the chief dispensing clerk in another part
of the building, and the ration to which he was entitled
was delivered, the order being filed for future reference.

In the selection of the kinds of food supplied the
committee sought to obtain the most wholesome and nutritious at the lowest cost. Wholesale dealers readily
agreed, when called upon, to sell to the committee at first
cost, thus saving the committee a large sum of money.
Purchasers were given the full benefit of this saving, the
charge being almost exact cost rate, exclusive of expenses
of administration. The charge for food at the market was
about half the usual price for the same article at any retail
store in the city. After some slight changes the ration
for four or five persons for one week was as follows: potatoes, 12 lbs.; corn meal, 10 lbs.; beans, 2 lbs., or hominy,
6 lbs.; bread, 6 loaves and 8 lbs. of flour, or 10 loaves of
bread; fresh pork, 4 lbs.; pickled pork, 2 lbs.; lard, $\frac{1}{2}$ lb.;
coffee, $\frac{1}{2}$ lb.; sugar, 1 lb.; syrup, 1 qt.; salt, $\frac{1}{2}$ lb.; soap,
1 bar. The charge for this ration was $1. The commit-
tee reports that there was general satisfaction with it
except in a few instances of persons of excessive appetite
who wanted a larger quantity. Soon after the market was
opened a committee representing one of the public meetings of the unemployed visited the market and inspected
the stock of supplies. They reported that the quality was
good and commended the managers of the market. Arrangements were also made to supply coal to those in need
of fuel. A regular allowance of 300 lbs. per week was
decided upon, and for this two tickets were issued, each
calling for 150 lbs. It was delivered to the purchasers in
wheelbarrows. A mining company gave thirteen car-loads
of coal, which was sufficient to meet all demands until the
latter part of February. A charge was made for the coal
as for other supplies, but opportunities were given to earn
it by work. The charge was fixed at ten cents per 100 lbs.
When the donation was exhausted, the committee purchased four car-loads, of which thirty tons were left
on hand at the close of the work and turned over to the
Charity Organization Society. Shoes were also supplied
from the market, principally, however, old shoes collected
by solicitors who made a house-to-house canvass for this

purpose. A repair shop was opened, and shoes were supplied at the exact cost of repairing, or at the price at which
they had 'been purchased. All together, about 1500 pairs
of shoes and boots, of various sizes, were collected and repaired, and 36 pairs were purchased. The latter were of
large sizes for which the demand exceeded the supply of
cast-off shoes. Six hundred and thirty-two pairs were on
hand at the close of the work, and were turned over to
the Charity Organization Society.

The expectation that the city might be able to provide
employment on public work with compensation from the
city treasury was not fulfilled. The committee finally
offered to furnish the labor at its command for public
work with the understanding that compensation would be
made from the relief funds. It was through this kind of
employment that credits were obtained at the market in
return for which food, fuel, and shoes were supplied. In
the beginning of the arrangement from fifty to sixty men
a day were directed to report to the street commissioner
for work, and they were sent by him to clean streets.
Later the board of public works wanted to use the labor
to make an excavation for a lake at Garfield Park. The
committee agreed to furnish the labor at their command
for this purpose, on the condition that the board would
provide transportation for the men from the central part
of the city to the park, and thus save those living in the
northern part of the city the hardship of walking several
miles in going to, and returning from, their day's work.
The board induced the Citizens' Railway Company to provide transportation without charge. While the street
commissioner continued to utilize some of the labor in
cleaning streets, a very much larger number of men were
sent to the park to work on the excavation of the lake.
The men seemed to prefer the work at the park for the
reason that they were subjected to less public notice than
when employed on the streets. The results of this particular work, however, were not satisfactory to the committee. Complaints were made from time to time that the
facilities and superintendence provided by the board of
public works were inadequate, and that many of the men
shirked. Finally the committee assigned a man to the

duty of looking after all labor, and daily reports were required from him regarding the conduct of the men. The information which was thus obtained enabled the committee to bring about better control of the men and compel more efficient work. A few discharges for insubordination and shirking had a wholesome effect. It was found that some of the men were sending their sons, from thirteen to sixteen years of age, to perform their work. This, however, was stopped, and for a time there were as many as three hundred men a day employed at the park, though the average was much below this.

At one time during the winter, immediately after a heavy snow-storm, several hundred men were put at work removing snow from the street gutters. Shovels were loaned for this purpose by the city and the natural gas companies. This was one of the most satisfactorily performed tasks to which the men were assigned. As there were more than a thousand men pledged to perform labor in payment of their accounts at the market, it was determined that they should be assigned to do only one day's work at a time, so that all should be given sufficient employment to pay for the ration charged to them each week, with the exception of those who drew supplies for families of more than four or five in number, who should be allowed to work two or three days a week. It was the purpose, in thus limiting the work, to avoid pledging the credit of the market in advance and possibly unnecessarily. The increasing number of applicants and the frequent interference with work by unfavorable weather, soon caused a large accumulation of indebtedness to the market. To clear up this the committee asked the board of public works to provide employment for a time for from two to three hundred men a day, which was done, and the debtors were required to work successively as many days as necessary to liquidate their accounts. Many of the men took advantage of the circumstances which brought about this condition, and did not perform the work required to pay for the rations which they had received. When called upon to give their labor, in accordance with the agreement, they stopped drawing rations from the market.

Later, when many of them again applied for credit, they were denied the benefit of the market until they had worked out the amount of their indebtedness. This accumulation of indebtedness was not due alone to the weather's interference with outdoor labor, but also to the necessity of supplying food to persons in need of it at the time the market was opened until they could be given an opportunity of doing it.

It became evident after the first three weeks that it was the disposition of a large number of men to avoid work if possible. It was therefore determined to require them to work before they could draw rations, and to present at the market cards of credit from the street commissioner or his foreman. No work, no rations, was the rule. Experience demonstrated that it was in every way a wholesome requirement, and later this was followed, when a system of inspection was instituted, with rigid insistence that no shirking should be permitted. The effect of this rule was good also in impressing the men with the idea of honestly endeavoring to earn all they received.

At the end of the season the books showed an aggregate indebtedness of a comparatively small amount — less than $1000, exclusive of the accounts with widows — from persons who had failed to perform the required work. The committee reports that many of the beneficiaries evinced eagerness to earn credit and manifestly appreciated the arrangement which gave them an opportunity of obtaining food in exchange for work when it was all they had to offer in payment for it.

The greatest difficulty in discriminating among applicants occurred in connection with those who were not absolutely destitute. Conditions were as different as the families to be aided. In the larger families some of the children or the mother were found to be earning something, possibly not more than three dollars a week, barely enough to pay rent and fuel bills. Relief was given in such cases. Then there were other applications from those holding an equity in their property through a loan association, or, indeed, in actual ownership of their property. To deny relief in the former case would be, perhaps, to cause a forfeit of equity and the home for which the nominal owner was struggling to pay. Relief was generally given in such cases. The same rule applied usually to those whose property was encumbered by mortgage. But relief was rarely given when the applicant owned his property free of debt. When it was done there were circumstances of advanced age or debility to be considered. The presence of sickness, insanity, or other grievous afflictions in the family also entered into conclusions of judgment. Many applications were from pensioners, and in these cases the age, health, size of family and of pension, were considered. Credit was not given to single men unless the need was extreme, and then it was the practice, as far as possible, to add them to the families of those who were patrons of the market.

There was a serious question in extending credit to those known to belong to the criminal or dissolute classes. It was thought best not to establish a standard of morality, but to let need have determining weight. Account was taken of the fact that relief had a motive of police protection as well as of humanity. This was illustrated in the answer of a young negro who was a willing worker: " What would you have done this winter except for the food market ? " was asked ; " Gone to stealin', " was the quick reply. " There would not have been jails enough in the county to hold all who would have been arrested. I'll steal before I'll starve." It is noteworthy that the arrests for larceny were not above the usual number during the winter.

The market at first proved highly attractive to women: widows, and those who were deserted by their husbands, and had children dependent on them. There was no way of providing work for them, as was done with the men, and before January closed there were nearly three hundred such persons on the list. The opportunity for deception as to the desertion of husbands was so great and the tax so heavy that it was decided to send all women from whom pay in work could not be expected to the Charity Organization Society for investigation, and also for the application of a work test. A requirement that labor should be performed by washing clothes at the Friendly Inn, where facilities were provided, had good results. A number of the women produced able-bodied sons who afterward worked out their accounts, and some husbands suddenly returned to their families. The market continued to supply rations to the worthy, but only on orders from the Charity Organization Society.

About two-fifths of those who received relief were Negroes, and this was estimated to be twenty per cent of the colored population of the city. The number of Negroes who asked merely for work was proportionately much less than the number of whites. Only forty per cent of the applicants were artisans, and these were largely carpenters or in other building trades.

The committee limited itself to the supply of food, fuel, clothing, and shoes; but distress requiring other forms of relief was continually brought to the committee's attention. The question of rents was especially troublesome, but the committee believed it to be impracticable to undertake to meet demands from landlords, which would exhaust the relief fund at once, and would have left the committee without means of providing food and other necessities of living for dependent people. Besides, even if there were sufficient funds, it would not have been right to divert to the benefit of landlords the money contributed by citizens for the relief of dependent people, and there would unavoidably have been much imposition. It was, therefore, the determined policy of the committee not to undertake to meet demands of this kind. Applicants for aid who were threatened with eviction were told that nothing could be done for them unless they were actually deprived of shelter, and then they must endeavor to find, if possible, temporary lodging with relatives or friends. Only two or three of these people ever returned to report themselves as homeless and helpless. While the moneyless people were pressed for payments and were under continual harassment from threats, there were, as a matter of fact, fewer evictions than usual at the same time of year. Landlords and rental agents strenuously endeavored to enforce the payments due them, but refrained finally from resorting to the usual extreme methods. In many cases advantage was taken by tenants who could have paid, but availed themselves of the excuse chargeable

to the times. Evictions were hardly to be expected, however, except in flagrant cases of untrustworthiness, for the
reason that both the landlords and rental agents realized
that if tenants were thrown out, they would certainly lose
the amount due them and their property would remain unoccupied ; if other tenants were secured, it was improbable that they would be more likely to pay than those
who were evicted. It seemed, therefore, wise for them to
permit property to be occupied by people who had paid
in the past when they were able to do so, and would probably liquidate their indebtedness when they again obtained
employment. Although there was constant annoyance on
account of the rent question, the burden of it was necessarily left to the people upon whom it already rested, and
in the end there were no serious results.

The market was gradually closed during the month of
March, with the coöperation of the Charity Organization
Society in taking over those who remained on the lists
when the closing was finally effected. Inasmuch as the
relief committee had exhausted its own funds, the county
commissioners were requested to make an appropriation
of $4000 to the Charity Organization Society to carry out
the arrangement which had been made that the society
should be reimbursed for the emergency relief supplied
in the early part of the winter.

In concluding its report, the committee quotes from an
article by Dr. Albert Shaw, on "Relief Measures in
America during the Winter of 1893 and 1894," a reference to the work in Indianapolis as the "model instance
of relief work." This praise is not undeserved, although
in the success with which employment was substituted for
relief, and in the ingenuity with which useful employment,
from the standpoint of the community, was devised, the
achievements of the New York East Side Relief Work Committee were at least equally instructive.

CHAPTER V

THE BALTIMORE FIRE[1]

THE Baltimore fire of Sunday, February 7, 1904, and the Monday following swept over an area estimated to be one hundred and fifty acres, the heart of the business section. Over thirteen hundred buildings were destroyed and probably four thousand firms, corporations, or individuals were burned out. Many of these went into new locations at once; some reduced their working force; some ceased to do business, for the time at least. No residence section was burned, but a few families, chiefly Hebrew and Italian, were driven from their homes. A good many lodging-houses were swept away, including some that had long been unsanitary shelters of homeless and depraved persons. All this came suddenly toward the close of an unusually cold winter, when there had been an unusual amount of illness.

The fire began Sunday noon, and was not wholly under control until Monday afternoon. At noon Monday, one hundred or more leading citizens met at the mayor's office. Little that was definite could be said or done about rehabilitation. The talk turned to the question of distress and its relief. A member of the legislature promised that the state would give a large sum; a member of congress suggested that the national government be asked for $1,000,000. Other cities were pledging aid. A few cool heads, saying that no residence section had been burned, urged that there was time to ascertain first what the needs were, before deciding how

---

[1] This account of the work of the Citizens' Relief Committee of Baltimore is condensed but slightly from an article contributed by Dr. Jeffrey R. Brackett to Charities of June 4, 1904. Dr. Brackett was not only president of the Board of Supervisors of City Charities, and a manager of the Charity Organization Society, but was chairman of the Relief Committee

to meet them and with what amounts.   These cool heads
were openly criticised by some as having cold hearts.
But the meeting adjourned without action in this matter.
The mayor was the key to the situation, and he, although
he had been under a great strain for twenty-four hours,
was calm and clear-headed, evidently disposed to agree
with the cooler heads.   As to the offers of aid for relief
of distress which came from many sources without the
city, the mayor did no more than courteously to acknowledge them ; such sums as were sent he placed in his safe,
to be used later as needed.   He conferred at once, however, with several leaders in charity work, including the
head of the city department of charities and correction,
who were watching conditions.   Meantime, some very
inflammatory reports as to conditions of distress were
being circulated, especially outside of Baltimore.   Several
of them came from well-meaning but injudicious religious
workers.   One of them was that homeless men and even
casual laborers from the lodging-houses burned were
unable to find shelter.   For one night only, the Friendly
Inn, a large and well-regulated temporary home for homeless men, used by the city for applicants to its offices, a
house where food and shelter and a bath must be earned
by work, had had a good many beds filled, but none had
had to be turned away ; three nights after the fire, there
were nearly one hundred vacant beds.   Strict orders
were issued by the marshal of police to the captains to
arrest all persons begging on the streets as fire sufferers,
and word was passed among the lodging-houses that persons who had no business in town had better leave.   The
mayor was soon informed that for homeless men no
special measures were required ; that the existing charitable agencies for dealing with homeless men could and
should deal with all such persons.

As to residents, the mayor was soon informed that
there was not then any such amount of unusual destitution as to call for unusual measures for immediate relief.
The few families who had been burned out had already
been cared for without delay and without publicity, by
neighbors and friends, or by the regular well-organized
charities of the city.   While the leaders in charitable

2 F

work were sure of this condition, no one ventured, of course, to prophesy what the extent of real distress caused by the fire would be, or how much money would be needed to meet it. The existing charities had been hard worked since autumn. While there was no immediate and great increase in pressure, all believed that there would be some unusual distress due to the fire which their regular workers and their usual income could hardly meet. The immediate question with their leaders was, should any extraordinary measures be taken for relieving in their homes persons who might soon become in actual need because of the fire. The judgment was that there was not need of any new mechanism for the administration of relief then, but that a large and representative relief committee had better be appointed by the mayor, in order to receive funds for the unusual demand, to decide what agencies should be used for administering relief, and to give confidence to the community that what needed to be done would be well done. Such a committee was appointed and organized February 13, the Saturday after the fire. The president of the Department of Charities and Correction was made its chairman, and a small executive committee was appointed to carry out all details. This consisted of two lawyers, two business men, and the chairman. They were all comparatively young men; three of them were actively interested in the work of the Charity Organization Society; one was president of the visitors to the jail.

The Citizens' Committee adopted and pronounced the following policy: There should be a clear understanding by all that the relief was to meet actual need, to secure the necessaries of living, and was not merely a reimbursement against losses by the fire. Persons in need were expected to try every resource available before applying for it. It might be in the form of a gift or loan, in order to start needy persons anew in occupations by which they could probably earn a living. Secondly, in so far as the fire sufferers might be persons who had already been aided by existing charities, they should be referred for further aid to those charities; the charities being reimbursed if necessary. As some of the suffering would fall upon persons who had never been aided, as some who would suffer most would be the last to make their needs known, the methods of administering relief should be such, as far as possible, as to avoid publicity. The hope of the committee was that, unless unusual measures were found to be absolutely necessary, its work of relief could be left to responsible charities. It believed that any unusual machinery if created would only cause confusion, duplicate agencies, and increase applications for aid. The churches and other bodies were expected to do much of themselves. The committee believed that many persons in need could best be cared for by those who knew well their language and ways of living — Hebrews by Hebrews, Italians by Italians, Germans by Germans.

In accordance with these principles, the executive committee was instructed to use the well-known, well-organized charities as agencies for the committee, the charities being reimbursed, in so far as they might ask it, for material relief given or extra services rendered because of the fire, in the approval of the executive committee. That committee was empowered also, if it deemed such action best, to deal directly, by gift or loan, with any cases of need. It took into its employ, therefore, three persons — a clerk and bookkeeper, who should also act as visitor, if needed, another man to give all his time to visiting, and a stenographer. This remained, practically, the full office force.

From the beginning, there was hope that men who had been accustomed to laboring might be placed at work in cleaning up the burnt district, work on a business basis, under the proper city officials. But the opportunity for such work for a considerable number of men never came. As a matter of fact, there are always a number of laboring men out of work in winter, and many of those who were seeking work were much more needy than most of those who had just lost work by the fire. The State Free Employment Bureau, located in Baltimore, seemed a proper agency to which persons asking merely for employment might be sent. Its use was urged upon employers, also.

The executive committee had to see at once that the

leading charities, which it wished to use for most applicants, were prepared to deal with them, to relieve needs
promptly, adequately, and without publicity. On Sunday the 14th, the chairman addressed a large meeting
of members of the Hebrew Benevolent Society. It had
been for years the one large general agency for relieving
Jews, but one or two smaller bodies had undertaken work
in the eastern part of the city. All were now urged to
work together under one representative committee with
which the Citizens' Relief Committee could promptly
deal. They were urged, also, to receive applications in
writing, so that persons who hesitated to apply need not
come to any public place, and to have inquiries made in
the homes of the needy. These requests were met with
enthusiasm. The next day a representative committee
came to the City Hall stating that they were prepared
to deal in future with all Jewish applicants, according to
particular needs, in the ways indicated. The society had,
since the fire, been relieving and caring for a considerable
number of burned-out families, and for all such unusual
expenses, over and above its receipts for fire sufferers from
citizens, it was promptly reimbursed. A number of Italian families had already gone to the Italian Consul, asking for aid, and he and several leading Italians were
planning to form a relief committee when the representative of the mayor's committee called upon them in turn
that Sunday afternoon. The next day, also, they reported
at the City Hall the formation of such a relief committee
whose members were willing to give much time and
thought to dealing with fire sufferers of their own people.
They were told to go ahead at once, to relieve in the
same way as the Hebrew society, with promise of reimbursement for necessary outlay. On the same Sunday
night a special meeting of the St. Vincent de Paul Society
was held, and its workers in the twenty and more conferences throughout the city promised to give prompt
attention to fire sufferers. The German society agreed
to coöperate also. Thus the committee was soon able
to publish in all the leading papers the following advertisement together with the names and addresses of the
leading charities, headed by the two large general ones —

the Association for the Improvement of the Condition of
the Poor and the Charity Organization Society, working
together as the Federated Charities, which maintain a
general application bureau in a central location, eight district offices, and fourteen agents in the field : —

"The Executive Committee of the Mayor's Advisory
Committee as to the relief of need owing to the fire,
wishes to announce to the public, on behalf of the leading
charitable agencies to which it is referring persons for
relief, that persons in need because of the fire, who have
never had to ask charitable aid, are not required to make
applications at any public office, but may state their needs
in writing through the mail to those charities, and inquiries
which may then be made will be made by visitors of the
charities, in the homes, without publicity.

"Applications in such cases may also be made in writing
to Jeffrey R. Brackett, chairman, City Hall, who will see
that they receive prompt attention. The relation of the
need to the fire should be plainly shown.

"The charities are expected by the Citizens' Committee
to act promptly, employing extra visitors if necessary for
the purpose ; and, if relief in unusual amounts is found
to be necessary in order to remove causes of need, the
charities are expected to spend whatever sums are really
needed for adequate relief, in gifts or loans."

All these charities went to work more actively than
ever, the Federated Charities employing several extra
agents. One of these was kindly loaned by the Washington society, and one who had formerly been an agent in
Baltimore returned from New York.

With all these agencies at work, and able to deal
promptly with applicants who came directly to them or
were sent to them by the relief committee, that committee
had its hands full during the following week in dealing
with a number of benevolent individuals, organizations,
and clubs, all wishing to do something for fire sufferers.
To convince some benevolent persons that there was no
great pressure of destitution, was a hard task indeed.
Yet most careful inquiries which were made from day
to day of various beneficial orders, of clergymen, of the
Salvation Army, of several deaconess' houses, of the visit-

ing nurses, and others not directly connected with the charities used, showed that there was no rush of applicants and no cause for further machinery for relief. Several of the agencies reporting had had no applications from fire sufferers. The three stations of the Salvation Army in Baltimore had had very few applications, and had referred those promptly to the usual charitable agencies. One Baltimore clergyman of many years' experience in a large parish, mostly of persons of little means, knew of some two hundred families with a member or members out of work because of the fire, but careful inquiry which he made brought to light six families only believed to be in immediate need, and only three of these were burned out. The family which he believed to be most in need had refused his offers of aid, on the ground that they were able to get on so far without it. The others he had referred to the Charity Organization Society or to the German Society. Some of the results of these careful inquiries were almost amusing. Two religious agencies which, the day of the fire, had spread inflammatory reports of dire distress, were called on one week after the fire. One had not heard of a single case of suffering ; the other had heard of several but had felt doubtful whether they were *bona fide* sufferers, and had referred them gladly to the proper agencies. One so-called missionary, who had written to a prominent citizen a plea for funds for " suffering ones," when asked to the office of the committee, in order that the committee might see that the families were relieved, named only one family which he wished the committee to aid, and that was found, on a prompt inquiry, to be in no way needy, because the wage-earner was again at work for the same wages received before.

There were very cheering reports from a number of societies and beneficial orders. The Royal Arcanum wrote that all needy members would be relieved. Leaders of the Federation of Labor, at its regular meeting ten days after the fire, had no unusual distress to report, declared that they would try to look out for their own members who might become needy, and voted to return to the federation of Washington, with their thanks, a check for $100 which had been sent over for the fire sufferers. One of their leaders was on the Citizens' Relief Committee. The chairman of the committee and the chairman of the Charity Organization Society executive committee had the pleasure of being at this meeting and of applauding this action of the federation. The Presbyterian clergy of the city very promptly appointed a special committee to deal with cases of need, especially those arising among their own people in congregations with limited resources. The Baptist clergy did the same. In order to give further publicity to the desire of the committee to help all *bona fide* cases of need, and to utilize every helpful agency in reaching the needy, representatives of all the religious denominations were invited to a meeting in the mayor's reception room. Many attended. The policy of the committee was talked over, and the clergy were asked to search for cases of need, especially for those who had not been in need before. At the same time a copy of the following circular letter was sent out, over the names of the executive committee, to three hundred and twenty-five ministers and religious leaders : —

"The Mayor's Advisory Committee on relief of need due to the fire, in promptly announcing to the public, by advertisement in six daily papers, the addresses of the leading charities, stated that persons in need because of the fire who have never applied to charitable agencies, are not required to make application at any public place, but may state their needs in writing to those charities, and that inquiries which are then made of them are made in their homes, without publicity. Announcement was made at the same time that applications in such cases might also be made to the chairman of the committee, J. R. Brackett, City Hall, in writing, plainly showing the relation of the need to the fire.

"The committee believes that the ministers and leaders of the many religious bodies in our city will find out the extreme needs of some persons of their congregations who will still hesitate to ask aid. It believes, too, that the congregations of all denominations will strive to provide through the ministers and leaders the means of relief for such persons ; that strong congregations will come to the aid of any weaker ones, whose resources are not equal to the demands upon them. The clergy of several denominations have already taken action to that end.

"In expressing the expectation that this will be done generally, the committee asks that cases of need due to the fire which may not be dealt with by the churches shall be referred to an appropriate charity or directly to the committee.

"One suggestion only is made in connection with religious bodies as sources of aid — that the persons aided be really known, that reasonable pains be taken to see that they are not being aided at the same time by others, in order that there may be the truest economy of energy and money. Such economy will allow relief, when given, to be more adequate.

"The committee will be glad to be of service in any possible way to the ministers and leaders of the religious bodies, whose part in the relief of unusual need and great distress is believed to be so valuable to the whole community."

An inquiry was made by the executive committee as to the need of the establishment of a special agency for making loans to fire sufferers of larger amounts than were being made by the committee itself, which were under $200. Correspondence was had with workers in other cities, and the decision was reached that no new agency had better be established for larger loans. Baltimore has an excellent chattel-loan association founded by philanthropic men, but strictly on business principles.

Thus the policy as to methods and agencies was adopted and carried out. The only modification was that the committee dealt directly with an increased number of cases. These were mostly applications for sums of a hundred dollars or more, or where uniformity in treatment was especially desirable. The executive committee gave hours to oversight of details. Through a system of frequent reports the committee had the addresses of all persons helped by the various agencies, and the amounts expended. Duplication was thus avoided and responsibility concentrated. An arrangement was made with a woman of refinement and experience for the use of her services,

if desired, as visitor to women applicants. But no case
arose in which she was needed, which apparently could
not properly be referred to the charities, especially to the
Charity Organization Society, whose agents are women,
or be dealt with by a member of the executive committee
or by its regular visitors. A few persons found fault
with the committee, but the majority and the public
press either spoke helpfully or said nothing. One or two
letters and published communications called for the provision of work, especially work for persons who had seen
better days, but no suggestion was made by which *bona
fide* employment could be created for fire sufferers, without publicity, which could be considered by a public relief
committee. The committee, while striving to avoid publicity and unnecessary formalities in administration, was
opposed to methods which would seem to recognize an
aristocracy among fire sufferers, or an aristocracy of fire
sufferers as compared with respectable persons in need
because of causes other than this particular fire, whose
only source of relief, now or later, would be the usual
charitable sources. In addition to the charitable agencies
used, as already stated, the Visiting Nurse Association was
employed for a while for nursing services rendered families with illness due to the exposure of the fire. Also, the
State Employment Bureau was requested to use temporarily several agents in trying by personal interviews with
employers to get places for applicants to the bureau who
had been burned out. A number of such persons asking
of the committee only work, not relief, were visited after
an interval by the committee's agents. Of two hundred, in
round numbers, thirty could not be found, nearly a third
were found to have secured work, more than a third reported no change in their situation, four had left the city,
five had been aided already with material relief, and only
eight said that they then needed such aid.

If the first strategic point to be won was the adoption
of a sound policy in methods of administration, the second
point was the prevention of an unwise financial policy.
Opinions differed as to what sources of money for relief
were best. Citizens were ready to give; other communities were sending offers of aid. But the mayor set-

tled the matter of outside aid by saying that Maryland
people would and could look out for their own. A bill
was soon introduced in the legislature, then in session, to
appropriate $250,000 for relief in Baltimore, after pay-
ment of some $40,000 from it for the militia which had
served at the fire. Opinions differed widely again as to
whether any such large sum could be needed. But the
mayor decided not to attempt to change the bill, especially
as the expenditure was placed in the hands of the governor
and a small special commission, and was made contingent
only upon the need, and as the members of the commission
were known to desire no unnecessary expenditure. For
nearly six weeks after its organization the Citizens' Relief
Committee did its work on money quietly borrowed, in an-
ticipation of action by the state ; every case of need known
of and believed to be genuine was relieved; and in that
time, in so doing, about $10,000 only was expended.

During those six weeks a good deal had been learned
by many persons as to actual conditions. The thousands
and thousands reported to be out of work had dwindled
constantly. Now, the estimate of the state bureau, based
on returns from four hundred business houses, was that
not over four thousand persons had been thrown out of
work, — a half of the number which had been estimated
three weeks before. Of the eight hundred applications
for work which the bureau had received during one month
after the fire, one-quarter only had given the fire as a
cause. Spring was at hand. Despite the delay in opening up the burned district for improvement, much laboring
work was beginning, as usual. Activity among artisans
would probably soon be great. Those who were now suffering by the fire were those who were willing to suffer in
silence. Many persons had been relieved by relatives or
churches or friends, in some of those many ways which
are the essence of true charity.

When, finally, the papers reported that the bill appropriating a quarter million of dollars for relief of distress
in Baltimore had become a law, somewhat of a " run " on
the committee was looked for. True, forty thousand went
to the militia, and another forty thousand was set aside, by
law, for the Johns Hopkins Hospital, but over two-thirds

was left. But no run came. The key to the situation
here was largely, as it had been at the other strategic
point, the good sense and honesty of public officials. The
governor, like the mayor, had known of the work previously done by the well-organized charities of Baltimore.
Both of them had been at the annual public meeting of
the Federated Charities in November. The governor had
intimated, before the passage of the bill, that the Citizens'
Relief Committee would be the natural advisers. So the
work went on quietly, without interruption. That the
work of the committee and the state appropriation were
not given more publicity in the daily press was probably
due largely to the exigencies for more interesting news
of the fire and of the doings of the legislators at Annapolis.

The total of families assisted up to the last week in
May, in fifteen weeks after the fire, was 1058. Of these,
by far the largest number were assisted through the
Federated Charities, the next through the Hebrew Benevolent Society. The Relief Committee assisted directly
about one-eighth of all. Aid was given in all sorts of
ways, in food, clothing, tools, transportation, by gifts and
loans, and of value ranging from $250 down. Some-
times it had to be given cautiously in small amounts
and repeated. Some persons came as fire sufferers who
had been well known to the charities as always rather
needy. Usually, when the person was well known as
responsible and reasonably resourceful, one considerable
sum would be given.

The total of money spent in those fifteen weeks was
about $21,600 only. Somewhat under a quarter of it was
spent directly by the committee in relief, mostly in gifts,
about a fifth was spent through the Hebrew Society,
about a fifth through the Italian committee, and as much
through the Federated Charities. The St. Vincent de
Paul Society called for less than a thousand dollars;
the German society for much less still. The expenses
for administration all told were under $1900, about
one thousand being spent by the committee directly, and
a half as much through the Federated Charities. It was
spent in saving the state many dollars and in seeing that
relief was brought intelligently to those in real need.

The total of money spent for fire sufferers from all
sources cannot, of course, be told. But the amounts
received by the charitable agencies from sources other
than the Relief Committee were not large. For instance,
the Federated Charities, up to May 1, spent about $600
received from special donations. The belief that the
state would make an appropriation cut off much giving
by individuals. Also, some persons felt that charitable
agencies, losing subscribers because of the fire, would need
their gifts for ordinary work in the future.

If there are lessons to be learned from this work for
emergency relief, they are indicated in the story itself.
Stress may be laid, in conclusion, on three. First, is the
value of having public officials who believe that enlightened administration of charity is a part of good government. Second, is the value in charity work of using the
experience of persons and agencies of experience in that
work. And third, and most of all, is the duty of protect-
ing the poor from patronage, of giving opportunity for
expression to the many forms of aid, from relatives,
churches, friends, etc., and to powers of self-help, which
in times of need show the real "strength of the people."

The Charities Record, the publication of the Baltimore
Charity Organization Society, in closing its account of fire
relief work, has spoken as follows, happily and justly: —

"The same spirit of self-help which has characterized
the mayor and his advisers, the business and professional
men of Baltimore, in meeting this disaster, has been mani-
fested by the working people who have shown equal courage and commendable independence. Those who have felt
compelled to ask for help have for the most part done so
only through stress of actual necessity, preferring to rely
upon their own efforts rather than to seek assistance even
from the public treasury. When the history of the city
is written and the story of its greatest conflagration is
told, no episode will furnish greater cause for pride to
its citizens, present and future, than that which has
demonstrated the courage and self-reliance of its own
people, not only the well-to-do, but those dependent upon
regular employment for their daily bread."

CHAPTER VI

THE "SLOCUM" DISASTER [1]

By the burning and sinking of the *General Slocum*, a steamboat of the Knickerbocker Steamboat Company, in the East River on June 15, 1904, 958 persons are known to have lost their lives ; 897 bodies having been identified, and 61 buried without identification.

The boat had been chartered for the day for a picnic by the Sunday school of St. Mark's Evangelical Church. The majority of those who were lost were of German birth or descent, communicants of the Lutheran Church, or their relatives or friends ; although, as tickets had been sold by members of the Sunday school to any who desired to attend the picnic, there was also a certain representation of other nationalities and of other religious faiths. The excursionists were mainly women and children, only nine male heads of families having been known to be lost, and in comparison with the appalling loss of life there was comparatively little loss of property. This was confined practically to the clothes worn by those on board who were naturally in holiday attire, their jewellery, which was valued in one instance at $800, and the money and bank books carried on the person—a surprisingly large amount, estimated by the coroner to amount in the aggregate to $200,000. While in some instances the mothers or older children who were lost in the disaster were wage-earners, even this was the exception rather than the rule, many of the grown daughters in the families affected not being engaged in wage-earning occupations. Two-thirds of the

---

[1] This is the text of the report of the Citizens' Relief Committee to Mayor George B. McClellan, of which committee the author was Acting Secretary when the report was made in September, 1904, on the conclusion of the active work of the Committee.

families subsequently aided in the burial of their dead
(255 families) carried insurance, and in 155 of these
families the amount of the insurance exceeded the total
funeral expenses. In the case of five other families there
were bank accounts which supplemented or took the place
of insurance, and in several cases the amount of life insurance obtained was upward of $1000.

These facts indicate clearly that the families affected
by the disaster were self-supporting and in many instances
prosperous members of the community, not likely to become dependent upon charitable relief even when overtaken by unexpected misfortune.

Even before the full extent of the calamity had been
made known, generous contributions to a relief fund for
the benefit of the survivors and the families of the victims
were offered, and on Thursday, June 16, Mayor McClellan
issued the following proclamation : —

"To the Citizens of New York : —

"The appalling disaster yesterday, by which more than five hundred
men, women, and children lost their lives by fire and drowning, has
shocked and horrified our city. Knowing the keen sympathy of the
people of the City of New York with their stricken fellows, I have
appointed a committee of citizens to receive contributions to a fund
to provide for the fit and proper burial of the dead, and for such other
relief as may be necessary.

"The following gentlemen have been asked to serve on the committee : —

Morris K. Jesup,	Jos. C. Hendrix,
Jacob H. Schiff,	Thomas M. Mulry,
Herman Ridder,	George Ehret,
Charles A. Dickey,	John Fox,
Robert A. Van Cortlandt,	H. B. Scharmann,
	Erskine Hewitt.

"Until the Committee has had an opportunity to organize, I shall
be glad to receive contributions at the Mayor's office.
"As a sign of mourning I have ordered the flags on the City Hall to
be put at half-mast.

"George B. McClellan, *Mayor.*"

On the following day, June 17, the committee held a
meeting at 12 o'clock at the office of the mayor, at which
all of the above-named gentlemen except Messrs. Ehret
and Jesup were present. Herman Ridder was duly elected
chairman of the committee, Jacob Schiff, treasurer, and

John C. Breckinridge, secretary.   It was then further decided to appoint a sub-committee to undertake the active
work of affording relief to the victims of the *General Slocum* disaster.   This sub-committee consisted of Messrs.
Weinacht, Scharmann, Mulry, Fox, Van Cortlandt, and
Hewitt, and also the officers of the General Committee who
should be *ex-officio* members of the sub-committee.

The meeting thereupon adjourned *sine die*, and the executive committee immediately had its first meeting, and
organized by the election of Mr. Scharmann as chairman,
and A. A. Hill of the Charity Organization Society as
secretary.

The following were subsequently added to the executive
committee : Rev. John J. Heischman, Rev. Jacob W.
Loch, Rev. E. C. J. Kræling, Rev. H. W. Hoffman,
William H. Allen, H. Cillis, Edward T. Devine, Julius
Harburger, Louis W. Kaufmann, Louis C. Rægener, Inspector Max F. Schmittberger, Gustav Straubenmiller.   A
committee was also appointed from the board of aldermen, some of whom attended the meetings of the executive committee from time to time, and its chairman, L. W.
Harburger, was made vice-chairman of the executive
committee.

Headquarters were opened in the basement of St. Mark's
Church, and the secretary was placed in full executive
charge of the work of receiving applications for relief, making the necessary visits and inquiry to establish their *bona
fide* character, and carrying into effect the decisions of the
committee.   The committee throughout realized and attempted in every way to make evident to those with whom
it was dealing, that it was engaged in the administration
of a fund which was not a charitable relief fund in the
ordinary sense, but a generous expression of heart-felt
sympathy on the part of the community toward those who
had been sorely stricken.   The secretary and his assistants
displayed in every way a personal sympathy for the
afflicted ; and, although there were irresponsible charges
to the contrary, the committee is confident that in no single instance was there a failure to attend promptly to
emergent needs, or harshness toward any person who came
to the committee for aid, or other ground for just com-

plaint. There were only five fraudulent applications, *i.e.*
from persons who were in no way affected by the disaster; but the number would doubtless have been much
larger if it had not been understood from the outset that
all applications would be carefully investigated. One
woman who was fraudulently collecting money on the ground
that she was a sufferer was arraigned in court by the
Mendicancy Officers of the Charity Organization Society,
convicted of obtaining money under false pretences, and
sentenced to one year's imprisonment.

The secretary was authorized to engage whatever visitors and office assistants might be required; the largest
number at work at any one time was twenty-nine, including volunteers, and the average for seven weeks over
twelve. The secretary himself, however, received no
financial remuneration, his services being placed at the
disposal of the committee by the Charity Organization
Society. A very considerable amount of volunteer service
was also supplied by the New York Association for Improving the Condition of the Poor. The total operating
expenses for the committee for the seven weeks over
which its active work extended were only $1062, or less
than one percent of the relief fund disbursed. The extraor-
dinarily low percentage was made possible only by the
large amount of expert assistance given to the committee
by the two societies named, and by the courtesy of the
New York City Mission and Tract Society, in providing
without charge commodious offices for the use of the
committee in the United Charities Building after the
removal of its headquarters from St. Mark's Church on
June 29.

The value of the aid rendered by the organized charities
is not, however, to be measured merely by the saving in
administrative expenses. It was through this coöperation
that the relief could be given promptly and to the right
persons, the element of imposition eliminated from the
beginning, and exact knowledge quickly obtained in
regard to each family for whom the committee was asked
to provide, on the basis of which action could be taken in
accordance with its own best judgment.

Members of the committee also gave a large amount of

time to its work, both at its headquarters and in their own places of business — of course entirely without compensation; and in the illness of the secretary after July 20, his entire duties fell upon Edward T. Devine of the executive committee. Rev. George C. F. Haas, pastor of St. Mark's Church, who himself lost three members of his family, served practically as a member of the committee, and gave at every step invaluable advice and coöperation.

For the first week the committee held daily meetings, and thereafter met at frequent intervals for the consideration of applications for relief and other business. In each individual case, on a full but confidential statement of the circumstances, the committee decided what kind and amount of assistance to give.

Except for its initiative in arranging a memorial meeting in Cooper Union, the committee limited its activities to questions of relief. It gave no consideration to questions relating to liability for the accident, to claims for pecuniary damages, to rewards for personal heroism in the rescues of June 15, or to any of the other aspects of the disaster in which the public has naturally been interested. It will be remembered that by the terms of the mayor's original proclamation the committee was appointed " to receive contributions to a fund for the fit and proper burial of the dead, and for such other relief as may be necessary." The burial expenses of those whose bodies were recovered have been in fact the principal item in the disbursements — almost exactly two-thirds of the fund having been used for this purpose.

Until it was definitely known what other relief would be necessary the committee felt warranted in paying funeral bills in full only in cases in which the families affected did not have other resources. If, therefore, there was insurance sufficient to meet the funeral expenses, or if there remained in the family any one of independent means, the funeral expenses were not paid by the committee, or were paid only in part. The committee finally fixed upon a date, July 21, after which further applications could not be considered, and within a few days thereafter full information was at hand on which could be based an accurate forecast of the provision required for orphan children,

2 G

aged persons, widows, or others left to any extent dependent by the disaster.

The number of such persons proved to be much less than many had anticipated, and after setting aside what was considered an adequate amount for all of them, there remained a sufficient sum to pay in full all funeral bills which in the judgment of the committee could properly, even on the most liberal basis, be met from the funds at its disposal.

On August 5, a meeting was held at which it was ascertained that about $85,000 had been paid or authorized to be paid for burials and other forms of relief, and that $20,000 would be required to meet the future needs of those who had been made to some extent dependent by the disaster, or had suffered so severely as to justify an appropriation in their behalf, leaving a balance of something over $15,000 unappropriated. In reference to the balance remaining in the hands of the treasurer, and the $20,000 already set aside for the future care of individual families made dependent by the disaster, the committee then adopted the following resolutions : —

" *Resolved :* that whenever the character and the circumstances of the family are such as to justify such action, immediate payment of the amount authorized by the Committee shall be made by an order on the Treasurer.

" That in the case of such families as should receive weekly or monthly payments, such payments shall be made through St. Mark's Evangelical Lutheran Church, — an order on the Treasurer, in favor of St. Mark's Church, being drawn, sufficient to cover such payments as have been authorized by the Committee.

" That a special committee, consisting of Messrs. Ridder, Scharmann, and Straubenmiller, be appointed to have a general oversight of such weekly and monthly payments on behalf of the Citizens' Relief Committee, and that such special committee shall have power to authorize any modifications of such grants as may seem to them, from time to time, advisable.

" That the balance remaining after such payments as are above specified have been made, shall be held by the Treasurer, subject to the order of the special committee above named, to care for any of the families from whom application was made prior to July 21, if in their opinion any further action in behalf of such families is required.

" That after July 15, 1905, any remaining balance still in the hands of the Treasurer may be disposed of by the special committee above named in such manner as may be approved by the Mayor of the City of New York."

For the small number of Roman Catholic families included in the list of beneficiaries it was arranged that the payments should be made through Thomas M. Mulry, president of the Society of St. Vincent de Paul.

In accordance with the resolutions the sum of $15,750 has been turned over to a special committee of St. Mark's Church appointed to receive this sum in trust for the families specified, and $1500 to Mr. Mulry for two families, the remainder of the $20,000 having been paid directly to the families for whom it was intended.

The number of families aided by the committee was 437, which is three-fourths of the 590 families known to have been represented on the *General Slocum* at the time of the disaster.

The 25 per cent who were not aided by the committee were those who were in better circumstances, or those who suffered least ; and very few of them made any application for aid. Only a little more than half (54 per cent) of those who were not aided lost even one member of the family, while 92 per cent of those who were aided lost one or more by death. In the 437 families aided by the committee, there were before the disaster 1913 persons, about two-thirds of whom were on the excursion. Of these 110 were injured, 61 were buried unidentified, 723 were recovered, identified, and buried, leaving only 1019, or 53 per cent of the whole, uninjured — and of these 1019 survivors probably less than one-fifth had been on the excursion. Besides this frightful loss of life the families suffered indescribably by shock, anxiety, and grief, to an extent which no statistics can represent. The numbers themselves are nevertheless an indication of the ravages which the little community sustained and which were the more severe because they were in many instances united by ties of blood-relationship as well as by those of religion and nativity.

The number of persons lost in the 437 families was 784. Of these, nine were male heads of families, 191 were mothers, 30 were wives without children, 155 were children of wage-earning age (not necessarily wage-earners), 356 were children under fourteen years of age, 31 were adults living with relatives, eighteen of whom were grandparents, seven were women living alone, and five were single men.

These numbers would indicate that the immediate economic loss was comparatively insignificant, — only twenty per cent of the whole number lost being present wage-earners. The actual loss, however, was much greater. Many of the children would have become wage-earners in a few years. Others not actually employed could have become wage-earners in case of necessity; and many who were not on the excursion lost valuable time from their business or occupation, searching for the dead, or even prostrated by illness or anxiety. Elder daughters were in some instances compelled to give up employment on the death of a mother, and the fathers of families found their expenses greatly increased by the death or injury of their wives.

One hundred and twenty men lost their entire family by the disaster. Of these, twenty-nine lost wife only; thirty-nine lost wife and one child; thirty-two, wife and two children; ten, wife and three children; three, wife and four children; and one, wife and five children; two widowers lost each two children, and one widower, four children, while the remaining three of the 120 men left alone as the result of the disaster lost other relatives with whom they were living. Twenty-one men, whose wives and one or more children were lost, were left with one child under fourteen; and eleven others were left with more than one small child, having lost wife and one or more children.

Forty-one men were left with children over fourteen, having lost wife or children or both. There were seventy-nine families in which only dependent members were taken, while there were thirty-nine families in which one or more wage-earning children were lost, although not the father or mother. Only two women were left alone, one of whom lost her husband and her only child. Three women who lost their husbands were left with from three to five children each, but in two of these families there were adult unmarried sons or daughters.

Among the 437 families there were sixty-three who were already widows with children, and ten mothers who had been deserted by their husbands. In forty of these seventy-three families no particular need resulted from the disaster aside from the expense of burials. In one instance the mother was lost with her only child, and in another with her entire family of five children, all of whom were under twelve years of age. In twenty instances only dependent children were taken ; and in eighteen others the mother was taken with one or more children, but only self-supporting children were left. In thirty-three of the cases of widows or deserted wives there was such economic loss as to make apparent a need for aid in addition to that given in burials, either because dependent children were left with relatives in moderate circumstances, or because the income of the family was reduced or entirely cut off by the loss of one or more wage-earning children.

In all there were twelve families in which, as a result of the disaster, orphan children were left. Seven of these were families of widows or deserted wives, and have therefore already been accounted for under that heading. The children left orphans in these twelve families numbered twenty-seven ; in six cases there was only one child left, in two cases two, in one case each three and four, and in two cases five. Fifteen of the twenty-seven were under fifteen years of age ; and two others, although of adult years, were defectives, and for that reason dependent. The other ten orphans were over fifteen years of age, and in most cases self-supporting. With one or two exceptions, the children who were made orphans by the disaster were found to be with relatives who were in position to give them suitable care. Two children were placed in institutions temporarily for special reasons, with a grant of money from the committee, and it was not deemed advisable or necessary to accept any of the numerous generous offers of foster-homes which were received by the committee.

Of the 437 families there were twenty-six in which physical injuries or money losses only were sustained, but in which there were no deaths.

The above analysis accounts for 420 of the families aided by the committee. Of the remainder, twelve were men or women living alone, and with no one immediately dependent upon them, and five were families in which collateral relatives had been lost, and little help was required aside from the payment of funeral bills.

The committee buried 705 persons belonging to 388

different families, at an expense of $81,279.99. The average cost of each funeral was $115.29 — the minimum $16, and the maximum $331.50. Medical attendance and supplies were furnished to 38 families at an expense of $1,264.17. Temporary aid was given to 133 families to the amount of $2,042.58. Transportation was provided for two persons costing $125, one of whom was sent to take a position in Chicago and the other to his father's home in Russia. Fourteen persons were reimbursed for the loss of clothing, musical instruments, etc., at an outlay of $571.65, and a tugboat injured in rescue work was repaired at a cost of $60.48. To care for dependent children and adults in 39 families appropriations of $18,281 were required, and $3520 was expended to assist 28 additional families in necessary readjustment after the loss of a wage-earner or because of illness or loss of work consequent on the disaster. There was expended for the Cooper Union Memorial Mass Meeting the sum of $275, and the operating expenses were $1062.

The total contributions to the relief fund, as shown in the report of the treasurer, were $124,205.80. The board of aldermen had indicated its willingness to appropriate $50,000 for relief; but on June 27 the executive committee, after full deliberation, announced to the public press that further contributions would not be required, and at the same time officially notified the board of aldermen that the appropriation would not be needed. As early as June 21, when the contributions amounted to over $60,000, Jacob H. Schiff, the treasurer, had expressed the opinion in a letter to the chairman that the amount received should suffice for the purpose for which the committee had been called into existence; but the resolution closing the subscription fund was deferred six days longer in order not to lay the committee open to the charge of premature action.

There are those who have felt considerable apprehension over the possible effect of the collection and disbursement of so large a relief fund for the benefit of families not in really destitute circumstances. The committee did not consider that it was at liberty to expend this money otherwise than for the direct pecuniary benefit of those for whom it had been subscribed. There were, of course, the possible alternatives of returning a portion of it to the donors, or of diverting it, after communicating with the donors, to some other allied purpose. Neither of these courses appeared to the committee feasible under all the circumstances, and it therefore remained to expend it for such of the *bona fide* sufferers from the disaster as were willing to accept aid, and to do this in such a manner as to run the least risk of injury to the character of those who received it, and to insure the nearest approach to equity among all concerned.

Because it was felt that liberal aid in meeting the extraordinary burdens caused directly by the disaster would be much less likely to prove harmful, the committee had less hesitation in meeting the full expenses for burial, even when there was left to the survivors a moderate life insurance, or a modest savings-bank account. With a view to this permanent effect upon character, the committee has attempted to give with just discrimination although at the same time with the liberality which donors to the fund have expected; and for this reason finally the committee has deemed it wise at the earliest practical moment to close its active work, leaving to other and more permanent bodies any responsibility for subsequent relief.

[NOTE. — A unique incident in connection with this disaster was the formal organization of the dissatisfied element among the survivors, with the avowed purpose of forcing the distribution of the funds according to their own ideas of their " rights," and, later, of securing from the federal treasury an allowance for each life lost. While this organization did not on any point influence the decisions of the committee, still it was an element to be reckoned with, for it had a perceptible effect on the group of families affected by the disaster. Many were stirred up to apply for aid who had little or no need for it and others who in spite of a just claim on the fund had at first sturdily declined all offers of assistance, were persuaded to accept it. This incident serves to emphasize the necessity of dealing with claimants individually and directly rather than through irresponsible representatives.]

Summary

Total number recovered		958
Identified	897	
Unidentified	61	

Number of families who lost one or more		590
Number of families aided by the Committee		437

(The numbers that follow refer only to the 437 families aided by the Committee.)

Number of persons lost in these 437 families		784
Of these 784, there were:		
Fathers	9	
Mothers	191	
Wives without children	30	
Children over 14	155	
Children under 14	356	
Women living alone	7	
Men living alone	5	
Other adults	31	

Number of men who lost entire family		120
Families in which children were made orphans by loss of both or only surviving parent		12
Number of orphans in these families		27
Of wage-earning age and self-supporting	10	
Number of persons buried by the Committee		705
Average cost of each burial		$115.29
Total cost of burials		$81,279.99
Families in which medical attendance was supplied		38
Cost of medical attendance, etc.		$1,264.17
Families given temporary aid		133
Expended for temporary aid		$2,042.58
Expended for transportation		$125.00
Expended for reimbursement of losses		$632.13
Appropriated for future needs in 67 families		$21,801.00
Expenses Cooper Union Memorial Meeting		$275.00
Total operating expenses		$1,062.00
For wages	$605.83	
For other expenses (including furniture, printing, postage, telephone, etc.)	$456.17	

CHAPTER VII

LESSONS TO BE LEARNED FROM EMERGENCY RELIEF IN DISASTERS

THE story of emergency relief work succeeding the great disasters at Chicago and Johnstown, the three minor but serious disasters coming in quick succession upon a single city, the hard times of 1893–1894, as seen in two cities with somewhat contrasting conditions, of the successful handling of the situation after the Baltimore fire with a relief fund of moderate size, and the expenditure of what may be felt to be an unnecessarily large sum for the benefit of the survivors of the *General Slocum* disaster, have been told in detail because they are typical, and together present many varied aspects of the problem of emergency relief. It will not be necessary to extend this study to the numerous disasters that have befallen other communities. Forest fires, as in Minnesota and other states ; inundations from the sea, as at Galveston and elsewhere ; earthquakes, as at Charleston ; cyclones, as at St. Louis ; lowland floods, as along the Ohio and the Mississippi, the Kansas and the Missouri ; droughts, and consequent failure of crops in limited areas in the West, and the various industrial crises through which the country has passed, present a greater variety in causes of disasters and in their attending circumstances, than in the relief problem, the character of which is sufficiently set forth by the examples which we have already studied.

The first lesson which is written large in the experience of those who have been called upon to deal with such disasters is the folly and wastefulness of relying upon inexperienced, untrained, or incompetent agents for the distribution of relief and for the constructive work without which relief distribution may easily be productive of more harm than good. There are always at such times novel problems to be solved, but the experience of other communities under similar or analogous conditions will aid in their solution if it can be brought to bear. It may be, as at Chicago after the great fire, that the problem is primarily one of relief pending the resumption of trade and industry. It may be, as at Johnstown and at Heppner,[1] that the problem of sanitation and public safety is equally important; or, as at Martinique, that the destruction of life is so complete that little relief is required except for the transportation of the few survivors for whom no means of livelihood remain. It may be that, as in Paterson after the fire and flood of March, 1902, and the tornado of 1903, and as in Baltimore after the devastating fire of 1904, the community as a whole remains self-supporting, even though one portion is severely taxed to supply the necessities of other portions that have especially suffered, and that as a consequence no outside relief is needed; or, on the other hand, as at Galveston after the inundation in September, 1900, and at Kansas City in 1903, that all classes have been so universally stricken that outside relief is imperative; it may be, as at East St. Louis after the inundations of May and June, 1903, that relief is provided in sufficient quantity from towns and cities in the immediate vicinity, although not in sufficient amount from the stricken town or city itself; it may be, as in Indianapolis, that there is a comparatively homogeneous and intelligent working population deprived of employment through a temporary paralysis of commerce and industry, and that, as in New York City, widespread unemployment is accompanied by unusual opportunities to perform public work which the local authorities are neglecting; or it may be, as in the case of the *General Slocum* disaster, that a very liberal relief fund is immediately subscribed and the chief problem of the committee responsible for its disbursement becomes one of applying the fund in such a way as to do as little injury as possible to families that have heretofore been independent, and in an exceptional degree, self-reliant.

[1] The county seat of Morrow County, Oregon, which was visited by a cloud-burst on June 14, 1903, in which two hundred persons, about one-seventh of the inhabitants of the town, lost their lives.

It is indispensable that there shall be a quick perception of the essential features of the existing situation in those who would lead a community and outside sympathizers to a wise conclusion in the face of impending or accomplished destruction of life and property.

When it has been decided that there is need for relief, whether in the form of money, of transportation, of labor, or in whatever direction, then there should be summoned an executive, if such a one can be found, who is endowed with financial capacity, a knowledge of human nature, experience in dealing with men, and acquaintance with the peculiar and difficult problems constantly arising in the attempt to relieve suffering and distress without injury to the self-respect of those who are to be aided, and without injury to their neighbors. If the problem is a large and complicated one, numerous sub-committees will be requisite and a staff of assistants. There should be searching inquiry into the claims for relief where the facts are not fully known. The Board of Inquiry inaugurated at Johnstown by Tom L. Johnson, of Cleveland, speedily became one of the most important features of the whole relief system, and upon it eventually devolved the real decision as to the persons to be aided and as to the amounts they should receive. The relief disbursed after the Baltimore fire, under the direction of Jeffrey R. Brackett, and after the *General Slocum* disaster, under the direction of A. A. Hill, Secretary of the Relief Committee, was similarly based upon accurate knowledge.

There should be an executive committee, whether called by that name, as in Chicago, or by some other designation, thoroughly acquainted with local conditions and in constant touch with the relief operations. Whether this committee should have the full responsibility, or should itself be responsible to a larger board or commission, will depend upon various conditions, and especially upon the extent of the area from which donations are received. If contributions are made from distant communities, it may be advisable that there should be representatives upon the controlling body from such communities, or at least there should be as members of it citizens of sufficient reputation and standing to inspire a feeling of confidence even in the most distant places. After the Johnstown Flood a commission was appointed by state authority on which there was comparatively little local representation, and the principal responsibility in Johnstown itself, during the period of greatest need, rested upon what was known as a finance committee. Although there are advantages in an authoritative and widely represented commission, such as that which was then created, it is doubtful whether the resulting delays and the lack of familiarity with the actual situation are not fatal objections. It is certain that decisions, if made at a distance, should be influenced by the opinion of those who are on the spot. In any event the real responsibility will naturally rest principally upon the local executive committee and its executive. The strictly local character of the New York East Side Relief Work Committee in 1893–1894 was one of its chief sources of strength. The committee should lay down the principles on which aid is to be extended, and full responsibility for carrying them into effect should devolve upon the executive.

Material should be preserved for the publication of a complete report, including a detailed financial record of both receipts and disbursements. This is not only due to contributors and to the public as a guide in future emergencies, but it is of advantage to those who are responsible for the relief measures, in order that, if criticisms or controversies arise, a full statement can be made. The Fire Report of the Chicago Relief and Aid Society and the report published in Calcutta of the Central Executive Committee of the Indian Famine Charitable Relief Fund of 1900 may be cited as models of most complete and elaborate reports; and, although of briefer compass, the Report of the Secretary of the Johnstown Relief Commission, the Report of the Jacksonville (1901) Relief Association, the Report of the Indianapolis Commercial Club Relief Committee of 1893–1894, the Report of the Minnesota State Commission for the Relief of Fire Sufferers (September, 1894; report printed 1895), and the Report of the *General Slocum* Relief Committee, printed as a chapter in this volume, are equally explicit and valuable as sources of information.

The failure to publish similar reports, or, indeed, anything that can be properly called a report or financial statement, is one of the just criticisms made against the American National Red Cross. This society has taken part in the relief of the sufferers from the forest fires in Michigan in 1881, from the overflow of the Mississippi River in 1882, and of the Ohio in 1883, from the Mississippi cyclone in the same year, from the overflow of the Ohio and Mississippi in 1884, from the drought in Texas in 1886, from the Charleston earthquake in the same year, from the Mount Vernon (Illinois) cyclone in 1888, from the yellow fever epidemic in Florida in the same year, from the Johnstown disaster in 1889, from the inundation, hurricane, and tidal wave of the South Carolina coast in 1893 and 1894, and from the Galveston Flood in 1900.

In connection with these various enterprises, and others in which the Red Cross has been interested, large sums of money have been contributed to the Red Cross Society, but for their disbursement no suitable public accounting appears to have been made in any instance. In the pamphlets and addresses issued by the society such paragraphs as the following take the place of definite statements concerning what was actually done and what relation such action bore to the relief work of other and often more important agencies : —

" The Secretary brought together the women of Johnstown, bowed to the earth with sorrow and bereavement, and the most responsible were formed into committees charged with definite duties toward the homeless and distraught of the community. Through them the wants of over three thousand families — more than twenty thousand persons — were made known in writing to the Red Cross, and by it supplied ; the white wagons with the red symbol fetching and carrying for the stricken people."

It is principally considerations of this kind that have led to the recent remonstrance from some of the most prominent members of the Red Cross Society, and to an attempt, thus far unsuccessful, to bring about a reorganization of its management, especially on the financial side.[1]

[1] It is reported, while the present volume is in press, that this reorganization, somewhat in the nature of a compromise, has been effected.

In times of great calamity, such as we have been considering, many who are ordinarily quite self-supporting find themselves suddenly bereft of property, of accumulated savings, of the means of livelihood, and even of the barest necessities of life. The disaster may befall a community of high industrial standards, with few, if any, paupers or public dependents — a community in which there is little lawlessness and crime. Under such conditions the principle of indemnity, as distinct from that of charity, may well have a very general application. The principle of indemnity is that of the fire insurance companies, and, in a modified form, also that of the life and accident insurance companies. It implies the reinstatement of the beneficiary as nearly as possible in the position from which he was hurled by the calamity which has befallen him. It implies that to the householder shall be given the use of a house, to the mechanic his tools, to the family its household furniture, to the laborer the opportunity of remunerative employment. For the community as a whole it means the speedy restoration of such commercial and industrial activities as have been temporarily suspended, the rebuilding of bridges, the reopening of streets, the reëstablishment of banks, business houses, churches, and schools. It requires that protection shall be given to the defenceless, food and shelter to the homeless, suitable guardianship to the orphan, and, as nearly as possible, normal social and industrial conditions to all. The charitable principle takes account only of the necessities of those who apply for aid; the principle of indemnity gives greater weight to their material losses and the circumstances under which they were previously placed. It is a vital question whether the principle of indemnity might not properly have a wider application to ordinary relief than has usually been given to it, but we may be certain that the pauperizing effects supposed to result from liberal relief have not been found to follow the most generous attempts to avert completely the paralyzing and direful consequences of such disasters as we are now considering. Both in Chicago and in Johnstown hundreds of families were placed, by gifts of money, or of house, furniture, clothing, or tools, in a position practically as

good as that which they had occupied before the fire or
the flood respectively, and in the former homeless persons
who owned or could rent a lot, or part of one, were given
money or lumber to build a "relief shanty." In this way
many people became house owners for the first time in
their lives. There is ample testimony that in practically
all instances good results were obtained from this policy.
In Chicago harmful consequences in the subsequent charitable history of the city have been traced, whether rightfully or not, to the appropriations made to charitable
institutions on the condition that the society which was
the custodian of the fund thereby acquired a right to control a proportionate number of admissions to their institutions; and in Johnstown there was unquestionable
hardship from the delay in its distribution and from
the early indiscriminate grants made without knowledge
of the circumstances of claimants; but in neither city
were there well-founded complaints of the results of discriminating and judicious disbursements in large amounts,
made with the avowed purpose of putting the recipients
in a position to carry on their former or equally appropriate
vocations.

In emergency relief made necessary by industrial depression, the prime necessity of providing suitable employment
for which wages are paid, rather than charitable relief, is apparent. Wages should not be placed so high as to discourage efforts to seek ordinary work, and it is essential that
there should be the least possible interference with ordinary business and industry. Various kinds of employment should be discovered, fitted to the physical capacity
of the various classes of laborers, and nothing should be
undertaken which is not in itself useful — which does not
meet a distinct public need. As the best example of success in meeting these conditions, the reader should study
the experience of the East Side Relief Committee, which,
in 1893–1894, provided employment for some five thousand persons in New York City. It is reported by the
charitable societies of the city that those who were aided
by that committee have very rarely been found since that
winter among applicants for charitable relief.

On several occasions the usefulness in great emergencies

of detachments of the standing army which have happened to be near at hand has been demonstrated. The perfect discipline and the organization constantly maintained in the army may save days at a time when even hours are of the greatest importance. The National Guard of the various states may render, and in some instances — notably, at East St. Louis, Missouri, in 1903 — has rendered, similar service. The suggestion made by Dr. F. H. Wines, in the Charities Review for June, 1898, that soldiers are of great utility as an aid in emergency relief work, was based upon an experience in the relief of sufferers from an overflow of the Ohio River at Shawneetown, Illinois. The detail which came to his assistance on that occasion consisted of a sergeant and nine men, and their special duty was that of patrol and other similar service. Dr. Wines found that even then twenty men would have been better. He recommends that where any portion of the population of a given community requires the shelter of tents, a temporary canvas city provided by the state or nation should be organized and remain under the control of the military authorities. By maintaining strict military discipline the inhabitants of the emergency camp at Shawneetown, slightly exceeding at one time two hundred in number, of whom two-thirds were Negroes, were at all times under thorough control. By the aid of the military force it became possible to provide for these refugees "a care so sympathetic and paternal that it produced no pauperizing impression."

For the temporary camp in Kansas City, Kansas, tents were supplied from the federal post at Fort Leavenworth, and for the similar but smaller camp on the Missouri side, for residents of Kansas City who had been driven from their homes by the flood, tents were supplied by the state militia; and in both cities detachments of the National Guard were called upon for patrol duty. One of the principal reasons for such a military patrol is the temporary disorganization of the community. The local constabulary is likely to be demoralized and excited, and the presence of state militia gives confidence and security to people who need temporary moral support.

While soldiers may profitably be employed in the man-

ner that has been indicated, it will not ordinarily be
found advantageous to place upon them responsibility for
relief or for remedial measures. Military discipline has
its limitations as well as its advantages, and it would
unfit the average soldier or petty officer to exercise that
discriminating judgment and personal influence which
are so essential in dealing with people who have suddenly
lost their possessions and require aid and counsel in read-
justing their affairs and regaining a foothold in the industrial system. This observation applies almost equally to
the use of policemen in the distribution of relief. At the
earliest practicable moment the ordinary municipal authority should be established and the necessity for military
patrol overcome.

At Johnstown one of the most instructive chapters in
the history of the few months succeeding the flood is that
which deals with the restoration of municipal borough
authorities to the full exercise of their functions. In
some of the boroughs affected by the flood there was left
no building in which a meeting of the borough council
could be held. Self-constituted committees had temporarily managed police, health, and fire departments, and
later such duties had been in part assumed by state
authorities. Gradually, however, the adjutant-general,
representing the state government, sought out those who
had been duly chosen to perform such duties, arranged
suitable meeting places for councils and public boards, and
transferred to them the duties which it had again become
possible for them to perform. No legal or other controversies arose in connection with these ultra-constitutional
arrangements, and no act of the legislature was thought
necessary to legalize what had been done in the interval
during which ordinary municipal activities were suspended, or the acts performed by the reorganized and
restored municipal authorities.

One suggestion which is frequently made is that relief
in emergencies should never be in money, but always in
an equivalent. This suggestion is not to be adopted
without consideration of the character of the proposed
beneficiaries. It is probable that, so far as disbursements
from public funds are concerned, the policy suggested is

2 H

wise, and that provision of employment where emergency relief measures are necessary is still better than relief in kind. Instead of opening free shelters, depots for free food and for the distribution of clothing, as early as possible a reliable list should be made, based upon a knowledge of the portion of the community affected by the disaster. When an accurate list of this kind has been prepared, applications may be compared with it and more intelligent decisions reached as to the relief required.

The conclusion reached by the Johnstown Flood Commission to make a distribution of money was eminently justified by the conditions that there prevailed. It was then proposed, and indeed at one time it had virtually been decided by the commission, instead of dividing the money in their hands after providing for various special needs, to establish large warehouses and fill them with clothing and other necessaries of life, to be distributed as occasion might require throughout the ensuing winter. A change of plan was made because of earnest and emphatic protests from prominent citizens of Johnstown who were personally acquainted with the people for whom this scheme of relief was proposed, and who appreciated the absurdity of applying to skilled mechanics and prosperous tradespeople conclusions based upon experiences with applicants for ordinary relief.

One cannot commend the methods of those almoners of Johnstown who, instead of placing their funds in the hands of the relief committees, passed through the streets handing ten-dollar bills to every one whom they met. The criticism, however, lies not against their use of money, but against their lack of discrimination and common sense. Many of those to whom grants of $1000 and upwards were made immediately engaged in active industry and trade, and within a few months, except for the loss of relatives, neighbors, and friends, might have looked upon their experience as a nightmare to be forgotten in the waking hours of renewed active life. It is probable that so large a sum has never before been poured into a community of equal size with so little damage to the personal character of the citizens and so complete an absence of any pauperizing or demoralizing influences.

In the opinion of good judges resident in the city both before and after the flood, this is due in part to the fact that money was given, and that those who received it were left free to decide for themselves how it should be expended.

Two other considerations may be suggested. Special emergencies display in a high degree the need of local coöperation. In meeting such distress as is caused in populous communities by a tornado or a serious fire, there is a place for the activity of the chamber of commerce, or merchants' association, or commercial club, or some other representative of the business interests of the community. The task of raising the large sums of money usually requisite can best be undertaken by some such body. Any appeal having their indorsement will be likely to meet with generous and quick response. There is a place also for the charity organization society, or bureau of charities, or provident association, or some other general agency whose officers and agents are trained in investigation and in the administration of funds.[1] It may also be expedient, if no such general agency is in existence, to call upon the churches or upon such denominational bodies as the Society of St. Vincent de Paul and the Hebrew Charities. There may also be a need for children's aid societies or the representatives of orphan asylums to care for children who are left without guardianship, and there is almost always an urgent demand for physicians, for a temporary ambulance and hospital service, and for trained nurses. The aid rendered by volunteer private citizens is sometimes as valuable as that of any organized agency, and often the absence of organized relief makes it imperative that private citizens shall undertake to do what is essential, whether from choice or not.

This leads to the final suggestion, which is that in the presence of even a serious disaster or an industrial crisis, leaders of public opinion should attempt to preserve in the

---

[1] Conspicuous illustrations of the value of training in the regular work of charity organization societies were supplied by the Chicago, Paterson, and Baltimore fire relief funds, and in the distribution of the *General Slocum* relief fund. The responsible direction of a committee composed of men of standing in business and professional circles is of course assumed.

public mind a due sense of proportion. When there comes an urgent call for aid from a distance, the continuing, and possibly equally imperative, needs at hand resulting from more ordinary causes should not be forgotten.

It is not surprising, in view of the frightful loss of life at Martinique and its proximity to our own shores, that the New York Committee should have received some $80,000 more than they could disburse, in spite of an announcement by the committee that it would not take additional contributions. This was in part due to the fact that the eruption occurred in foreign territory, and that public appropriations were made both in the United States and France.

This is not to be understood as discountenancing large and immediate responses to special appeals. By no means all that is given to meet special emergencies is deducted from ordinary charitable resources. There should, however, be cultivated a sane and reasonable examination of the probable need ; and the citizen who gives, even with great liberality, should not on that account consider himself free from the obligation to consider also the needs of his immediate neighbor. The city, even in prosperous times, through its quick industrial changes and by the very conditions of life which it imposes, places upon some weak shoulders burdens which are not rightfully theirs, and which it is the duty — and it is an agreeable duty — of their neighbors to share.

APPENDICES

APPENDIX I

CONSTITUTION OF A CHARITY ORGANIZATION SOCIETY[1]

ARTICLE I

NAME

This Society shall be known as THE CHARITY ORGANIZATION SOCIETY OF THE CITY OF ———.

ARTICLE II

STATEMENT OF PURPOSES AND OBJECTS

SECTION 1. — To extirpate pauperism, mendicancy, and such social conditions as create preventable dependency.

SEC. 2. — To provide, as far as lies in its power to obtain it, adequate material assistance and intelligent care for needy families in their homes and for homeless persons.

SEC. 3. — In accomplishing the objects above named, to obtain the coöperation of other agencies and of charitable individuals.

SEC. 4. — To promote the general welfare by social reform affecting the living condition of wage-earners.

ARTICLE III

MEMBERSHIP

The Society shall be composed of the following persons: —

I. Annual Members: Those who contribute annually [$5] to the funds of the Society and are approved by the Finance Committee.

[1] This draft of a Constitution may readily be modified to meet the needs of either a large or a small society. The portions which especially require to be modified to meet local needs or which may be omitted are enclosed in brackets [ ]. In the preparation of this draft the author has been assisted by Frank Tucker, formerly General Agent of the New York Association for Improving the Condition of the Poor.

II. Associate Members: Those who contribute annually [$20] to the funds of the Society and are approved by the Finance Committee.

III. Life Members: Those who contribute [$100] to the funds of the Society at any one time and are approved for life membership by the Finance Committee.

ARTICLE IV

MEETINGS OF THE SOCIETY

The annual meeting of the Society shall be held on the [second Wednesday of October], when a report of the work and condition of the Society for the past year shall be submitted and members of the Council shall be elected to fill vacancies caused by expiration of term. No person shall be eligible for election as a member of the Council unless his name shall have been posted for ten successive days prior to the date of holding the election in the Central Office of the Society.

The President may call a special meeting whenever seven members of the Society request him in writing to do so. Such written request shall specify the business to be transacted, and the meeting requested shall be called within twenty days after receipt of the request.

Seven members shall constitute a quorum at the annual and at any special meeting of the Society.

At any special meeting only such business shall be transacted as was specified in the notice of the meeting.

ARTICLE V

THE COUNCIL

[BOARD OF MANAGERS. BOARD OF TRUSTEES]

SECTION 1. — The management of the Society shall be vested in a Council which shall consist of [thirty] members of the Society who shall be elected by ballot and hold office until their successors shall be elected.

At the first regular meeting of the Council the membership shall be divided by lot into three classes as nearly equal in number as possible. The terms of those in the first class shall expire at the next annual meeting of the Society following this meeting of the Council; of the second class at the second annual meeting of the Society, and of the third class at the third annual meeting of the Society. At each annual meeting thereafter [ten members] shall be elected as members of the Council to replace the outgoing class, the term of office being [three years] and until their successors are elected; provided, however, that the absence of a member from three consecutive meetings of the Council without satisfactory excuse may be considered by the President as equivalent to a resignation, and the vacancy so caused by such resignation may be filled by the Council as hereinafter provided.

SEC. 2. — The officers of the Council shall consist of a President, a Vice-President, a Treasurer, and a Secretary. All, excepting the Secretary, shall be members of the Council and shall be elected by ballot at the first meeting of the Council after the Annual Meeting of the Society. The Secretary shall be appointed by the Council. They shall continue in office until their successors are chosen. The officers of the Council shall also be the officers of the Society.

SEC. 3. — The Council shall have power to fill vacancies occurring in its own body.

SEC. 4. — There shall be a regular meeting of the Council on the [second Wednesday of the month]. Special meetings may be called by the President at any time and shall be called on a written request of five members of the Council. Two days' notice shall be given of any special meeting, and the call shall specify the object thereof. No other business than that named in the call shall be presented at the special meeting.

SEC. 5. — At any meeting of the Council [seven] elective members shall constitute a quorum.

SEC. 6. — The Council shall make such by-laws as it may deem necessary governing the direction of the Society, and may also alter or suspend such by-laws.

ARTICLE VI

DUTIES OF OFFICERS

SECTION 1. — The President and the Vice-President shall perform the duties which usually pertain to their respective offices.

SEC. 2. — The Treasurer shall have charge of the funds of the Society. He shall make monthly reports to the Council and shall give such security as the Council may require. His duties are more fully defined in Article VIII.

SEC. 3. — The Secretary shall keep the minutes of the Council and shall notify officers and members of the Council of their appointment. He shall be, under the direction of the Council, the general executive officer of the Society. He shall attend all committee meetings so far as practicable, and shall act as Secretary of the Executive Committee [of the Finance Committee, of the Committee on the Care and Relief of the Dependent, of the Committee on Legislation and Legal Questions], and of other standing committees so far as practicable. His further duties are set forth in Article VIII.

ARTICLE VII

DISTRIBUTION OF WORK

SECTION 1. — I. The various activities of the Society shall be under the direction of standing and special committees subject to the control of the Council.

II. The standing committees of the Council shall consist of not less than [three] persons, and shall be appointed annually by the President, who shall also designate the chairman. It shall be the duty of each committee to present a report at each meeting of the Council.

SEC. 2. — The Executive Committee shall act for the Council in the interim of its sessions, and shall approve of all appointments of employees and regulate their compensation. It shall transact any business for the Society which in its judgment cannot await the action of the Council and does not involve an expenditure of over [$500]. It shall make nominations to the Council to fill vacancies in that body.

SEC. 3. — The Committee on Finance shall be charged with the duty of raising and caring for the funds of the Society as set forth in Article VIII, and shall also pass upon the names of all persons qualified for membership, pursuant to Article I.

SEC. 4. — I. The Committee on the Care and Relief of the Dependent shall have immediate charge of all work relating to applications for assistance, the investigation of applications made to the Society or referred to the Society for investigation, the keeping of records relating to dependent families and the making of reports from such records, and the material relief of families and homeless persons.

[II. The city shall be divided, for the purpose of the Society, into such districts as the Committee on the Care and Relief of the Dependent shall designate; but the Committee may unite any two or more of such districts into one, and may at any time rearrange such districts subject to the approval of the Council.]

[III. In each district, or combination of districts, there shall be a District Committee, consisting of twelve or more persons, preferably residents of the district. The Committee on the Care and Relief of the Dependent shall appoint the original members of such Committee, and said Committee shall thereafter have power to fill vacancies in its own number, subject to the approval of the Committee on the Care and Relief of the Dependent. In case a rearrangement of districts shall be made at any time by the Committee, it shall appoint the original members of the District Committee for the newly combined districts.]

[IV. Each District Committee shall perform such duties as shall be assigned to it by the Committee on the Care and Relief of the Dependent.]

[V. An office shall be established in a convenient position for each district, or combination of districts, for the meetings of the committees, for receiving applications, and for facility of reference.]

[VI. The Committee on the Care and Relief of the Dependent may appoint sub-committees to deal with homeless persons, and such other sub-committees as it may, from time to time, find necessary.]

[VII. Whenever any particular group of dependents shall become an object of special interest and inquiry, or shall appear to demand exceptional treatment, the care of such group may be retained by the Committee on the Care and Relief of the Dependent without reference to the District Office.]

SEC. 5. — The Committee on Industrial Employment shall have charge of [the Industrial Building, of the Wood Yard, Laundry, Workrooms, Sewing Bureau, and other forms of] industrial employment, and may appoint sub-committees for each department of industrial employment.

SEC. 6. — The Committee on Fresh Air Work shall have charge of the fresh air activities of the Society.

SEC. 7. — The Committee on Mendicancy shall be charged with the duty of suppressing mendicancy. [Any special officers appointed for this purpose shall report to this Committee and be under its direction.]

SEC. 8. — The Committee on the Prevention of Tuberculosis shall be charged with the work of securing and disseminating information on means of preventing the spread of tuberculosis, and of any other activities undertaken by the Society within the scope indicated by the title of the Committee.

SEC. 9. — The Committee on Housing Reform shall be charged with the duty of improving the condition of tenement-houses by securing proper legislation, by securing the enforcement of the existing laws, by encouraging the building of improved tenements and otherwise.

SEC. 10. — The Committee on Publications shall have charge of the publications of the Society.

SEC. 11. — The Committee on Provident Habits shall endeavor to promote the general welfare of the poor by the inculcation of habits of prudence and thrift, and by supplying facilities therefor.

SEC. 12. — The Committee on Statistics shall be charged with the collection and treatment of charitable and correctional statistics relating to the work of the Society, subject to the approval of the Council.

ARTICLE VIII

SUBSCRIPTIONS AND FUNDS

SECTION 1. — The fiscal year of the Society shall begin on the first day of July in each year, but all annual subscriptions shall become due upon the first day of January in each year.

SEC. 2. — No appeal for contributions to the funds of the Society shall be issued without the sanction of the Finance Committee; provided, however, that the Secretary may make, from time to time, in the daily press, such special appeals for contributions as exceptional conditions may require.

SEC. 3. — The funds of the Society shall be divided into three parts, known as : —

(1) *The Endowment Fund.*
(2) *The Reserve Fund.*
(3) *The General Fund.*

SEC. 4. — *The Endowment Fund:* The Endowment Fund shall consist of such contributions and legacies as shall be given with the restriction that the income only shall be used for the purposes of the Society.

SEC. 5. — *The Reserve Fund:* The Reserve Fund shall consist of such sums as may be set aside from the General Fund, from time to time, by the Council, for investment. Whenever any part of the Reserve Fund shall be appropriated by the Council, such sum shall be immediately transferred to the General Fund.

The Endowment and Reserve Funds shall be under the immediate direction and control of the Committee on Finance, and all investments of these funds shall be ordered by the Committee.

The Treasurer of the Society shall be a member of and act as the Treasurer of the Committee on Finance, and shall be responsible for the safe keeping of the securities of the Endowment and Reserve Funds.

Any uninvested balance of the Endowment and Reserve Funds shall be kept each in separate trust companies, in the name of the Society, subject to the check of the Treasurer, and shall, whenever possible, bear interest.

All income from the Endowment and Reserve Funds shall be transferred to the General Fund as soon as received.

No part of the Reserve Fund shall be used for any purpose except by resolution of the Council, and whenever any part shall be appropriated by the Council it shall be immediately transferred' to the General Fund.

SEC. 6. — *The General Fund:* The term General Fund shall cover all receipts of the Society not constituting a Special Fund or specified for the Endowment Fund; the intention being that all income, including legacies, donations for general purposes, and income from Endowment, Reserve, and Special Funds, shall be credited to the General Fund, to which the authorized disbursements of each activity of the Society shall be charged at the close of the fiscal year.

SEC. 7. — Whenever an appeal shall be authorized for a particular purpose or activity of the Society, the donations received in response to such appeal shall be credited to a fund the title of which shall be descriptive of the work done, and the proportion of the donations so received to be transferred to the General Fund as a proper share of the general administration expense of the Society shall be decided by the Committee on Finance.

All special funds, unless otherwise specified by the donor, shall be under control of the Committee on Finance, in like manner as the Endowment and Reserve Funds, and the securities or money making up such fund shall be placed in the hands of the Treasurer of the Committee on Finance, who shall be responsible for the safe keeping of the same; all income from any such funds shall be transferred to the General Fund on its receipt by the Treasurer, to be used in accordance with the terms of the several trusts.

SEC. 8. — The Treasurer shall notify the Secretary at once of all transfers of income from the Endowment and Reserve Funds or from any Special Fund to the General Fund.

The Treasurer shall notify the Secretary immediately on the receipt by him of any sum for the account of the Society, that such receipt may be entered at once to the credit of the proper account on the books of the Society.

SEC. 9. — The Secretary shall be the only disbursing agent of the Society, the object of this provision being to keep in the Central

Offices of the Society all receipts for payments by the Society, of any kind, nature, or description, and to have in the Central Offices immediate record of any disbursement. This provision shall not necessarily apply to the investment of the Endowment and Reserve Funds, nor of any special fund.

SEC. 10. — All donations shall be received by the Treasurer, or by the Secretary as his representative, entered by him on the proper books of the Society, and then deposited in such trust company as is directed by the Treasurer.

SEC. 11. — Whenever the Council shall make an appropriation out of either the Reserve or General Fund, the Secretary shall send to the Treasurer a copy of the resolution, making the appropriation, certified by the Secretary, which certified copy shall be the Treasurer's authority for transferring the appropriated amount to the Secretary.

SEC. 12. — The Treasurer shall keep an account in the name of the Society, subject to his check as Treasurer, in such trust company as may be selected by him and approved by the Committee on Finance, and such account shall draw interest whenever possible. Such account shall be separate and distinct from those accounts opened for the uninvested balances of the Endowment, Reserve, or Special Funds.

ARTICLE IX

AMENDMENTS

This Constitution shall not be amended except by either (1) the resolution of a two-thirds vote of a meeting of the Council, at which at least [seven] elective members shall be present, notice of such amendment having been already given at a previous stated meeting of the Council, and a copy thereof sent to each member of the Council at least five days previous to the meeting at which it is to be considered; or (2) the unanimous vote of such a meeting without notice having been given at a previous stated meeting, but after the five days' notice to each member of the Council hereinbefore provided.

The Secretary shall keep a bank account in the name of the Society, subject to his check as Secretary, for current disbursements.

SEC. 13. — No resolution appropriating money for any purpose other than the ordinary expenses of the Society, as provided for by the regular appropriations, shall be acted upon at the meeting at which it is introduced, except when such resolution, making an appropriation, shall be recommended to the Council by the Committee on Finance.

SEC. 14. — The Committee on Finance may employ an expert accountant to audit the accounts at such times as may be deemed necessary.

SEC. 15. — At each regular meeting of the Council the Treasurer shall make a detailed statement of the receipts and disbursements for the preceding calendar month; he shall make a statement showing the investments and the receipts and disbursements of the Endowment, Reserve, and Special Funds. He shall make, at the annual meeting of the Society, a detailed statement of the receipts and disbursements for the fiscal year.

APPENDIX II

CHARITABLE TRANSPORTATION

RULES AND SUGGESTIONS ADOPTED BY THE COMMITTEE
ON CHARITABLE TRANSPORTATION APPOINTED AT THE
TWENTY-NINTH NATIONAL CONFERENCE OF CHARI-
TIES AND CORRECTION

EXPLANATORY. — *A.* The word "transportation" as used in the following
paragraphs includes both free transportation and the recommendation of
charity rates, even if the latter are to be paid by the applicant.

B. The word "he" means he, she, or they, as the context in any case will
suggest, and the word "applicant" includes the family group for whom transportation is desired.

C. "Public Charity" includes not only the official charities supported by
taxation, but any general charitable organization upon which the applicant in
question has no claim through membership, blood relationship, or through the
Society's definite promise to aid the specific applicant.

D. In some of the following paragraphs "shall" is used, in others
"should" or "may." The former word is mandatory and the phrases in
which it is used are to be accepted as binding upon all signers of these rules.
Where "should" or "may" is used, the paragraph is only a suggestion which
signers may observe or not, at their discretion.

RULES AND SUGGESTIONS

1. Before any charitable transportation shall be granted, the organization or official having the matter under consideration must be
satisfied by adequate and reliable evidence : —

First: That the applicant is unable to pay the regular fare.

Second: That the applicant's condition and prospects will be sub-
stantially improved by sending him to the place in question.

Third: That the applicant will have such resources for maintenance at the point of destination as will prevent him from dependence
on public charity.

2. An applicant's statements must in every case be substantiated
by other definite, reliable evidence. When this is lacking, the applicant should be taken care of, if necessary, until the needful testimony
is secured.

3. In all cases an appropriate charitable organization or official, if
such exists, at the point of destination, should be promptly advised

478

that the applicant's transportation to that place is under consideration, or has already been determined upon.

When a signer of these rules is listed as being located at the proposed point of destination, it shall not be legitimate to send the applicant thither unless notification is sent to the signer in advance of the transportation being furnished, or upon the day when it is provided.

4. It is strongly recommended that a report be secured from an appropriate charitable organization or official in the city to which transportation is desired, before any applicant is sent thither. This is especially urged when a signer of these rules is listed as being located at the point of destination.

All signers have definitely announced themselves as willing to coöperate with other signers by making reasonable efforts to secure needful information and to determine whether transportation ought to be provided in any given case. Other charitable agencies, also, are usually willing to make any legitimate inquiries and reports which fall within the range of their customary activities.

5. All charitable transportation provided shall, in every instance, be *adequate;* that is, the initial or original sender shall provide for the applicant through to his ultimate destination. When through tickets cannot be secured at charity rates, the initial sender may enlist the services of some charitable agency at an intermediate point, all expenses to be borne by the initial sender.

6. If an applicant has been aided to reach a place intermediate to the point of his proper destination, without means having been provided for forwarding him to the latter, then no further transportation should be granted without inquiry of the charitable organization or individual who sent the applicant thither. This correspondent should be requested to remit the amount necessary either to forward the applicant to his destination or to return him to the starting-point. If a satisfactory response is not promptly made, the applicant should be returned to the place where his charitable transportation originated.

7. If an applicant who has been provided with charitable transportation to a given place shall there become dependent on public charity within nine months after his arrival, or within the time there specified by law as necessary for the establishment of a legal residence, then the charitable organization or individual who sent him thither should be notified and requested to provide for the applicant's necessities or to remit the money necessary to return him to the place from which his transportation was provided.

8. In case an applicant has been forwarded in violation of these rules or has become dependent upon public charity within the time specified above, then the reasonable expense of providing for him temporarily, pending investigation and the proper disposal of the case, should be considered as a proper charge against the charitable organization or individual from whom the applicant secured his transportation.

9. The society or official through whom charitable transportation is procured shall in each case preserve a full record of all the essential facts upon which the granting of transportation has been based.

A copy or summary of such record should be furnished promptly on request to any charitable organization or official interested in the case. When such request for a digest of the record comes from a signer of these rules, it shall be considered mandatory upon any other signer.

10. In case of persons asking charitable transportation on the ground of being able to secure employment in the place to which transportation is desired, definite, reliable assurances of employment must be obtained as part of the necessary evidence. A general report that conditions of employment are better, or that the applicant would be "better off" in the place specified, shall not be considered sufficient grounds for the granting of transportation.

11. Organizations and individuals who agree to these rules thereby pledge themselves to keep a copy of the rules and the telegraphic code conveniently at hand, and to use all due diligence in making reasonable inquiries requested by other signers of the rules and in replying to communications regarding transportation cases.

12. Persons forwarded by charitable agencies or officials from places where any contagious or infectious disease is known to be epidemic, must be provided with the proper health certificates.

13. When disagreement, as to facts or decisions, arises in regard to any transportation case, one or both the parties concerned may appeal to: —

(1) The secretary of the State Board of Charities, if both disputants are located in the same State; or, if not,

(2) Their two State secretaries working jointly or to either one of them, or,

(3) The general secretary of the National Conference of Charities and Correction.

CHARLES F. WELLER,
F. W. BLACKMAR,
JAMES L. DAWSON,
MAX SENIOR.
}
Committee.

INDEX

not to be exaggerated, 25; modern charity, 26; new conception of relief funds, 26; modern charity and government, 27.
See also Emergency relief measures.
Evolution and charity, 6.
Experience, value in emergency relief, 457.
Experimental relief, private philanthropy in, 129.
Extradition for desertion, 139.

FAMILIES, THE BREAKING UP OF, 97–106.
See BREAKING UP OF FAMILIES, THE.
FAMILIES AT HOME, THE RELIEF OF, 73–79.
See RELIEF OF FAMILIES AT HOME, THE.
FAMILY DESERTION, 135–143.
Some exceptional cases, 136; age and economic position of deserters, 138; lack of moral responsibility, 138; causes, 139; existing laws, 139; National Conference resolutions on extradition, 139; relief and desertion, 140; types of deserters, 141; analysis of deserted families in Boston, 141; Illinois law, 142; Pennsylvania law, 143.
Family, the unit of social organization, 96, 97.
Farm colony for inebriates, 149.
Feeble-minded, removal from the almshouse, 130.
Financial problem of the hospitals, 39.
FIRE AND FLOOD IN PATERSON, 405–411, 458.
The fire in February, 1902, 405; Central Relief Committee organized, 405; offers of outside assistance declined, 405; an office opened, 406; relief orders given, 407; discontent, 407; change in method, 407; end of the period of distress, 408; the first flood, in March, 408; expenditures, 408; the second flood, in October, 1903, 409; untrained investigators, 409; substitution of cash for relief orders, 410; relief given, 411.
Fitler, Edwin H., 386.

Folks, Homer, 119, 120, 131, 278.
Folks, Ralph, 60.
Food as an element in the standard of living, 29, 30.
Food, fuel, and clothing, Distribution in times of disaster, 376, 389, 422.
Food market in Indianapolis, 423.
Foraker, J. B., 393.
Foundling asylum and illegitimacy, 91.
Fox, John, 446, 447.
Fraud, prevention of.
See Deception.
Fresh-air agencies, 44.
Frothingham, Edward, 322, 355.
Fulton, John, 386.
Funds for relief, 311, 312.
New conception of, 26.
See also Emergency relief measures.

Garrett, Philip C., 301.
Girls, homeless, 85.
Gladstone, William E., 272.
Goodwin, A. G., 322.
Gould, E. R. L., 72.
Gould, Jay, 365.
Government and modern charity, 27.

Haas, George C. F., 449.
Hadley, Arthur Twining, 269.
Hale, George Silsbee, 325, 332.
Hamilton, David Stuart, 405, 409.
"Handbook on the Prevention of Tuberculosis," 58, 67.
Hanna, H. H., 413.
Harburger, Julius, 447.
Harburger, L. W., 447.
Harrison, Benjamin, 384.
Harrison, Thomas S., 301.
Hartley, Robert M., 277, 316.
Hastings, Gen. Daniel H., 387, 394.
Health insurance, 127.
Hebberd, Robert W., 278.
Hebrew charities, 324, 467.
Henderson, C. Hanford, 47.
Heischman, John J., 447.
Hewitt, Erskine, 446, 447.
Hill, A. A., 447, 459.
Historical interpretation of the English Poor Law, 275–277.
Historical survey of relief, 269–357.
Hoffman, H. W., 447.
Holden, Charles C. P., 363.
Homeless boys and men, 83, 84.

POVERTY, U. S. A.

THE HISTORICAL RECORD

An Arno Press/New York Times Collection

Adams, Grace. **Workers on Relief.** 1939.

The Almshouse Experience: Collected Reports. 1821-1827.

Armstrong, Louise V. **We Too Are The People.** 1938.

Bloodworth, Jessie A. and Elizabeth J. Greenwood.
The Personal Side. 1939.

Brunner, Edmund de S. and Irving Lorge.
**Rural Trends in Depression Years: A Survey of
Village-Centered Agricultural Communities, 1930-1936.**
1937.

Calkins, Raymond.
**Substitutes for the Saloon: An Investigation Originally
made for The Committee of Fifty.** 1919.

Cavan, Ruth Shonle and Katherine Howland Ranck.
**The Family and the Depression: A Study of
One Hundred Chicago Families.** 1938.

Chapin, Robert Coit.
**The Standard of Living Among Workingmen's Families
in New York City.** 1909.

**The Charitable Impulse in Eighteenth Century America:
Collected Papers.** 1711-1797.

Children's Aid Society.
Children's Aid Society Annual Reports, 1-10.
February 1854-February 1863.

Conference on the Care of Dependent Children.
**Proceedings of the Conference on the Care
of Dependent Children.** 1909.

Conyngton, Mary.
How to Help: A Manual of Practical Charity. 1909.

Devine, Edward T. **Misery and its Causes.** 1909.

Devine, Edward T. **Principles of Relief.** 1904.

Dix, Dorothea L.
On Behalf of the Insane Poor: Selected Reports. 1843-1852.

Douglas, Paul H.
**Social Security in the United States: An Analysis and
Appraisal of the Federal Social Security Act.** 1936.

Farm Tenancy: Black and White. Two Reports. 1935, 1937.

Feder, Leah Hannah.
**Unemployment Relief in Periods of Depression:
A Study of Measures Adopted in Certain American
Cities, 1857 through 1922.** 1936.

Folks, Homer.
**The Care of Destitute, Neglected, and
Delinquent Children.** 1900.

Guardians of the Poor.
**A Compilation of the Poor Laws of the State of
Pennsylvania from the Year 1700 to 1788, Inclusive.** 1788.

Hart, Hastings, H.
Preventive Treatment of Neglected Children.
(Correction and Prevention, Vol. 4) 1910.

Herring, Harriet L.
**Welfare Work in Mill Villages: The Story of Extra-Mill
Activities in North Carolina.** 1929.

The Jacksonians on the Poor: Collected Pamphlets.
1822-1844.

Karpf, Maurice J.
Jewish Community Organization in the United States.
1938.

Kellor, Frances A.
Out of Work: A Study of Unemployment. 1915.

Kirkpatrick, Ellis Lore.
The Farmer's Standard of Living. 1929.

Komarovsky, Mirra.
**The Unemployed Man and His Family: The Effect of
Unemployment Upon the Status of the Man in
Fifty-Nine Families.** 1940.

Leupp, Francis E. **The Indian and His Problem.** 1910.

Lowell, Josephine Shaw.
Public Relief and Private Charity. 1884.

More, Louise Bolard.
**Wage Earners' Budgets: A Study of Standards and
Cost of Living in New York City. 1907.**

New York Association for Improving
the Condition of the Poor.
AICP First Annual Reports Investigating Poverty.
1845-1853.

O'Grady, John.
**Catholic Charities in the United States:
History and Problems.** 1930.

Raper, Arthur F.
Preface to Peasantry: A Tale of Two Black Belt Counties.
1936.

Raper, Arthur F. **Tenants of The Almighty.** 1943.

Richmond, Mary E.
What is Social Case Work? An Introductory Description.
1922.

Riis, Jacob A. **The Children of the Poor.** 1892.

Rural Poor in the Great Depression: Three Studies. 1938.

Sedgwick, Theodore.
Public and Private Economy: Part I. 1836.

Smith, Reginald Heber. **Justice and the Poor.** 1919.

Sutherland, Edwin H. and Harvey J. Locke.
**Twenty Thousand Homeless Men: A Study of
Unemployed Men in the Chicago Shelters.** 1936.

Tuckerman, Joseph.
On the Elevation of the Poor: A Selection From His Reports as Minister at Large in Boston. 1874.

Warner, Amos G. **American Charities.** 1894.

Watson, Frank Dekker.
The Charity Organization Movement in the United States: A Study in American Philanthropy. 1922.

Woods, Robert A., et al. **The Poor in Great Cities.** 1895.